Apache Oozie

Mohammad Kamrul Islam & Aravind Srinivasan

Beijing · Cambridge · Farnham · Köln · Sebastopol · Tokyo

SHROFF PUBLISHERS & DISTRIBUTORS PVT. LTD.
Mumbai Bangalore Kolkata New Delhi

Apache Oozie

by Mohammad Kamrul Islam and Aravind Srinivasan

ISBN: 978-1-449-36992-7
Originally Printed in the United States of America.

Published by O'Reilly Media, Inc., 1005 Gravenstein Highway North, Sebastopol, CA 95472.

O'Reilly books may be purchased for educational, business, or sales promotional use. Online editions are also available for most titles (*http://safari.oreilly.com*). For more information, contact our corporate/institutional sales department: (800) 998-9938 or *corporate@oreilly.com*.

Editors: Mike Loukides and Marie Beaugureau
Production Editor: Colleen Lobner
Copyeditor: Gillian McGarvey
Proofreader: Jasmine Kwityn
Indexer: Lucie Haskins
Interior Designer: David Futato
Cover Designer: Ellie Volckhausen
Illustrator: Rebecca Demarest

Printing History:
May 2015: First Edition

Revision History for the First Edition 2015-05-08: First Release

See http://oreilly.com/catalog/errata.csp?isbn=9781449369927 for release details.

First Indian Reprint: June 2015

ISBN 13: 978-93-5213-092-4

Published by **Shroff Publishers and Distributors Pvt. Ltd.** C-103, TTC Industrial Area, MIDC, Pawane, Navi Mumbai - 400 703 • TEL: (91 22) 4158 4158 • FAX: (91 22) 4158 4141• E-mail : spdorders@shroffpublishers.com Web : www.shroffpublishers.com CIN : U22200MH1992PTC067760 Printed at Jasmine Art Printers Pvt. Ltd. Navi Mumbai.

Table of Contents

Foreword

First developed when I was at Yahoo! in 2008, Apache Oozie remains the most sophisticated and powerful workflow scheduler for managing Apache Hadoop jobs. Although simpler open source alternatives have been introduced, Oozie is still my recommended workflow scheduler due to its ability to handle complexity, ease of integration with established and emerging Hadoop components (like Spark), and the growing ecosystem of projects, such as Apache Falcon, that rely on its workflow engine.

That said, Oozie also remains one of the more challenging schedulers to learn and master. If ever a system required a comprehensive user's manual, Oozie is it. To take advantage of the full power that Oozie has to offer, developers need the guidance and advice of expert users. That is why I am delighted to see this book get published.

When Oozie was first developed, I was Chief Architect of Yahoo!'s Search and Advertising Technology Group. At the time, our group was starting to migrate the event-processing pipelines of our advertising products from a proprietary technology stack to Apache Hadoop.

The advertising pipelines at Yahoo! were extremely complex. Data was processed in batches that ranged from 5 minutes to 30 days in length, with aggregates "graduating" in complex ways from one time scale to another. In addition, these pipelines needed to detect and gracefully handle late data, missing data, software bugs tickled by "black swan" event data, and software bugs introduced by recent software pushes. On top of all of that, billions of dollars of revenue—and a good deal of the company's growth prospects—depended on these pipelines, raising the stakes for data quality, security, and compliance. We had about a half-dozen workflow systems in use back then, and there was a lot of internal competition to be selected as the standard for Hadoop. Ultimately, the design for Oozie came from ideas from two systems: PacMan, a system already integrated with Hadoop, and Lexus, a system already in place for the advertising pipelines.

Oozie's origins as a second-generation system designed to meet the needs of extremely complicated applications are both a strength and a weakness. On the positive side, there is no use case or scenario that Oozie can't handle—and if you know what you're doing, handle well. On the negative side, Oozie suffers from the over-engineering that you'd expect from second-system effect. It has complex features that are great for handling complicated applications, but can be very nonintuitive for inexperienced users. For these newer users, I want to let you know that Oozie is worth the investment of your time. While the newer, simpler workflow schedulers are much easier for simple pipelines, it is in the nature of data pipelines to grow more sophisticated over time. The simpler solutions will ultimately limit the solutions that you can create. Don't limit yourself.

As guides to Oozie, there can be no better experts than Aravind Srinivasan and Mohammad Kamrul Islam. Aravind represents the "voice of the user," as he was one of the engineers who moved Yahoo!'s advertising pipelines over to Oozie, bringing the lessons of Lexus to the Oozie developers. Subsequently, he has worked on many other Oozie applications, both inside and outside of Yahoo!. Mohammad represents the "voice of the developer," as a core contributor to Oozie since its 1.x days. Mohammad is currently Vice President of the Oozie project at the Apache Software Foundation, and he also makes significant contributions to other Hadoop-related projects such as YARN and Tez.

In this book, the authors have striven for practicality, focusing on the concepts, principles, tips, and tricks necessary for developers to get the most out of Oozie. A volume such as this is long overdue. Developers will get a lot more out the Hadoop ecosystem by reading it.

—Raymie Stata, CEO, Altiscale

Preface

Hadoop is fast becoming the de facto big data platform across all industries. An entire ecosystem of tools, products, and services targeting every functionality and requirement have sprung up around Hadoop. Apache Oozie occupies an important space in this ever-expanding ecosystem. Since Hadoop's early days at Yahoo!, it has been a natural platform for Extract, Transform, and Load (ETL) and other forms of data pipelines. Without a mature workflow management and scheduling system, implementing such pipelines can be a challenge. Oozie satisfies these requirements and provides a viable tool to implement complex, real-world data pipelines. In this book, we have tried our best to introduce readers to all the facets of Oozie and walk them through the intricacies of this rather powerful and flexible platform.

Software workflow systems are ubiquitous and each system has its own idiosyncrasies. But Oozie is a lot more than just another workflow system. One of Oozie's strengths is that it was custom built from the ground up for Hadoop. This not only means that Oozie works well on Hadoop, but that the authors of Oozie had an opportunity to build a new system incorporating much of their knowledge about other legacy workflow systems. Although some users view Oozie as just a workflow system, it has evolved into something more than that. The ability to use data availability and time-based triggers to schedule workflows via the Oozie coordinator is as important to today's users as the workflow. The higher-level concept of *bundles*, which enable users to package multiple coordinators into complex data pipelines, is also gaining a lot of traction as applications and pipelines moving to Hadoop are getting more complicated.

We are both very lucky to have been involved in Oozie's journey from its early days. We have played several roles in its evolution, ranging from developer, architect, open source committer, Project Management Committee (PMC) member, product manager, and even demanding customer. We have tried to leverage all of that perspective to present a comprehensive view of Oozie in this book. We strongly believe in the vision of Oozie and its potential to make Hadoop a more powerful platform. Hadoop's use is expanding and we notice that users want to use it in smarter and more interesting ways. We have seen many projects in the past getting bogged down with writing, operating, and debugging the workflow system meant to manage the business application. By delegating all of the workflow and scheduling complexities to Oozie, you can focus on developing your core business application.

This book attempts to explain all the technical details of Oozie and its various features with specific, real-world examples. The target audience for this book is Oozie users and administrators at all levels of expertise. Our only requirement for the reader is a working knowledge of Hadoop and the ecosystem tools. We are also very aware of the challenges of operating a Hadoop cluster in general and Oozie in particular, and have tried our best to cover operational issues and debugging techniques in depth. Last but not the least, Oozie is designed to be very flexible and extensible and we want to encourage users to get comfortable with the idea of becoming an Oozie developer if they so desire. We would love to grow the Oozie community and continue the innovation in this part of the Hadoop ecosystem. While it would be nice to achieve all of these goals with this book, the most fundamental hope is that readers find it helpful in using Oozie and Hadoop more effectively every day in their jobs.

Contents of This Book

We start the book off with a brief introduction to Oozie in Chapter 1 and an overview of the important concepts in Chapter 2. Chapter 3 gets your hands dirty right away with detailed instructions on installing and configuring Oozie. We want this book to be a hands-on experience for our readers, so deployment must be mastered early.

Oozie is primarily a workflow system in most users' worlds. Chapters 4 and 5 take you on an in-depth journey through the world of writing and configuring workflows. These chapters also explain parameterization and variable substitution in detail. This will establish a very good basis for the rest of the book, as the other major Oozie features are built on top of the workflow system.

Chapter 6 covers the concepts of the coordinator and helps you to start writing coordinator apps. We then look at the data dependency mechanism in Chapter 7. Data triggers are a powerful and distinguishing feature of Oozie and this chapter explains all the intricacies of managing data dependencies.

Bundles are the higher-level pipeline abstraction and Chapter 8 delves deep into the world of bundles with specific examples and use cases to clarify some of the advanced concepts. It also introduces concepts and challenges like reprocessing, which production pipelines routinely deal with.

In Chapter 9, we cover the powerful security features in Oozie, including Kerberos support and impersonation. This chapter also explains the management of shared libraries in Oozie and cron-based scheduling, which comes in handy for a certain class of use cases.

We cover the developer aspects regarding extending Oozie in Chapter 10. Readers can learn how to implement custom extensions to their Oozie systems. It teaches them how to write their own Expression Language (EL) functions and custom actions.

Last, but not the least, we realize that debugging Oozie workflows and managing the operational details of Oozie are an important part of mastering Oozie. Thus, Chapter 11 focuses exclusively on these topics. We start by explaining the command-line interface (CLI) tool and the REST API and then discuss monitoring and debugging. We also cover the purge service, reprocessing, and other operational aspects in this chapter.

Conventions Used in This Book

The following typographical conventions are used in this book:

Italic
: Indicates new terms, URLs, email addresses, filenames, and file extensions.

`Constant width`
: Used for program listings, as well as within paragraphs to refer to program elements such as variable or function names, databases, data types, environment variables, statements, and keywords.

`Constant width bold`
: Shows commands or other text that should be typed literally by the user.

`Constant width italic`
: Shows text that should be replaced with user-supplied values or by values determined by context.

This icon signifies a tip, suggestion, or general note.

This icon indicates a warning or caution.

Using Code Examples

The source code for all the examples in the book is available on GitHub.

This book is here to help you get your job done. In general, you may use the code in your programs and documentation. You do not need to contact us for permission unless you're reproducing a significant portion of the code. For example, writing a program that uses several chunks of code from this book does not require permission. Selling or distributing a CD-ROM of examples from O'Reilly books does require permission. Answering a question by citing this book and quoting example code does not require permission. Incorporating a significant amount of example code from this book into your product's documentation does require permission.

We appreciate, but do not require, attribution. An attribution usually includes the title, author, publisher, and ISBN. For example: "*Apache Oozie* by Mohammad Kamrul Islam and Aravind Srinivasan (O'Reilly). Copyright 2015 Mohammad Islam and Aravindakshan Srinivasan, 978-1-449-36992-7."

If you feel your use of code examples falls outside fair use or the permission given above, feel free to contact us at *permissions@oreilly.com*.

Safari® Books Online

Safari Books Online (*www.safaribooksonline.com*) is an on-demand digital library that delivers expert content in both book and video form from the world's leading authors in technology and business.

Technology professionals, software developers, web designers, and business and creative professionals use Safari Books Online as their primary resource for research, problem solving, learning, and certification training.

Safari Books Online offers a range of product mixes and pricing programs for organizations, government agencies, and individuals. Subscribers have access to thousands of books, training videos, and prepublication manuscripts in one fully searchable database from publishers like O'Reilly Media, Prentice Hall Professional, Addison-Wesley Professional, Microsoft Press, Sams, Que, Peachpit Press, Focal Press, Cisco Press, John Wiley & Sons, Syngress, Morgan Kaufmann, IBM Redbooks, Packt, Adobe Press, FT Press, Apress, Manning, New Riders, McGraw-Hill, Jones & Bartlett, Course Technology, and dozens more. For more information about Safari Books Online, please visit us online.

How to Contact Us

Please address comments and questions concerning this book to the publisher:

O'Reilly Media, Inc.
1005 Gravenstein Highway North
Sebastopol, CA 95472

800-998-9938 (in the United States or Canada)
707-829-0515 (international or local)
707-829-0104 (fax)

We have a web page for this book, where we list errata, examples, and any additional information. You can access this page at *http://bit.ly/apache-oozie*.

To comment or ask technical questions about this book, send email to *bookquestions@oreilly.com*.

For more information about our books, courses, conferences, and news, see our website at *http://www.oreilly.com*.

Find us on Facebook: *http://facebook.com/oreilly*

Follow us on Twitter: *http://twitter.com/oreillymedia*

Watch us on YouTube: *http://www.youtube.com/oreillymedia*

Acknowledgments

As the saying goes, it takes a village to raise a child. After working on this book, we now realize it takes an even bigger crowd to finish a book! We would like to take this opportunity to thank everybody who helped us with this book. There are a lot of people we would like to thank and we apologize if we have missed a name or two (it's certainly not our intention to forget anybody here). We will start with our family and personal friends because without their understanding, support, encouragement, and patience, this book would not have been possible.

At the top of our list is Robert Kanter from Cloudera. We thank him for his unwavering support. His in-depth knowledge and contributions to the Oozie code base and the community were a major source of information for us both directly and indirectly. He was our "go to" reviewer and sounding board throughout the process. We are very thankful for his incredible attention to detail and for his commitment to this project. We are convinced that without Robert's involvement, this book would have been a lesser product.

A sincere vote of thanks goes out to Mona Chitnis and Virag Kothari from Yahoo! for all the detailed review comments and also for being there to answer any and all of our questions about various areas of the Oozie code. In addition, we also received a lot of comments and suggestions from a few other key reviewers. Their extensive and insightful thoughts definitely enhanced both the technical depth and the readability of this book. Hien Luu (LinkedIn), Jakob Homan (Microsoft), Denis Sheahan (Facebook), and William Kang (LinkedIn) deserve special mention in this regard. Special thanks to Raymie Stata (Altiscale) for his encouragement and support for this book.

We also thank David Chaiken (Altiscale), Barbara Lewis (Altiscale), and Ann McCown (Altiscale) for their support.

We would also like to thank Sumeet Singh from Yahoo!, who initially encouraged us to write a book on Oozie and Santhosh Srinivasan from Cloudera for helping the two of us come together to work on this book. Santhosh has spent some time in the past as a manager of Yahoo!'s Oozie team and his perspective and understanding of this area was a major help to us.

None of this would have been possible without Alejandro Abdelnur, the cocreator of Oozie. Alejandro was personally involved with the contents of the early chapters and without his involvement, this project would have been a much harder endeavor. We sincerely thank him for his direct and indirect help and for serving as a sounding board and inspiration for us.

Finally, we thank all the O'Reilly folks for their support and resources. There are too many to thank individually, but they are the true owners of this project and deserve all the credit for making this happen. They were there every step of the way and helped us realize the vision of a book on Oozie.

CHAPTER 1

Introduction to Oozie

In this chapter, we cover some of the background and motivations that led to the creation of Oozie, explaining the challenges developers faced as they started building complex applications running on Hadoop.[1] We also introduce you to a simple Oozie application. The chapter wraps up by covering the different Oozie releases, their main features, their timeline, compatibility considerations, and some interesting statistics from large Oozie deployments.

Big Data Processing

Within a very short period of time, Apache Hadoop, an open source implementation of Google's *MapReduce* paper and Google File System, has become the de facto platform for processing and storing big data.

Higher-level domain-specific languages (DSL) implemented on top of Hadoop's MapReduce, such as Pig[2] and Hive, quickly followed, making it simpler to write applications running on Hadoop.

A Recurrent Problem

Hadoop, Pig, Hive, and many other projects provide the foundation for storing and processing large amounts of data in an efficient way. Most of the time, it is not possible to perform all required processing with a single MapReduce, Pig, or Hive job.

1 Tom White, *Hadoop: The Definitive Guide, 4th Edition* (Sebastopol, CA: O'Reilly 2015).

2 Olga Natkovich, "Pig - The Road to an Efficient High-level language for Hadoop," Yahoo! Developer Network Blog, October 28, 2008.

Multiple MapReduce, Pig, or Hive jobs often need to be chained together, producing and consuming intermediate data and coordinating their flow of execution.

Throughout the book, when referring to a MapReduce, Pig, Hive, or any other type of job that runs one or more MapReduce jobs on a Hadoop cluster, we refer to it as a *Hadoop job*. We mention the job type explicitly only when there is a need to refer to a particular type of job.

At Yahoo!, as developers started doing more complex processing using Hadoop, multistage Hadoop jobs became common. This led to several ad hoc solutions to manage the execution and interdependency of these multiple Hadoop jobs. Some developers wrote simple shell scripts to start one Hadoop job after the other. Others used Hadoop's JobControl class, which executes multiple MapReduce jobs using topological sorting. One development team resorted to Ant with a custom Ant task to specify their MapReduce and Pig jobs as dependencies of each other—also a topological sorting mechanism. Another team implemented a server-based solution that ran multiple Hadoop jobs using one thread to execute each job.

As these solutions started to be widely used, several issues emerged. It was hard to track errors and it was difficult to recover from failures. It was not easy to monitor progress. It complicated the life of administrators, who not only had to monitor the health of the cluster but also of different systems running multistage jobs from client machines. Developers moved from one project to another and they had to learn the specifics of the custom framework used by the project they were joining. Different organizations within Yahoo! were using significant resources to develop and support multiple frameworks for accomplishing basically the same task.

A Common Solution: Oozie

It was clear that there was a need for a general-purpose system to run multistage Hadoop jobs with the following requirements:

- It should use an adequate and well-understood programming model to facilitate its adoption and to reduce developer ramp-up time.
- It should be easy to troubleshot and recover jobs when something goes wrong.
- It should be extensible to support new types of jobs.
- It should scale to support several thousand concurrent jobs.
- Jobs should run in a server to increase reliability.
- It should be a multitenant service to reduce the cost of operation.

Toward the end of 2008, Alejandro Abdelnur and a few engineers from Yahoo! Bangalore took over a conference room with the goal of implementing such a system. Within a month, the first functional version of Oozie was running. It was able to run multistage jobs consisting of MapReduce, Pig, and SSH jobs. This team successfully leveraged the experience gained from developing PacMan, which was one of the ad hoc systems developed for running multistage Hadoop jobs to process large amounts of data feeds.

Yahoo! open sourced Oozie in 2010. In 2011, Oozie was submitted to the Apache Incubator. A year later, Oozie became a top-level project, Apache Oozie.

Oozie's role in the Hadoop Ecosystem

In this section, we briefly discuss where Oozie fits in the larger Hadoop ecosystem. Figure 1-1 captures a high-level view of Oozie's place in the ecosystem. Oozie can drive the core Hadoop components—namely, MapReduce jobs and Hadoop Distributed File System (HDFS) operations. In addition, Oozie can orchestrate most of the common higher-level tools such as Pig, Hive, Sqoop, and DistCp. More importantly, Oozie can be extended to support any custom Hadoop job written in any language. Although Oozie is primarily designed to handle Hadoop components, Oozie can also manage the execution of any other non-Hadoop job like a Java class, or a shell script.

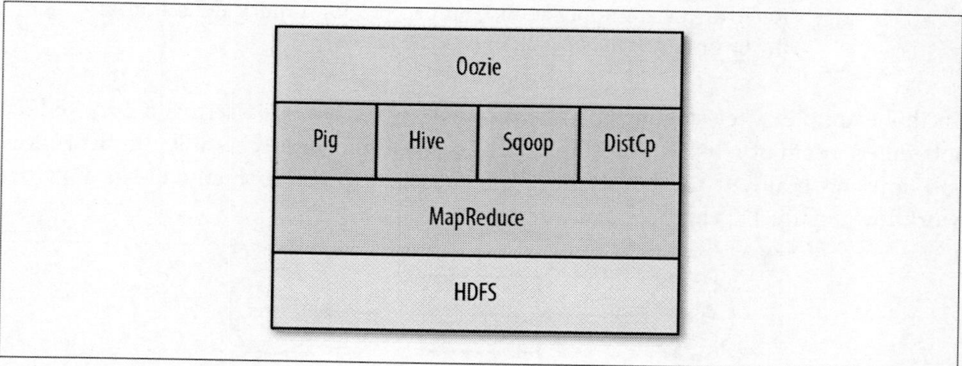

Figure 1-1. Oozie in the Hadoop ecosystem

What exactly is Oozie?

Oozie is an orchestration system for Hadoop jobs. Oozie is designed to run multistage Hadoop jobs as a single job: an Oozie job. Oozie jobs can be configured to run on demand or periodically. Oozie jobs running on demand are called *workflow jobs*. Oozie jobs running periodically are called *coordinator jobs*. There is also a third type of Oozie job called *bundle jobs*. A bundle job is a collection of coordinator jobs managed as a single job.

The name "Oozie"

Alejandro and the engineers were looking for a name that would convey what the system does—managing Hadoop jobs. Something along the lines of an elephant keeper sounded ideal given that Hadoop was named after a stuffed toy elephant. Alejandro was in India at that time, and it seemed appropriate to use the Hindi name for elephant keeper, *mahout*. But the name was already taken by the Apache Mahout project. After more searching, *oozie* (the Burmese word for elephant keeper) popped up and it stuck.

A Simple Oozie Job

To get started with writing an Oozie application and running an Oozie job, we'll create an Oozie workflow application named `identity-WF` that runs an identity MapReduce job. The identity MapReduce job just echoes its input as output and does nothing else. Hadoop bundles the `IdentityMapper` class and `IdentityReducer` class, so we can use those classes for the example.

The source code for all the examples in the book is available on GitHub.

For details on how to build the examples, refer to the README.txt file in the GitHub repository.

Refer to "Oozie Applications" on page 13 for a quick definition of the terms *Oozie application* and *Oozie job*.

In this example, after starting the `identity-WF` workflow, Oozie runs a MapReduce job called `identity-MR`. If the MapReduce job completes successfully, the workflow job ends normally. If the MapReduce job fails to execute correctly, Oozie kills the workflow. Figure 1-2 captures this workflow.

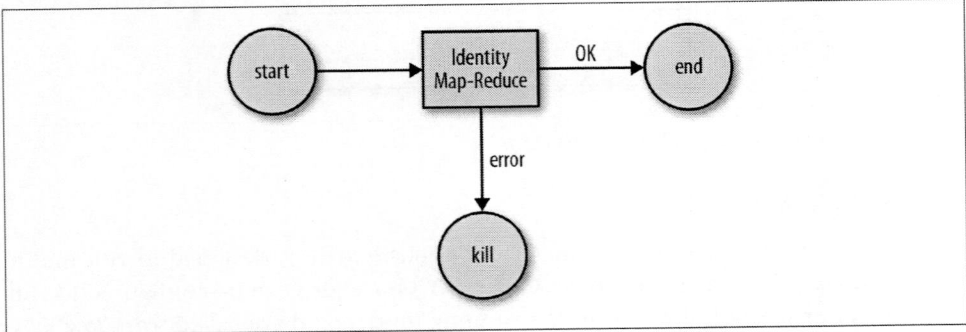

Figure 1-2. identity-WF Oozie workflow example

The example Oozie application is built from the *examples/chapter-01/identity-wf/* directory using the Maven command:

```
$ cd examples/chapter-01/identity-wf/
$ mvn package assembly:single
...
[INFO] BUILD SUCCESS
...
```

The `identity-WF` Oozie workflow application consists of a single file, the *workflow.xml* file. The Map and Reduce classes are already available in Hadoop's classpath and we don't need to include them in the Oozie workflow application package.

The *workflow.xml* file in Example 1-1 contains the workflow definition of the application, an XML representation of Figure 1-2 together with additional information such as the input and output directories for the MapReduce job.

A common question people starting with Oozie ask is *Why was XML chosen to write Oozie applications?* By using XML, Oozie application developers can use any XML editor tool to author their Oozie application. The Oozie server uses XML libraries to parse and validate the correctness of an Oozie application before attempting to use it, significantly simplifying the logic that processes the Oozie application definition. The same holds true for systems creating Oozie applications on the fly.

Example 1-1. identity-WF Oozie workflow XML (workflow.xml)

```
<workflow-app xmlns="uri:oozie:workflow:0.4" name="identity-WF">

  <start to="identity-MR"/>

  <action name="identity-MR">
    <map-reduce>
      <job-tracker>${jobTracker}</job-tracker>
      <name-node>${nameNode}</name-node>
      <prepare>
        <delete path="${exampleDir}/data/output"/>
      </prepare>
      <configuration>
        <property>
          <name>mapred.mapper.class</name>
          <value>org.apache.hadoop.mapred.lib.IdentityMapper</value>
        </property>
        <property>
          <name>mapred.reducer.class</name>
          <value>org.apache.hadoop.mapred.lib.IdentityReducer</value>
        </property>
        <property>
          <name>mapred.input.dir</name>
```

```
          <value>${exampleDir}/data/input</value>
        </property>
        <property>
          <name>mapred.output.dir</name>
          <value>${exampleDir}/data/output</value>
        </property>
      </configuration>
    </map-reduce>
    <ok to="success"/>
    <error to="fail"/>
  </action>

  <kill name="fail">
    <message>The Identity Map-Reduce job failed!</message>
  </kill>

  <end name="success"/>

</workflow-app>
```

The workflow application shown in Example 1-1 expects three parameters: `jobTracker`, `nameNode`, and `exampleDir`. At runtime, these variables will be replaced with the actual values of these parameters.

In Hadoop 1.0, `JobTracker` (JT) is the service that manages MapReduce jobs. This execution framework has been overhauled in Hadoop 2.0, or YARN; the details of YARN are beyond the scope of this book. You can think of the YARN `ResourceManager` (RM) as the new JT, though the RM is vastly different from JT in many ways. So the `<job-tracker>` element in Oozie can be used to pass in either the JT or the RM, even though it is still called as the `<job-tracker>`. In this book, we will use this parameter to refer to either the JT or the RM depending on the version of Hadoop in play.

When running the workflow job, Oozie begins with the `start` node and follows the specified transition to `identity-MR`. The `identity-MR` node is a `<map-reduce>` action. The `<map-reduce>` action indicates where the MapReduce job should run via the `job-tracker` and `name-node` elements (which define the URI of the `JobTracker` and the `NameNode`, respectively). The `prepare` element is used to delete the output directory that will be created by the MapReduce job. If we don't delete the output directory and try to run the workflow job more than once, the MapReduce job will fail because the output directory already exists. The `configuration` section defines the `Mapper` class, the `Reducer` class, the input directory, and the output directory for the MapReduce job. If the MapReduce job completes successfully, Oozie follows the transition defined in the `ok` element named `success`. If the MapReduce job fails, Oozie follows the transition specified in the `error` element named `fail`. The `success` transition takes the job to the end node, completing the Oozie job successfully. The fail transition takes the job to the kill node, killing the Oozie job.

The example application consists of a single file, *workflow.xml*. We need to package and deploy the application on HDFS before we can run a job. The Oozie application package is stored in a directory containing all the files for the application. The *workflow.xml* file must be located in the application root directory:

```
app/
  |
  |-- workflow.xml
```

We first need to create the workflow application package in our local filesystem. Then, to deploy it, we must copy the workflow application package directory to HDFS. Here's how to do it:

```
$ hdfs dfs -put target/example/ch01-identity ch01-identity
$ hdfs dfs -ls -R ch01-identity

/user/joe/ch01-identity/app
/user/joe/ch01-identity/app/workflow.xml
/user/joe/ch01-identity/data
/user/joe/ch01-identity/data/input
/user/joe/ch01-identity/data/input/input.txt
```

To access HDFS from the command line in newer Hadoop versions, the hdfs dfs commands are used. Longtime users of Hadoop may be familiar with the hadoop fs commands. Either interface will work today, but users are encouraged to move to the hdfs dfs commands.

The Oozie workflow application is now deployed in the *ch01-identity/app/* directory under the user's HDFS home directory. We have also copied the necessary input data required to run the Oozie job to the *ch01-identity/data/input* directory.

Before we can run the Oozie job, we need a *job.properties* file in our local filesystem that specifies the required parameters for the job and the location of the application package in HDFS:

```
nameNode=hdfs://localhost:8020
jobTracker=localhost:8032
exampleDir=${nameNode}/user/${user.name}/ch01-identity
oozie.wf.application.path=${exampleDir}/app
```

The parameters needed for this example are jobTracker, nameNode, and exampleDir. The oozie.wf.application.path indicates the location of the application package in HDFS.

Users should be careful with the `JobTracker` and `NameNode` URI, especially the port numbers. These are cluster-specific Hadoop configurations. A common problem we see with new users is that their Oozie job submission will fail after waiting for a long time. One possible reason for this is incorrect port specification for the `JobTracker`. Users need to find the correct `JobTracker` RPC port from the administrator or Hadoop site XML file. Users often get this port and the `JobTracker` UI port mixed up.

We are now ready to submit the job to Oozie. We will use the **`oozie`** command-line tool for this:

```
$ export OOZIE_URL=http://localhost:11000/oozie
$ oozie job -run -config target/example/job.properties
job: 0000006-130606115200591-oozie-joe-W
```

We will cover Oozie's command-line tool and its different parameters in detail later in "Oozie CLI Tool" on page 203. For now, we just need to know that we can run an Oozie job using the `-run` option. And using the `-config` option, we can specify the location of the *job.properties* file.

We can also monitor the progress of the job using the `oozie` command-line tool:

```
$ oozie job -info 0000006-130606115200591-oozie-joe-W
Job ID : 0000006-130606115200591-oozie-joe-W
-----------------------------------------------------------------
Workflow Name : identity-WF
App Path      : hdfs://localhost:8020/user/joe/ch01-identity/app
Status        : RUNNING
Run           : 0
User          : joe
Group         : -
Created       : 2013-06-06 20:35 GMT
Started       : 2013-06-06 20:35 GMT
Last Modified : 2013-06-06 20:35 GMT
Ended         : -
CoordAction ID: -

Actions
-----------------------------------------------------------------
ID                                                   Status
-----------------------------------------------------------------
0000006-130606115200591-oozie-joe-W@:start:          OK
-----------------------------------------------------------------
0000006-130606115200591-oozie-joe-W@identity-MR      RUNNING
-----------------------------------------------------------------
```

When the job completes, the **`oozie`** command-line tool reports the completion state:

```
$ oozie job -info 0000006-130606115200591-oozie-joe-W
Job ID : 0000006-130606115200591-oozie-joe-W
```

```
------------------------------------------------------------------------
Workflow Name : identity-WF
App Path      : hdfs://localhost:8020/user/joe/ch01-identity/app
Status        : SUCCEEDED
Run           : 0
User          : joe
Group         : -
Created       : 2013-06-06 20:35 GMT
Started       : 2013-06-06 20:35 GMT
Last Modified : 2013-06-06 20:35 GMT
Ended         : 2013-06-06 20:35 GMT
CoordAction ID: -

Actions
------------------------------------------------------------------------
ID                                                   Status
------------------------------------------------------------------------
0000006-130606115200591-oozie-joe-W@:start:        OK
------------------------------------------------------------------------
0000006-130606115200591-oozie-joe-W@identity-MR    OK
------------------------------------------------------------------------
0000006-130606115200591-oozie-joe-W@success        OK
------------------------------------------------------------------------
```

The output of our first Oozie workflow job can be found in the *ch01-identity/data/output* directory under the user's HDFS home directory:

```
$ hdfs dfs -ls -R ch01-identity/data/output

/user/joe/ch01-identity/data/output/_SUCCESS
/user/joe/ch01-identity/data/output/part-00000
```

The output of this Oozie job is the output of the MapReduce job run by the workflow job. We can also see the job status and detailed job information on the Oozie web interface, as shown in Figure 1-3.

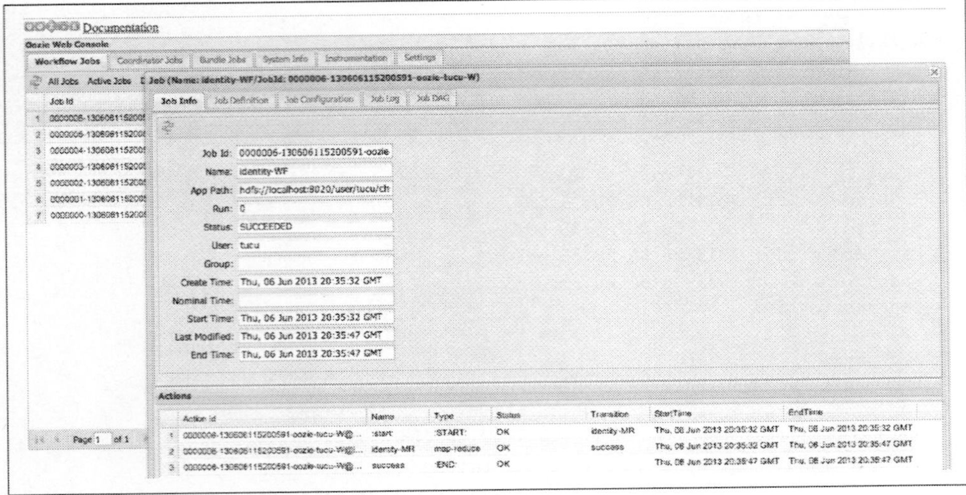

Figure 1-3. Oozie workflow job on the Oozie web interface

This section has illustrated the full lifecycle of a simple Oozie workflow application and the typical ways to monitor it.

Oozie Releases

Oozie has gone through four major releases so far. The salient features of each of these major releases are listed here:

1.x
: Support for workflow jobs

2.x
: Support for coordinator jobs

3.x
: Support for bundle jobs

4.x
: Hive/HCatalog integration, Oozie server high availability, and support for service-level agreement (SLA) notifications

Several other features, bug fixes, and improvements have also been released as part of the various major, minor, and micro releases. Support for additional types of Hadoop and non-Hadoop jobs (SSH, Hive, Sqoop, DistCp, Java, Shell, email), support for different database vendors for the Oozie database (Derby, MySQL, PostgreSQL, Oracle), and scalability improvements are some of the more interesting enhancements and updates that have made it to the product over the years.

Timeline and status of the releases

The 1.x release series was developed by Yahoo! internally. There were two open source code drops on GitHub in May 2010 (versions 1.5.6 and 1.6.2).

The 2.x release series was developed in Yahoo!'s Oozie repository on GitHub. There are nine releases of the 2.x series, the last one being 2.3.2 in August 2011.

The 3.x release series had eight releases. The first three were developed in Yahoo!'s Oozie repository on GitHub and the rest in Apache Oozie, the last one being 3.3.2 in March 2013.

4.x is the newest series and the latest version (4.1.0) was released in December 2014.

The 1.x and 2.x series are are no longer under development, the 3.x series is under maintenance development, and the 4.x series is under active development.

The 3.x release series is considered stable.

Current and previous releases are available for download from Apache Oozie, as well as a part of Cloudera, Hortonworks, and MapR Hadoop distributions.

Compatibility

Oozie has done a very good job of preserving backward compatibility between releases. Upgrading from one Oozie version to a newer one is a simple process and should not affect existing Oozie applications or the integration of other systems with Oozie.

As we discussed in "A Simple Oozie Job" on page 4, Oozie applications must be written in XML. It is common for Oozie releases to introduce changes and enhancements to the XML syntax used to write applications. Even when this happens, newer Oozie versions always support the XML syntax of older versions. However, the reverse is not true, and the Oozie server will reject jobs of applications written against a later version.

As for the Oozie server, depending on the scope of the upgrade, the Oozie administrator might need to suspend all jobs or let all running jobs complete before upgrading. The administrator might also need to use an upgrade tool or modify some of the configuration settings of the Oozie server.

The `oozie` command-line tool, Oozie client Java API, and the Oozie HTTP REST API have all evolved maintaining backward compatibility with previous releases.[3]

3 Roy Thomas Fielding, "REST: Representational State Transfer" (PhD dissertation, University of California, Irvine, 2000)

Some Oozie Usage Numbers

Oozie is widely used in several large production clusters across major enterprises to schedule Hadoop jobs. For instance, Yahoo! is a major user of Oozie and it periodically discloses usage statistics. In this section, we present some of these numbers just to give readers an idea about Oozie's scalability and stability.

Yahoo! has one of the largest deployments of Hadoop, with more than 40,000 nodes across several clusters. Oozie is the primary workflow engine for Hadoop clusters at Yahoo! and is responsible for launching almost 72% of 28.9 million monthly Hadoop jobs as of January 2015. The largest Hadoop cluster processes 60 bundles and 1,600 coordinators, amounting to 80,000 daily workflows with 3 million workflow nodes. About 25% of the coordinators execute at frequencies of either 5, 10, or 15 minutes. The remaining 75% of the coordinator jobs are mostly hourly or daily jobs with some weekly and monthly jobs. Yahoo's Oozie team runs and supports several complex jobs. Interesting examples include a single bundle with 200 coordinators and a workflow with 85 fork/join pairs.

Now that we have covered the basics of Oozie, including the problem it solves and how it fits into the Hadoop ecosystem, it's time to learn more about the concepts of Oozie. We will do that in the next chapter.

CHAPTER 2

Oozie Concepts

This chapter covers the basic concepts behind the workflow, coordinator, and bundle jobs, and how they relate to one another. We present a use case for each one of them. Throughout the book, we will elaborate on these concepts and provide more detailed examples. The last section of this chapter explains Oozie's high-level architecture.

Oozie Applications

In Unix, the */bin/echo* file is an executable. When we type `/bin/echo Hello` in a terminal session, it starts a process that prints `Hello`. Oozie applications are analogous to Unix executables, and Oozie jobs are analogous to Unix processes. Oozie users develop applications, and one execution of an application is called a job.

Throughout the book, unless explicitly specified, we do not differentiate between applications and jobs. Instead, we simply call them a workflow, a coordinator, or a bundle.

Oozie Workflows

An Oozie workflow is a multistage Hadoop job. A workflow is a collection of action and control nodes arranged in a directed acyclic graph (DAG) that captures control dependency where each action typically is a Hadoop job (e.g., a MapReduce, Pig, Hive, Sqoop, or Hadoop DistCp job). There can also be actions that are not Hadoop jobs (e.g., a Java application, a shell script, or an email notification).

The order of the nodes in the workflow determines the execution order of these actions. An action does not start until the previous action in the workflow ends. Control nodes in a workflow are used to manage the execution flow of actions. The *start* and *end control nodes* define the start and end of a workflow. The *fork* and *join control nodes* allow executing actions in parallel. The *decision control node* is like a `switch/case` statement that can select a particular execution path within the workflow using information from the job itself. Figure 2-1 represents an example workflow.

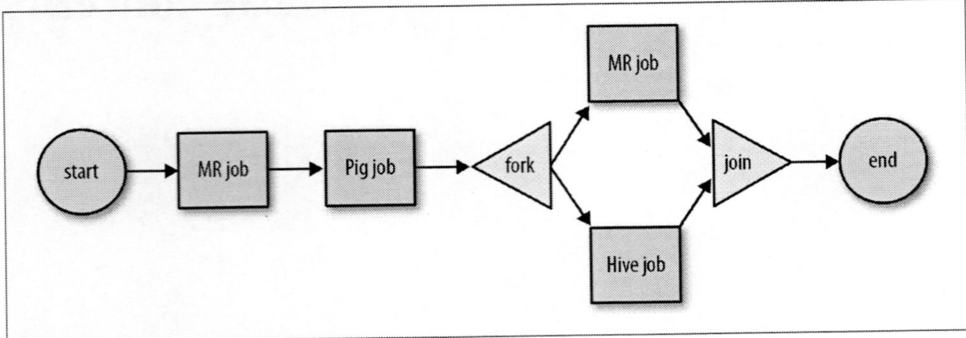

Figure 2-1. Oozie Workflow

Because workflows are directed acyclic graphs, they don't support loops in the flow.

Workflow use case

For this use case, we will consider a site for mobile applications that keeps track of user interactions collecting the timestamp, username, and geographic location of each interaction. This information is written to log files. The logs files from all the servers are collected daily. We would like to process all the logs for a day to obtain the following information:

- ZIP code(s) for each user
- Interactions per user
- User interactions per ZIP code

First, we need to convert geographic locations into ZIP codes. We do this using a `to-ZIP` MapReduce job that processes the daily logs. The input data for the job is `(timeStamp, geoLocation, userName)`. The map phase converts the geographic location into ZIP code and emits a ZIP and username as key and 1 as value. The intermediate data of the job is in the form of `(ZIP + userName, 1)`. The reduce phase adds up and emits all the occurrences of the same ZIP and username key. Each output record of the job is then `(ZIP, userName, interactions)`.

Using the `(ZIP, userName, interactions)` output from the first job, we run two additional MapReduce jobs, the `user-ZIPs` job and `user-interactions` job.

The map phase of the `user-ZIPs` job emits `(userName, ZIP)` as intermediate data. The reduce phase collects all the ZIP codes of a `userName` in an array and emits `(userName, ZIP[])`.

For the `user-interactions` job, the map phase emits `(userName, 1)` as intermediate data. The reduce phase adds up all the occurrences for the same `userName` and emits `(userName, number-of-interactions)`.

The `to-ZIP` job must run first. When it finishes, we can run the `user-ZIPs` and the `user-interactions` MapReduce jobs. Because the `user-ZIPs` and `user-interactions` jobs do not depend on each other, we can run both of them in parallel.

Figure 2-2 represents the `daily-logs-workflow` just described.

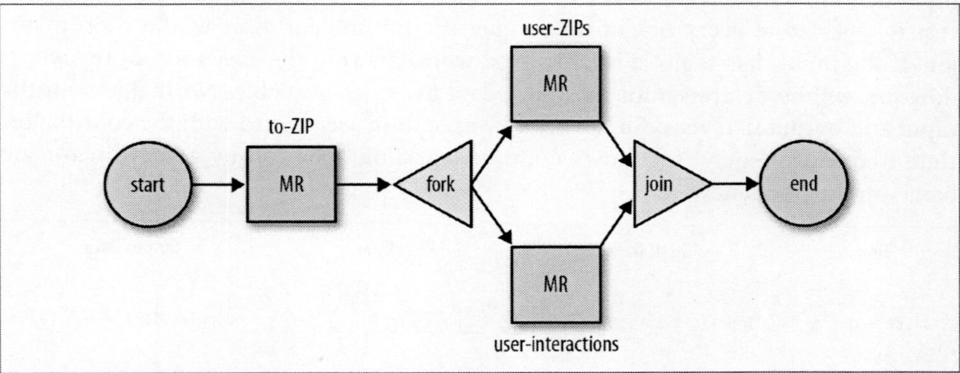

Figure 2-2. The daily-logs-workflow Oozie workflow

Oozie Coordinators

An Oozie coordinator schedules workflow executions based on a *start-time* and a *frequency parameter*, and it starts the workflow when all the necessary input data becomes available. If the input data is not available, the workflow execution is delayed until the input data becomes available. A coordinator is defined by a start and end time, a frequency, input and output data, and a workflow. A coordinator runs periodically from the start time until the end time, as shown in Figure 2-3.

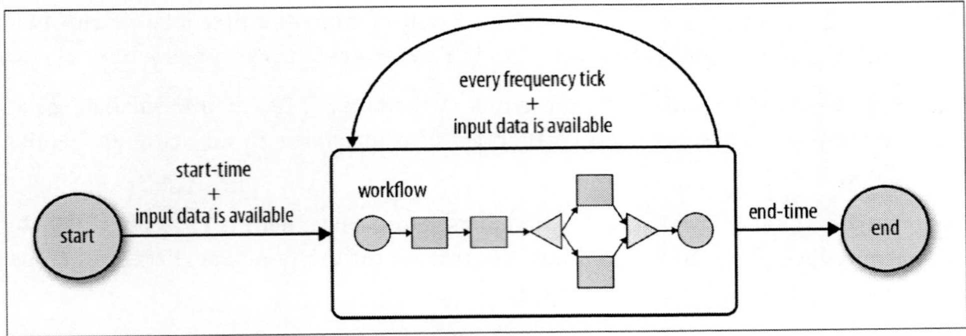

Figure 2-3. Lifecycle of an Oozie coordinator

Beginning at the start time, the coordinator job checks if the required input data is available. When the input data becomes available, a workflow is started to process the input data, which on completion, produces the corresponding output data. This process is repeated at every tick of the frequency until the end time of the coordinator job. If the input data is not available for a workflow run, the execution of the workflow job will be delayed until the input data becomes available. Normally, both the input and output data used for a workflow execution are aligned with the coordinator time frequency. Figure 2-4 shows multiple workflow jobs run by a coordinator job based on the frequency.

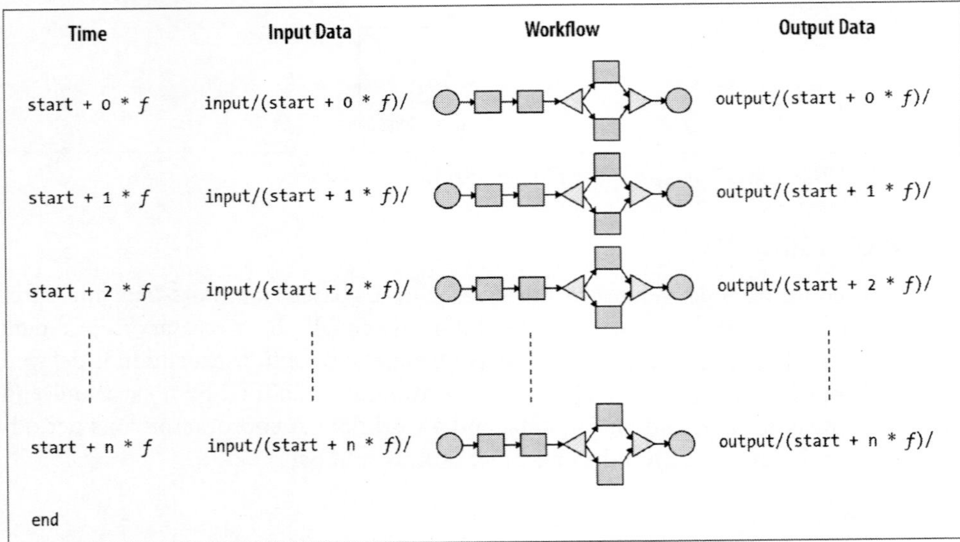

Figure 2-4. An Oozie coordinator job

It is possible to configure a coordinator to wait for a maximum amount of time for the input data to become available and timeout if the data doesn't show up.

If a coordinator does not define any input data, the coordinator job is a time-based scheduler, similar to a Unix *cron* job.

Coordinator use case

Building on the "Workflow use case" on page 14, the `daily-logs-workflow` needs to run on a daily basis. It is expected that the logs from the previous day are ready and available for processing at 2:00 a.m.

To avoid the need for a manual submission of the `daily-logs-workflow` every day once the log files are available, we use a coordinator job, the `daily-logs-coordinator` job.

To process all the daily logs for the year 2013, the coordinator job must run every day at 2:00 a.m., starting on January 2, 2013 and ending on January 1, 2014.

The coordinator defines an input data dependency on logs files: `rawlogs`. It produces three datasets as output data: `zip_userName_interactions`, `userName_interactions`, and `userName_ZIPs`. To differentiate the input and output data that is used and produced every day, the date of the logs is templatized and is used as part of the input data and output data directory paths. For example, every day, the logs from the mobile site are copied into a *rawlogs/YYYYMMDD/* directory. Similarly, the output data is created in three different directories: *zip_userName_interactions/YYYYMMDD/*, *userName_interactions/YYYYMMDD/*, and *userName_ZIPs/YYYYMMDD/*. For both the input and the output data, YYYYMMDD is the day of the logs being processed. For example, for May 24, 2013, it is `20130524`.

When the `daily-logs-coordinator` job is running and the daily `rawlogs` input data is available at 2:00 a.m. of the next day, the workflow is started immediately. However, if for any reason the `rawlogs` input data is not available at 2:00 a.m., the coordinator job will wait until the input data becomes available to start the workflow that processes the logs. If the daily `rawlogs` are not available for a few days, the coordinator job keeps track of all the missed days. And when the `rawlogs` for a missing day shows up, the workflow to process the logs for the corresponding date is started. The output data will have the same date as the date of the input data that has been processed. Figure 2-5 captures some of these details.

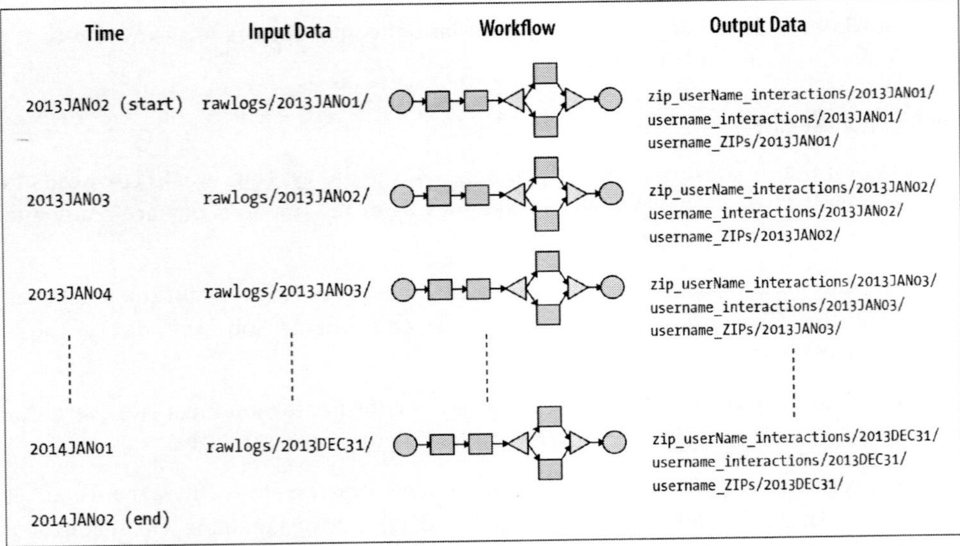

Figure 2-5. daily-logs-coordinator Oozie coordinator

Oozie Bundles

An Oozie bundle is a collection of coordinator jobs that can be started, stopped, suspended, and modified as a single job. Typically, coordinator jobs in a bundle depend on each other. The Output data produced by a coordinator job becomes input data for other coordinator jobs. These types of interdependent coordinator jobs are also called *data pipelines*.

Bundle use case

We will extend the "Coordinator use case" on page 17 to explain the concept of a bundle. Specifically, let's assume that in addition to the daily processing, we need to do a weekly and a monthly aggregation of the daily results.

For this aggregation, we use an `aggregator-workflow` workflow job that takes three different inputs for a range of dates: `zip_userName_interactions`, `userName_interactions`, and `userName_ZIPs`.

The weekly aggregation is done by the `weekly-aggregator-coordinator` coordinator job with a frequency of one week that aggregates data from the previous week.

The monthly aggregation is done by the `monthly-aggregator-coordinator` coordinator job with a frequency of one month that aggregates data from the previous month.

We have three coordinator jobs: `daily-logs-coordinator`, `weekly-aggregator-coordinator`, and `monthly-aggregator-coordinator`. Note that we are using the same workflow application to do the reports aggregation. We are just running it using different date ranges.

A `logs-processing-bundle` bundle job groups these three coordinator jobs. By running the bundle job, the three coordinator jobs will run at their corresponding frequencies. All workflow jobs and coordinator jobs are accessible and managed from a single bundle job.

This `logs-processing-bundle` bundle job is also known as a data pipeline job.

Parameters, Variables, and Functions

Most jobs running on a regular basis are parameterized. This is very typical for Oozie jobs. For example, we may need to run the same workflow on a daily basis, each day using different input and output directories. In this case, we need two parameters for our job: one specifying the input directory and the other specifying the output directory.

Oozie parameters can be used for all type of Oozie jobs: workflows, coordinators, and bundles. In "A Simple Oozie Job" on page 4, we specified the parameters for the job in the *job.properties* file used to submit the job:

```
nameNode=hdfs://localhost:8020
jobTracker=localhost:8032
exampleDir=${nameNode}/user/${user.name}/ch01-identity
oozie.wf.application.path=${exampleDir}/app
```

In "Oozie Coordinators" on page 15, we saw a coordinator that triggers a daily workflow to process the logs from the previous day. The coordinator job needs to pass the location of the logs to process for the corresponding day to each workflow. This is done using parameters as well.

Variables allow us to use the job parameters within the application definition. For example, in "A Simple Oozie Job" on page 4, the MapReduce action uses the three parameters of the job to define the cluster URIs as well as the input and output directories to use for the job:

```
...
  <action name="identity-MR">
    <map-reduce>
      <job-tracker>${jobTracker}</job-tracker>
      <name-node>${nameNode}</name-node>
      <prepare>
        <delete path="${exampleDir}/data/output"/>
      </prepare>
      <configuration>
```

```
        ...
        <property>
          <name>mapred.input.dir</name>
          <value>${exampleDir}/data/input</value>
        </property>
        <property>
          <name>mapred.output.dir</name>
          <value>${exampleDir}/data/output</value>
        </property>
      </configuration>
    </map-reduce>
    ...
  </action>
...
```

In addition to variables, Oozie supports a set of functions that can be used to carry out sophisticated logic for resolving variable values during the execution of the Oozie job. For example, the `${wf:id()}` function resolves to the workflow job ID of the current job. The `${hadoop:counters('identity-MR')}` function returns the counters of the MapReduce job run by the `identity-MR` action. We cover these functions in detail in Chapters 5, 6, and 7.

Application Deployment Model

An Oozie application is comprised of one file defining the logic of the application plus other files such as configuration and JAR files and scripts. A workflow application consists of a *workflow.xml* file and may have configuration files, Pig scripts, Hive scripts, JAR files, and more. Coordinator applications consist of a *coordinator.xml* file. Bundle applications consist of a *bundle.xml* file.

In most of our examples, we use the filename *workflow.xml* for the workflow definition. Although the default filename is *workflow.xml*, you can choose a different name if you wish. However, if you use a different filename, you'll need to specify the full path including the filename as the workflow app path in *job.properties*. In other words, you can't skip the filename and only specify the directory. For example, for the custom filename *my_wf.xml*, you would need to define `oozie.wf.application.path=${exampleDir}/app/my_wf.xml`. The same convention is true for coordinator and bundle filenames.

Oozie applications are organized in directories, where a directory contains all files for the application. If files of an application need to reference each other, it is recommended to use relative paths. This simplifies the process of relocating the application to another directory if and when required. The JAR files required to execute the Hadoop jobs defined in the action of the workflow must be included in the classpath of Hadoop jobs. One basic approach is to copy the JARs into the *lib/* subdirectory of the application directory. All JAR files in the *lib/* subdirectory of the application directory are automatically included in the classpath of all Hadoop jobs started by Oozie. There are other efficient ways to include JARs in the classpath and we discuss them in Chapter 9.

Oozie Architecture

Figure 2-6 captures the Oozie architecture at a very high level.

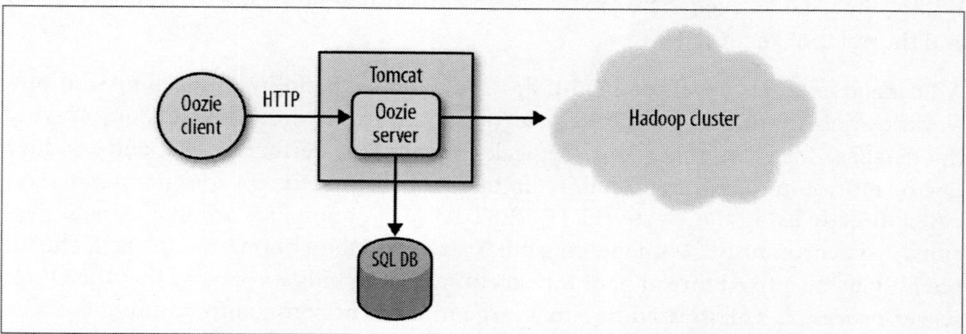

Figure 2-6. Oozie server architecture

When Oozie runs a job, it needs to read the XML file defining the application. Oozie expects all application files to be available in HDFS. This means that before running a job, you must copy the application files to HDFS. Deploying an Oozie application simply involves copying the directory with all the files required to run the application to HDFS. After introducing you to all aspects of Oozie, additional advice is given in "Application Deployment Tips" on page 236.

The Oozie server is a Java web application that runs in a *Java servlet container*. By default, Oozie uses Apache Tomcat, which is an open source implementation of the Java servlet technology. Oozie clients, users, and other applications interact with the Oozie server using the `oozie` command-line tool, the Oozie Java client API, or the Oozie HTTP REST API. The `oozie` command-line tool and the Oozie Java API ultimately use the Oozie HTTP REST API to communicate with the Oozie server.

The Oozie server is a stateless web application. It does not keep any user or job information in memory between user requests. All the information about running and completed jobs is stored in a SQL database. When processing a user request for a job, Oozie retrieves the corresponding job state from the SQL database, performs the requested operation, and updates the SQL database with the new state of the job. This is a very common design pattern for web applications and helps Oozie support tens of thousands of jobs with relatively modest hardware. All of the job states are stored in the SQL database and the transactional nature of the SQL database ensures reliable behavior of Oozie jobs even if the Oozie server crashes or is shut down. When the Oozie server comes back up, it can continue to manage all the jobs based on their last known state.

Oozie supports four types of databases: Derby, MySQL, Oracle, and PostgreSQL. Oozie has built-in purging logic that deletes completed jobs from the database after a period of time. If the database is properly sized for the expected load, it can be considered maintenance-free other than performing regular backups.

Within the Oozie server, there are two main entities that do all the work, the `Command` and the `ActionExecutor` classes.

A `Command` executes a well-defined task—for example, handling the submission of a workflow job, monitoring a MapReduce job started from a workflow job, or querying the database for all running jobs. Typically, commands perform a task and produce one or more commands to do follow-up tasks for the job. Except for commands executed directly using the Oozie HTTP REST API, all commands are queued and executed asynchronously. A queue consumer executes the commands using a thread pool. By using a fixed thread pool for executing commands, we ensure that the Oozie server process is not stressed due to a large number of commands running concurrently. When the Oozie server is under heavy load, the command queue backs up because commands are queued faster than they can be executed. As the load goes back to normal levels, the queue depletes. The command queue has a maximum capacity. If the queue overflows, commands are dropped silently from the queue. To handle this scenario, Oozie has a background thread that re-creates all dropped commands after a certain amount of time using the job state stored in the SQL database.

There is an `ActionExecutor` for each type of action you can use in a workflow (e.g., there is an `ActionExecutor` for MapReduce actions, and another for Pig actions). An `ActionExecutor` knows how to start, kill, monitor, and gather information about the type of job the action handles. Modifying Oozie to add support for a new type of action in Oozie requires implementing an `ActionExecutor` and a Java main class, and defining the XML syntax for the action (we cover this topic in detail in Chapter 10).

Given this overview of Oozie's concepts and architecture, you should now feel fairly comfortable with the overall idea of Oozie and the environment in which it operates. We will expand on all of these topics as we progress through this book. But first, we will guide you through the installation and setup of Oozie in the next chapter.

CHAPTER 3

Setting Up Oozie

In this chapter, we describe how to build and install Oozie on a single machine. This is suitable for installing evaluation and development environments while also introducing Oozie's general deployment architecture. Later in this chapter, we also cover advanced installation topics required for a production environment.

Oozie Deployment

In this section, we outline how to deploy and configure Oozie and its related modules on a real system. As explained in "Oozie Architecture" on page 21, there are four basic systems in a standard Oozie setup. A short overview of each of those systems will help you to better understand the Oozie setup and installation.

The Oozie server runs in a web container (e.g., Tomcat) and manages Oozie job scheduling and execution. The Oozie server is actually a Hadoop client and a database client while it acts as a server for Oozie clients. It also provides an optional web user interface for basic monitoring of jobs. This web UI utilizes a JavaScript library called *extJS*, which is not Apache compliant. The Oozie server needs to package all these required libraries into an *oozie.war* file. Although the Oozie server can be installed on any machine collocated with any other system, we recommend installing it on a separate machine to ensure its stability, especially in large production systems.

The Oozie client can connect to the Oozie server in multiple ways. The Oozie command-line interface (CLI) is the most popular and convenient way of interacting with the Oozie server. In addition, the Oozie server provides a standard REST API, enabling you to write a client application in any language. Finally, Oozie also provides a Java client library that could be used in any JVM-based application. The three types of client applications can run on any machine provided it has network access to the Oozie web service.

Typically, the Oozie server works with any recent Hadoop version. Oozie requires two things to connect to any Hadoop system. First, Oozie should use the same version of the Hadoop JARs as the installed Hadoop services. Second, Hadoop's *core-site.xml* should be configured to allow the Oozie service user (`oozie`) account to act as a proxy user for Hadoop services (details explained later in this chapter).

Oozie supports multiple DBMSes for its internal use, including Derby, PostgreSql, MySQL, and Oracle. The Oozie server requires two things to support any DBMS. First, the appropriate JDBC JAR should be included in the *oozie.war* file. Second, the *oozie-site.xml* must be configured with the relevant JDBC connection details. By default, the Oozie package includes the required JAR and configurations for Derby. Deploying and configuring a different DBMS system is the user's responsibility. Although the DBMS can be installed on any machine, we recommend that you install the DB server on a separate machine than the Oozie server in production environments.

Basic Installations

In this section, we explain the steps required to build and install Oozie on a single machine. This discussion focuses primarily on the open source Apache version. Most commercial Hadoop vendors also include Oozie as part of their distributions. If you are using one of those, you can skip this section and follow the specific vendor-provided installation instructions instead.

Requirements

The following tools are required in order to build and install Oozie:

- Unix-like operating system (Oozie has been tested on Linux and Mac OS X)
- Oracle Java JDK 1.6+
- Maven 3.0.1+ (only required if you are building Oozie)

Make sure the Java and Maven commands such as `java`, `javac`, and `mvn` are available in your Unix path. Your machine might already have those tools installed. You can verify the correct version of Java and Maven by running the following commands from your terminal window.

```
$ java -version
$ mvn -version
```

Build Oozie

The best way to install Oozie is to build it locally from an Oozie source release. You'll need to follow these steps:

1. Download and unpack the Oozie source code release from Apache:

```
$ cd <BUILD_BASE_PATH>
$ curl -O http://www.us.apache.org/dist/oozie/4.0.1/oozie-4.0.1.tar.gz
$ tar xvf oozie-4.0.1.tar.gz
$ cd oozie-4.0.1
```

2. Build the Oozie binary package:

```
$ bin/mkdistro.sh -DskipTests
[INFO] Scanning for projects...
....
[INFO] BUILD SUCCESS
[INFO] ------------------------------------------------------------
[INFO] Total time: 5:05.467s
[INFO] Finished at: Mon Oct 27 00:43:14 PDT 2014
[INFO] Final Memory: 68M/306M
[INFO] ------------------------------------------------------------

Oozie distro created, DATE[2014.10.27-07:38:06GMT] VC-REV[unavailable],
available at [/Users/joe/apache/oozie/book_oozie-4.0.1/oozie-4.0.1/
  distro/target]
```

You can build and verify all test cases by not specifying the `-DskipTests` option:

```
$ bin/mkdistro.sh
```

In some cases, the build may fail due to insufficient memory. You can execute `export MAVEN_OPTS=-Xmx1024m` to increase the memory for Maven. The build might also fail due to a missing or inconsistent JAR file downloaded into the local Maven cache. You can remove the Maven cache using `rm -rf ~/.m2/` and start a new build.

Install Oozie Server

As mentioned in "Oozie Deployment" on page 23, the Oozie web application archive (*.war*) file found in the Oozie binary package doesn't contain all the required JAR or library files. The missing JARs and libraries mainly come from three sources: Hadoop JARs, JDBC JARs, and extJS package. You need to explicitly inject those into *oozie.war*. The following steps show you how to inject the JARs, install Oozie, and configure it:

1. Copy the Oozie binary package:

   ```
   $ cd <INSTALLATION_DIR>
   $ cp <BUILD_BASE_PATH>/
     oozie-4.0.1/distro/target/
     oozie-4.0.1-distro.tar.gz .
   $ tar xvf oozie-4.0.1-distro.tar.gz
   $ cd oozie-4.0.1
   ```

2. Collect third-party libraries.

   Oozie provides a convenient way to inject any library into the original *oozie.war* file. You can create a directory called *libext/* in the same directory where the TAR file is unpacked. Then, you copy all missing library and JAR files into the *libext/* directory. The Oozie setup script will then inject the libraries into the original WAR file and finally create a new self-contained WAR file that you can deploy in any web server.

   a. You can gather Hadoop JARs from either of these sources:

      - The Oozie build directory contains the required JARs from major Hadoop releases.
      - Copy the Hadoop JAR from any Hadoop package or any installed Hadoop system:

        ```
        $ mkdir libext
        $ cd libext
        $ cp <BUILD_BASE_PATH>/oozie-4.0.1/hadooplibs/target/
            oozie-4.0.1-hadooplibs/oozie-4.0.1/\
          hadooplibs/hadooplib-2.3.0.oozie-4.0.1/* .
        ```

      Or:

        ```
        Copy JARs from <HADOOP_INSTALLATION_DIR>/ directory.
        ```

   b. Download extJS 2.2 from *http://extjs.com/deploy/ext-2.2.zip* and copy it into the *libext/* directory:

      ```
      $ cd <INSTALLATION_DIR>/oozie-4.0.1/libext
      $ cp <EXT_JS_DIR>/ext-2.2.zip .
      $ ls -1
      ```

```
...
commons-codec-1.4.jar
commons-collections-3.2.1.jar
...
ext-2.2.zip
guava-11.0.2.jar
hadoop-annotations-2.3.0.jar
hadoop-auth-2.3.0.jar
hadoop-client-2.3.0.jar
hadoop-common-2.3.0.jar
hadoop-hdfs-2.3.0.jar
hadoop-mapreduce-client-app-2.3.0.jar
hadoop-mapreduce-client-common-2.3.0.jar
hadoop-mapreduce-client-core-2.3.0.jar
hadoop-mapreduce-client-jobclient-2.3.0.jar
hadoop-mapreduce-client-shuffle-2.3.0.jar
hadoop-yarn-api-2.3.0.jar
hadoop-yarn-client-2.3.0.jar
hadoop-yarn-common-2.3.0.jar
hadoop-yarn-server-common-2.3.0.jar
...
```

3. Create a self-contained Oozie WAR file:

```
$ cd ..
$ bin/oozie-setup.sh prepare-war
  setting CATALINA_OPTS="$CATALINA_OPTS -Xmx1024m"

  INFO: Adding extension: <INSTALLATION_DIR>/libext/activation-1.1.jar
  INFO: Adding extension: <INSTALLATION_DIR>/libext/avro-1.7.4.jar
  INFO: Adding extension: <INSTALLATION_DIR>/libext/
      commons-beanutils-1.7.0.jar
   ..elided
  INFO: Adding extension: <INSTALLATION_DIR>/libext/
      guava-11.0.2.jar
  INFO: Adding extension: <INSTALLATION_DIR>/libext/
      hadoop-annotations-2.3.0.jar
  INFO: Adding extension: <INSTALLATION_DIR>/libext/
      hadoop-auth-2.3.0.jar
  INFO: Adding extension: <INSTALLATION_DIR>/libext/
      hadoop-client-2.3.0.jar
  INFO: Adding extension: <INSTALLATION_DIR>/libext/
      hadoop-common-2.3.0.jar
  INFO: Adding extension: <INSTALLATION_DIR>/libext/hadoop-hdfs-2.3.0.jar
  INFO: Adding extension: <INSTALLATION_DIR>/libext/
  hadoop-mapreduce-client-app-2.3.0.jar
  INFO: Adding extension: <INSTALLATION_DIR>/libext/
  hadoop-mapreduce-client-common-2.3.0.jar
  INFO: Adding extension: <INSTALLATION_DIR>/libext/
  hadoop-mapreduce-client-core-2.3.0.jar
  INFO: Adding extension: <INSTALLATION_DIR>/libext/
```

```
hadoop-mapreduce-client-jobclient-2.3.0.jar
INFO: Adding extension: <INSTALLATION_DIR>/libext/
hadoop-mapreduce-client-shuffle-2.3.0.jar
INFO: Adding extension: <INSTALLATION_DIR>/libext/
    hadoop-yarn-api-2.3.0.jar
INFO: Adding extension: <INSTALLATION_DIR>/libext/
    hadoop-yarn-client-2.3.0.jar
INFO: Adding extension: <INSTALLATION_DIR>/libext/
    hadoop-yarn-common-2.3.0.jar
INFO: Adding extension: <INSTALLATION_DIR>/libext/
    hadoop-yarn-server-common-2.3.0.jar
 .. elided

New Oozie WAR file with added 'ExtJS library, JARs' at
<INSTALLATION_DIR>/oozie-server/webapps/oozie.war


INFO: Oozie is ready to be started
```

4. Configure the Oozie server. In this basic installation, you can use the default configurations provided in the Oozie package. For advanced installation, you may need to modify the configuration (we'll discuss this later in this chapter).
5. Finally, create the Oozie DB:

```
$ bin/ooziedb.sh create -sqlfile oozie.sql -run
setting CATALINA_OPTS="$CATALINA_OPTS -Xmx1024m"
Validate DB Connection
DONE
..
Create SQL schema
DONE
Create OOZIE_SYS table
DONE
Oozie DB has been created for Oozie version '4.0.1'

The SQL commands have been written to: oozie.sql
```

Hadoop Cluster

This book assumes that you have a fundamental knowledge of Hadoop. You can learn more about Hadoop from *Hadoop: The Definitive Guide* (O'Reilly) and from the online Apache Hadoop documentation. In this section, we primarily describe the specific Hadoop configuration required for Oozie.

Hadoop installation

If Hadoop is already installed, you can skip this section. Otherwise, use the online instructions to install Hadoop in a pseudodistributed mode. In this book, most of the examples assume a Hadoop deployment on `localhost` in a pseudodistributed mode.

Configuring Hadoop for Oozie. Oozie runs all Hadoop jobs as the end user, not as the Unix user (*oozie*) who owns the Oozie service. In other words, the Oozie service owner (*oozie*) serves as a proxy user for accessing Hadoop.[1] So you need to configure Hadoop to allow *oozie* as a proxy user. More specifically, the following two properties must be added to *$HADOOP_HOME/etc/hadoop/core-site.xml* and Hadoop must be restarted subsequent to those changes:

```
<!-- OOZIE -->
<property>
      <name>hadoop.proxyuser.[OOZIE_SERVICE_OWNER].hosts</name>
      <value>[OOZIE_SERVICE_HOSTNAME]</value>
</property>

<property>
      <name>hadoop.proxyuser.[OOZIE_SERVICE_OWNER].groups</name>
      <value>[OOZIE_SERVICE_OWNER_GROUP] </value>
</property>
```

Following are the typical example values for these variables.

`[OOZIE_SERVICE_OWNER]`	*oozie*
`[OOZIE_SERVICE_OWNER_GROUP]`	*users*
`[OOZIE_SERVICE_HOSTNAME]`	*localhost*

Both properties can have multiple values, comma-separated. The wildcard * might work for newer Hadoop versions. However, we highly discourage using that value in production systems due to potential security holes.

Start and Verify the Oozie Server

You'll need to follow these steps:

1. Start the Oozie server:

```
$ bin/oozied.sh start

Setting OOZIE_HOME:          <INSTALLATION_DIR>
```

1 "Secure Impersonation in Hadoop."

```
Setting OOZIE_CONFIG:        <INSTALLATION_DIR>/conf
Sourcing:                    <INSTALLATION_DIR>/conf/oozie-env.sh
  setting CATALINA_OPTS="$CATALINA_OPTS -Xmx1024m"
..
Setting OOZIE_LOG:            <INSTALLATION_DIR>/logs
..
Setting OOZIE_HTTP_PORT: 11000
..
Setting OOZIE_BASE_URL: http://<local-machine-name>:11000/oozie
..
Using CATALINA_HOME: <INSTALLATION_DIR>/oozie-server
...
Using CATALINA_PID: <INSTALLATION_DIR>/oozie-server/temp/oozie.pid
```

If a previous instance of the Oozie server was not stopped properly, you might see the following error message:

```
Existing PID file found during start. Remove/clear
stale PID file
```

You can follow these steps to resolve the issue:

a. Stop Oozie using:

```
bin/oozied.sh stop
```

b. Check to see whether any Oozie process is still running:

```
ps -ef | grep oozie
```

c. If a process is running, kill it:

```
kill <PID>
```

d. Remove the PID file:

```
rm <INSTALLATION_DIR>/oozie-server/temp/oozie.pid
```

2. Check Oozie's server status:

```
$ bin/oozie admin -oozie http://localhost:11000/oozie -status

  System mode: NORMAL
```

If it returns `Error: IO_ERROR : java.net.ConnectException: Connection refused`, it means the Oozie server did not start properly. You can check the *logs/* directory to find the root cause.

3. Verify through the web UI.

Go to *http://localhost:11000/oozie*.

4. Check the log files.

The *logs/* directory contains multiple log files. The main log is *oozie.log*. The *catalina.** files contain Tomcat web server logs and they are very important and useful for debugging startup errors and any `OutOfMemory` exception.

If the error message in the *catalina.out* file says, `SEVERE: Error initializing endpoint java.net.BindException: Address already in use <null>:11000`, it means that another instance of Oozie server is running. You can either stop or kill the process and clean up the PID file.

Advanced Oozie Installations

In the previous section, we described how to install an Oozie server on a single machine, which is useful as a proof of concept or in development. In this section, we discuss various advanced installation topics that are often required for a production setup.

Configuring Kerberos Security

If the Hadoop cluster is secured with Kerberos authentication, the Oozie server needs to provide the appropriate credentials to access Hadoop resources such as the `JobTracker/ResourceManager` and `NameNode`. The Oozie server uses a `keytab` file for user *oozie* to get the Kerberos credentials. We describe Oozie security in detail in "Oozie Security" on page 154. At a minimum, you need to add the following properties in *conf/oozie-site.xml* to support Kerberos authentication to Hadoop in Oozie:

```
<property>
    <name>oozie.service.HadoopAccessorService.kerberos.enabled</name>
    <value>true</value>
    <description>Indicates if Oozie is configured to use Kerberos.
   </description>
</property>
 <property>
    <name>oozie.service.HadoopAccessorService.keytab.file</name>
    <value>${user.home}/oozie.keytab</value>
    <description>Location of the Oozie user keytab file in Oozie server
    box </description>
</property>
<property>
    <name>oozie.service.HadoopAccessorService.kerberos.principal</name>
    <value>${user.name}/localhost@${local.realm}</value>
    <description>Kerberos principal for Oozie service.</description>
</property>
```

DB Setup

In this section, we describe how to configure the Oozie server to use MySQL and Oracle. These substeps should be added to the steps described in "Install Oozie Server" on page 26 if you want to use one of these databases.

MySQL configuration

For the MySQL configuration, you'll need to follow these steps:

1. MySQL installation. Oozie has been tested against MySQL 5.1.x. If MySQL is already installed, you can skip this step. Otherwise, download MySQL and follow the online instructions to set up the MySQL server. At the end, make sure the MySQL *bin/* directory is in your Unix path.
2. Create the MySQL Oozie database:

   ```
   $ mysql -u root
   mysql> create database oozie;

                   Query OK, 1 row affected (0.00 sec)
   ```

3. Create the MySQL Oozie user:

   ```
   mysql> grant all privileges on oozie.* to 'oozie'@'localhost'
                   identified by 'oozie';
   Query OK, 0 rows affected (0.01 sec)

   mysql> grant all privileges on oozie.* to 'oozie'@'%'
   identified by 'oozie';
   Query OK, 0 rows affected (0.00 sec)
   ```

4. Download the MySQL JDBC driver. You can download the package using the following command:

   ```
   $ curl -O http://cdn.mysql.com/Downloads/Connector-J/\
   mysql-connector-java-5.1.25.tar.gz
   ```

   You can extract the required *mysql-connector-java-5.1.25-bin.jar* file from the downloaded TAR file.
5. Inject JDBC driver. The Oozie server needs the JDBC driver to access the database. You need to copy the *mysql-connector-java-5.1.25-bin.jar* into the *libext/* directory (as described in step 3 in "Install Oozie Server" on page 26).
6. Configure the Oozie server. Add the following properties to *oozie-site.xml* to make sure the Oozie server uses MySQL:

   ```
   <property>
        <name>oozie.db.schema.name</name>
        <value>oozie</value>
   </property>
   ```

```
<property>
    <name>oozie.service.JPAService.create.db.schema</name>
    <value>false</value>
</property>
<property>
    <name>oozie.service.JPAService.jdbc.driver</name>
    <value>com.mysql.jdbc.Driver</value>
</property>
<property>
    <name>oozie.service.JPAService.jdbc.url</name>
    <value>jdbc:mysql://localhost:3306/oozie</value>
</property>
<property>
    <name>oozie.service.JPAService.jdbc.username</name>
    <value>oozie</value>
</property>
<property>
    <name>oozie.service.JPAService.jdbc.password</name>
    <value>oozie</value>
</property>
```

Oracle configuration

The steps needed to install and use Oracle are very similar to the ones just outlined for MySQL. Oracle 11g is the most commonly used version with Oozie. After installing Oracle, you can follow these steps to configure Oozie to use it:

1. Create the Oracle Oozie user:

   ```
   $ sqlplus system@localhost
   SQL> create user oozie identified by oozie default tablespace users
        temporary tablespace temp;

   User created.

   SQL> grant all privileges to oozie;

   Grant succeeded.
   ```

2. Download the Oracle JDBC driver. Download the JDBC driver for Oracle Database 11g Release 2 (*ojdbc6.jar*).
3. Inject JDBC driver. The Oozie server needs the JDBC driver to access the database. Copy the *ojdbc6.jar* into the *libext/* directory (as described in step 3 in "Install Oozie Server" on page 26).
4. Configure the Oozie server.

   You need to add the following properties in *oozie-site.xml* to make sure the Oozie server uses the Oracle database:

```
<property>
    <name>oozie.db.schema.name</name>
    <value>oozie</value>
</property>
<property>
    <name>oozie.service.JPAService.create.db.schema</name>
    <value>false</value>
</property>
<property>
    <name>oozie.service.JPAService.jdbc.driver</name>
    <value>oracle.jdbc.driver.OracleDriver</value>
</property>
<property>
    <name>oozie.service.JPAService.jdbc.url</name>
    <value>jdbc:oracle:thin:@localhost:1521:oozie</value>
</property>
<property>
    <name>oozie.service.JPAService.jdbc.username</name>
    <value>oozie</value>
</property>
<property>
    <name>oozie.service.JPAService.jdbc.password</name>
    <value>oozie</value>
</property>
```

Shared Library Installation

As described in the previous chapter, Oozie schedules and executes various types of actions such as MapReduce, Pig, Hive, DistCp, and Sqoop. Each type requires a separate set of JAR files for its execution. Oozie provides multiple ways to make those JARs available during execution. We will discuss the details of managing shared libraries later in "Managing Libraries in Oozie" on page 147. In this section, we describe a convenient way to make those action-specific JAR files available to Oozie right from the time of installation.

The Oozie binary distribution includes a shared library TAR file (*oozie-sharelib-<VERSION>.tar.gz*). It contains the versions of JARs that are currently supported for the different action types. During installation, untar this file and upload the shared library directory to HDFS. This directory is known as the Oozie `sharelib` and must be owned by the Oozie service user (*oozie*). The following commands executed as user *oozie* will accomplish this:

```
$ cd <INSTALLATION_DIR>
$ tar xvf oozie-4.0.1/oozie-sharelib-4.0.1.tar.gz
$ hdfs dfs -put share share
```

Oozie, by default, looks into the */user/${oozie_service_user}/share/lib* directory on HDFS for any system JAR file. If you want to deploy them into a different location, specify the new location in *conf/oozie-site.xml* as shown here:

```
<property>
   <name>oozie.service.WorkflowAppService.system.libpath</name>
   <value><OOZIE_SYSTEM_LIBRARY>/share/lib</value>
</property>
```

Sharelib since version 4.1.0

Oozie 4.1.0 made a significant change to support an important feature. The goal of this change is to support seamless upgrades of the Oozie `sharelib` even when the Oozie service is up and running. In earlier versions, Oozie was looking for the shared library for each action under, for example, the */user/oozie/share/lib* directory. In newer releases, Oozie looks for a different directory pattern (*/user/oozie/share/lib/lib_$timestamp$*), and picks the directory with the newest timestamp. Oozie will pick up the shared library from the old directory path (without *_timestamp*) only if the timestamped lib directories don't exist. This raises some interesting questions:

What is the ideal process for uploading a new `sharelib`*?*
: In Oozie 4.1.0 and newer versions, uploading the `sharelib` JARs using the `hdfs dfs` command is not a good option. Oozie provides an option in *oozie-setup.sh* command to upload the JARs transparently. This command ensures that the *lib_$timestamp$* directory is created using the current time and copies the JARs into that directory. The following command is used to achieve this:

```
$ oozie-setup.sh sharelib create -fs FS_URI [-locallib SHARED_LIBRARY]
$ oozie-setup.sh sharelib create -fs
hdfs://namenode01.grid.mycompany.com:8020 -locallib /tmp/share/lib
```

Here are the details of the arguments for this command:

`FS_URI`
: The HDFS URI where the script uploads the `sharelib`. Generally, it is just *hdfs://NN_SERVER_NAME:port*. The rest of it is the full path, and it is determined either by the value of the property `oozie.serviceWorkflowAppService.system.libpath` defined in the *oozie-site.xml* file or the default path (*/user/${oozie_service_user}/share/lib*).

`SHARED_LIBRARY`
: This optional parameter determines the location of the shared library tarball or its expanded directory in the local filesystem. If this is omitted, Oozie looks for the shared library in the Oozie installation directory.

When Oozie is running, is there a way to upgrade the `sharelib`*?*
: Yes. Once the `sharelib` directory is uploaded, the admin can upgrade to this new `sharelib` even when Oozie is running. The command `oozie admin -sharelibupdate` is the way to do it and ensures that Oozie uses the latest version.

How do you clean up shared libraries that are not used?
: It can become an operational challenge to manage multiple sets of shared libraries with different timestamps. Oozie enforces a mechanism to clean up the directories with older timestamps. During the Oozie server startup, it removes any shared library directory that is older than seven days *and* is not the latest two instances. The seven-day retention can be overridden using the property `ShareLibService.temp.sharelib.retention.days` in *oozie-site.xml*. The old-style `sharelib` directory without the `_timestamp` (e.g., */user/oozie/share/lib*) will not be cleaned up if it exists.

How can I see the currently used `sharelib`*?*
: Users can check the active `sharelib` path at any time without going to HDFS. There are convenient commands available for this, which are listed here:

```
$ oozie admin -shareliblist
$ oozie admin -shareliblist pig
$ oozie admin -shareliblist hive
```

It's often the case that older `sharelibs` do not work correctly with newer Oozie servers, so you should update the `sharelib` as part of every version upgrade.

Oozie Client Installations

As you already know, Oozie provides client tools and libraries and these are bundled as a separate TAR and included as part of the Oozie binary package. The Oozie single-node server setup described in "Install Oozie Server" on page 26 also installs the Oozie client. The primary CLI tool is called `oozie` and you will need to install the client to get access to it. This section lists the steps required to install the Oozie client on any machine (and location) because the server and client are typically deployed on different machines, especially in a production setup. First, `untar` the Oozie client archive to deploy it under a directory of your choice:

```
$ tar xvf oozie-client-4.0.1.tar.gz
$ cd oozie-client-4.0.1
```

After this deployment, you will find the command-line tool in the *bin/* directory and all the JARs in the *lib/* directory. You should add this *bin/* directory to your Unix path:

```
export
      PATH=<CURRENT_WORKING_DIR>/oozie-client-4.0.1/bin:$PATH
```

Lastly, you can verify that the Oozie client is installed properly by running a sample command:

```
oozie admin -status
      -oozie <OOZIEURL>
```

If the Oozie command throws the following error message, it means the command did not find the Oozie web server URL to connect to:

```
Oozie URL is not available neither in command option or
in the environment
```

The `oozie` command-line utility looks for the Oozie server URL in two places: in the command-line option `-oozie <URL>`, and in the shell environment. If you use the `oozie` command frequently against the same Oozie instance, it is a good idea to add this:

```
export OOZIE_URL=<Oozie_Server_URL>
```

In this chapter, we saw how to build, configure, and deploy an Oozie server and client. In addition to the step-by-step installation guide, this chapter also exposed you to the various internal components of a working Oozie system along with some practical configuration tips. The next chapter will focus on building workflow applications, the fundamental building block of Oozie.

CHAPTER 4

Oozie Workflow Actions

The previous chapter took us through the Oozie installation in detail. In this chapter, we will start looking at building full-fledged Oozie applications. The first step is to learn about Oozie workflows. Many users still use Oozie primarily as a workflow manager, and Oozie's advanced features (e.g., the coordinator) are built on top of the workflow. This chapter will delve into how to define and deploy the individual action nodes that make up Oozie workflows. The individual action nodes are the heart and soul of a workflow because they do the actual processing and we will look at all the details around workflow actions in this chapter.

Workflow

As explained earlier in "A Recurrent Problem" on page 1, most Hadoop projects start simple, but quickly become complex. Let's look at how a Hadoop data pipeline typically evolves in an enterprise. The first step in many big data analytic platforms is usually data ingestion from some upstream data source into Hadoop. This could be a weblog collection system or some data store in the cloud (e.g., Amazon S3). Hadoop DistCp, for example, is a common tool used to pull data from S3. Once the data is available, the next step is to run a simple analytic query, perhaps in the form of a Hive query, to get answers to some business question. This system will grow over time with more queries and different kinds of jobs. At some point soon, there will be a need to make this a recurring pipeline, typically a daily pipeline. The first inclination of many users is to schedule this using a Unix cron job running a script to invoke the pipeline jobs in some sequence.

As new requirements and varied datasets start flowing into this Hadoop system, this processing pipeline quickly becomes unwieldy and complicated. It can't be managed in a cron job anymore. This is when people start exploring Oozie and they start by implementing an Oozie workflow.

"A Simple Oozie Job" on page 4 showed a simple workflow and "Oozie Workflows" on page 13 defined it as a collection of action and control nodes arranged in a directed acyclic graph (DAG) that captures control dependency where each action typically is a Hadoop job. Workflows are defined in an XML file, typically named *workflow.xml*. Each job, like the `DistCp` or the subsequent Hive query in the previous example, ends up as an action node in this workflow XML. They can be chained together using the workflow definition language. If you want a recurring pipeline you can also make this a daily coordinator job, but we won't cover the coordinator until later in the book (for more information, refer to Chapter 6). The first and the most important part of writing such pipelines is to learn to write workflows and to learn how to define and package the individual actions that make up these workflows.

Actions

Action nodes define the jobs, which are the individual units of work that are chained together to make up the Oozie workflow. Actions do the actual processing in the workflow. An action node can run a variety of jobs: MapReduce, Pig, Hive, and more.

Actions in a workflow can either be Hadoop actions or general-purpose actions that allow execution of arbitrary code. Not all of the required processing fits into specific Hadoop action types, so the general-purpose action types come in handy for a lot of real-life use cases. We will cover them both in this chapter.

Action Execution Model

Before we get into the details of the Oozie actions, let's look at how Oozie actually runs these actions. A clear understanding of Oozie's execution model will help us to design, build, run, and troubleshoot workflows.

When a user runs a Hadoop job from the command line, the client executable (e.g., Hadoop, Pig, or Hive) runs on the node where the command is invoked. This node is usually called the *gateway*, or an *edge node* that sits outside the Hadoop cluster but can talk to the cluster. It's the responsibility of the client program to run the underlying MapReduce jobs on the Hadoop cluster and return the results. The Hadoop environment and configuration on the edge node tell the client programs how to reach the `NameNode`, `JobTracker`, and others. The execution model is slightly different if you decide to run the same job through an Oozie action.

Oozie runs the actual actions through a launcher job, which itself is a Hadoop MapReduce job that runs on the Hadoop cluster. The launcher is a map-only job that runs only one mapper. Let's assume the Oozie job is launched by the `oozie` CLI. The `oozie` CLI client will submit the job to the Oozie server, which may or may not be on the same machine as the client. But the Oozie server does not launch the Pig or Hive client locally on its machine. The server first launches a job for the aforementioned launcher job on the Hadoop cluster, which in turn invokes the appropriate client libraries (e.g., Hadoop, Pig, or Hive).

Users new to Oozie usually have questions about the need for a launcher job and wonder about the choice of this architecture. Let's see how and why the launcher job helps. Delegating the client responsibilities to the launcher job makes sure that the execution of that code will not overload or overwhelm the Oozie server machine. A fundamental design principle in Oozie is that the Oozie server never runs user code other than the execution of the workflow itself. This ensures better service stability by isolating user code away from Oozie's code. The Oozie server is also stateless and the launcher job makes it possible for it to stay that way. By leveraging Hadoop for running the launcher, handling job failures and recoverability becomes easier for the stateless Oozie server. Hadoop is built to handle all those issues, and it's not smart to reinvent the wheel on the Oozie server.

This architecture also means that the action code and configuration have to be packaged as a self-contained application and must reside on HDFS for access across the cluster. This is because Hadoop will schedule the launcher job on any cluster node. In most cases, the launcher job waits for the actual Hadoop job running the action to finish before exiting. This means that the launcher job actually occupies a Hadoop task slot on the cluster for the entire duration of the action. Figure 4-1 captures how Oozie executes a Hive action in a workflow. The Hive action also redirects the output to the Hive launcher job's `stdout/stderr` and the output is accessible through the Oozie console. These patterns are consistent across most asynchronous action types (covered in "Synchronous Versus Asynchronous Actions" on page 73), except the `<map-reduce>` action. The `<map-reduce>` launcher is the exception and it exits right after launching the actual job instead of waiting for it to complete.

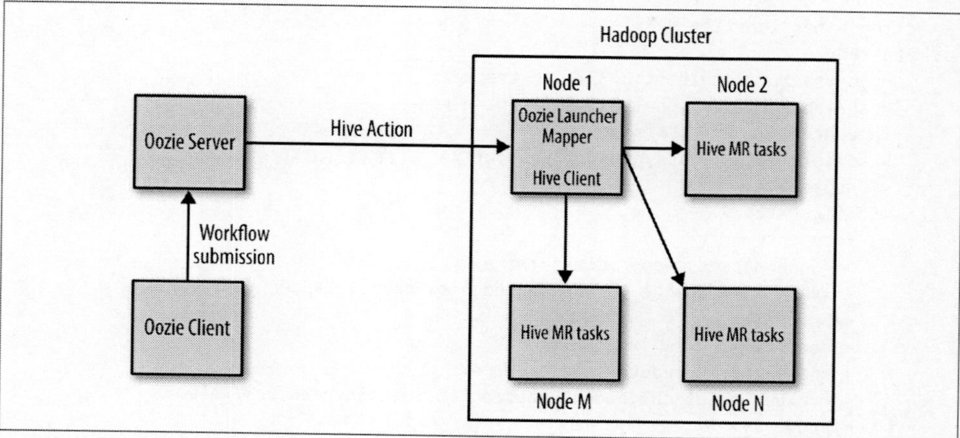

Figure 4-1. Action execution model

If many Oozie actions are submitted simultaneously on a small Hadoop cluster, all the task slots could be occupied by the launcher jobs. These launchers will then be waiting forever to run the action's Hadoop jobs that can't be scheduled due to unavailability of slots, causing a messy deadlock. This deadlock can be solved by configuring the launcher and the actual action to run on different Hadoop queues and by making sure the launcher queue cannot fill up the entire cluster. The topic of launcher configuration is covered in detail in "Launcher Configuration" on page 85.

Action Definition

Oozie's XML specification for each action is designed to define and deploy these jobs as self-contained applications. The key to mastering Oozie is to understand how to define, configure, and parameterize the individual actions in a workflow. In this section, we will cover all of the different action types and cover the details of their specification.

Actions are defined in the workflow XML using a set of elements that are specific and relevant to that action type. Some of these elements are common across many action types. For example, all Hadoop actions need the `<name-node>` and `<job-tracker>` elements. But some of the other XML elements are specific to particular actions. For example, the Pig action needs a `<script>` element, but the Java action does not. As a workflow system custom built for Hadoop, Oozie makes it really easy and intuitive for users to define all these actions meant for executing various Hadoop tools and processing paradigms. Before looking at all the actions and their associated elements, let's look at an example action again in Example 4-1.

Example 4-1. Action node

```
<action name="identity-MR">
 <map-reduce>
     <job-tracker>localhost:8032</job-tracker>
     <name-node>hdfs://localhost:8020</name-node>
     <prepare>
       <delete path="/user/joe/data/output"/>
     </prepare>
     <configuration>
         <property>
           <name>mapred.mapper.class</name>
           <value>org.apache.hadoop.mapred.lib.IdentityMapper</value>
         </property>
         <property>
           <name>mapred.reducer.class</name>
           <value>org.apache.hadoop.mapred.lib.IdentityReducer</value>
         </property>
         <property>
             <name>mapred.input.dir</name>
              <value>/user/joe/data/input</value>
```

```
            </property>
            <property>
                <name>mapred.output.dir</name>
                <value>/user/joe/data/input</value>
            </property>
        </configuration>
    </map-reduce>
    <ok to="success"/>
    <error to="fail"/>
</action>
```

All action nodes start with an `<action>` element with a `name` attribute that indicates the action name. Action nodes have three subelements: the *`<action-type>`* encapsulating the definition and all of the configuration for the action, `<ok>`, and the `<error>` subelements that indicate the transitions to follow depending on the exit status of the action. We will now dig further into the various action types required for building workflows.

As explained in "Application Deployment Model" on page 20, the *workflow.xml* file and all the required binaries, scripts, archives, files, and configuration are packaged and deployed in an HDFS directory. The *workflow.xml* file is under the workflow application root directory on HDFS (`oozie.wf.application.path`).

Action Types

This section will cover all Oozie action types, but we will first look at a couple of actions in great detail and the other action types will fall in place rather easily after that. We will focus on the `<map-reduce>` Hadoop action and the general-purpose `<java>` action at first.

We encourage you to read through these two action types (`<map-reduce>` and `<java>`) closely even if they are not of interest to you, as we will cover all of the common XML elements in the context of these two actions. The usage and meaning of most elements repeat across the other action types and can just be borrowed and replicated. There is a lot of boilerplate XML content explained here that won't need further explanation in other action types.

MapReduce Action

We already saw a sample Oozie `<map-reduce>` action in Example 4-1. We will analyze it in more detail in this section. This action type supports all three variations of a Hadoop MapReduce job: Java, streaming, and pipes. The Java MapReduce job is the most typical of the three and you can think of the other two as special cases. Let's look at the different XML elements needed to configure and define a `<map-reduce>` action through Oozie. The following is an ordered sequence of XML elements; you must specify them in order when writing the action definition in your workflows (elements can be omitted, but if present, they should be in sequence):

- `job-tracker` (required)
- `name-node` (required)
- `prepare`
- `streaming` or `pipes`
- `job-xml`
- `configuration`
- `file`
- `archive`

The Oozie XML has a well-defined schema definition (XSD), as most XMLs do. These schema definitions are verbose and can be found in the Oozie documentation. One way to understand the action definition is to look at the schema definition. It's not always easy to read but can come in handy sometimes as the source of truth for the list of elements supported and their sequence.

The action needs to know the `JobTracker` (JT) and the `NameNode` (NN) of the underlying Hadoop cluster where Oozie has to run the MapReduce job. The first two elements in the previous list are meant for specifying them. These are required elements for this action:

```
...
    <job-tracker>localhost:8032</job-tracker>
    <name-node>hdfs://localhost:8020</name-node>
...
```

As already explained in "A Simple Oozie Job" on page 4, the `<job-tracker>` element can refer to either the `JobTracker` or the ResourceManager based on the Hadoop version in use. Also, there are ways to globally specify common elements like the JT and NN to be shared among multiple actions in a workflow. We cover this in "Global Configuration" on page 83.

You should not use the Hadoop configuration properties <mapred.job.tracker> (JobTracker) and <fs.default.name> (NameNode) as part of an Oozie workflow action definition. Oozie will throw an error on those because it expects the <job-tracker> and <name-node> elements instead. This is true for all Hadoop action types, including the <map-reduce> action.

The <prepare> section is optional and is typically used as a preprocessor to delete output directories or *HCatalog* table partitions or to create some directories required for the action. This delete helps make the action repeatable and enables retries after failure. Without this cleanup, retries of Hadoop jobs will fail because Hadoop checks for nonexistence of the output directories and tries to create them for the job. So deleting them before running the action is a common use case for this element. Using <prepare> to create directories is also supported, but not as common as the delete in usage:

```
...
    <prepare>
        <delete path="hdfs://localhost:8020/user/joe/output"/>
    </prepare>
...
```

The <job-xml> element(s) and/or the <configuration> section can be used to capture all of the Hadoop job configuration properties. The worker code for the MapReduce action is specified as part of this configuration using the mapred.mapper.class and the mapred.reducer.class properties. These properties specify the actual Java classes to be run as map and reduce as part of this action:

```
...
    <configuration>
        <property>
            <name>mapred.mapper.class</name>
            <value>org.myorg.FirstJob.Map</value>
        </property>
        <property>
            <name>mapred.reducer.class</name>
            <value>org.myorg.FirstJob.Reduce</value>
        </property>
    </configuration>
...
```

Hadoop supports two distinct API packages, commonly referred to as the `mapred` and `mapreduce` APIs. The old `org.apache.hadoop.mapred` package and the newer `org.apache.hadoop.mapreduce` package are functionally very similar, but the newer `mapreduce` API has cleaner abstractions and is better organized though less mature and stable at this point. Refer to the Hadoop documentation for more details. By default, Oozie supports only the older `mapred` API. There is a way to use the new API with Oozie (covered in "Supporting New API in MapReduce Action" on page 165).

When you write a Hadoop Java MapReduce program, you need to write a main driver class that specifies the job configuration, mapper class, reducer class, and so on. Oozie simplifies things by handling this responsibility for you. You can just write the mapper and reducer classes, package them as a JAR, and submit the JAR to the Oozie action. Oozie takes care of the Hadoop driver code internally and uses the older `mapred` API to do so. However, you must be careful not to mix the new Hadoop APIs in their mapper/reducer class with the old API in Oozie's driver code. This is one of the reasons why Oozie only supports the older `mapred` API out of the box. Refer to the Hadoop examples to learn more about the MapReduce driver code.

Oozie also supports the `<file>` and `<archive>` elements for actions that need them. This is the native, Hadoop way of packaging libraries, archives, scripts, and other data files that jobs need, and Oozie provides the syntax to handle them. Refer to the Hadoop documentation for more information on `files` and `archives`. Users can specify symbolic links to files and archives using the # symbol in the workflow, as the following code fragment will show. The links themselves can't have slashes (/) in them. Oozie creates these `symlinks` in the workflow root directory, and other files in the application can refer to and access them using relative paths.

Oozie does not support the `libjars` option available as part of the Hadoop command line. But Oozie does provide several ways to handle JARs and shared libraries, which are covered in "Managing Libraries in Oozie" on page 147.

In the following example, the *myFile.txt* file referred to by the `<file>` element needs to be deployed in the *myDir1* subdirectory under the *wf/* root directory on HDFS. A `symlink` named *file1* will be created in the workflow root directory. The archive file *mytar.tgz* also needs to be copied to the workflow root directory on HDFS and Oozie will unarchive it into a subdirectory called *mygzdir/* in the current execution directory on the Hadoop compute nodes. This is how Hadoop generally distributes files and archives using the distributed cache. Archives (TARs) are packaged and deployed, and the specified directory (*mygzdir/*) is the path where your MapReduce code can find the files in the archive:

```
...
    <file>hdfs://localhost:8020/user/myUser/wf/myDir1/myFile.txt#file1</file>
    <archive>hdfs://localhost:8020/user/myUser/wf/mytar.tgz#mygzdir</archive>
...
```

Now, putting all the pieces together, a sample `<map-reduce>` action is shown here:

```
...
    <action name="myMapReduceAction">
        <map-reduce>
            <job-tracker>${jobTracker}</job-tracker>
            <name-node>${nameNode}</name-node>
            <prepare>
                <delete path="${myMapReduceActionOutput}"/>
            </prepare>
            <job-xml>/myfirstjob.xml</job-xml>
            <configuration>
                <property>
                    <name>mapred.mapper.class</name>
                    <value>org.myorg.FirstJob.Map</value>
                </property>
                <property>
                      <name>mapred.reducer.class</name
                      <value>org.myorg.FirstJob.Reduce</value>
                </property>
                <property>
                    <name>mapred.input.dir</name>
                    <value>${myMapReduceActionInput}</value>
                </property>
                <property>
                    <name>mapred.output.dir</name>
                    <value>${myMapReduceActionOutput}</value>
                </property>
                <property>
                    <name>mapred.reduce.tasks</name>
                    <value>${JobNumReducers}</value>
                </property>
            </configuration>
            <file>myDir1/myFile.txt#file1</file>
            <archive>mytar.tgz#mygzdir</archive>
        </map-reduce>
    </action>
...
```

The preceding example uses typical conventions for variable substitution and parameterization (we will look at this in detail in "Parameterization" on page 86). This example illustrates some of the best practices in writing an action definition.

Streaming and pipes are special kinds of MapReduce jobs, and this action supports both. They are both mechanisms that Hadoop supports to help run non-Java code as MapReduce jobs. This is to help users who might have to port existing code written in other languages like Python or C++ to Hadoop's MapReduce framework in Java. Also, some users might just prefer other programming languages.

Depending on whether you want to execute streaming or pipes, you can have either of those elements or neither. But you cannot specify both `<streaming>` and `<pipes>` as part of a single `<map-reduce>` action. Also, if they are present, they require some special subelements specific to those execution modes.

Streaming

Streaming jobs support the following elements in addition to the `<map-reduce>` elements we saw previously (these are subelements under the `<streaming>` element):

- `mapper`
- `reducer`
- `record-reader`
- `record-reader-mapping`
- `env`

Streaming jobs run binaries or scripts and obviously need a mapper and reducer executable. These are packaged through the `<file>` and `<archive>` elements as explained in the previous section. If the `<file>` element is missing for a streaming job, the executables are assumed to be available in the specified path on the local Hadoop nodes. If it's a relative path, it's assumed to be relative to the workflow root directory.

You might have noticed that the `mapred.mapper.class` and/or `mapred.reducer.class` properties can be defined as part of the configuration section for the action as well. If present, those will have higher priority over the `<mapper>` and `<reducer>` elements in the streaming section and will override the values in the streaming section.

You can optionally give a `<record-reader>` and `<record-reader-mapping>` through those elements to the streaming MapReduce job. Refer to the Hadoop documentation for more information on those properties. The `<env>` element comes in handy to set some environment variables required by the scripts. Here is an example of a streaming section:

```
...
    <streaming>
        <mapper>python MyCustomMapper.py</mapper>
        <reducer>python MyCustomReducer.py</reducer>
        <record-reader>StreamXmlRecordReader</record-reader>
        <env>output_dir=/tmp/output</env>
    </streaming>
...
```

Pipes

While streaming is a generic framework to run any non-Java code in Hadoop, pipes are a special way to run C++ programs more elegantly. Though not very popular, Oozie's `<map-reduce>` action does support a `<pipes>` section for defining pipes jobs and it includes the following subelements:

- `map`
- `reduce`
- `inputformat`
- `partitioner`
- `writer`
- `program`

The `<program>` element is the most important in the list and it points to the C++ executable to be run. This executable needs to be packaged with the workflow application and deployed on HDFS. You can also optionally specify the `<map>` class, `<reduce>` class, `<inputformat>`, `<partitioner>`, and `<writer>` elements. Refer to the Hadoop documentation on pipes for more details. Here is an example of a pipes section in the Oozie action:

```
...
    <pipes>
        <program>hdfs://localhost:8020/user/myUser/wf/bin/
                 wordcount-simple#wordcount-simple</program>
    </pipes>
...
```

As a general rule in Oozie, the exit status of the Hadoop MapReduce job and the job counters must be available to the workflow job after the Hadoop job completes. Without this, the workflow may not be able to decide on the next course of action. Oozie obviously needs to know if the job succeeded or failed, but it is also common for the workflow to make decisions based on the exit status and the counters.

MapReduce example

Now, let's look at a specific example of how a Hadoop MapReduce job is run on the command line and convert it into an Oozie action definition. You're likely already familiar with running basic Hadoop jobs from the command line. Using that as a starting point and converting it to an action definition in Oozie will make it easier for you to become familiar with the workflow syntax. Here's an example:

```
$ hadoop jar /user/joe/myApp.jar myAppClass
  -Dmapred.job.reduce.memory.mb=8192 /hdfs/user/joe/input
  /hdfs/user/joe/output prod
```

The command just shown runs a Java MapReduce job to implement some business logic. The *myApp.jar* file packages the code that runs the mapper and the reducer class. The job requires 8 GB memory for its reducers (and that is) defined in the command line above using the `-D` option). The job also takes three command-line arguments. The first one is the input directory on HDFS (*/hdfs/user/joe/input*), the second argument is the output directory (*/hdfs/user/joe/output*), and the last one is the execution type (prod), which is some application-specific argument. The arguments and the directory paths themselves are just examples; it could be anything in reality.

In "Action Types" on page 43, we covered how a typical Java MapReduce program has a main driver class that is not needed in Oozie. You just need to specify the mapper and reducer class in the action definition. But this also requires knowing the actual mapper and reducer class in the JAR to be able to write the Oozie `<map-reduce>` action. In the command line above, `myAppClass` is the main driver class. This is part of the main driver code for the preceding Hadoop example:

```
...
 /**
   * The main driver for the map/reduce program.
   * Invoke this method to submit the map/reduce job.
   */
  public static void main(String[] args) throws IOException {
    JobConf conf = new JobConf(myAppClass.class);
    conf.setJobName("myAppClass");

    conf.setOutputKeyClass(Text.class);
    conf.setOutputValueClass(IntWritable.class);

    conf.setMapperClass(MyMapClass.class);
    conf.setReducerClass(MyRedClass.class);
...
```

Given this, the command line for the preceding Hadoop job submission can be specified in an Oozie workflow action as shown here:

```
<map-reduce>
    <job-tracker>jt.mycompany.com:8032</job-tracker>
    <name-node>hdfs://nn.mycompany.com:8020</name-node>
```

```
        <prepare>
            <delete path="hdfs://nn.mycompany.com:8020/hdfs/user/joe/output"/>
        </prepare>
        <configuration>
            <property>
                <name>mapred.mapper.class</name>
                <value>com.myBiz.mr.MyMapClass</value>
            </property>
            <property>
                <name>mapred.reducer.class</name>
                <value>com.myBiz.mr.MyRedClass</value>
            </property>
            <property>
                <name>mapred.job.reduce.memory.mb</name>
                <value>8192</value>
            </property>
            <property>
                <name>mapred.input.dir</name>
                <value>/hdfs/user/joe/input</value>
            </property>
            <property>
                <name>mapred.output.dir</name>
                <value>/hdfs/user/joe/output</value>
            </property>
        </configuration>
    </map-reduce>
    <ok to="success"/>
    <error to="fail"/>
</action>
```

You might notice that the preceding Oozie action definition does not have any reference to the main JAR (*/user/joe/myApp.jar*) that you saw in the Hadoop command line. This is because of the way Oozie workflows are packaged and deployed. Oozie knows where to look for and find this JAR. The JAR has to be copied to the *lib/* subdirectory under the workflow application root directory on HDFS.

Due to the implicit handling of the main driver code in Oozie, some users who are new to Hadoop are likely to be confused when they try to switch between the Hadoop command line and the Oozie `<map-reduce>` action. This is a little subtle and tricky, but the translation to an Oozie action is a lot more straightforward with all the other action types that we cover later in this chapter.

For the sake of clarity, the example discussed in this section specifically skips variable substitution and parameterization. It would be a good exercise for readers to parameterize this example using variables ("EL Variables" on page 87 provides insight on how to do this).

Streaming example

Let's look at a Python streaming job invoked using the Hadoop client:

```
$ hadoop jar /opt/hadoop/share/hadoop/tools/lib/hadoop-*streaming*.jar
  -file /home/joe/mapper.py -mapper /home/joe/mapper.py
  -file /home/joe/reducer.py -reducer /home/joe/reducer.py
  -input hdfs://nn.mycompany.com:8020/hdfs/user/joe/input/
  -output hdfs://nn.mycompany.com:8020/hdfs/user/joe/output/
```

This command-line example runs a Python streaming job to implement a Hadoop MapReduce application. The Python script *mapper.py* is the code it runs for the mapper, and *reducer.py* is the Python script it runs for the reducer. The job reads its input from the */hdfs/user/joe/input/* directory on HDFS and writes the output to */hdfs/user/joe/output/*. The previous example can be specified in Oozie as shown in Example 4-2.

Example 4-2. MapReduce streaming action

```
<action name="myStreamingMRAction">
    <map-reduce>
        <job-tracker>jt.mycompany.com:8032</job-tracker>
        <name-node>hdfs://nn.mycompany.com:8020</name-node>
        <prepare>
            <delete path="hdfs://nn.mycompany.com:8020/hdfs/user/joe/output"/>
        </prepare>
        <streaming>
            <mapper>python mapper.py</mapper>
            <reducer>python reducer.py</reducer>
        </streaming>
        <configuration>
            <property>
                <name>mapred.input.dir</name>
                <value>/hdfs/user/joe/input</value>
            </property>
            <property>
                <name>mapred.output.dir</name>
                <value>/hdfs/user/joe/output</value>
            </property>
        </configuration>
        <file>wfDir/mapper.py#mapper.py</file>
        <file>wfDir/redcer.py#reducer.py</file>
    </map-reduce>
    <ok to="success"/>
    <error to="fail"/>
</action>
```

Java Action

Oozie's Java action is a great way to run custom Java code on the Hadoop cluster. The Java action will execute the `public static void main(String[] args)` method of the specified Java main class. It is technically considered a non-Hadoop action. This action runs as a single mapper job, which means it will run on an arbitrary Hadoop worker node.

While it's not recommended, Java action can be used to run Hadoop MapReduce jobs because MapReduce jobs are nothing but Java programs after all. The main class invoked can be a Hadoop MapReduce driver and can call Hadoop APIs to run a MapReduce job. In that mode, Hadoop spawns more mappers and reducers as required and runs them on the cluster. The reason this approach is not ideal is because Oozie does not know about or manage the MapReduce job spawned by the Java action, whereas it does manage the job run by the `<map-reduce>` action we saw in the previous section. There are distinct advantages to being tightly integrated as a `<map-reduce>` action in Oozie instead of being just another Java program:

- Because Oozie knows that the `<map-reduce>` action runs a Hadoop job, it provides easy access to Hadoop counters for this job. We will learn more about these counters in "EL Variables" on page 87. It's a lot harder to save and access the counters of a Hadoop job if it is invoked as a `<java>` action.
- The launcher map task that launches the `<map-reduce>` action completes immediately and Oozie directly manages the MapReduce job. This frees up a Hadoop slot for a MapReduce task that would have otherwise been occupied by the launcher task in the case of a `<java>` action.

We saw in "MapReduce Action" on page 43 that Oozie supports only the older, `mapred` Java API of Hadoop. However, the Java class invoked via the `<java>` action could use the newer `mapreduce` API of Hadoop. This is not recommended, but is still a potential workaround for people committed to using the newer Hadoop API.

The Java action is made up of the following elements:

- `job-tracker` (required)
- `name-node` (required)
- `prepare`
- `configuration`
- `main-class` (required)
- `java-opts`
- `arg`
- `file`

- `archive`
- `capture-output`

We have seen the `<job-tracker>`, `<name-node>`, `<prepare>`, `<configuration>`, `<file>`, and `<archive>` elements in the context of a `<map-reduce>` action, which work exactly the same with the `<java>` action or any other action for that matter. Let's look at the elements specific to the `<java>` action.

The key driver for this action is the Java main class to be run plus any arguments and/or JVM options it requires. This is captured in the `<main-class>`, `<arg>`, and `<java-opts>` elements, respectively. Each `<arg>` element corresponds to one argument and will be passed in the same order, as specified in the workflow XML to the main class by Oozie.

The `<capture-output>` element, if present, can be used to pass the output back to the Oozie context. The Java program has to write the output in Java properties file format and the default maximum size allowed is 2 KB. Instead of `stdout`, the Java program should write to a file path defined by the system and accessible via the system property `oozie.action.output.properties`. Other actions in the workflow can then access this data through the EL function `wf:actionData(String java-node-name)`, which returns a map (EL functions are covered in "EL Functions" on page 88). The following piece of code in the Java action generates some output shareable with Oozie:

```
{
      File outputFile = new File(System.getProperty(
        "oozie.action.output.properties"));
      Properties outputProp = new Properties();
      outputProp.setProperty("OUTPUT_1", "007");

      OutputStream oStream = new FileOutputStream(outputFile);
      outputProp.store(oStream, "");
      oStream.close();
      System.out.println(outputFile.getAbsolutePath());
  }
```

The `oozie.action.max.output.data` property defined in *oozie-site.xml* on the Oozie server node controls the maximum size of the output data. It is set to 2,048 by default, but users can modify it to suit their needs. This change will require a restart of the Oozie server process.

The Java main class has to exit gracefully to help the Oozie workflow successfully transition to the next action, or throw an exception to indicate failure and enable the error transition. The Java main class must not call `System.exit(int n)`, not even `exit(0)`. This is because of Oozie's execution model and the launcher mapper process. It is this mapper that invokes the Java main class to run the Java action. An `exit()` call will force the launcher mapper process to quit prematurely and Oozie will consider that a failed action.

The Java action also builds a file named *oozie-action.conf.xml* and puts it in the running directory of the Java class for it to access. Here is an example of a Java action:

```
...
    <action>
        <java>
            <job-tracker>localhost:8032</job-tracker>
            <name-node>hdfs://localhost:8020</name-node>
            <prepare>
                <delete path="${myJavaActionOutput}"/>
            </prepare>
            <configuration>
                <property>
                    <name>mapred.queue.name</name>
                    <value>default</value>
                </property>
            </configuration>
            <main-class>org.apache.oozie.MyJavaMainClass</main-class>
            <java-opts>-DmyOpts</java-opts>
            <arg>argument1</arg>
            <arg>argument2</arg>
            <capture-output/>
        </java>
    </action>
...
```

You will see that a lot of the XML elements become repetitive across actions now that we have seen the `<map-reduce>` and `<java>` action. Settings like `<name-node>`, `<job-tracker>`, and `<queue>` are required by most actions and are typically the same across a workflow or even many workflows. You can just cut and paste them across actions or centralize them using some approaches that we will see in the next chapter.

Java example

Let's look at an example of how a Hadoop job is converted into a custom Oozie Java action. The example below is the same MapReduce job that we saw in "MapReduce example" on page 50, but we will convert it into a `<java>` action here instead of the `<map-reduce>` action:

```
$ hadoop jar /user/joe/myApp.jar myAppClass
  -Dmapred.job.reduce.memory.mb=8192 /hdfs/user/joe/input
  /hdfs/user/joe/output prod
```

The complete Java action definition is shown here:

```
<action name="myJavaAction">
    <java>
        <job-tracker>jt.mycompany.com:8032</job-tracker>
        <name-node>hdfs://nn.mycompany.com:8020</name-node>
        <prepare>
            <delete path="hdfs://nn.mycompany.com:8020/hdfs/user/joe/output"/>
        </prepare>
        <main-class>myAppClass</main-class>
        <arg>-D</arg>
        <arg>mapreduce.reduce.memory.mb=8192</arg>
        <arg>hdfs://nn.mycompany.com:8020/hdfs/user/joe/input</arg>
        <arg>hdfs://nn.mycompany.com:8020/hdfs/user/joe/output</arg>
        <arg>prod</arg>
        <file>myApp.jar#myApp.jar</file>
        <capture-output/>
    </java>
    <ok to="success"/>
    <error to="fail"/>
</action>
```

It's customary and useful to set `oozie.use.system.libpath=true` in the *job.properties* file for a lot of the actions to find the required jars and work seamlessly. We cover library management in detail in "Managing Libraries in Oozie" on page 147.

Pig Action

Oozie's Pig action runs a Pig job in Hadoop. Pig is a popular tool to run Hadoop jobs via a procedural language interface called Pig Latin. The Pig framework translates the Pig scripts into MapReduce jobs for Hadoop (refer to the Apache Pig documentation for more details). Pig action requires you to bundle the Pig script with all the necessary parameters. Here's the full list of XML elements:

- `scrjob-tracker` (required)
- `name-node` (required)
- `prepare`
- `job-xml`
- `configuration`
- `script` (required)
- `param`
- `argument`
- `file`

- archive

The following is an example of a Pig action with the Pig script, parameters, and arguments. We will look at Oozie's variable substitution in detail in "Parameterization" on page 86, but the script can be parameterized in Pig itself because Pig supports variable substitution as well. The values for these variables can be defined as `<argument>` in the action. Oozie does its parameterization before submitting the script to Pig, and this is different from the parameterization support inside Pig. It's important to understand the two levels of parameterization. Let's look at an example:

```
...
    <action name=" myPigAction">
        <pig>
            ...
            <script>/mypigscript.pig</script>
            <argument>-param</argument>
            <argument>TempDir=${tempJobDir}</argument>
            <argument>-param</argument>
            <argument>INPUT=${inputDir}</argument>
            <argument>-param</argument>
            <argument>OUTPUT=${outputDir}/my-pig-output</argument>
        </pig>
    </action>
            ...
```

Oozie will replace `${tempJobDir}`, `${inputDir}`, and `${outputDir}` before submission to Pig. And then Pig will do its variable substitution for `TempDir`, `INPUT`, and `OUTPUT` which will be referred inside the Pig script as `$TempDir`, `$INPUT`, and `$OUTPUT` respectively (refer to the parameterization section in the Apache Pig documentation for more details).

The argument in the example above, `-param INPUT=${inputDir}`, tells Pig to replace `$INPUT` in the Pig script and could have also been expressed as `<param>INPUT=${inputDir}</param>` in the action. Oozie's Pig action supports a `<param>` element, but it's an older style of writing Pig actions and is not recommended in newer versions, though it is still supported.

Pig example

Let's look at a specific example of how a real-life Pig job is run on the command line and convert it into an Oozie action definition. Here's an example of a simple Pig script:

```
REGISTER myudfs.jar;
data = LOAD '/user/joe/pig/input/data.txt' USING PigStorage(',') AS
       (user, age, salary);
filtered_data = FILTER data BY age > $age;
```

```
ordered_data = ORDER filtered_data BY salary;
final_data = FOREACH ordered_data GENERATE (user, age,
             myudfs.multiply_salary(salary));
STORE final_data INTO '$output' USING PigStorage();
```

It is common for Pig scripts to use user-defined functions (UDFs) through custom JARs. In the preceding example, there is a Java UDF JAR file (*myudfs.jar*) on the local filesystem. The JAR is first registered using the `REGISTER` statement in Pig before using the UDF `multiply_salary()` (refer to the Pig documentation on how to write, build, and package the UDFs; we will only cover how to use it via Oozie here).

This Pig script is also parameterized using variables—`$age` and `$ouput`. This is typically run in Pig using the following command (this invocation substitutes these two variables using the `-param` option to Pig):

```
$ pig -Dmapreduce.job.queuename=research -f pig.script -param age=30
  -param output=hdfs://nn.mycompany.com:8020/hdfs/user/joe/pig/output
```

We will now see an example Oozie Pig action to run this Pig script. The easiest way to use the UDF in Oozie is to copy the *myudfs.jar* file to the *lib/* subdirectory under the workflow root directory on HDFS. You can then remove the `REGISTER` statement in the Pig script before copying it to HDFS for the Oozie action to run it. Oozie will automatically add the JAR to the classpath and the Pig action will have no problem finding the JAR or the UDF even without the `REGISTER` statement:

```
<action name="myPigAction">
    <pig>
        <job-tracker>jt.mycompany.com:8032</job-tracker>
        <name-node>hdfs://nn.mycompany.com:8020</name-node>
        <prepare>
            <delete path="hdfs://nn.mycompany.com:8020/hdfs/user/
              joe/pig/output"/>
        </prepare>
        <configuration>
            <property>
                <name>mapred.job.queue.name</name>
                <value>research</value>
            </property>
        </configuration>
        <script>pig.script</script>
        <argument>-param</argument>
        <argument>age=30</argument>
        <argument>-param</argument>
        <argument>output=hdfs://nn.mycompany.com:8020/hdfs/user/
           joe/pig/output</argument>
    </pig>
    <ok to="end"/>
    <error to="fail"/>
</action>
```

There are multiple ways to use UDFs and custom JARs in Pig through Oozie. The UDF code can be distributed via the `<archive>` and `<file>` elements, as always, but copying it to the *lib/* subdirectory is the easiest and most straightforward approach.

FS Action

Users can run HDFS commands using Oozie's FS action. Not all HDFS commands are supported, but the following common operations are allowed: `delete`, `mkdir`, `move`, `chmod`, `<touchz>`, `chgrp`. The elements that make up the FS action are as follows:

- `name-node` (required)
- `job-xml`
- `configuration`
- `delete`
- `mkdir`
- `move`
- `chmod`
- `touchz`
- `chgrp`

FS action commands are launched by Oozie on its server instead of the launcher. This is something to keep in mind, because a long-running, resource-intensive FS action can affect the performance of the Oozie server and impact other Oozie applications. This is also the reason why not all HDFS commands (e.g., `copy`) are supported through this action.

Here's an example of an FS action in a real workflow:

```
...
    <action name="myFSAction">
        <fs>
            <delete path='hdfs://foo:8020/usr/joe/temp-data'/>
            <mkdir path='myDir/${wf:id()}'/>
            <move source='${jobInput}' target='myDir/${wf:id()}/input'/>
            <chmod path='${jobOutput}' permissions='-rwxrw-rw-'
              dir-files='true'/>
        </fs>
```

```
    </action>
...
```

Depending on the operation, Oozie will check to make sure source directories exist and target directories don't to reduce the chance of failure of the HDFS commands. To be more specific, Oozie checks for the following:

- Existence of the path for `<delete>`, `<chmod>`, and `<chgrp>`.
- The existence of the source path for the `<move>` command.
- The nonexistence of the target file path for the `<move>` (existence of a directory path is fine).
- The nonexistence of the path for the `<mkdir>` and `touchz>`.

Both `move` and `chmod` use the same conventions as typical Unix operations. For `move`, the existence of the target path is fine if it's a directory because the `move` will drop the source files or the source directory underneath this target directory. However, the target can't be a path of an existing file. The parent of the target path must exist. The target for the `move` can also skip the filesystem URI (e.g., *hdfs://{nameNode}*) because the source and the target Hadoop cluster must be the same.

Permissions for `chmod` are specified using the Unix symbolic representation (e.g., `-rwxrw-rw-`) or an octal representation (`755`). When doing a `chmod` command on a directory, by default the command is applied to the directory and the files one level within the directory. To apply the `chmod` command to the directory, without affecting the files within it, the `dir-files` attribute must be set to `false`. You can also optionally add a `<recursive>` element to `chmod` to change the permissions recursively in the given directory.

Filesystem example

This is the easiest example to illustrate among all the Oozie actions. Imagine that we want to do the following three simple filesystem tasks on HDFS: `delete`, `mkdir`, and `chmod`. Let's first see the command-line way of doing this (the example uses both the `hadoop` and `hdfs` CLI tools, but they support the same functionality and are equivalent; the `hdfs` CLI is the recommended tool moving forward):

```
$ hadoop fs -rm -r /hdfs/user/joe/logs
$ hdfs dfs -mkdir /hdfs/user/joe/logs
$ hdfs dfs -chmod -R 755 /hdfs/user/joe/
```

This can be implemented using an Oozie FS action as shown here:

```
<action name="myFSAction">
    <fs>
        <name-node>hdfs://nn.mycompany.com:8020</name-node>
        <delete path='/hdfs/user/joe/logs'/>
```

```
        <mkdir path='/hdfs/user/joe/logs'/>
        <chmod path='/hdfs/user/joe/' permissions='755' dir-files='true'>
                          <recursive/></chmod>
    </fs>
    <ok to="success"/>
    <error to="fail"/>
</action>
```

The entire action is not atomic. This means that if the <chmod> command fails in this example, the action does not rollback the <delete> and <mkdir> commands that happened just prior to that. So it's important to handle the cleanup and reset if you want to rerun the action in its entirety.

Sub-Workflow Action

The sub-workflow action runs a child workflow as part of the parent workflow. You can think of it as an embedded workflow. From a parent's perspective, this is a single action and it will proceed to the next action in its workflow if and only if the sub-workflow is done in its entirety. The child and the parent have to run in the same Oozie system and the child workflow application has to be deployed in that Oozie system:

- `app-path` (required)
- `propagate-configuration`
- `configuration`

The properties for the sub-workflow are defined in the `<configuration>` section. The `<propagate_configuration>` element can also be optionally used to tell Oozie to pass the parent's job configuration to the sub-workflow. Note that this is to propagate the job configuration (*job.properties* file). The following is an example of a simple but complete `<sub-workflow>` action:

```
<action name="mySubWorkflow">
    <sub-workflow>
        <app-path>hdfs://nn.mycompany.com:8020/hdfs/user/joe/
          sub_workflow</app-path>
        <propagate-configuration/>
    </sub-workflow>
    <ok to="success"/>
    <error to="fail"/>
</action>
```

Hive Action

Hive actions run a Hive query on the cluster and are not very different from the Pig actions as far as Oozie is concerned. Hive is a SQL-like interface for Hadoop and is probably the most popular tool to interact with the data on Hadoop today (refer to the Apache Hive documentation for more information). The Hive query and the required configuration, libraries, and code for user-defined functions have to be packaged as part of the workflow bundle and deployed to HDFS:

- `job-tracker` (required)
- `name-node` (required)
- `prepare`
- `job-xml`
- `configuration`
- `script` (required)
- `param`
- `argument`
- `file`
- `archive`

Hive requires certain key configuration properties, like the location of its metastore (`hive.metastore.uris`), which are typically part of the *hive-site.xml*. These properties have to be passed in as configuration to Oozie's Hive action.

One common shortcut people take for Hive actions is to pass in a copy of the *hive-site.xml* from the Hive client node (edge node) as the `<job-xml>` element. This way, the *hive-site.xml* is just reused in its entirety and no additional configuration settings or special files are necessary. This is an overkill and considered a little lazy, but it works most of the time.

Be careful with any directory and file path settings copied or borrowed from the *hive-site.xml* file, because the directory layout on the edge node and the Hadoop worker nodes may not be the same and you might hit some filesystem and permission errors.

The `script` element points to the actual Hive script to be run with the `<param>` elements used to pass the parameters to the script. Hive supports variable substitution similar to Pig, as explained in "Pig Action" on page 56. The same rules from the Pig action apply here as far as using the `<argument>` element instead of the old-style

<param> element and also understanding the two levels of parameterization with Oozie and Hive. Here's a simple example:

```
...
    <action name=" myHiveAction ">
         <hive>
              ...
              <script>myscript.sql</script>
              <argument>-hivevar</argument>
              <argument>InputDir=/home/joe/input-data</argument>
              <argument>-hivevar</argument>
              <argument>OutputDir=${jobOutput}</argument>
         </hive>
    </action>
...
```

Hive example

Let's look at an example of how a real-life Hive job is run on the command line. The following is a simple Hive query saved in a file called *hive.hql*. This query also uses a UDF from the JAR file */tmp/HiveSwarm-1.0-SNAPSHOT.jar* on the local filesystem. The Hive statement `ADD JAR` is invoked before using the UDF `dayofweek()` (refer to the Hive documentation for information on Hive UDFs; we will just see how to run it in Oozie here):

```
ADD JAR /tmp/HiveSwarm-1.0-SNAPSHOT.jar;
create temporary function dayofweek as 'com.livingsocial.hive.udf.DayOfWeek';
select *, dayofweek(to_date('2014-05-02')) from test_table
       where age>${age} order by name;
```

This Hive query is also parameterized using the variable `$age`. This is typically run in Hive using the following command line (this invocation substitutes the variable using the `-hivevar` option):

```
$ hive -hivevar age=30 -f hive.hql
```

We will now see a Hive action to operationalize this example in Oozie. As with Pig UDFs, copy the JAR file (*HiveSwarm-1.0-SNAPSHOT.jar*) to the *lib/* subdirectory under the workflow root directory on HDFS. You can then remove the `ADD JAR` statement in the Hive query before copying it to HDFS for the Oozie action to run it. Oozie will automatically add the JAR to the classpath and the Hive action will have no problem finding the JAR or the UDF even without the `ADD JAR` statement. Alternatively, the UDF code can be distributed via the `<archive>` and `<file>` elements as well, but that will involve more work:

```
<action name="myHiveAction">
    <hive>
        <job-tracker>jt.mycompany.com:8032</job-tracker>
        <name-node>hdfs://nn.mycompany.com:8020</name-node>
        <job-xml>hive-config.xml</job-xml>
```

```
            <script>hive.hql</script>
            <argument>-hivevar</argument>
            <argument>age=30</argument>
        </hive>
        <ok to="success"/>
        <error to="fail"/>
    </action>
```

The *hive-config.xml* file in the example needs to be on HDFS in the workflow root directory along with the Oozie workflow XML and the *hive.hql* file. The config file can be a simple copy of the entire *hive-site.xml* or a file with a subset of the Hive configuration handcrafted for the specific query.

In older versions of Oozie and Hive, we could use the `oozie.hive.defaults` configuration property to pass in the default settings for Hive. This setting no longer works with newer versions of Oozie (as of Oozie 3.4) and will be ignored even if present in the workflow XML file. You should use the `<job-xml>` element instead to pass the settings.

DistCp Action

DistCp action supports the Hadoop distributed copy tool, which is typically used to copy data across Hadoop clusters. Users can use it to copy data within the same cluster as well, and to move data between Amazon S3 and Hadoop clusters (refer to the Hadoop DistCp documentation for more details).

Here are the elements required to define this action:

- `job-tracker` (required)
- `name-node` (required)
- `prepare`
- `configuration`
- `java-opts`
- `arg`

Here is an example of a DistCp action:

```
<action name=" myDistCpAction ">
    <distcp>
            ...
            <arg> hdfs://localhost:8020/path/to/input.txt</arg>
            <arg>${nameNode2}/path/to/output.txt</arg>
      </distcp>
</action>
```

The first argument passed in via the `<arg>` element points to the URI for the full path for the source data and the second `<arg>` corresponds to the full path URI for the target for the distributed copy. Do note the different `NameNodes`.

The following configuration property is required if the DistCp is copying data between two secure Hadoop clusters:

```
oozie.launcher.mapreduce.job.hdfs-servers
```

The DistCp action might not work very well if the two clusters are running different Hadoop versions or if they are running secure and nonsecure Hadoop. There are ways to make it work by using the WebHDFS protocol and setting some special configuration settings for Hadoop. Those details about DistCp are beyond the scope of this book, but it's fairly straightforward to implement them in Oozie if you want to research and incorporate those tricks and tips.

DistCp Example

Let's look at a specific example of how a real-life DistCp job is run on the command line and convert it into an Oozie action definition. The following is an example of a typical DistCp command:

```
$ /opt/hadoop/bin/hadoop distcp -m 100  s3n://my-logfiles/2014-04-15/*
  /hdfs/user/joe/logs/2014-04-15/
```

This example copies data from an Amazon S3 bucket to the local Hadoop cluster, which is a common usage pattern. Copying from one Hadoop cluster to another follows the same concepts. This DistCp is configured to run 100 mappers through the `-m=100` option.

Let's convert this command line example to an Oozie action:

```
<action name="myDistcpAction">
    <distcp xmlns="uri:oozie:distcp-action:0.1">
        <job-tracker>jt.mycompany.com:8032</job-tracker>
        <name-node>hdfs://nn.mycompany.com:8020</name-node>
        <prepare>
            <delete path="hdfs://nn.mycompany.com:8020/hdfs/user/joe/
              logs/2014-04-15/"/>
        </prepare>
        <arg>-Dfs.s3n.awsAccessKeyId=XXXX</arg>
        <arg>-Dfs.s3n.awsSecretAccessKey=YYYY</arg>
        <arg>-m</arg>
        <arg>100</arg>
        <arg>s3n://my-logfiles/2014-04-15/*</arg>
        <arg>/hdfs/user/joe/logs/2014-04-15/</arg>
    </distcp>
    <ok to="success"/>
```

```
    <error to="fail"/>
</action>
```

As you can see, the `<distcp>` action definition in Oozie has the Amazon (AWS) access key and secret key, while the command-line example does not. This is because the AWS keys are typically saved as part of the Hadoop *core-site.xml* configuration file on the edge node where the DistCp command line is invoked. But they need to be defined explicitly in the Oozie action either through the `-D` option, the `<job-xml>` file, or the configuration section because those keys need to be propagated to the launcher job running on one of the nodes, which may or may not have the same Hadoop configuration files as the edge node.

The DistCp command-line example shown here assumes the keys are in the Hadoop *core-site.xml* file. Also, the keys in the Oozie example are obviously fake. There is another way to pass in the AWS keys by embedding them in the s3n URI itself using the syntax `s3n://ID:SECRET@BUCKET` (refer to the Hadoop documentation for more details; Oozie supports this syntax as well).

Email Action

Sometimes there is a need to send emails from a workflow application. It might be to notify users about the state of the workflow or error messages or whatever the business need dictates. Oozie's email action provides an easy way to integrate this feature into the workflow. It takes the usual email parameters: `to`, `cc`, `subject`, and `body`. Email IDs of multiple recipients can be comma separated.

The following elements are part of this action:

- `to` (required)
- `cc`
- `subject` (required)
- `body` (required)

This is one of the few actions that runs on the Oozie server and not through an Oozie launcher on one of the Hadoop nodes. The assumption here is that the Oozie server node has the necessary SMTP email client installed and configured, and can send emails. In addition, the following SMTP server configuration has to be defined in the *oozie-site.xml* file for this action to work:

- `oozie.email.smtp.host` (default: localhost)
- `oozie.email.smtp.port` (default: 25)
- `oozie.email.from.address` (default: oozie@localhost)

- `oozie.email.smtp.auth` (default: false)
- `oozie.email.smtp.username` (default: empty)
- `oozie.email.smtp.password` (default: empty)

Here is an example of an email action:

```
...
    <action name=" myEmailAction ">
        <email>
            <to>joe@initech.com,the_other_joe@initech.com</to>
            <cc>john@initech.com</cc>
            <subject>Email notifications for ${wf:id()}</subject>
            <body>The wf ${wf:id()} successfully completed.</body>
        </email>
    </action>
...
```

Shell Action

Oozie provides a convenient way to run any shell command. This could be Unix commands, Perl/Python scripts, or even Java programs invoked through the Unix shell. The shell command runs on an arbitrary Hadoop cluster node and the commands being run have to be available locally on that node. It's important to keep the following limitations and characteristics in mind while using the `<shell>` action:

- Interactive commands are not allowed.
- You can't run `sudo` or run as another user.
- Because the shell command runs on any Hadoop node, you need to be aware of the path of the binary on these nodes. The executable has to be either available on the node or copied by the action via the distributed cache using the `<file>` tag. For the binaries on the node that are not copied via the cache, it's perhaps safer and easier to debug if you always use an absolute path.
- It's not unusual for different nodes in a Hadoop cluster to be running different versions of certain tools or even the operating system. So be aware that the tools on these nodes could have slightly different options, interfaces, and behaviors. While built-in shell commands like `grep` and `ls` will probably work fine in most cases, other binaries could either be missing, be at different locations, or have slightly different behaviors depending on which node they run on.
- On a nonsecure Hadoop cluster, the shell command will execute as the Unix user who runs the *TaskTracker* (Hadoop 1) or the YARN container (Hadoop 2). This is typically a system-defined user. On secure Hadoop clusters running Kerberos,

the shell commands will run as the Unix user who submitted the workflow containing the <shell> action.

The elements that make up this action are as follows:

- job-tracker (required)
- name-node (required)
- prepare
- job-xml
- configuration
- exec (required)
- argument
- env-var
- file
- archive
- capture-output

The <exec> element has the actual shell command with the arguments passed in through the <argument> elements. If the excutable is a script instead of a standard Unix command, the script needs to be copied to the workflow root directory on HDFS and defined via the <file> element as always. The <shell> action also includes an <env-var> element that contains the Unix environment variable, and it's defined using the standard Unix syntax (e.g., PATH=$PATH:my_path).

Be careful not to use the ${VARIABLE} syntax for the environment variables, as those variables will be replaced by Oozie.

This action also adds a special environment variable called OOZIE_ACTION_CONF_XML, which has the path to the Hadoop configuration file that Oozie creates and drops in the <shell> action's running directory. This environment variable can be used in the script to access the configuration file if needed.

Just like Java action, if the <capture_output> element is present here, Oozie will capture the output of the shell command and make it available to the workflow application. This can then be accessed by the workflow through the action:output() EL function. The one difference between the <java> action and <shell> action is that Oozie captures the stdout of the <shell> action whereas with the Java action, the program has to write the output to a file (`oozie.action.output.properties`). Here is a typical `<shell>` action:

```
...
    <action name=" myShellAction ">
        <shell>
            ...
            <exec>${EXEC}</exec>
            <argument>A</argument>
            <argument>B</argument>
            <file>${EXEC}#${EXEC}</file>
        </shell>
    </action>
...
```

While Oozie does run the shell command on a Hadoop node, it runs it via the launcher job. It does not invoke another MapReduce job to accomplish this task.

Shell example

Let's say there is a Python script that takes today's date as one of the arguments and does some basic processing. Let's assume it also requires an environment variable named `TZ` to set the time zone. This is how you will run it on the shell command line:

```
$ export TZ=PST
$ python test.py 07/21/2014
```

Let's convert this example to an Oozie `<shell>` action:

```
<action name="myShellAction">
    <shell xmlns="uri:oozie:shell-action:0.2">
        <job-tracker>jt.mycompany.com:8032</job-tracker>
        <name-node>hdfs://nn.mycompany.com:8020</name-node>
        <exec>/usr/bin/python</exec>
        <argument>test.py</argument>
        <argument>07/21/2014/argument>
        <env-var>TZ=PST</env-var>
        <file>test.py#test.py</file>
        <capture-output/>
    </shell>
    <ok to="success"/>
    <error to="fail"/>
</action>
```

Users often use the Python Virtual Environment and distribute it via the Hadoop distributed cache using the `<archive>` element. This is a nice and self-contained approach to isolate your Python environment from what's available on the node and also to make sure you have access to all the packages your job needs.

SSH Action

The `<ssh>` action runs a shell command on a specific remote host using a secure shell. The command should be available in the path on the remote machine and it is executed in the user's home directory on the remote machine. The shell command can be run as another user on the remote host from the one running the workflow. We can do this using typical `ssh` syntax: `user@host`. However, the `oozie.action.ssh.allow.user.at.host` should be set to true in *oozie-site.xml* for this to be enabled. By default, this variable is false. Here are the elements of an `<ssh>` action:

- `host` (required)
- `command` (required)
- `args`
- `arg`
- `capture-output`

The `<command>` element has the actual command to be run on the remote host and the `<args>` element has the arguments for the command. Either `<arg>` or `<args>` can be used in the action, but not both. The difference between the two is as follows. If there is a space in the `<args>`, it will be handled as separate arguments, while `<arg>` will handle each value as one argument. The `<arg>` element was basically introduced to handle arguments with white spaces in them. Here is an example `<ssh>` action:

```
...
    <action name=" mySSHAction ">
        <ssh>
            <host>foo@bar.com<host>
            <command>uploaddata</command>
            <args>jdbc:derby://bar.com:1527/myDB</args>
            <args>hdfs://foobar.com:8020/usr/joe/myData</args>
        </ssh>
    </action>
...
```

It's important to understand the difference between the `<ssh>` action and the `<shell>` action. The `<shell>` action can be used to run shell commands or some custom scripts on one of the Hadoop nodes. The `<ssh>` action can be used to run similar commands, but it's meant to be run on some remote node that's not part of the Hadoop cluster. Also, the `<shell>` action runs through an Oozie launcher while the `<ssh>` action is initiated from the Oozie server.

Sqoop Action

Apache Sqoop is a Hadoop tool used for importing and exporting data between relational databases (MySQL, Oracle, etc.) and Hadoop clusters. Sqoop commands are structured around connecting to and importing or exporting data from various relational databases. It often uses JDBC to talk to these external database systems (refer to the documentation on Apache Sqoop for more details). Oozie's `sqoop` action helps users run Sqoop jobs as part of the workflow.

The following elements are part of the Sqoop action:

- `job-tracker` (required)
- `name-node` (required)
- `prepare`
- `job-xml`
- `configuration`
- `command` (required if `arg` is not used)
- `arg` (required if `command` is not used)
- `file`
- `archive`

The arguments to Sqoop are sent either through the `<command>` element in one line or broken down into many `<arg>` elements. The following example shows a typical usage:

```
...
    <action name=" mySqoopAction ">
        <sqoop>
            ...
            <command>import  --connect jdbc:hsqldb:file:db.hsqldb --table
            test_table--target-dir hdfs://localhost:8020/user/joe/sqoop_tbl
            -m 1</command>
        </sqoop>
    </action>
...
```

Sqoop example

Let's look at an example of an import from a MySQL database into HDFS using the Sqoop command line. We are using Sqoop version 1.4.5 here. Also known as Sqoop 1, it is a lot more popular than the newer Sqoop 2 at this time. The command shown here is connecting to a MySQL database called `MY_DB` and importing all the data from the table `test_table`. The output is written to the HDFS directory */hdfs/joe/sqoop/output-data* and this Sqoop job runs just one mapper on the Hadoop cluster to accomplish this import. Here's the actual command line:

```
$ /opt/sqoop-1.4.5/bin/sqoop import --connect jdbc:mysql://mysqlhost.mycompany
.com/MY_DB --table test_table -username mytestsqoop -password password
--target-dir /hdfs/joe/sqoop/output-data -m 1
```

Example 4-3 converts this command line to an Oozie `sqoop` action:

Example 4-3. Sqoop import

```
<action name="sqoop-import">
        <sqoop xmlns="uri:oozie:sqoop-action:0.2">
           <job-tracker>jt.mycompany.com:8032$lt;/job-tracker>
           <name-node>hdfs://nn.mycompany.com:8020$lt;/name-node>
            <prepare>
                <delete path=" hdfs://nn.mycompany.com:8020/hdfs/joe/sqoop/
                output-data"/>
            </prepare>
            <configuration>
                <property>
                    <name>mapred.job.queue.name</name>
                    <value>default</value>
                </property>
            </configuration>
             <command>import --connect jdbc:mysql://mysqlhost.mycompany.com/MY_DB
               --table test_table -username mytestsqoop -password password
               --target-dir /user/alti-test-01/ara/output-data/sqoop -m 1</command>
        </sqoop>
        <ok to="end"/>
        <error to="fail"/>
    </action>
```

The Sqoop `eval` option runs any random and valid SQL statement on the target (relational) DB and returns the results. This command does not run a MapReduce job on the Hadoop side and this caused some issues for Oozie. The `eval` option via the Oozie `<sqoop>` action used to fail. This bug has been fixed in Oozie version 4.1.0 and it now supports the `eval` option as well.

Let's see another example using the <arg> element instead of the <command> element in the <sqoop> action. Example 4-4 shows how to run a Sqoop eval in Oozie 4.1.0:

Example 4-4. Sqoop eval

```
<action name="ara_sqoop_eval">
    <sqoop xmlns="uri:oozie:sqoop-action:0.2">
        <job-tracker>jt.mycompany.com:8032$lt;/job-tracker>
        <name-node>hdfs://nn.mycompany.com:8020$lt;/name-node>
        <arg>eval</arg>
        <arg>--connect</arg>
        <arg>jdbc:mysql://mysqlhost.mycompany.com/MY_DB</arg>
        <arg>--username</arg>
        <arg>mytestsqoop</arg>
        <arg>--password</arg>
        <arg>password</arg>
        <arg>-e</arg>
        <arg>SELECT count(*) FROM test_table</arg>
    </sqoop>
    <ok to="end"/>
    <error to="fail"/>
</action>
```

The example shows the username and password in clear text just for convenience. This is not the recommended way to pass them via Oozie. These values are usually parameterized using variables and saved in a secure fashion.

Synchronous Versus Asynchronous Actions

All Hadoop actions and the <shell> action follow the "Action Execution Model" on page 40. These are called asynchronous actions because they are launched via a launcher as Hadoop jobs. But the filesystem action, email action, SSH action, and sub-workflow action are executed by the Oozie server itself and are called synchronous actions. The execution of these synchronous actions do not require running any user code—just access to some libraries.

As seen earlier, the Oozie filesystem action performs lightweight filesystem operations not involving data transfers and is executed by the Oozie server itself. The email action sends emails; this is done directly by the Oozie server via an SMTP server. The sub-workflow action is executed by the Oozie server also, but it just submits a new workflow. The SSH action makes Oozie invoke a secure shell on a remote machine, though the actual shell command itself does not run on the Oozie server. These actions are all relatively lightweight and hence safe to be run synchronously on the Oozie server machine itself.

Table 4-1 captures the execution modes for the different action types.

Table 4-1. Action modes

Action	Type
MapReduce	Asynchronous
Java	Asynchronous
Pig	Asynchronous
Filesystem	Synchronous
Sub-Workflow	Synchronous
Hive	Asynchronous
DistCp	Asynchronous
Email	Synchronous
Shell	Asynchronous
SSH	Synchronous
Sqoop	Asynchronous

This wraps up the explanation of all action types that Oozie supports out of the box. In this chapter, we learned about all the details and intricacies of writing and packaging the different kinds of action types that can be used in a workflow. We will cover parameterization and other advanced workflow topics in detail in Chapter 5.

CHAPTER 5

Workflow Applications

We learned about action types, the basic building blocks of an Oozie workflow, in the last chapter. In this chapter, we will get into the various aspects of authoring a complete workflow application comprised of those actions. We will learn all the tricks and techniques, like parameterization and variable substitution, that come in handy when assembling actions into a functional workflow. We will also see how to manage and drive the control flow among those actions.

Outline of a Basic Workflow

As we have already seen, workflows are defined in an XML file that is typically named *workflow.xml*. Example 5-1 shows an outline of a typical Oozie workflow XML, which captures some of the relevant components and the most common sections.

Example 5-1. Outline of a basic workflow

```
<workflow-app xmlns="uri:oozie:workflow:0.5" name="simpleWF">
  <global>
     ...
  </global>
  <start to="echoA"/>
  <action name="echoA">
    <shell xmlns="uri:oozie:shell-action:0.2">
      ...
    </shell>
    <ok to="echoB"/>
    <error to="done"/>
  </action>
  <action name="echoB">
    <shell xmlns="uri:oozie:shell-action:0.2">
      ...
    </shell>
```

```
    <ok to="done"/>
    <error to="done"/>
</action>
  <end name="done"/>
</workflow-app>
```

At the very beginning of the XML is the `<workflow-app>` root element with an `xmlns` and a `name` attribute specifying the name of the workflow application.

Oozie performs XML schema validation on all XML files used to define workflows, coordinators, and bundles. So you must specify a schema URI (the `xmlns` attribute in the root element). Oozie schemas have evolved and newer versions have been introduced. While Oozie supports older schemas, it is recommended to always use the latest schema, as it supports the latest Oozie features. Older schemas will eventually be deprecated in newer versions of Oozie.

The workflow name must be a word consisting of any combination of letters, numbers, underscores (_), and dashes (-). Within this `<workflow-app>` element, the complete workflow application is defined. As you can see, the following sections are captured in Example 5-1:

- `Global configuration`
- `Control nodes`
- `Action nodes`

The action nodes in the example shown here are represented as simple `<shell>` actions meant only to `echo` something on the screen. Real workflows will have real actions, mostly Hadoop actions that we covered in the last chapter. We will go with `<shell>` actions here for simplicity. When users start writing their first Oozie workflows, it's a good idea to start small with something like a one-line `<shell>` action and expand from there.

First, we cover the control nodes in the next section. We look at configuration details later in this chapter.

Control Nodes

Workflow control nodes define the start and end of a workflow and they define any control changes in the execution flow. All nodes except for the `<start>` node have a name attribute. Node names must be a valid Java identifier with a maximum length of 40 characters. Node names can also use dashes.

<start> and <end>

The <start> node is the starting point of a workflow. When Oozie starts a workflow, it looks for the <start> node and transitions to the node specified in the to attribute.

The <end> node is the completion point of the workflow. When a workflow transitions to an <end> node, it completes its execution with a SUCCEEDED status.

The preceding workflow example has a <start> node that transitions to a <shell> action echoA, then transitions to the <shell> action echoB, and then transitions to the done <end> node, which ends the workflow successfully. This simple workflow is captured in Figure 5-1.

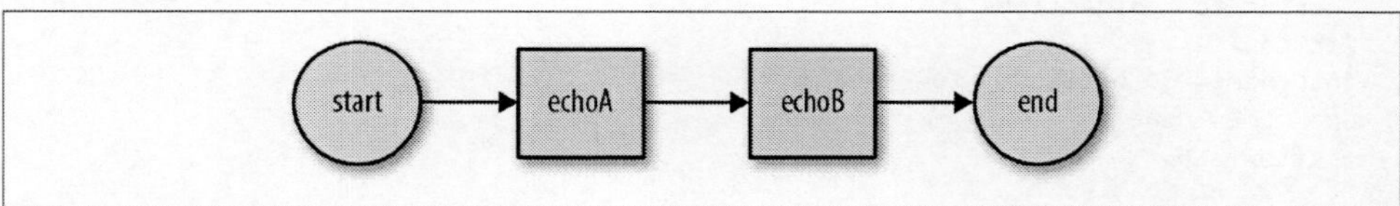

Figure 5-1. Simple workflow example

<fork> and <join>

Simple workflows execute one action at a time. In the previous section, we saw that the echoA action is executed first and the echoB action is not executed until after echoA completes successfully.

When actions don't depend on the result of each other, it is possible to execute actions in parallel using the <fork> and <join> control nodes to speed up the execution of the workflow.

When Oozie encounters a <fork> node in a workflow, it starts running all the paths defined by the fork in parallel. These parallel execution paths run independent of each other. All the paths of a <fork> node must converge into a <join> node. A workflow does not proceed its execution beyond the <join> node until all execution paths from the <fork> node reach the <join> node. Example 5-2 captures the <fork>-<join> syntax.

Example 5-2. Workflow with <fork> and <join> control nodes

```
<workflow-app xmlns="uri:oozie:workflow:0.5" name="forkJoinNodeWF">
  <global>
    ...
  </global>
```

```
  <start to="forkActions"/>
  <fork name="forkActions">
    <path name="echoA"/>
    <path name="echoB"/>
  </fork>
  <action name="echoA">
    <shell xmlns="uri:oozie:shell-action:0.2">
      ...
    </shell>
    <ok to="joinActions"/>
    <error to="joinActions"/>
  </action>
  <action name="echoB">
    <shell xmlns="uri:oozie:shell-action:0.2">
      ...
    </shell>
    <ok to="joinActions"/>
    <error to="joinActions"/>
  </action>
  <join name="joinActions" to="done"/>
  <end name="done"/>
</workflow-app>
```

The `<path>` elements within the `<fork>` node define the parallel execution paths of the `<fork>` node. Each `<path>` element indicates the first node in the parallel execution path being created. In the example above, each parallel path happens to have only one action node. But in reality, it could be a sequence of nodes. The last node of each such execution path should transition to the `<join>` node.

It is possible to have nested `<fork>` and `<join>` nodes. The only constraint is that `<fork>` and `<join>` nodes always go in pairs and all execution paths starting from a given `<fork>` must end in the same `<join>` node. Figures 5-2 and 5-3 depict both invalid and valid nesting of `<fork>` and `<join>` nodes.

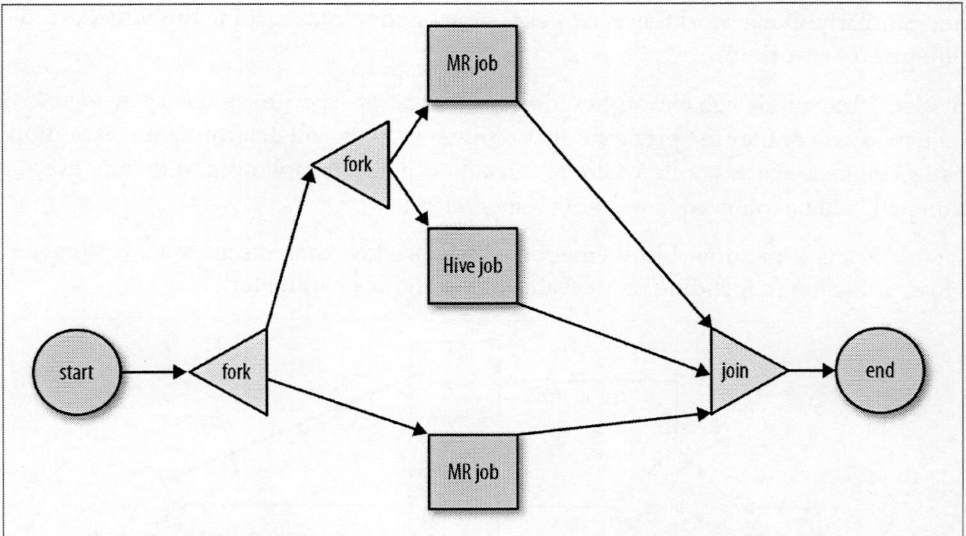

Figure 5-2. Workflow with invalid nesting of <fork> and <join> nodes

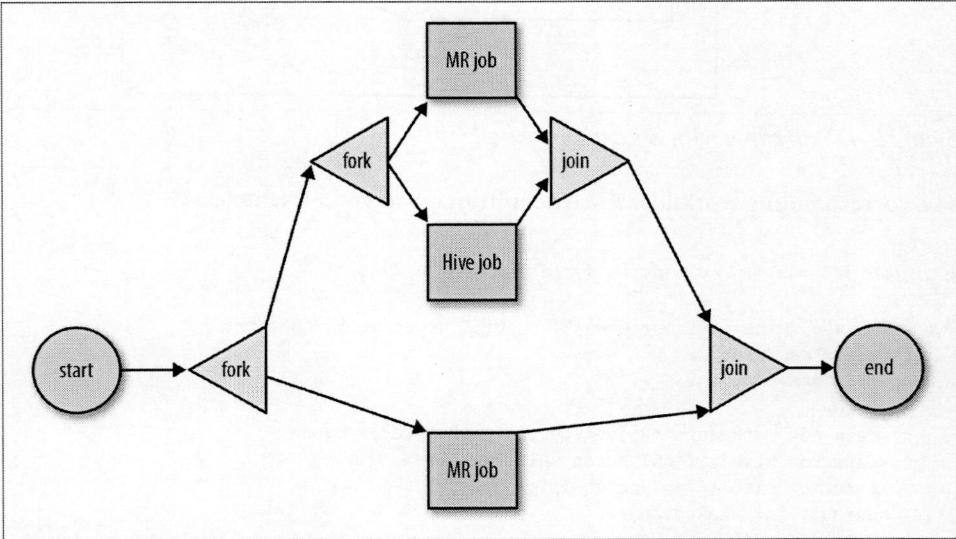

Figure 5-3. Workflow with valid nesting of <fork> and <join> nodes

<decision>

In programming languages, `if-then-else` and `switch-case` statements are usually used to control the flow of execution depending on certain conditions being met or not. Similarly, Oozie workflows use `<decision>` nodes to determine the actual execution path of a workflow.

A `<decision>` node behavior is best described as an `if-then-else-if-then-else...` sequence, where the first predicate that resolves to `true` will determine the execution path. Unlike a `<fork>` node where all execution paths are followed, only one execution path will be followed in a `<decision>` node.

Figure 5-4 is a pictorial representation of a workflow that executes a MapReduce, Hive, or Pig job (depending on the value of a workflow parameter).

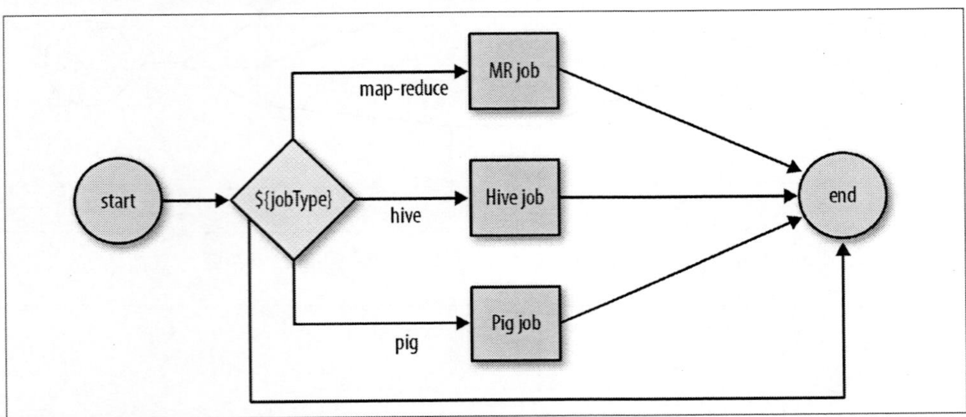

Figure 5-4. Workflow with a <decision> node

The corresponding workflow XML definition is shown in Example 5-3.

Example 5-3. Workflow with a <decision> node

```
<workflow-app xmlns="uri:oozie:workflow:0.5" name="decisionNodeWF">
  <start to="decision"/>
  <decision name="decision">
    <switch>
      <case to="mapReduce">${jobType eq "mapReduce"}</case>
      <case to="hive">${jobType eq "hive"}</case>
      <case to="pig">${jobType eq "pig"}</case>
      <default to="mapReduce"/>
    </switch>
  </decision>
  <action name="mapReduce">
    ...
    <ok to="done"/>
    <error to="done"/>
  </action>
  <action name="hive">
    ...
```

```
    <ok to="done"/>
    <error to="done"/>
  </action>
  <action name="pig">
    ...
    <ok to="done"/>
    <error to="done"/>
  </action>
  <end name="done"/>
</workflow-app>
```

Each `<case>` element has a `to` attribute indicating the execution path to follow if the content of the <case> element (`${jobType eq "mapReduce"}` in the example) evaluates to `true`. If none of the `<case>` contents evaluates to `true`, the execution path specified by the `<default to>` attribute will be followed.

Expressions like `${jobType eq "mapReduce"}` are explained in detail in "EL Functions" on page 88.

<kill>

The `<kill>` node allows a workflow to kill itself. If any execution path of a workflow reaches a `<kill>` node, Oozie will terminate the workflow immediately, failing all running actions (it could be multiple running actions if the workflow execution is currently within a `<fork>`-`<join>` block) and setting the completion status of the workflow to `KILLED`. It is worth noting that Oozie will not explicitly kill the currently running MapReduce jobs on the Hadoop cluster that corresponds to those actions. They will be allowed to complete, though the action will be set to `FAILED` and no downstream actions of those jobs in their respective `<fork>`-`<join>` block will be run. Example 5-4 illustrates the use of a `<kill>` node.

Example 5-4. Workflow with a <kill> node

```
<workflow-app xmlns="uri:oozie:workflow:0.4" name="killNodeWF">
  <start to="mapReduce"/>
  <action name="mapReduce">
    ...
    <ok to="done"/>
    <error to="error"/>
  </action>
  <kill name="error">
    <message>The 'mapReduce' action failed!</message>
  <end name="done"/>
</workflow-app>
```

Using a <kill> node in a workflow is similar to doing a `System.exit(1)` (any non-zero exit code) in Java. We have already seen in previous examples that action nodes have two possible transitions: <ok> and <error>. Typically, <error> transitions to a <kill> node indicating that something went wrong.

<OK> and <ERROR>

When an action completes, its status is typically in either `OK` or `ERROR` status depending on whether or not the execution was successful. If an action ends in `OK` status, the workflow execution path transitions to the node specified in the <ok> element. If the action ends in `ERROR` status, the workflow execution path transitions to the node specified in the <error> element. Even when the action exit status is `ERROR`, the workflow still continues to execute. Typically, the node specified for transition in case of an `ERROR` is the <kill> node, but it's not required to be. In that case, the workflow will stop running and it will end up in the `KILLED`.

If desired, you have the option to continue the workflow execution even in case of an `ERROR` state for an action. There are legitimate reasons to continue running the workflow even after an action ends with an error. For example, you might want to transition to an <email> action on an error and send mails to a group of people before actually failing the workflow. In some use cases, there might be expected errors that can be handled and you may chose to transition to an action that cleans up or recovers some state and retries the failed action again. In short, just because an action ended up in the `ERROR` state doesn't mean the containing workflow also exits with an error right away.

Figure 5-5 captures the typical flow of control from an action node.

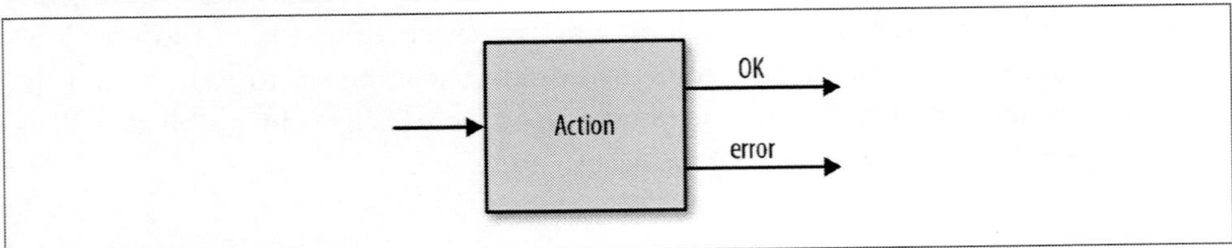

Figure 5-5. Workflow action node

<OK> and <ERROR> nodes in a workflow are considered action nodes, though they are funtionally different from the action worker nodes we saw in the previous chapter. Also, there are several other action states and we will see them in detail later in the chapter. But for simplicity here, we will assume actions either end up in <OK> or <ERROR>.

Job Configuration

As we have seen in the last chapter, there are several configuration settings that are required for defining workflow actions, especially Hadoop actions. Oozie provides multiple ways to specify them. It's important to understand Oozie's approach to configuration and parameterization if you want to become efficient at writing workflows.

Oozie's workflow XML supports several elements for each action type and we looked at these elements in detail in the previous chapter. For instance, every Hadoop job needs a `JobTracker` and `NameNode` and Oozie supports the `<name-node>` and `<job-tracker>` as top-level XML elements for all Hadoop action types. Most actions, especially Hadoop actions, also support a `<configuration>` section where job configurations can be defined. This can include system settings like `mapred.job.queue.name` or can also be user-defined keys that they want to send to the job.

Oozie provides multiple ways—some users may say too many ways—to pass in all of these configuration settings to the workflow. Here are three ways in which configuration can be passed to the workflow actions, listed in order of increasing priority:

- Global configuration
- Job XML file(s) specified in `<job-xml>`
- Inline `<configuration>` section in *workflow.xml*

There is actually a fourth, rarely used way to predefine most of the job configuration per action type, but it requires changing the Oozie server settings. The following setting in *oozie-site.xml* can be used to specify a set of configuration files:

```
oozie.service.HadoopAccessorService.
  action.configurations
```

Refer to the Oozie documentation for more details.

Global Configuration

Most actions in a workflow need several of the same settings (e.g., the `JobTracker` URI, `NameNode` URI, Hadoop scheduler queue, etc.). Users can avoid repeating all these settings and job configuration values in every action of the workflow by defining them once in the workflow's `<global>` section. The properties defined in the `<global>` section are available to all actions of the workflow. The sample workflow we saw in Example 5-1 introduced this `<global>` section, but Example 5-5 provides a more detailed example. As you can see, this makes the individual action definitions short and sweet.

Example 5-5. Global configuration for workflow applications

```
<workflow-app name="globalConfigurationWF" xmlns="uri:oozie:workflow:0.5">
  <global>
    <job-tracker>localhost:8032</job-tracker>
    <name-node>hdfs://localhost:8020</name-node>
    <configuration>
        <property>
            <name>mapred.job.queue.name</name>
            <value>development</value>
        </property>
    </configuration>
  </global>

  <action>
    <java>
        <main-class>org.apache.oozie.MyJavaMainClass</main-class>
        <arg>argument1</arg>
        <capture-output/>
    </java>
  </action>
  ...
</workflow-app>
```

Make sure you are using the right schema version for both the workflow and the specific action types when using the `<global>` section. Workflow schema version 0.4 and above supports the `<global>` section. In fact, schema version is always something to check and verify when certain workflow features and syntax throw errors.

Readers are strongly encouraged to use the `<global>` section liberally in their workflows to reduce clutter and confusion.

Job XML

Most actions supports a `<job-xml>` element, which is specifically meant for passing in Hadoop job configuration in XML format. This file has to be packaged with the workflow app and deployed on HDFS. Different action nodes in the workflow can include `different job-xml` file(s). With the later versions of the Oozie schema (version 0.4 and above), multiple `<job-xml>` elements are supported, which means that an action can have multiple files packaged and made available with the job configuration information split across them. Example 5-6 shows multiple job XMLs listed for a single action.

Example 5-6. Multiple job XML files

```
<map-reduce>
    <job-tracker>${jobTracker}</job-tracker>
    <name-node>${nameNode}</name-node>
    <job-xml>/conf_A_job.xml</job-xml>
    <job-xml>/conf_B_job.xml</job-xml>
    <job-xml>/conf_C_job.xml</job-xml>
...
```

What happens if the same configuration property is defined in multiple `<job-xml>` files? Settings from the later files in the list of files override the earlier ones. In this example, if the property `mapred.queue.name` is defined in all three job XML files, the value in *conf_C_job.xml* will take precedence over the value in the first two files.

Inline Configuration

Inline configuration in the body of the workflow action holds higher priority than the `<global>` section and the `<job-xml>` files. Example 5-7 shows a `<configuration>` section. The format and syntax are the same regardless of whether these properties are defined in the body of the action in the workflow XML or in a separate job XML file. It's only the priority and precedence that will be different.

Example 5-7. Configuration properties

```
<configuration>
    <property>
        <name>hive.metastore.local</name>
        <value>true</value>
        <description>controls whether to connect to a remote metastore
                                          server</description>
    </property>
    <property>
        <name>javax.jdo.option.ConnectionURL</name>
        <value>jdbc:postgresql://localhost/hive</value>
        <description>JDBC connect string for a JDBC metastore</description>
    </property>
</configuration>
```

Launcher Configuration

We saw in "Action Execution Model" on page 40 how the Oozie launcher job itself is a MapReduce job. You can specify the configuration settings for this launcher job in the action by prefixing `oozie.launcher` to any Hadoop configuration property. This way, you can override the default settings Oozie uses for the launcher job. Hadoop configuration properties like the job queue specified for the action are applied as defaults to the launcher job as well. These defaults help keep the action definition short and clean by avoiding specifying several redundant properties, but they can be explicitly overridden using the `oozie.launcher.*` properties.

One of the common settings users change for the launcher is `oozie.launcher.mapred.job.queue.name` to run it in a different Hadoop queue from the actual action itself. This will help avoid the deadlock situation explained in "Action Execution Model" on page 40.

Parameterization

Oozie applications are often parameterized at all levels: workflow, coordinator, and bundle. Typically, the same workflow is often required to run in different contexts and it's too inefficient to modify the workflow and action definition for each of those runs. For example, you might want to run the same workflow every day on a different date partition of the same input dataset. You might do this through a coordinator application or by using cron or may be even run it manually every day. In all of these scenarios, you don't want to have to modify the *workflow.xml* and update the HDFS directory every day to run this job. It's much more efficient to parameterize the workflow using variables or functions than to hardcode everything.

This section explains configuration, parameterization, and EL functions in the context of an Oozie workflow. But the concepts, patterns, and techniques are exactly the same when it comes to parameterization of Oozie coordinator and bundle applications that we will come across in later chapters. Specific functions and variables will be different, but the concept and methodology are the same.

Oozie supports the JSP Expression Language syntax from the JSP 2.0 Specification for parameterization. This allows Oozie to support variables, functions, and complex expressions as parameters. We will see each one of them in detail below. Oozie's parameterization framework is extensible and we will cover how to add user-defined EL functions in "Developing Custom EL Functions" on page 177. Do note that you can't just submit code for user-defined functions dynamically as part of a workflow at runtime. It needs to be preconfigured and added to the Oozie system and requires a server restart.

EL Variables

The most common technique for parameterization in Oozie is through EL variables. Various settings like `NameNode`, `JobTracker`, Hadoop queue, application path, and the date for the datasets can all be defined and parameterized using EL variables. We have seen user-defined variables in a workflow as early as Example 1-1; this is reproduced here:

```
<job-tracker>${jobTracker}</job-tracker>
<name-node>${nameNode}</name-node>
```

The values for these user-defined variables `${jobTracker}` and `${nameNode}`) need to be specified before the job submission. These variables are valid throughout the entire life of the workflow.

EL constants and system-defined variables

In addition to user-defined variables, Oozie also provides a set of system-defined variables and EL constants for your convenience. For example, `KB`, `MB`, `GB`, `TB`, and `PB` are all predefined long integers representing KiloBytes, MegaBytes, GigaBytes, TeraBytes, and PetaBytes, respectively. These are EL constants. Oozie also supports variables like ${YEAR}, ${MONTH}, and ${DAY} that you will use often in Oozie coordinators. Think of them as system-defined variables. Unlike the user-defined variables, system variables are evaluated during job execution. In some cases, the system variables have a predefined scope. In other words, those variables are valid only in certain parts of the Oozie job specification. We will run across system-defined variables in various contexts throughout the book.

Hadoop counters

It's also very common to use Hadoop counters as parameters in a workflow. If `myMRNode` is a MapReduce node in a workflow, the subsequent actions could refer to its counters using the following syntax. It could use it as an action argument or make some decisions based on it:

```
${hadoop:counters("myMRNode")["FileSystemCounters"]["FILE_BYTES_READ"]}

${hadoop:counters("myPigNode")["RECORD_WRITTEN"]}
```

There are system variables representing some of the common Hadoop counters: `RECORDS`, `MAP_IN`, `MAP_OUT`, `REDUCE_IN`, and `REDUCE_OUT`. `RECORDS` is the Hadoop counter group name and those other variables refer to the record's in-and-out counters for mappers and reducers. These variables refer to the counters from the particular action and can come in handy when making decisions after the action's processing completes.

EL Functions

Applications also have a need for handling dynamic values during runtime that cannot be statically defined through variables. For example, you may want to print the workflow ID as part of some `<shell>` action. This ID is available only at runtime and the developer had no way to specify the value when she was writing the workflow or even when she was submitting it. This is where Oozie's EL functions come in handy. They are convenience functions that are available for a lot of common use cases. For instance, Oozie has a `wf:id()` function that returns the ID of the current workflow execution. The workflow can be parameterized using the `${FUNC}` syntax `${wf:id()}` for this use case. While Oozie verifies the syntax of any function during job submission, it eventually evaluates the functions during the workflow execution.

EL expressions can be used in all XML element values, all configuration values (for both action and decision nodes), and attribute values. They cannot be used in a XML element name, attribute name, node name, and within the transition elements of a node (“`ok to`”, “`error to`”, etc.).

There are several built-in EL functions that Oozie supports and they are all listed in the Oozie documentation. They are roughly classified as basic, Hadoop, HDFS, and HCatalog functions and constants. We will now look at a few common and useful ones.

String timestamp()

Current UTC time in W3C format up to seconds granularity; this takes the format *(YYYY-MM-DDThh:mm:ss.sZ)* (e.g., a timestamp from July 17, 2014, taken around 5 p.m. looks like *2014-07-17T17:10:50.45Z*).

String wf:id()

This is a useful workflow EL function that returns the job ID for the current workflow job. This is often useful in reporting and printing status messages.

String wf:errorCode(String node)

Given a node name, this EL function returns the error code or an empty string if the action node did not exit with an error. Each type of action node must define its complete error code list, which the standard actions do anyways. It's something to keep in mind if you are writing your own custom action. This function is very useful in error reporting as well as in transition nodes and decision nodes where you may want to take different courses of action in the workflow depending on errors and error types.

boolean fs:fileSize(String path)

This is an HDFS EL function that returns the size in bytes of the specified file. If the path is not a file, or if it does not exist, it returns -1.

The preferred syntax for Oozie variables is `${VAR}`. But this only works for variable names that follow Java naming conventions. There is another way to specify these variables and that's by using the `{wf:conf('VAR')}` function. If a variable name has spaces or dots, `wf:conf()` is the way to go. Some users prefer this because it's consistent with the syntax for EL functions while most users like the `${VAR}` syntax because it's simpler and also helps differentiate between variables and functions.

EL Expressions

In addition to the EL variables and functions, EL expressions are supported as well. A common use case for this is the decision nodes in a workflow. It's not uncommon to check the output of the previous action against some condition and branch the workflow based on that. But that's not the only use for EL expressions and they can be used wherever the EL variables and functions are supported. Example 5-3 illustrates the use of EL expressions in the context of a decision node.

As you can see, EL variable, function, and expression substitution are a very powerful and fundamental feature of Oozie and users are encouraged to make good use of it. This will make their workflows more flexible and dynamic.

The job.properties File

When and how do we set the values for the EL variables? As we saw in Chapter 1, Oozie workflows are typically invoked with the following command (the command is similar for coordinator and bundle jobs, but let's restrict the scope of this discussion to workflows):

```
oozie job -oozie http://localhost:4080/oozie/ -config ~/job.properties -run
```

The *job.properties* file is on the local filesystem and not on HDFS. The filename *job.properties* conforms to Oozie conventions, but a different name can be used if you wish (because this file is explicitly passed to the Oozie command line). The file contains the job configuration that you send to Oozie for this invocation of the workflow application. Think of the *job.properties* as the set of arguments for the *workflow.xml*, which is the application. This file can be used to pass in all the variables required to parameterize the *workflow.xml*. For example, - `${nameNode}`. This var can be defined in the *job.properties* file used for a particular run.

The *workflow.xml* can define the `NameNode` as follows:

```
<name-node>${nameNode}</name-node>
```

And the *job.properties* file can pass in an actual value to the workflow as follows:

```
nameNode=hdfs://abc.xyz.com:8020
```

If the Hadoop `NameNode` crashes and is replaced by another node (`efg.qrs.com`), we don't have to modify the *workflow.xml* on HDFS for making this update. We can just replace the variable in *job.properties* for the next run of the workflow. It's good practice to handle the application XMLs like code rather than configuration and the less often we modify "code," the better.

Oozie accepts both the XML syntax and the properties file syntax (`key=value`) as shown above. But do note the file extension matters. If you're using the XML syntax, you should name the file*file_name.xml*; if you're using the properties file syntax, you should name the file *file_name.properties*. The properties (`key=value`) file syntax is simpler and much more popular among users.

Example 5-8 contains a simple example of a typical *job.properties* file.

Example 5-8. Sample job.properties file

```
nameNode= hdfs://localhost:8020
jobTracker=localhost:8032

queueName=research
oozie.use.system.libpath=true

oozie.wf.application.path=${nameNode}/user/joe/oozie/mrJob/firstWorkflow.xml
```

Example 5-9 shows the same file using the XML syntax.

Example 5-9. Sample job.xml file

```
<configuration>
    <property>
        <name>nameNode</name>
        <value>hdfs://localhost:8020</value>
    </property>
    <property>
        <name>jobTracker</name>
        <value>localhost:8032</value>
    </property>
    <property>
        <name>queueName</name>
        <value>research</value>
    </property>
```

```
    <property>
        <name>oozie.use.system.libpath</name>
        <value>true</value>
    </property>
    <property>
        <name>oozie.wf.application.path</name>
        <value>${nameNode}/user/joe/oozie/mrJob/firstWorkflow.xml</value>
    </property>
</configuration>
```

There are three variables defined in this file: `jobTracker`, `nameNode`, and `queueName`; and they will be substituted during the workflow submission. Oozie will throw an error if the variables cannot be substituted due to missing values. The most important property in the *job.properties* file is the application root pointing to the HDFS directory where the workflow files reside. It must be specified as `oozie.wf.application.path`. This tells Oozie where to find the workflow XML file on HDFS and everything follows from there. If you choose to go with the default *workflow.xml* filename for the workflow XML, the `oozie.wf.application.path` can just be a directory.

The other interesting setting in the *job.properties* file is the `oozie.use.system.libpath=true`. This tells Oozie to look for JARs and libraries in the `sharelib` path, and many actions like `<distcp>` and `<hive>` require this setting. Oozie `sharelib` is an important topic and is explained in detail in "Managing Libraries in Oozie" on page 147.

Command-Line Option

Passing parameter values using the `-D` command-line option is pretty much the same as defining them through the *job.properties*, except the `-D` overrides the properties file and is of the highest priority. Example 5-10 contains an example of using `-D` on the command line to pass in a variable.

Example 5-10. Calling the Oozie CLI with the -D option

```
oozie job -oozie http://localhost:4080/oozie/ -DqueueName=research
  -config job.properties -run
```

The config-default.xml File

The optional *config-default.xml* file can be packaged with the workflow and deployed in the workflow app directory on HDFS. This file has default values for variables that are not defined via the *job.properties* file or the `-D` option. You can use the same *job.properties* file for all invocations of the workflow or use a different properties file for different runs. But the *config-default.xml* file is valid for all invocations of the workflow and serves as the default for all missing variables in other places. A sample is shown here:

```
<configuration>
    <property>
        <name>queueName</name>
        <value>default</value>
    </property>
</configuration>
```

Note that a *config-default.xml* file in a directory can act as the default for all workflow XMLs in that directory, though the normal convention is to have one workflow per directory. This file has the least priority and is often overridden by the *job.properties* file and/or the `-D` option.

The <parameters> Section

Another convenient feature for parameterization is the `<parameters>` section at the top of the workflow. This optional section allows users to declare the EL variables in the workflow XML. This lets Oozie validate the XML and the parameters before submission to the server rather than after. This is similar to a compile time check versus a runtime check in programming languages. Users can declare just a `<name>` or also specify a `<value>`. If there is just a name, Oozie will check for the value defined either in the *job.properties* file or through `-D` . It will throw an error if the variable is not defined. If the `<parameters>` section also includes a `<value>` element, that value will be used as the default value if the variable is not defined elsewhere. It is similar to the *config-default.xml* and can be used for handling defaults, though the `<parameters>` section is confined to only that workflow file.

Oozie's validation of the `<parameters>` section ignores the entries in the *config-default.xml* file. So use the *config-default.xml* file approach or the `<parameters>` section for providing the defaults, but don't try to mix both for a given workflow.

Example 5-11 contains an example of a `<parameters>` usage in a workflow.

Example 5-11. Parameters section in a workflow

```
...
<workflow-app name="parametersWF" xmlns="uri:oozie:workflow:0.5">
<parameters>
    <property>
        <name>queueName</name>
        <value>production</value>
```

```
    </property>
    <property>
        <name>outputDir</name>
    </property>
</parameters>
...
```

Configuration and Parameterization Examples

Let's take a look at a couple of concrete examples to understand all the configuration and parameterization concepts we have seen so far. In Example 5-12, the value for the Hadoop configuration property `mapred.job.queue.name` will be evaluated as "`integration`".

Example 5-12. Configuration example

```
workflow.xml file:
...
<job-xml>my-job.xml</job-xml>
...
<configuration>
    <property>
        <name>mapred.job.queue.name</name>
        <value>integration</value>
    </property>
</configuration>
...

my-job.xml file:

...
<property>
    <name>mapred.job.queue.name</name>
    <value>staging</value>
</property>
...
```

Basically, the inline definition in the body of the workflow overrides the definition in the *my-job.xml* file.

Example 5-13 is a little more complicated and pulls in parameterization concepts. The value for the Hadoop property `mapred.job.queue.name` will be evaluated as "`production`" in this case.

Example 5-13. Parameterization example

```
config-default.xml:
<property>
    <name>queue_var</name>
```

```
    <value>default</value>
</property>

job.properties:
queue_var=research

workflow.xml:
<job-xml>my-job.xml</job-xml>
...
<property>
    <name>queue_var</name>
    <value>production</value>
</property>

my-job.xml

<property>
    <name>mapred.job.queue.name</name>
    <value>${queue_var}</value>
</property>
...
```

The variable `queue_var` is defined in three places and that variable is used in *my-job.xml* to define the `mapred.job.queue.name` property. The inline definition in *workflow.xml* overrides the *config-default.xml* and *job.properties*. So the value for the `mapred.job.queue.name` property will be evaluated as "`production`".

Lifecycle of a Workflow

Now that we have looked at all aspects of a workflow specification, it's good to understand the lifecycle of a workflow. As you know, once a workflow application is deployed and copied to HDFS, we can run the jobs. A workflow job has a well-defined set of state transitions from submission until completion.

Workflow statuses are: `PREP`, `RUNNING`, `SUCCEEDED`, `KILLED`, `FAILED`, and `SUSPENDED`.

When a workflow is submitted, its initial status is `PREP`. When the workflow is started, it transitions from `PREP` to `RUNNING`.

The transition from `PREP` to `RUNNING` is not automatic. If you want the workflow to start running immediately on submission without having to perform an additional step to start it, use the `-run` option instead of the `-submit` option when submitting the job with the `Oozie` command-line tool. If the `-submit` option is used, the workflow will be in `PREP` status until it is explicitly started using the `-start` option of the `Oozie` command-line tool.

On completion, a workflow transitions to SUCEEDED, KILLED, or FAILED status depending on the end result of its execution. If the execution completed successfully, the end status of the workflow is SUCCEEDED. If the execution failed due to an error in the workflow, the end status of the workflow is KILLED. If the execution failed due to an error in Oozie itself, the end status of the workflow is FAILED.

It is a common practice to write a workflow to kill itself if it encounters an application error; for example, if the input directory for a Hadoop job does not exist.

A workflow in RUNNING status can be suspended. In that case, the workflow status changes to SUSPENDED. When a workflow has been suspended, it does not make any further progress. A workflow in SUSPENDED status can be resumed or killed. If the workflow is resumed, its status changes back to RUNNING. If the workflow is killed, its status changes to KILLED.

When a workflow is SUSPENDED, if the workflow was executing a Hadoop job, the Hadoop job will continue running until completion. Hadoop jobs cannot be paused. When the Hadoop job completes, Oozie will update the workflow with the completion information of the Hadoop job, but the workflow job itself will still not make any further progress until resumed.

When a workflow reaches SUCCEEDED, KILLED, or FAILED status, there is no further processing performed by Oozie for the workflow. Any of these three statuses indicates the completion status of the workflow. Figure 5-6 captures workflow state transitions.

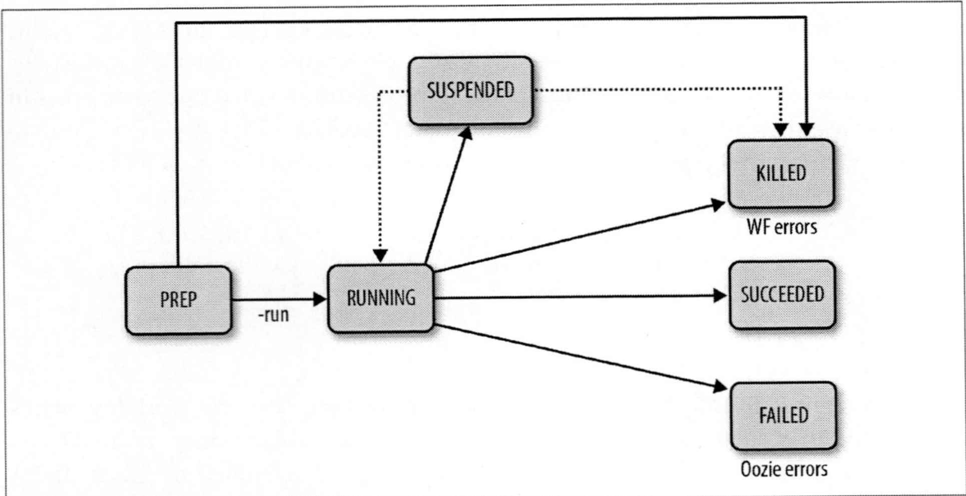

Figure 5-6. Workflow state transitions

Action States

Much like the workflow, individual actions go through their own state transitions, too. We won't cover the action states in detail because users don't usually manage the action states at that level of granularity. It's more practical to manage complete workflows or even coordinators or bundles. The list of action states is captured here just for your reference:

- `DONE`
- `END_MANUAL`
- `END_RETRY`
- `ERROR`
- `FAILED`
- `KILLED`
- `OK`
- `PREP`
- `RUNNING`
- `START_MANUAL`
- `START_RETRY`
- `USER_RETRY`

In this chapter, we saw the various practical aspects of writing an Oozie workflow application. This chapter, combined with the coverage of various action types in Chapter 4, should give you enough ammunition for writing efficient, production-quality workflow applications. We will now move on to the Oozie coordinator in the next chapter.

CHAPTER 6

Oozie Coordinator

In the previous two chapters, we covered the Oozie workflow in great detail. In addition to the workflow, Oozie supports another abstraction called the coordinator that schedules and executes the workflow based on triggers. We briefly introduced the coordinator in Chapter 2. In this chapter, we will cover the various aspects of the Oozie coordinator in a comprehensive fashion using real-life use cases. We present multiple scenarios to demonstrate how the Oozie coordinator can be utilized to trigger workflows based on time. We also describe the various operational knobs that the coordinator provides to control the execution of the workflow. We will get into the data availability–based workflow trigger in Chapter 7.

Coordinator Concept

As described in Chapter 5, an Oozie workflow can be invoked manually and on demand using the Oozie command-line interface (CLI). This is sufficient for a few basic use cases. However, for most of the practical use cases, this is inadequate and very difficult to manage. For instance, consider a scenario where a workflow needs to be started based on some external trigger or condition. In other words, as soon as some predefined condition or predicate is satisfied, the corresponding workflow should be executed. For example, we could have a requirement to run the workflow every day at 2 a.m. It is very hard to achieve this behavior using just the CLI and basic scripting. There are two main reasons for this:

- The specification of multifaceted predicates (such as time and data dependency) can often get very complex.
- The scheduling of workflows based on such predicates is a challenging task.

Oozie coordinator helps handle these trigger-based workflow executions. First, Oozie provides a flexible framework to specify the triggers or predicates. Second, it schedules the workflow based on those predefined triggers. In addition, it enables administrators to monitor and control the workflow execution depending on cluster conditions and application-specific restrictions.

Triggering Mechanism

As of now, the Oozie coordinator supports two of the most common triggering mechanisms, namely time and data availability. These triggering mechanisms allow recurrent and interdependent workflow executions that can create an implied data pipeline application.

Time Trigger

Time-based triggers are easy to explain and resembles the Unix cron utility. In a time-aware coordinator, a workflow is executed at fixed intervals or frequency. A user typically specifies a time trigger in the coordinator using three attributes:

Start time (ST)
: Determines when to execute the first instance of the workflow

Frequency (F)
: Specifies the interval for the subsequent executions

End time (ET)
: Bounds the last execution start time (i.e., no new execution is permitted on or after this time)

In other words, the first execution occurs at the *ST* and subsequent executions occur at *(ST + F)*, *(ST + 2F)*, *(ST + 3F)* , and so on until the *ET* is reached.

Data Availability Trigger

Workflow jobs usually process some input data and produce new output data. Therefore, it is very common to hold off the workflow execution until all of the required input data becomes available. For instance, you want to execute a workflow at 1 a.m., but you also want to make sure the required input data is available before the workflow starts. You ideally want the job to wait even past 1 p.m. if any of the input data is missing.

The Oozie coordinator supports a very flexible data dependency–based triggering framework. It is important to note that the concept of data availability–based scheduling is a little more involved than time-based triggering. Therefore, we introduce the concept here but explain data triggers in detail in Chapter 7.

Coordinator Application and Job

A coordinator application is a template to define the triggers or predicates to launch a workflow. In particular, it has three components: triggers (time and/or data triggers), a reference to the workflow to be launched, and the workflow execution parameters. Coordinator applications are usually parameterized to allow flexibility. When a coordinator application is submitted to Oozie with all its parameters and configurations, it is called a coordinator job. A coordinator application can be submitted multiple times with the same or different parameters that create multiple and independent coordinator jobs. As explained in "Oozie Applications" on page 13, Oozie executes coordinator jobs whereas users write coordinator applications.

Coordinator Action

A coordinator job regularly creates/materializes a new coordinator action for each time instance based on its start time and frequency. For example, if a coordinator job has a start time of January 1, 2014, and an end time of December 31, 2014, with a frequency of one day, there will be a total of 365 actions, one created each day. More importantly, the coordinator action actually checks for data availability and ultimately submits the workflow.

Our First Coordinator Job

In this section, we describe a basic coordinator job that is very similar to a Unix cron job. This example introduces the common terminologies and concepts of a time-triggered coordinator job. As mentioned earlier, the time-triggered coordinator launches the workflow starting from the *start time* and continuously launches one at every predefined interval (a.k.a. `frequency`) until it reaches the *end time*. In this example, we want to execute the *identity-WF* (explained in Chapter 1) daily starting from 2 a.m., January 1, 2014 to 2 a.m., December 31, 2014. That means the first coordinator action will start at *2014-01-01T02:00Z*, the second instance will start at *2014-01-02T02:00Z*, and the last instance at *2014-12-31T02:00Z*. Each of these time instances is called the *nominal time* of that specific action. In other words, each coordinator action must have a nominal time. Here's the formal XML definition of such a coordinator:

```
<coordinator-app name="my_first_coord_job" start="2014-01-01T02:00Z "
      end="2014-12-31T02:00Z" frequency="1440"  timezone="UTC"
      xmlns="uri:oozie:coordinator:0.4">
   <action>
      <workflow>
         <app-path>${appBaseDir}/app/</app-path>
         <configuration>
         <property>
            <name>nameNode</name>
```

```
              <value>${nameNode}</value>
            </property>
            <property>
              <name>jobTracker</name>
              <value>${jobTracker}</value>
            </property>
            <property>
              <name>exampleDir</name>
              <value>${appBaseDir}</value>
            </property>
          </configuration>
        </workflow>
    </action>
</coordinator-app>
```

Nominal time specifies when a workflow execution should ideally start. For various reasons, it might not start on time but the nominal time of that coordinator action is unchanged regardless of when the workflow actually starts. In our example, nominal time for the first coordinator action is *2014-01-01T02:00Z* and for the second action is *2014-01-02T02:00Z*, irrespective of their actual execution time. It's important that you have a clear understanding of nominal time.

For ease of explanation, we artificially divide the above coordinator XML into two segments: specification of the trigger(s) and definition of the triggered workflow. The first segment primarily describes the triggering conditions including both time and data dependencies.

As mentioned earlier, there are three main attributes required to specify a coordinator job. The *start time* defines when to start the execution and the value could be some time in the future or some time from the past. The *end time* defines the time when a coordinator should stop the creation of new coordinator actions. Both start and end times are defined in a combined date and time format as defined by ISO 8601. The frequency of the job is 1,440 minutes or one day. Although the default unit of coordinator frequency is minutes, there are other convenient ways to specify the frequency using EL functions that we describe in "Parameterization of the Coordinator" on page 110. More specifically, for daily jobs, we recommend you use `${coord:days(1)}` instead of 1,440 minutes for frequency.

In addition, there are two other self-explanatory attributes that are not directly related to the triggering mechanism. The first attribute is `name` with value `my_first_coord_job` that can later be used for querying Oozie. The second attribute is `xmlns`, which specifies the coordinator namespace used for coordinator XML versioning. The namespace plays a critical role in ensuring backward compatibility of the coordinator. For example, the new/updated features added for namespace `oozie:coordinator:0.4` might break or modify the functionality of a coordinator written with an older namespace (e.g., `oozie:coordinator:0.3`). Alternatively, if you want to use some of the new/updated features, the new namespace should be used.

The next segment of the coordinator XML specifies what type of job to execute when the triggering conditions are met. As of now, Oozie coordinator only supports launching Oozie workflows and a coordinator application can only include one workflow application. In the future, the scope could be extended to other types of jobs as well.

The workflow tag here is the same as the one we used to define a standalone submission in "A Simple Oozie Job" on page 4. coordinator uses these values to parameterize and automate the workflow submission as we do with any standalone workflow submission. The main difference is in the representation. In a standalone workflow execution, we typically use a property file in key-value format, though the XML syntax is also supported. But for the workflow execution via a coordinator, we have to define it inline in XML format. In both cases, these key-value pairs are passed to the workflow at its start.

It is important to note that the propagation of coordinator properties down to the workflow is not automatic; you need to define and specify these key value pairs under `<action>` configuration. As shown in the example, we specify `app-path` to point to the workflow application path, whereas in a standalone CLI-based workflow submission we define the property `oozie.wf.application.path` in the property file to specify the same thing. The rest of the parameters are optional and defined as configuration properties. The properties defined in this example are similar to the properties defined in "A Simple Oozie Job" on page 4.

Coordinator Submission

There are multiple ways to submit a coordinator. In this section, we only explain job submission using the `oozie` CLI. Other approaches are described later in Chapter 11. At first, we will need to create a local properties file (say *job.properties*) and pass this filename during submission as an argument to the CLI:

```
$ cat job.properties
nameNode=hdfs://localhost:8020
jobTracker=localhost:8032
appBaseDir=${nameNode}/user/${user.name}/ch06-first-coord
oozie.coord.application.path=${appBaseDir}/app
```

In addition, we will need to upload the coordinator job definition to HDFS. It primarily includes the job's XML definition (i.e., *coordinator.xml*):

```
$ hdfs dfs -put ch06-first-coord/ .
$ hdfs dfs -ls -R ch06-first-coord/
drwxr-xr-x   - joe supergroup        0 2014-03-29 12:24 ch06-first-coord/app
```

```
-rw-r--r--   1 joe supergroup    705 2014-03-29 12:24 ch06-first-coord/app/
coordinator.xml
-rw-r--r--   1 joe supergroup   2141 2014-03-29 12:24 ch06-first-coord/app/
workflow.xml
drwxr-xr-x   - joe supergroup      0 2014-03-29 12:24 ch06-first-coord/data
drwxr-xr-x   - joe supergroup      0 2014-03-29 12:24 ch06-first-coord/data/
input
-rw-r--r--   1 joe supergroup     25 2014-03-29 12:24 ch06-first-coord/data/
input/input.txt
```

Similar to the workflow XML convention explained in "Application Deployment Model" on page 20, the coordinator definition file doesn't have to be named *coordinator.xml*. Using different names allows users to host multiple definitions in one directory, which has more of a practical value for coordinators than workflows.

The command in Example 6-1 submits the coordinator and returns a coordinator job ID if successful. The subsequent commands show the most common operations that users typically run for monitoring and managing the coordinator jobs through the Oozie CLI.

Example 6-1. Running and managing coordinator jobs

```
$ export OOZIE_URL=http://localhost:11000/oozie
$ oozie   job -run -config  job.properties
job: 0000003-140329120933279-oozie-joe-C
$ oozie job -info 0000003-140329120933279-oozie-joe-C
Job ID : 0000003-140329120933279-oozie-joe-C
------------------------------------------------------------------------------
Job Name    : my_first_coord_job
App Path    : hdfs://localhost:8020/user/joe/ch06-first-coord/app
Status      : RUNNING
Start Time  : 2014-01-01 02:00 GMT
End Time    : 2014-12-31 02:00 GMT
Pause Time  : -
Concurrency : 1
------------------------------------------------------------------------------
ID                                        Status    Ext ID
Err Code  Created                 Nominal Time
0000003-140329120933279-oozie-joe-C@1     SUCCEEDED 0000004-140329120933279-
  oozie-joe-W
-         2014-03-29 23:14 GMT 2014-01-01 02:00 GMT
------------------------------------------------------------------------------
0000003-140329120933279-oozie-joe-C@2     SUCCEEDED 0000005-140329120933279-
  oozie-joe-W
-         2014-03-29 23:16 GMT 2014-01-02 02:00 GMT
------------------------------------------------------------------------------

$ oozie job -info 0000003-140329120933279-oozie-joe-C@1
```

```
ID : 0000003-140329120933279-oozie-joe-C@1
------------------------------------------------------------------------
Action Number            : 1
Console URL              : -
Error Code               : -
Error Message            : -
External ID              : 0000004-140329120933279-oozie-joe-W
External Status          : -
Job ID                   : 0000003-140329120933279-oozie-joe-C
Tracker URI              : -
Created                  : 2014-03-29 23:14 GMT
Nominal Time             : 2014-01-01 02:00 GMT
Status                   : SUCCEEDED
Last Modified            : 2014-03-29 23:15 GMT
First Missing Dependency : -
------------------------------------------------------------------------

$ oozie job -kill 0000003-140329120933279-oozie-joe-C
$ oozie job -info 0000003-140329120933279-oozie-joe-C
Job ID : 0000003-140329120933279-oozie-joe-C
------------------------------------------------------------------------
Job Name    : my_first_coord_job
App Path    : hdfs://localhost:8020/user/joe/ch06-first-coord/app
Status      : KILLED
Start Time  : 2014-01-01 02:00 GMT
End Time    : 2014-12-31 02:00 GMT
Pause Time  : -
Concurrency : 1
------------------------------------------------------------------------
ID                                         Status    Ext ID
Err Code  Created              Nominal Time
0000003-140329120933279-oozie-joe-C@1     SUCCEEDED 0000004-140329120933279-
  oozie-joe-W
-         2014-03-29 23:14 GMT 2014-01-01 02:00 GMT
------------------------------------------------------------------------
0000003-140329120933279-oozie-joe-C@2     SUCCEEDED 0000005-140329120933279-
  oozie-joe-W
-         2014-03-29 23:16 GMT 2014-01-02 02:00 GMT
------------------------------------------------------------------------
```

Upon successful submission, Oozie returns a unique coordinator job ID. Each coordinator ID has a `-C` at the end. At the start time for this job, Oozie initiates the creation of the coordinator action. Oozie also assigns an ID for each new action. coordinator action IDs are generated by concatenating the coordinator job ID, the `@` sign, and a sequentially incrementing action number. For example, if the coordinator job ID is `0000003-140329120933279-oozie-joe-C`, the first two action IDs will be `0000003-140329120933279-oozie-joe-C@1` and `0000003-140329120933279-oozie-joe-C@2`.

Oozie Web Interface for Coordinator Jobs

Oozie provides a basic, read-only user interface for coordinator jobs very similar to what it provides for workflows and bundles. Users can click on the Coordinator Jobs tab on the Oozie web interface at any time. It displays the list of recent coordinator jobs in a grid-like UI as shown in Figure 6-1. This UI captures most of the useful information about the coordinator jobs. The last column titled Next Materialization shows the nominal time for the next coordinator action to be materialized for any running coordinator job.

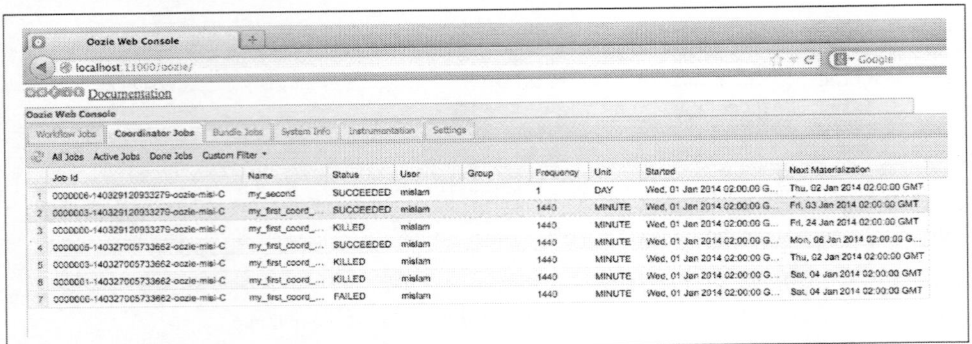

Figure 6-1. Oozie web interface for coordinator jobs

Users can drill down into a specific coordinator job by clicking on the row of that job. This will display a new window presenting the details of that coordinator job, as shown in Figure 6-2. As you can see, there are four tabs: Coord Job Info, Coord Job Definition, Coord Job Configuration, and Coord Job Log. You can select any of these tabs as necessary (the Coord Job Info tab is displayed by default). The first tab shows the current job status, including all the spawned coordinator actions listed in the bottom half of the window. Users can click on the reload icon located at the top-left of the window to refresh the contents. The second tab, Coord Job Definition, displays the original coordinator XML that you submitted.

All of the configuration settings passed as part of the CLI and the properties file are displayed in the third tab (the Coord Job Configuration tab). The fourth tab shows the Oozie log generated for this specific coordinator job. Since coordinator jobs typically create a lot of coordinator actions, they tend to be long running and the logs may be huge. It can take a long time to load all the logs from the Oozie backend. That's why it is better to retrieve only the logs for a subset of coordinator actions. For this purpose, there is a "Retrieve log" button where the user can specify a set of coordinator action numbers such as "1,2" or "1-3," and so on. This will ensure that Oozie retrieves the logs only for those actions.

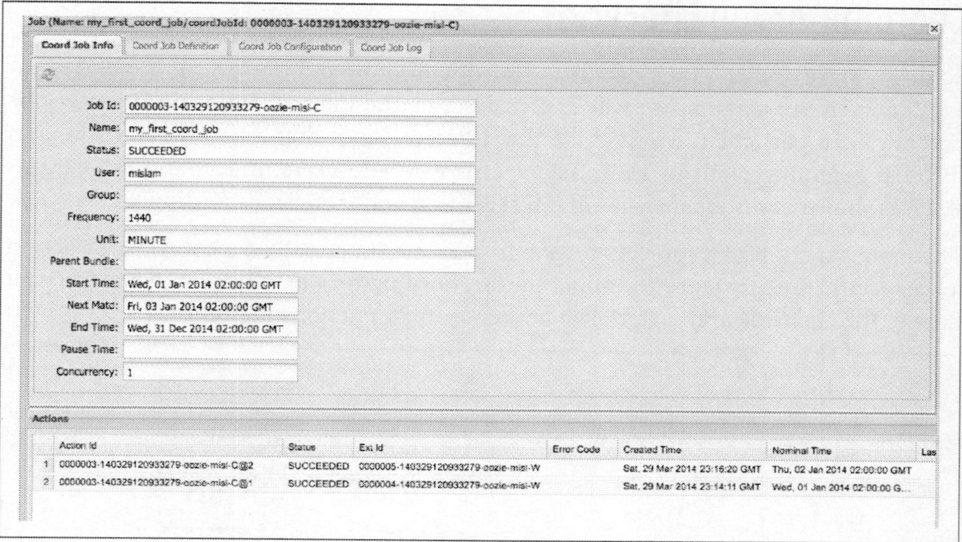

Figure 6-2. Oozie web interface for coordinator jobs

From the first tab (Coord Job Info) of the coordinator job window, users can further drill down to the corresponding workflow by clicking on the row of the coordinator action. This displays the workflow window shown in Figure 6-3. This window is essentially the same as the one explained in "A Simple Oozie Job" on page 4.

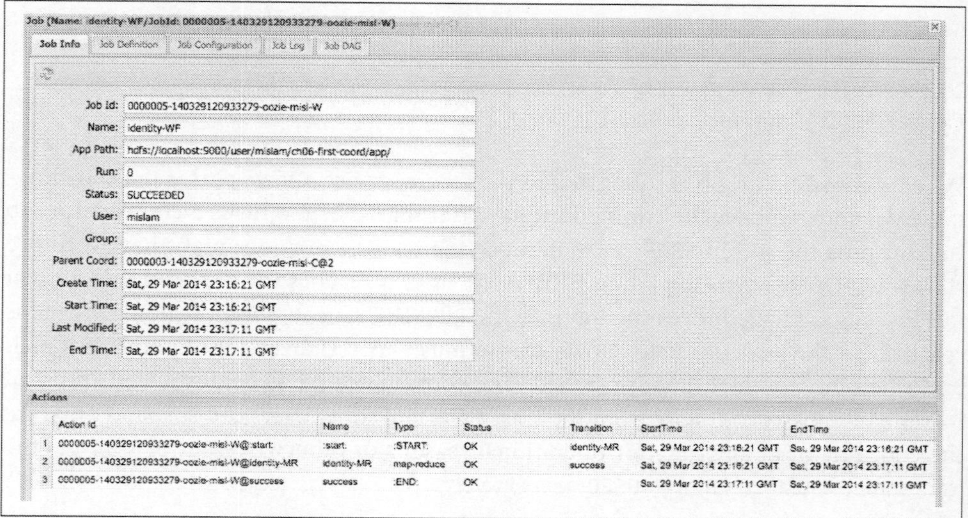

Figure 6-3. A workflow job launched by coordinator

Coordinator Job Lifecycle

So far we have discussed the details of coordinator jobs and how to submit and manage them. In this section, we will briefly describe the internals of a coordinator job's execution. In particular, we describe the different states that a coordinator job goes through beginning with its submission. This will help users understand the various statuses shown at different stages of job execution and then act accordingly.

The main function of a coordinator job is to create (materialize) a coordinator action for a specific time instance (nominal time). coordinator jobs often run from the start time to the end time and materialize new coordinator actions periodically.

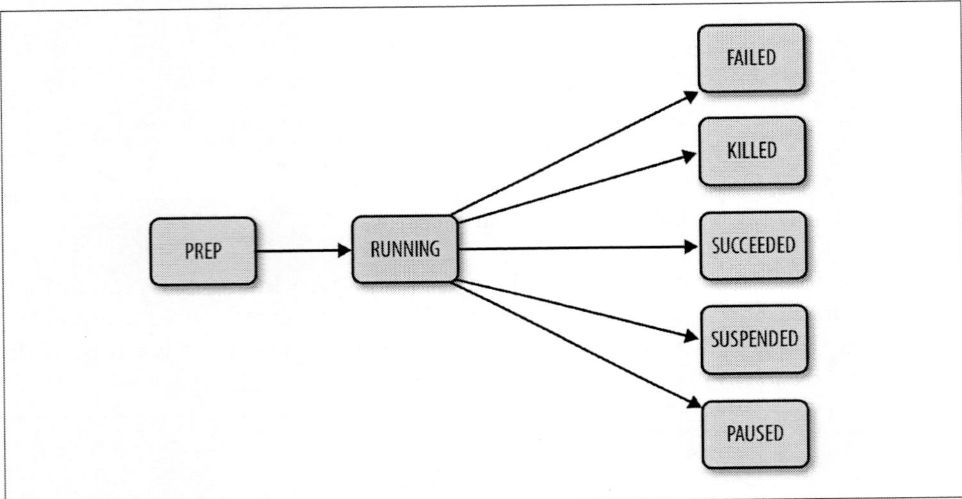

Figure 6-4. Coordinator job lifecycle

When a coordinator job is submitted to the Oozie service, Oozie parses the coordinator XML and validates the configurations. After that, Oozie returns a coordinator job ID and puts the job in `PREP` state. Because the coordinator job might have a future start time, Oozie keeps the job in PREP state until it reaches the start time. As shown in Figure 6-4, Oozie moves the job into the `RUNNING` state as soon as the start time is reached. In the `RUNNING` state, Oozie continuously materializes coordinator actions if and when the nominal time is reached. The coordinator job generally spends most of its time in the `RUNNING` state from the start to its end time. Users can suspend or pause the coordinator at any time for operational reasons or otherwise, and that moves the job's state to `SUSPENDED` or `PAUSED`, respectively.

The final state of a coordinator job depends on the states of all the spawned coordinator actions. For example, if and when all coordinator actions are materialized and all actions complete successfully, Oozie moves the job to the `SUCCEEDED` state. Likewise, if all the actions end up in the `FAILED` state, the coordinator job also moves to the `FAILED` state. Figure 6-4 shows the basic transition diagram. The actual transitions are much more complex: if one of the coordinator actions fails, times out, or is killed as the job is still running, Oozie moves the job from `RUNNING` to `RUNNING_WITH_ERROR`. Similarly, there are other states such as `DONE_WITH_ERROR`, `SUSPENDED_WITH_ERROR`, and `PAUSED_WITH_ERROR`. Also, it's possible to explicitly kill a coordinator job in any state, which transitions the job to the `KILLED` state.

Coordinator Action Lifecycle

As mentioned earlier, a coordinator job creates or materializes a coordinator action for a specific time instance (a.k.a. nominal time). The coordinator action waits until the dependent data (if any) is available and then submits the actual workflow. In this section, we briefly describe the different coordinator action states and their transitions.

When a coordinator job materializes a coordinator action, Oozie assigns the action to the `WAITING` state. In this initial state, the action waits for any dependent data for the duration of the timeout period (configurable and described in "Execution Controls" on page 112). If any of the dependent data is still missing after the timeout period, Oozie transitions the action to the `TIMEDOUT` state. On the other hand, if all the data become available, Oozie moves the action's state to `READY`. At this state, Oozie enforces the throttling mechanism as defined by the concurrency setting. This setting specifies the maximum number of coordinator actions of a coordinator job that can run simultaneously. If the action fits under the concurrency constraint, Oozie just transfers the action to the `SUBMITTED` state. This is when Oozie submits the corresponding workflow. Figure 6-5 captures all the important state transitions.

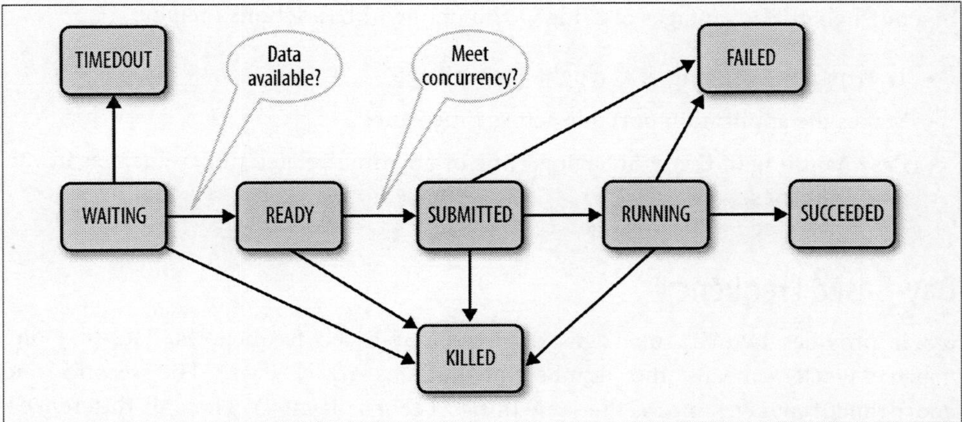

Figure 6-5. Coordinator action lifecycle

If the submission fails, Oozie moves the action to the `FAILED` state. Otherwise, it moves it to the `RUNNING` state and waits for the workflow to finish. At this stage, the state of the workflow dictates the state of the corresponding coordinator action. More specifically, depending on whether the workflow fails, succeeds, or gets killed, Oozie transitions the state of the coordinator action to `FAILED`, `SUCCEEDED`, or `KILLED`, respectively. A user can kill a coordinator action at any state and that transitions the action to the `KILLED` state.

Parameterization of the Coordinator

The coordinator XML can be parameterized using the same techniques we discussed in "Parameterization" on page 86 for the workflow. It supports both variable and function parameters in exactly the same way as seen before. In this section, we explain time- and frequency-related EL functions. We explain other EL functions as needed in subsequent sections.

EL Functions for Frequency

In "Our First Coordinator Job" on page 101, we used `frequency="1440"` for daily jobs. This frequency was expressed in minutes. However, there are some scenarios where frequencies can't be easily expressed in absolute minutes. For example, a frequency of one day may not always translate to 24 hours. Some days could be 23 hours or 25 hours due to Daylight Saving Time. Similarly, every month does not correspond to 30 days. It could be anything between 28 and 31 days. To help you handle these intricacies easily, Oozie provides a set of functions to define the frequency. We strongly encourage you to utilize those functions instead of using absolute value in minutes.

In a nutshell, the advantages of using Oozie-defined EL functions include:

- Transparent handling of Daylight Saving Time
- Makes the application portable across time zones
- Easy handling of Daylight Saving Time or any time-related policy changes in various countries

Day-Based Frequency

Oozie provides two EL functions to specify day-based frequencies. The first one, `coord:days(N)`, means the number of minutes in *N* days. The second one, `coord:endOfDays(N)`, means the same thing as `coord:days(N)`. The only difference is that `endOfDays` shifts the first occurrence to the end of the day and then adds *N* days to get the next occurrence. Table 6-1 explains the different scenarios.

Table 6-1. Day-based frequency

EL function	Start time	Time zone	In minutes	First instance	Second instance
days(1)	2014-01-01T08:00Z	UTC	1440	2014-01-01T08:00Z	2014-01-02T08:00Z
days(2)	2014-01-01T08:00Z	America/Los_Angeles	1440 X 2	2014-01-01T08:00Z	2014-01-03T08:00Z
days(1)	2014-03-08T08:00Z	UTC	1440	2014-03-08T08:00Z	2014-03-09T08:00Z
days(1)	2014-03-08T08:00Z	America/Los_Angeles	**1380**	2014-03-08T08:00Z	2014-03-09T07:00Z
days(2)	2014-03-08T08:00Z	America/Los_Angeles	1380 +1440	2014-03-08T08:00Z	2014-03-10T07:00Z
endOfDays(1)	2014-01-01T08:00Z	UTC	1440	**2014-01-02T00:00Z**	**2014-01-03T00:00Z**
endOfDays(1)	2014-01-01T08:00Z	America/Los_Angeles	1440	**2014-01-01T08:00Z**	**2014-01-02T08:00Z**
endOfDays(1)	2014-01-01T09:00Z	America/Los_Angeles	1440	**2014-01-02T08:00Z**	**2014-01-03T08:00Z**
endOfDays(1)	2014-03-07T09:00Z	America/Los_Angeles	**1380**	**2014-03-08T08:00Z**	**2014-03-09T08:00Z**

Month-Based Frequency

Any month-based frequency also has its own issues similar to a day-based frequency. These include:

- Number of days in a month is not a constant, but changes month to month. It also depends on whether the year is a leap year or not.
- Number of hours in the individual days of a month might not be the same due to Daylight Saving Time.

There are two month-based EL functions for frequency. `coord:months(N)` returns the number of minutes in *N* months starting from the current nominal time. `coord:endOfMonths(N)` is very similar to `coord:months(N)`. The difference is that `endOfMonths()` first moves the current nominal time to the end of this month and then calculates the number of minutes for *N* months from that point. Table 6-2 demonstrates the various scenarios with real values.

Table 6-2. Month-based frequency

EL function	Start time	Time zone	In minutes	First instance	Second instance
months(1)	2014-01-01T08:00Z	UTC	1440 x 31	2014-02-01T08:00Z	2014-02-01T08:00Z
months(2)	2014-01-01T08:00Z	America/ Los_Angeles	1440 X (31 +28)	2014-03-01T08:00Z	2014-03-01T08:00Z
months(1)	2014-03-01T08:00Z	UTC	1440 x 31	2014-04-01T08:00Z	2014-04-01T08:00Z
months(1)	2014-03-01T08:00Z	America/ Los_Angeles	1440 x 30 + 1380	2014-04-01T07:00Z	2014-04-01T08:00Z
endOfMonths(1)	2014-01-01T08:00Z	UTC	1440 x 31	**2014-02-01T00:00Z**	**2014-03-01T00:00Z**
endOfMonths(1)	2014-01-01T08:00Z	America/ Los_Angeles	1440 x 31	**2014-01-01T08:00Z**	**2014-02-01T08:00Z**

Execution Controls

A coordinator job continuously creates coordinator actions until it reaches the end time. In an ideal situation, a coordinator job will have only one active coordinator action in Oozie at any give time. Let's assume that each action completes before the nominal time of the next action under normal processing conditions. However, there are still many circumstances that result in a lot of coordinator actions being concurrently active in the system. Let's call this a "backlog," which could occur for the following reasons:

Delayed data
: When any dependent data for a coordinator is not available, Oozie has to wait. This could build up a backlog.

Reprocessing
: It is very common to rerun the job after its original start time due to either bad input data or a bug in the processing logic. This reprocessing scenario could cause a significant backlog.

Late submission
: Users could submit the coordinator job late for various practical reasons. The size of the backlog of coordinator actions in such situations depends on how late the submission was. The system might take a long time to catch up to the current processing time depending on various factors.

Whatever the root cause is, this backlog creates potential system instability for Oozie, as well as the Hadoop services. In particular, each active coordinator action increases the load on Oozie and Hadoop system resources, such as the database, memory, CPU, and the `NameNode`. To address these catch-up scenarios, Oozie provides four control parameters for any coordinator. Having a good understanding of the coordinator action lifecycle explained in "Coordinator Action Lifecycle" on page 109 will help you comprehend the control parameters explained here:

`throttle`
: A coordinator job periodically creates coordinator actions. Therefore, if we can regulate this materialization, the ultimate number of outstanding actions can be controlled. Oozie provides a user-level control knob called `throttle`, which a user can specify in her coordinator XML. This controls how many maximum coordinator actions can be in the `WAITING` state for a coordinator job at any instant. If no value is specified, the system default value of 12 is used. While a user can specify any value for this, there is also a system-level upper limit that an administrator can tune. This system-level limit is calculated by multiplying the throttling factor (property `oozie.service.coord.materialization.throttling.factor`) and the maximum internal processing

queue size (property `oozie.service.CallableQueueService.queue.size`) defined in *oozie-site.xml*. In short, this setting can be tuned both at the system and the user level through the *oozie-site.xml* and coordinator XML, respectively.

`timeout`
: While `throttle` restricts how many actions can be in the `WAITING` state, `timeout` enforces how long each coordinator action can be in `WAITING`. Like `throttle`, there are both user- and system-level limits to the `timeout` value. A user can specify a `timeout` in minutes in the coordinator XML. If no `timeout` value is specified, Oozie defaults to 7 days. In addition, Oozie enforces the maximum value that a user can specify for the `timeout`. Oozie system administrators can specify this using the property `oozie.service.coord.default.max.timeout` in *oozie-site.xml*. The default maximum `timeout` is 60 days.

`execution order`
: If there are multiple actions in the `READY` state, Oozie needs to determine which workflow to submit first. This `execution` knob specifies which order Oozie should follow. There are three possible values: `FIFO`, `LIFO`, and `LAST_ONLY`. The default is `FIFO` (First in First Out), which means start the earliest action first. The `LIFO` (Last In First Out) asks Oozie to execute the latest action first. `LAST_ONLY` means execute *only* the last one and discard the rest.

As of the time of writing this book, `FIFO` is the only fully tested option.

`concurrency`
: This dictates how many coordinator actions of a job can run simultaneously. It restricts the maximum number of actions that can be in the `RUNNING` state for a coordinator job at the same time. In other words, it regulates the transition from the `READY` state to the `RUNNING` state of a coordinator action. This setting primarily impacts the load on the Hadoop cluster. The default value is 1. A value of -1 means infinite.

An Improved Coordinator

Our initial example ("Our First Coordinator Job" on page 101) was very simple and straightforward. In Example 6-2, we extend it with more parameterization and by adding the `<controls>` section.

Example 6-2. Improved coordinator

```
<coordinator-app name="my_second" start="${startTime}" end="${endTime}"
      frequency="${coord:days(1)}"  timezone="UTC"
      xmlns="uri:oozie:coordinator:0.4">
  <controls>
    <timeout>${my_timeout}</timeout>
    <concurrency>${my_concurrency}</concurrency>
    <execution>${execution_order}</execution>
    <throttle>${materialization_throttle}</throttle>
  </controls>
  <action>
     <workflow>
        <app-path>${appBaseDir}/app/</app-path>
        <configuration>
        <property>
           <name>nameNode</name>
           <value>${nameNode}</value>
         </property>
         <property>
           <name>jobTracker</name>
           <value>${jobTracker}</value>
         </property>
         <property>
           <name>exampleDir</name>
           <value>${appBaseDir}</value>
         </property>
        </configuration>
      </workflow>
  </action>
</coordinator-app>
```

```
$ cat job.properties
nameNode=hdfs://localhost:8020
jobTracker=localhost:8032
appBaseDir=${nameNode}/user/${user.name}/ch06-second-coord
startTime=2014-01-01T02:00Z
endTime=2014-12-31T02:00Z
my_timeout=60
my_concurrency=2
execution_order=FIFO
materialization_throttle=5
oozie.coord.application.path=${appBaseDir}/app

$ hdfs dfs -put ch06-second-coord .

$ hdfs dfs -ls -R ch06-second-coord
drwxr-xr-x   - joe supergroup   0 2014-03-29 16:46 ch06-second-coord/app
-rw-r--r--   1 joe supergroup   914 2014-03-29 16:46 ch06-second-coord/app/
  coordinator.xml
-rw-r--r--   1 joe supergroup   2141 2014-03-29 16:46 ch06-second-coord/app/
  workflow.xml
drwxr-xr-x   - joe supergroup   0 2014-03-29 16:48 ch06-second-coord/data
```

```
drwxr-xr-x   - joe supergroup   0 2014-03-29 16:46 ch06-second-coord/data/input
-rw-r--r--   1 joe supergroup   25 2014-03-29 16:46 ch06-second-coord/data/
  input/input.txt
drwxr-xr-x   - joe supergroup   0 2014-03-29 16:48 ch06-second-coord/data/output
-rw-r--r--   3 joe supergroup   0 2014-03-29 16:48 ch06-second-coord/data/
  output/_SUCCESS
-rw-r--r--   3 joe supergroup   31 2014-03-29 16:48 ch06-second-coord/data/
  output/part-00000

$ oozie job -run -config job.properties
<COORDINATOR-JOB ID>
```

In this chapter, we covered the basic concepts of the coordinator with a primary focus on time-based triggers. The next chapter will continue to dig deeper into the coordinator framework with a focus on data dependencies.

CHAPTER 7

Data Trigger Coordinator

In Chapter 6, we primarily discussed how Oozie materialized coordinator actions at periodic intervals and subsequently executed the workflow. In other words, we only considered the *time-based trigger* to start workflows. However, time is not the only dependency that determines when to launch a workflow for many use cases. A common use case is to wait for input data. If a workflow is started before its required data is available, the workflow execution will either produce wrong results or fail. The Oozie coordinator allows users to express both data and time dependency together and to kick off the workflow accordingly. There are many diverse use cases based on data dependency that poses serious challenges to the design of the coordinator. In this chapter, we explain how to express both data and time dependency in a coordinator and how Oozie manages the workflow executions.

Expressing Data Dependency

It's important to understand the three terms, `dataset`, `input-events`, and `output-events`, that Oozie uses to describe data dependencies in a coordinator XML.

Dataset

A dataset is a logical entity to represent a set of data produced by an application. A user can define a dataset either using its directory location or using metadata. Oozie has always supported directory-based data dependency. Recently, Oozie introduced metadata-based data dependency as well. This book primarily focuses on the directory-based dataset, as that's the most commonly used approach. The metadata-based dependency will be covered later, in "HCatalog-Based Data Dependency" on page 174.

Furthermore, the data in a dataset can be produced in two ways:

- In a fixed interval
- Ad hoc/random, without following any time pattern

In Oozie, the dataset produced in regular frequency is called *synchronous* and the dataset produced randomly is known as *asynchronous*. Oozie currently supports only the synchronous datasets, so this is the type we will focus on in this chapter. We will explore an approach to handle asynchronous datasets later in "Emulate Asynchronous Data Processing" on page 172. In a nutshell, a dataset in Oozie is a template to represent a set of directory-based data produced at fixed time intervals.

Defining a dataset

There are five attributes to define a dataset in Oozie:

`name`
: This specifies the logical name of a dataset. There can be more than one dataset in a coordinator. The name of a dataset must be unique within a coordinator.

`initial-instance`
: This specifies the first time instance of valid data in a dataset. This time instance is specified in a combined date and time format. Any reference to data earlier than this time is meaningless.

`frequency`
: This determines the interval of successive data instances. A user can utilize any EL functions mentioned in "Parameterization of the Coordinator" on page 110 to define the frequency.

`uri-template`
: This specifies the template of the data directory in a dataset. The data directory of most batch systems often contains year, month, day, hour, and minute to reflect the effective data creation time. Oozie provides a few system-defined variables to specify the template. These are `YEAR`, `MONTH`, `DAY`, `HOUR`, and `MINUTE`. These system variables are only valid in defining `uri-template`. During execution, Oozie replaces these using the timestamp of a specific dataset instance.

In a synchronous dataset, every data instance is associated with a time instance. For example, if the time instance of a dataset is `2014-07-15T10:25Z`, the variables `YEAR`, `MONTH`, `DAY`, `HOUR`, and `MINUTE` will be replaced with `2014`, `07`, `15`, `10`, and 25, respectively. However, it's not required to utilize all these system variables to define a `uri-template`.

`done-flag`
: This specifies the filename that is used to indicate whether the data is ready to be consumed. This file is used as a signal to prevent the dependent process from starting too early with only partial data as input. The `done-flag` is optional and defaults to `_SUCCESS` if it's not specified. Usually, a Hadoop MapReduce job creates a zero-size file called `_SUCCESS` at the end of processing to indicate data completeness. If `done-flag` exists, but the value is specified as empty, Oozie just checks for the existence of the directory and uses that as a signal for completion.

The following example shows a dataset definition. The dataset `ds_input1` is produced by some other application every six hours starting from 2 a.m. on December 29. The first three instances of the `ds_input1` dataset are in directories: *hdfs://localhost:8020/user/joe/revenue_feed/2014-12-29-02*, *hdfs://localhost:8020/user/joe/revenue_feed/2014-12-29-08*, and *hdfs://localhost:8020/user/joe/revenue_feed/2014-12-29-14*, respectively. The producer of the data creates a file called *_trigger* (defined as `done-flag`) when the data for the previous six hours is complete and ready. For example, if any coordinator action depends of the first data instance, coordinator will particularly wait for the file *hdfs://localhost:8020/user/joe/revenue_feed/2014-12-29-02/**_trigger***. Instead, if the `done-flag` contains an *empty* value, the coordinator will wait until the directory *hdfs://localhost:8020/user/joe/revenue_feed/2014-12-29-02/* is created:

```
<dataset name="ds_input1" frequency="${coord:hours(6)}"
      initial-instance="2014-12-29T02:00Z">
  <uri-template>
     ${baseDataDir}/revenue_feed/${YEAR}-${MONTH}-${DAY}-${HOUR}
   </uri-template>
   <done-flag>_trigger</done-flag>
</dataset>
```

In practice, there could be multiple datasets defined in a coordinator. Oozie provides a `<datasets>` section where a user can define all the relevant datasets. In addition, Oozie allows users to include a *separate* XML file within the `<datasets>` section that includes a set of dataset definitions. This enables users to define the datasets in one file and reuse them in multiple coordinators. If a dataset with the same name is defined in both places, the one defined in the coordinator XML supersedes the one in the other file. The following example shows how to include a dataset file:

```
<datasets>
  <include>hdfs://localhost:8020/user/joe/shares/common_datasets.xml</include>
  <dataset name="ds_input1" frequency="${coord:hours(6)}"
       initial-instance="2014-12-29T02:00Z">
    <uri-template>
      ${baseDataDir}/revenue_feed/${YEAR}-${MONTH}-${DAY}-${HOUR}
    </uri-template>
    <done-flag>_trigger</done-flag>
  </dataset>
</datasets>
```

The example *common_datasets.xml* could be as follows:

```
<datasets>
  <dataset name="ds_input2" frequency="${coord:hours(6)}"
      initial-instance="2014-12-29T02:00Z">
    <uri-template>
      ${baseDataDir}/revenue_feed/${YEAR}-${MONTH}-${DAY}-${HOUR}
    </uri-template>
    <done-flag>_trigger</done-flag>
  </dataset>
</datasets>
```

It's becoming increasingly common to access datasets on Amazon S3 from Hadoop. To enable data dependency on datasets on S3 in Oozie, set the following property:

```
oozie.service.HadoopAccessorService.
  supported.filesystems
```

to value `hdfs,s3,s3n` in the *oozie-site.xml* file. Also add the `jets3t` JAR to the Oozie webapp during Oozie deployment.

Timelines: coordinator versus dataset

So far, we have introduced two independent timelines, one for the coordinator and one for the datasets. These multiple time-based terminologies might be confusing and overwhelming, so some clarification will be helpful here. The notion of a coordinator itself is founded on time and we have introduced a handful of concepts related to time in the previous chapter. The time parameters explained there helps to manage the workflow execution and controls things like the start and stop of the action materialization and the frequency of materialization. In contrast, the `initial-instance` and `frequency`, introduced in the dataset definition in this chapter, controls a different timeline for the data produced by upstream jobs. These dataset settings might not have any direct association with the timeline defined for the coordinator itself.

input-events

Whereas `datasets` declare data items of interest, `<input-events>` describe the actual instance(s) of dependent dataset for this coordinator. More specifically, a workflow will not start until all the data instances defined in the `input-events` are available.

There is only one `<input-events>` section in a coordinator, but it can include one or more `data-in` sections. Each `data-in` handles one dataset dependency. For instance, if a coordinator depends on two different datasets, there will be two `data-in` definitions in the `input-events` section. In turn, a `data-in` can include one or more data instances of that dataset. Each data instance typically corresponds to a time interval and has a direct association with one directory on HDFS.

A `data-in` definition needs the following three attributes:

`name`
: Can be used to uniquely identify this `data-in` section.

`dataset`
: Indicates the name of a dataset that the application depends on. The referred dataset must be defined in the `<datasets>` definition section.

The `instance` *definition*
: Specifies the data instance that the application will wait for. There are two ways to denote the instance(s). A user can define each instance using an individual `<instance>` tag. Alternatively, a user can specify the range of instances using `<start-instance>` and `<end-instance>` tags. Each instance is basically a timestamp that will eventually be used to replace the variables defined in the `<uri-template>` of a dataset definition. Defining an absolute timestamp is valid, but it is neither practical nor convenient for a long-running coordinator. Therefore, Oozie provides several EL functions (explained later in "Parameterization of Dataset Instances" on page 124) to conveniently specify the batch instance(s).

In summary, the `input-events` allows a user to define the list of required datasets and the corresponding data instances. Example 7-1 shows an `<input-events>` section with one `<data-in>` item. In this example, the `data-in`, named `event_input1`, refers to the last four instances of the dataset using the EL function `current()` (described in "Parameterization of Dataset Instances" on page 124). This means that the coordinator will wait for the previous four batch instances of data coming from the dataset named `ds_input1`.

Example 7-1. Input-events section

```
<input-events>
  <data-in name="event_input1" dataset="ds_input1">
    <start-instance>${coord:current(-4)}</start-instance>
    <end-instance>${coord:current(-1)}</end-instance>
  </data-in>
</input-events>
```

output-events

In an Oozie coordinator, `<output-events>` specifies the data instance produced by a coordinator action. It is very similar to `input-events`. The similarities and differences are explained in Table 7-1.

Table 7-1. Similarities and differences between input-events and output-events

Similarities	Differences
There can be at most one `<input-events>` and one `<output-events>` in a coordinator.	There are one or more `<data-in>` sections under `input-events`. On the other hand, there can be only one `<data-out>` section under `output-events`.
There are two attributes (`name` and `data set`) required to define a `data-in`, as well as a `data-out`.	Each `data-in` contains a single instance or a range of instances. Conversely, each `data-out` can contain only one instance and multiple instances are not allowed.
Like `input-events`, a user can pass the output directory to the workflow as well.	Oozie waits for the data instances defined in the`input-events`. Oozie expects and supports the passing of the dependent directories to the launched workflow. However, Oozie generally doesn't perform any special processing like data availability checks for the `output-events`. Oozie refers to the `output-events` mostly for cleaning up the output data during coordinator reprocessing (discussed in "Coordinator Reprocessing" on page 224).

The following example shows the declaration of `output-events`:

```
<output-events>
  <data-out name="event_output1" dataset="daily-feed">
    <instance>${coord:current(0)}</instance>
  </data-out>
</output-events>
```

Example: Rollup

This example is an extension of our previous time-triggered coordinator described in "Our First Coordinator Job" on page 101 with data dependency added to it. The previous example executed a workflow once every day. In Example 7-2, we add a new condition. The workflow runs every day and waits for the previous four instances of a dataset produced every six hours by an upstream application. The workflow uses the preceding four instances of a "six-hourly" dataset as input and produces the daily output. These types of jobs are commonly known as *rollup jobs* where datasets produced in a smaller frequency are combined into a higher frequency.

Example 7-2. A rollup job

```
<coordinator-app name="my_first_rollup_job" start="2014-01-01T02:00Z"
     end="2014-12-31T02:00Z" frequency="${coord:days(1)}"
     xmlns="uri:oozie:coordinator:0.4">
  <datasets>
    <dataset name="ds_input1" frequency="${coord:hours(6)}"
             initial-instance="2014-12-29T02:00Z">
      <uri-template>
        ${baseDataDir}/revenue_feed/${YEAR}-${MONTH}-${DAY}-${HOUR}
```

```
      </uri-template>
      <done-flag>_trigger</done-flag>
    </dataset>
  </datasets>
  <input-events>
    <data-in name="event_input1" dataset="ds_input1">
      <start-instance>${coord:current(-4)}</start-instance>
      <end-instance>${coord:current(-1)}</end-instance>
    </data-in>
  </input-events>
  <action>
    <workflow>
      <app-path>${appBaseDir}/basic-cron</app-path>
      <property>
        <name>nameNode</name>
        <value>hdfs://localhost:8020</value>
      </property>
      <property>
        <name>jobTracker</name>
        <value>localhost:8032</value>
      </property>
    </workflow>
  </action>
</coordinator-app>
```

This example XML has two new sections `<datasets>` and `<input-events>` that we discussed in "Defining a dataset" on page 118 and "input-events" on page 120, respectively. Each coordinator action waits for four dataset directories produced for the times 2:00, 8:00, 14:00, and 20:00 of the previous day. Figure 7-1 captures these timelines. It's worth noting there are two independent timelines, one for the coordinator and one for the dataset. The dataset timeline in Figure 7-1 shows that the data is produced every 6 hours by some other process at 2:00, 8:00, 14:00, and 20:00. On the other hand, the coordinator timeline shows that the coordinator job runs every day at 2:00 a.m. Each coordinator action depends on data from the previous four instances of the dataset with respect to its nominal time. The nominal time of the action acts as the bridge between the two timelines. As shown in the figure, the coordinator action with nominal time `2014-01-01T02:00Z` waits for the following dataset instances:

- `hdfs://localhost:8020/user/joe/revenue_feed/2014-12-31-02/_trigger`
- `hdfs://localhost:8020/user/joe/revenue_feed/2014-12-31-08/_trigger`
- `hdfs://localhost:8020/user/joe/revenue_feed/2014-12-31-14/_trigger`
- `hdfs://localhost:8020/user/joe/revenue_feed/2014-12-31-20/_trigger`

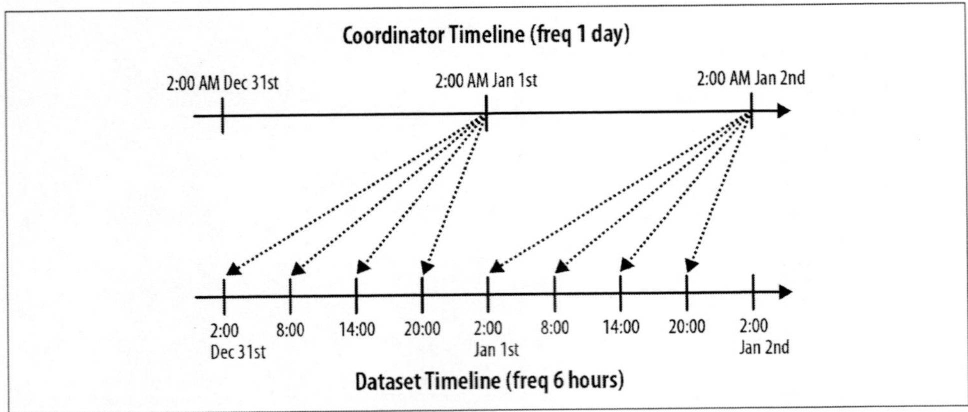

Figure 7-1. Coordinator job rolling up six-hourly data into daily data

Parameterization of Dataset Instances

Each coordinator action waits for data instances defined in `<data-in>`. Each data instance ultimately needs the absolute timestamp to evaluate the exact directory provided in `uri-template`. Since this timestamp is usually relative to the nominal and execution times, users often can't specify it in absolute values. So Oozie provides several EL functions to express and parameterize the data instances. These EL functions are used to support a variety of complex use cases and hence require close attention.

The instance timestamp primarily depends on two time parameters from the coordinator action and the dependent datasets. First and foremost, coordinator action's nominal time plays a critical role in determining the data instance. coordinator action's nominal time, in turn, depends on the time-related attributes in the coordinator job specifications such as `start` time and `frequency`. For example, if the start time of a coordinator job is `cS` and the frequency is `cF`, the nominal time of the nth coordinator action is calculated as follows (not considering Daylight Saving Time):

```
Nominal Time (caNT) = cS + n * cF
```

Second, the dataset definition has two time attributes, initial-instance (`dsII`) and frequency (`dsF`), which also play an important role in determining the actual data instance.

Apart from the time attributes just discussed, the `instance` expressed in the `data-in` section of a coordinator XML plays a direct role in determining the actual dependent data directories. An instance is usually defined using EL functions like `current(n)`, `latest(n)`, `offset(n, timeunit)`, and `future(n)`. Among them, `current(n)` is the most frequently used, followed by `latest(n)`. The usage of `offset(n, timeunit)` and `future(n)` are rare. We will discuss the first two functions in detail here with examples (refer to the Oozie coordinator specification for the other, less commonly used functions).

current(n)

This EL function returns the timestamp of the nth instance of a dataset *relative* to a specific coordinator action's nominal time (`caNT`). The value of n can be any integer number. Any negative value for n refers to an instance earlier than the nominal time. While any positive value for n refers to some instance after the nominal time. The simplest equation to approximately calculate the timestamp of the nth instance is as follows:

```
current(n) = dsII + dsF * (n + (caNT - dsII) / dsF)
```

The following example further clarifies the concept with real values. Assume the coordinator job has the start time of `2014-10-18T06:00Z` and a frequency of one day. This means Oozie will materialize coordinator actions with the following nominal times (in order): `2014-10-18T06:00Z`, `2014-10-19T06:00Z`, `2014-10-20T06:00Z`, and so on. Let's also assume that there are four datasets with the attributes in Table 7-2 to demonstrate the different scenarios.

Table 7-2. Example datasets

Dataset name	Initial instance	Frequency
ds1	2014-10-06T06:00Z	1 day
ds2	2014-10-06T06:00Z	12 hours
ds3	2014-10-06T06:00Z	3 days
ds4	2014-10-06T**07**:00Z	1 day

We explain below how to calculate some of the time instances of these datasets. This calculation is in the context of the second coordinator action with a nominal time of `2014-10-19T06:00Z`.

current(0) of ds1: The `current(0)` of any dataset specifies the dataset instance/timestamp that is closest to and no later than the coordinator action's nominal time. In general, finding `current(0)` is the first step in understanding any other data instance. Most instance calculations are based on the coordinator action's nominal time. Conceptually, we can start from the dataset's initial instance and go forward to the coordinator action's nominal time with an increment of dataset frequency. In this example, we start with `dsII=2014-10-06T06:00Z` and go toward `caNT= 2014-10-19T06:00Z` with a frequency of one day. The dataset instances will correspond to 10/6, 10/7, 10/8, and so on (in order). In this example, the nominal time and the dataset (ds1) initial timestamp have the same time component (6 a.m.) and that makes the calculation a little easier. So the closest dataset timestamp is the same as the nominal time and is

2014-10-19T06:00Z. Hence this time represents current(0) as well. We can also calculate the same using the following equation:

```
current(n) = dsII + dsF * (n + (caNT - dsII) / dsF)
           = 2014-10-06T06:00Z + 1 day x
               (0 + (2014-10-19T06:00Z - 2014-10-06T06:00Z))/ 1 day
           = 2014-10-06T06:00Z + 13 day = 2014-10-19T06:00Z
```

Similarly, we can calculate current(-1), which is the immediate previous instance of current(0), and current(1), which is the immediate next instance of current(0). We also describe the same concept in Figure 7-2.

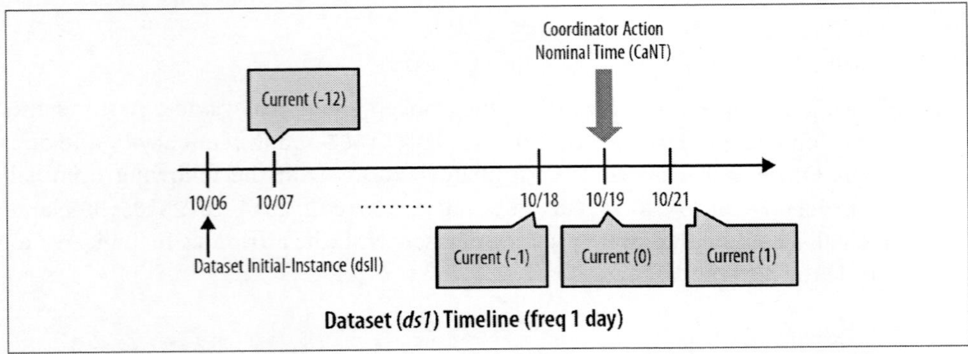

Figure 7-2. Timestamps of current() EL function for dataset ds1

current(0) of ds3: We use dataset ds3 to explain the same idea in a slightly different scenario. In this example, the dataset instances starts with dsII=2014-10-06T06:00Z and moves toward caNT= 2014-10-19T06:00Z with a frequency of *three days*. Dataset instances will be 10/6, 10/9, 10/12, 10/15, 10/18, 10/21, and so on (in order). So the closest instance to nominal time is 10/18, which becomes current(0) for this scenario. Notably, the nominal time 2014-10-19T06:00Z and current(0) do not exactly match in this example. Figure 7-3 displays the different data instances including current(-1), current(1), and so on.

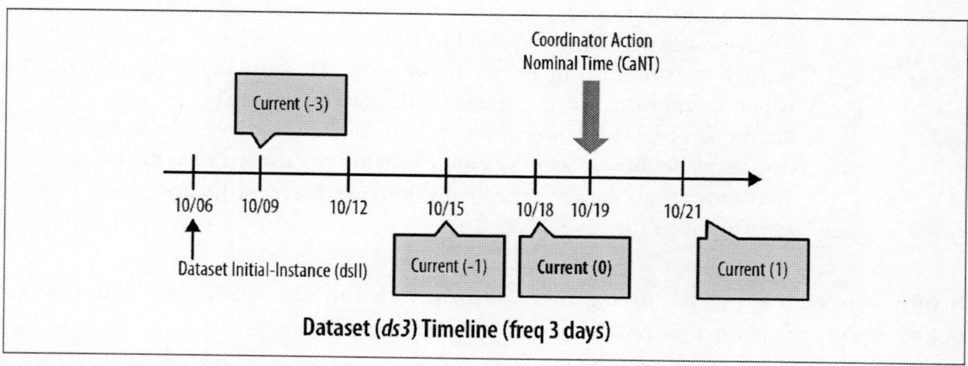

Figure 7-3. Timestamps of current() EL function for dataset ds3

Table 7-3 shows the return value of `current(n)` given different values of *n* for all of the example datasets in Table 7-2.

Table 7-3. current(n) instances of datasets

Instance	ds1	ds2	ds3	ds4
current(0)	2014-10-19T06:00Z	2014-10-19T06:00Z	**2014-10-18T06:00Z**	**2014-10-18T07:00Z**
current(-1)	2014-10-18T06:00Z	2014-10-18T018:00Z	2014-10-15T06:00Z	2014-10-17T07:00Z
current(-2)	2014-10-17T06:00Z	2014-10-18T06:00Z	2014-10-12T06:00Z	2014-10-16T07:00Z
current(1)	2014-10-20T06:00Z	2014-10-19T18:00Z	2014-10-21T06:00Z	2014-10-19T07:00Z

Instances before the dataset's `initial-instance`: The data instances before the `initial-instance` of any dataset doesn't count. So if the EL function (e.g., *current()*) refers to any such dataset instance, coordinator doesn't really check the existence of that data. In other words, there could be some data on HDFS before the dataset's `initial-instance` as defined in the dataset definition, but Oozie disregards those data instances. However, Oozie returns an `empty ("")` string for any such instance. For instance, `current(-14)` for dataset `ds1` points to `2014-10-05T06:00Z`, which is earlier than the declared `initial-instance (2014-10-06T06:00Z)` of `ds1`. In this case, Oozie returns an empty string ("") without checking for the existence of the data.

During initial testing, users are frequently confused with this behavior and are often surprised to find that their workflows have started to run with an empty input path. This usually happens when the coordinator start time and the dataset `initial-instance` are the same or close to each other. This can be solved and the tests can be made more useful by either moving the dataset's `initial-instance` to an earlier time or by moving the coordinator start time to a later time.

Scope: The `current()` EL function is valid only within the `<data-in>` and `<data-out>` sections of a coordinator XML.

latest(n)

This EL function returns the timestamp of the nth latest *available* dataset. Evaluating this "latest" available data instance happens with respect to either one of the two points in time listed here:

`present time`
: The wall-clock time when Oozie evaluates the `latest()` function

`actual time`
: The time when Oozie actually materializes a coordinator action

Oozie selects this option based on the property `oozie.service.ELService.latest-el.use-current-time` defined in the *oozie-site.xml* file. The default is to evaluate "latest" based on the action's actual time.

The `latest(n)` function does not support positive integers (n) and cannot be used to look "forward" in time. Unlike the `curent(n)` function, specifications like `latest(1)` and `latest(2)` are not supported.

Nominal versus actual versus present time

Before going further into the explanation of the `latest()` function, we need to clarify the newly introduced terms related to time. We are already familiar with the action `nominal time`. We just introduced two new terms, `present time` and `actual time`. Present time represents the current wall clock time when the `latest` evaluation logic is executed. In other words, if the same `latest` function is executed multiple times, it will obviously use different `present` (wall-clock) times for its dataset evaluations.

On the other hand, the action's actual time represents the time when the action is materialized by Oozie. Although this sounds very similar to nominal time, there are subtle but important differences. For instance, when a coordinator is delayed and is running in catch-up mode, an action may be *actually* created at 6 p.m. but it should have been *ideally* created at 2 p.m. In other words, action's nominal time is 2 p.m., but the action's actual time is 6 p.m.

Now let's also assume this delayed action has a `latest()` dependency and is checking and waiting for data availability. For example, at 10 p.m., the coordinator evaluates the `latest()` function. At that moment, the `present` time on the wall clock is 10 p.m. whereas the nominal time (2 p.m.) and the actual time (6 p.m.) remain unchanged. In short, the nominal time of an action is *always* fixed, the actual time becomes fixed once the action is created, and the present time is *always changing* and follows the wall clock.

latest() evaluation

As already mentioned, Oozie evaluates `latest(n)` based on either the coordinator action's actual time or the present wall clock time. Let's generalize this time as *look-back start time* denoted by T_{lbs}. At first, Oozie determines the closest time instance of the dataset to T_{lbs}. Oozie starts from the dataset's initial-instance (dsII) and increments it by the dataset's frequency (`dsF`) until it reaches T_{lbs}. Let's assume the closest timestamp value to T_{lbs} is determined to be T_{ds}. Oozie first checks if the data directory for time T_{ds} is available. If it is available, it will consider it as the first available data instance or `latest(0)`. If the data for T_{ds} is not available yet, Oozie will walk back and look for data for time T_{ds} `- dsF` (dataset frequency). If that data is available, Oozie will consider this second time instance as the first available data instance or `latest(0)`. If data is not available for that instance as well, Oozie will skip it and keep walking back.

Continuing with this example, if all previous data instances are available, the nth available instance (`latest(n)`) will be the data instance for time T_{ds} `- n x dsF`. If any one data instance between time T_{ds} and T_{ds} `- n x dsF` is not available for whatever reason, Oozie needs to look back further to find (`latest(n)`. If it can't get to the nth instance after searching backward all the way to the `initial-instance` of the dataset (`dsII`), Oozie will go to sleep and start the evaluation process again in the next cycle starting with the calculation of the time T_{lbs}. Finally, when Oozie finds the nth *available* instance, it returns the corresponding timestamp.

The following detailed example attempts to further clarify the concept with real values. Assume the coordinator job specifies the *start time* as `2014-10-18T06:00Z` and the frequency as one day. Oozie materializes the first coordinator action with a nominal time of `2014-10-18T06:00Z`.

Let's further assume that the dependent dataset has the following attributes:

- `Initial-instance` = `2014-10-06T06:00Z`

- `frequency` = `1 day`
- `uri-template` = `hdfs://foo:8020/logs/${YEAR}-${MONTH}-${DAY}`

Let's consider the scenario where Oozie is evaluating `latest()`for this dataset at two different times on the wall clock: `2014-10-19T10:00Z` and `2014-10-19T11:00Z`. At these times, let's also assume that the actual data availability is as it appears in Table 7-4.

Table 7-4. Data availability at time t

Wall Clock Time = 2014-10-19T10:00Z	Wall Clock Time = 2014-10-19T11:00Z
hdfs://foo:8020/logs/2014-10-19	hdfs://foo:8020/logs/2014-10-19
Missing	hdfs://foo:8020/logs/2014-10-18
Missing	Missing
hdfs://foo:8020/logs/2014-10-16	hdfs://foo:8020/logs/2014-10-16
Missing	Missing
hdfs://foo:8020/logs/2014-10-14	hdfs://foo:8020/logs/2014-10-14

Table 7-5 shows the return value of the `latest(n)` timestamp for various values of *n* given the above example scenario. The example assumes that the property `oozie.service.ELService.latest-el.use-current-time` is set to `true`. In other words, it utilizes the present wall-clock time (instead of the `actual` time) in evaluating `latest()`.

Table 7-5. latest(n) instances at time t

Instance	Wall Clock Time = 2014-10-19T10:00Z	Wall Clock Time = 2014-10-19T11:00Z
latest(0)	2014-10-19T06:00Z	2014-10-19T06:00Z
latest(-1)	2014-10-**16**T06:00Z	2014-10-18T06:00Z
latest(-2)	2014-10-**14**T06:00Z	2014-10-**16**T06:00Z

`latest()` at 10 a.m.: At first, Oozie determines the closest timestamp that could be the candidate for `latest(0)`. It starts from `2014-10-06T06:00Z` (dataset `initial-instance`, dsII) and increments the timestamp using the frequency (dsF) until it reaches the `present` time (2014-10-19T10:00Z). In this example, that instance evaluates to 2014-10-19T06:00Z and that's where Oozie starts its data availability checks. Since the data from 10/19 is available at wall-clock time 10 a.m., that instance is determined to be the `latest(0)`. But for `latest(-1)`, Oozie looks for the 10/18 data, which is actually missing at wall-clock time 10 a.m. So Oozie continues to look backward and finds there is no data for 10/17 either. However, it finds data for 10/16 and returns that as the `latest(-1)`. Using the same approach, it looks backwards for latest(-2) and skips 10/15 due to missing data. Oozie finally finds data in 10/14 and returns that instance as the `latest(-2)`. We demonstrate this pictorially in Figure 7-4.

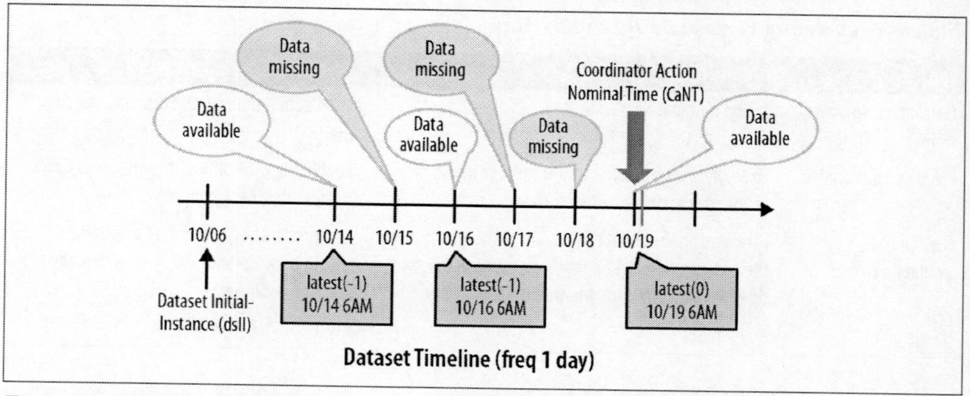

Figure 7-4. Timestamps of latest() EL function at wall-clock time 10 a.m.

`latest()` at 11 a.m.: The only context change between wall clock time 10 a.m. and 11 a.m. is the arrival of new data for 10/18. This changes the timestamp evaluations for `latest(-1)` and `latest(-2)`. Specifically, if Oozie evaluates at 11 a.m., it will return 10/18 as `latest(-1)` and 10/16 as `latest(-2)`.

Scope: The `latest()` EL function is valid only within the `<data-in>` and `<data-out>` sections of the coordinator XML.

Comparison of current() and latest()

The `latest()` and `current()` functions have subtle but important differences. It's important that you have a good understanding of both these concepts so that you can pick the correct EL function for your application. Broadly, if you want to process the same dependent datasets irrespective of when the job executes, you should use `current()`. In other words, for every run for a specific nominal time if you want to process the same input datasets, the right function is `current()`. For example, if you execute the February 1, 2014 instance of your job and *always* want to process the previous 3 days of data (i.e., 01/29/14. 01/30/2014, and 01/31/2014), you should use the `current()` EL function. On the other hand, if you want to process the latest available data at the time of execution irrespective of the nominal time, you should use the `latest()` function. Note that if you run the same coordinator action multiple times, your job may end up processing different datasets with `latest()`. With the preceding example, if you run the job on February 14, 2015 and use `current()`, you will still process the same three days (01/29/2014, 01/30/2014, and 01/31/2014) of data. On the other hand, if you use `latest()`, Oozie will pick more recent datasets, probably

02-11-2015, 02-12-2015, and 02-13-2015 if they are available. Table 7-6 compares some of the key properties of these two functions.

Table 7-6. current() versus latest() comparison

Topics	current(n)	latest(n)
Data checking starts from	Action nominal time	Action actual time OR the present wall clock time
Fixed versus Variable	Fixed. Returns the same timestamp for the same action irrespective of when it checks.	Variable. Returns different timestamps based on when the check happens.
Gaps in data availability	Disregards gaps in data availability. Always returns the same instance(s) of data for a given action and does not skip any data whether it exists or not.	Accounts for the gaps in data availability. Skips missing data instances. Only considers the available instances.
Range of 'n'	Any integer	Only '0' OR negative integer.

Parameter Passing to Workflow

An Oozie workflow, launched by a coordinator action, doesn't directly deal with any time-dependent parameters such as nominal time or actual time. The coordinator primarily deals with these aspects. Nevertheless, workflows frequently need those parameters for its execution. For instance, the dependent data directories checked by a coordinator action is typically directly used by some workflow action as input. Therefore, Oozie provides the following EL functions to easily pass those parameters to the launched workflow. The workflow can refer to the parameters as EL variables in its XML definition.

dataIn(eventName):

This function evaluates all input data directories of a dataset for a specific time instance and returns the directories as a string. The `dataIn()` function doesn't really check if the data is available or not. This function takes `eventName` as a parameter. First, Oozie identifies `data-in` from the `input-events` definition using the `eventName`. Second, Oozie finds the name of the dataset from the `data-in` definition. Last, Oozie takes the `uri-template` from the dataset definition and resolves the paths corresponding to the particular time instance. Oozie evaluates the time instance based on nominal time and the instance number defined in the EL function. We already saw the details of this process in "Parameterization of Dataset Instances" on page 124. If there are multiple instances (e.g., `current(0)`, `current(-1)`, etc.) in `data-in`, Oozie concatenates them using `,` as a separator.

For instance, consider the EL function `${coord:dataIn('event_input1')}` in the context of the example `dataset` and `input-events` defined in "Defining a dataset" on page 118 and "input-events" on page 120, respectively. Let's also assume the nominal time of the coordinator action is `2015-01-01T02:00Z`. Using the event name `event_input1`, Oozie initially determines the corresponding dataset name `ds_input1` from the `data-in` definition. Then using the nominal time and instance count (such as `-1` for `current(-1)`), Oozie calculates the exact time instance of the data and ultimately resolves the `uri-template` defined in the dataset. For example, `current(-1)` returns `2014-12-31T20:00Z` for this coordinator action. Finally, Oozie resolves the `uri-template` with this time instance and evaluates the final directory as *hdfs://localhost:8020/user/joe/revenue_feed/2013-12-31-20*. Oozie follows the same process for each current instance and concatenates them with a comma (,). The EL function `dataIn()` finally returns the following string:

```
hdfs://localhost:8020/user/joe/revenue_feed/2014-12-31-02,
hdfs://localhost:8020/user/joe/revenue_feed/2014-12-31-08,
hdfs://localhost:8020/user/joe/revenue_feed/2014-12-31-14,
hdfs://localhost:8020/user/joe/revenue_feed/2014-12-31-20
```

You could take the input directory and add wildcards to it in the workflow XML. For example, */part**. This will work well for a single directory returned, but for a list like the one shown above, the wildcard will be added only to the last directory in the list, and this probably is not what you want.

Scope: `dataIn()` is valid within the <workflow> section of a coordinator XML.

dataOut(eventName)

This function is similar to `dataIn()`. The key difference is that `dataOut()` utilizes the `output-events` and `data-out` sections whereas the `dataIn()` uses `input-events` and `data-in`.

Scope: `dataOut()` is valid within the <workflow> section of a coordinator XML.

nominalTime()

This function returns the nominal time or the action creation time (explained in section "Our First Coordinator Job" on page 101) of a particular coordinator action.

Scope: `nominalTime()` is valid within the <workflow> section of a coordinator XML.

actualTime()

This function calculates the *actual* time of a coordinator action as defined in "Parameterization of Dataset Instances" on page 124. In an ideal world, the nominal time and the actual time of an action will be the same. But during catch-up scenarios, where the coordinator action execution is delayed, the actual time of a coordinator action is different and later than its nominal time.

Scope: *actualTime()* is valid within the <workflow> section of a coordinator XML.

dateOffset(baseTimeStamp, skipInstance, timeUnit)

This utility function returns a date as a string using the base time and offset. Oozie calculates the new date using the following equation (not considering Daylight Saving Time).

```
New Date = baseTimeStamp + skipInstance * timeUnit
```

Scope: `dateOffset()` is valid within the <workflow> section of a coordinator XML.

formatTime(timeStamp, formatString)

This utility function formats a standard ISO8601 compliant timestamp into another timestamp string based on `formatString`. The `formatString` should follow the conventions used in Java's SimpleDateFormat .

Scope: `formatTime()` is valid within the `<workflow>` and `<input-events>` sections of a coordinator XML.

A Complete Coordinator Application

We now extend the rollup window example described in "Example: Rollup" on page 122. The additional features of this example include the following:

- Extensive parameterization using appropriate EL functions
- Demonstration of the EL functions to pass parameters to the launched workflow

The example code is as follows:

```
<coordinator-app name="my_rollup_job" start="2014-01-01T02:00Z "
    end="2014-12-31T02:00Z" frequency="${coord:days(1)}"
    xmlns="uri:oozie:coordinator:0.4">
  <datasets>
    <dataset name="ds_input1" frequency="${coord:hours(6)}"
           initial-instance="2013-12-29T02:00Z">
      <uri-template>
        hdfs://localhost:8020/user/joe/revenue_feed/${YEAR}-${MONTH}-${DAY}-
        ${HOUR}
      </uri-template>
      <done-flag>_trigger</done-flag>
    </dataset>
    <dataset name="daily-feed" frequency="${coord:days(1)}"
```

```
            initial-instance="2013-12-29T02:00Z">
          <uri-template>
            hdfs://localhost:8020/user/joe/revenue_daily_feed/${YEAR}-${MONTH}-
            ${DAY}
          </uri-template>
        </dataset>
      </datasets>
      <input-events>
          <data-in name="event_input1" dataset="ds_input1">
              <start-instance>${coord:current(-4)}</start-instance>
              <end-instance>${coord:current(-1)}</end-instance>
          </data-in>
      </input-events>
      <output-events>
          <data-out name="event_output1" dataset="daily-feed">
             <instance>${coord:current(0)}</instance>
          </data-out>
      </output-events>
      <action>
         <workflow>
            <app-path>${myWFHomeInHDFS}/app</app-path>
            <property>
              <name>myInputDirs</name>
              <value>${coord:dataIn('event_input1')}</value>
            </property>
            <property>
              <name>myOutputDirs</name>
              <value>${coord:dataOut('event_output1')}</value>
            </property>
            <property>
              <name>myNominalTime</name>
              <value>${coord:nominalTime()}</value>
            </property>
            <property>
              <name>myActualTime</name>
              <value>${coord:actualTime()}</value>
            </property>
            <property>
              <name>myPreviousInstance</name>
              <value>${coord:dateOffset(coord:nominalTime(), -1, 'DAY')}</value>
            </property>
            <property>
              <name>myFutureInstance</name>
              <value>${coord:dateOffset(coord:nominalTime(), 1, 'DAY')}</value>
            </property>
            <property>
                <name>nameNode</name>
                <value>hdfs://localhost:8020</value>
            </property>
            <property>
                <name>jobTracker</name>
                <value>localhost:8032</value>
```

```
            </property>
        </workflow>
    </action>
</coordinator-app>
```

For evaluating the function `dataIn()`, Oozie uses the event name `event_input1` that was passed in to find the dataset `ds_input1` from the `data-in` definition. After translating the `myInputDirs` into an actual list of directories, Oozie passes it to the launched workflow where the workflow refers to it using the variable `${myInputDirs}`. Workflows generally use this as input data for its actions.

For the first coordinator action, Oozie returns `2014-01-01T02:00Z` as the value of `myNominalTime`. For the second action, `myNominalTime` is `2014-01-02T02:00Z`.

For the second action with nominal time `2014-01-02T02:00Z`, the value of `myPreviousInstance` is `2014-01-01T02:00Z`, and the value of `myFutureInstance` is `2014-01-03T02:00Z`.

The value of property `myOutputDir` is resolved as `hdfs://localhost:8020/user/joe/revenue_daily_feed/2014-01-01` for the first coordinator action with nominal time `2014-01-01T02:00Z`. Again, this variable is passed to the workflow where it is often used as application output.

This concludes our explanation of data availability triggers, which is as important as time-based triggers for the Oozie coordinator. This chapter, along with the previous chapter, discusses the details of a coordinator application in a comprehensive fashion. We covered when and how to launch a workflow based on user-defined time and data triggers. In the next chapter, we will introduce another abstraction on top of the coordinator called the `bundle`, which helps users easily manage multiple coordinator jobs.

CHAPTER 8

Oozie Bundles

Leading up to this chapter, we have covered two important and basic Oozie concepts, namely the workflow and the coordinator, and everything that goes into authoring and implementing them. Workflows are at the core of any Oozie application and coordinators are the next level of abstraction that allows the orchestration of these workflows through time and data triggers, as explained in Chapters 6 and 7. In this chapter, we will cover Oozie bundles, the highest level of abstraction in Oozie that helps users package a bunch of coordinator applications into a single entity, often called a *data pipeline*.

Bundle Basics

Oozie's evolutionary path gives us a lot of context on how bundles were born. Oozie version 1.0 was all about workflows and the basic features around it. Version 2.0 introduced coordinators and triggers. Bundle became the next step for Oozie and was introduced in version 3.0. As you can see, there is a nice rhythm to this evolutionary arc and users wanted higher abstractions and more features for a Hadoop-based workflow engine at every stage. Bundle was the direct result of users wanting Oozie to support large data pipelines involving many workflows with complex interdependencies.

Bundle Definition

An Oozie bundle is a collection of Oozie coordinator applications with a directive on when to kick off those coordinators. As with the other parts of Oozie, bundles are also defined via an XML-based language called the Bundle Specification Language. Bundles can be started, stopped, suspended, and managed as a single entity instead of managing each individual coordinator that it's composed of. This is a very useful level of abstraction in many large enterprises. These data pipelines can get rather large and complicated, and the ability to manage them as a single entity instead of meddling with the individual parts brings a lot of operational benefits. Figure 8-1 shows a pictorial representation of an Oozie bundle.

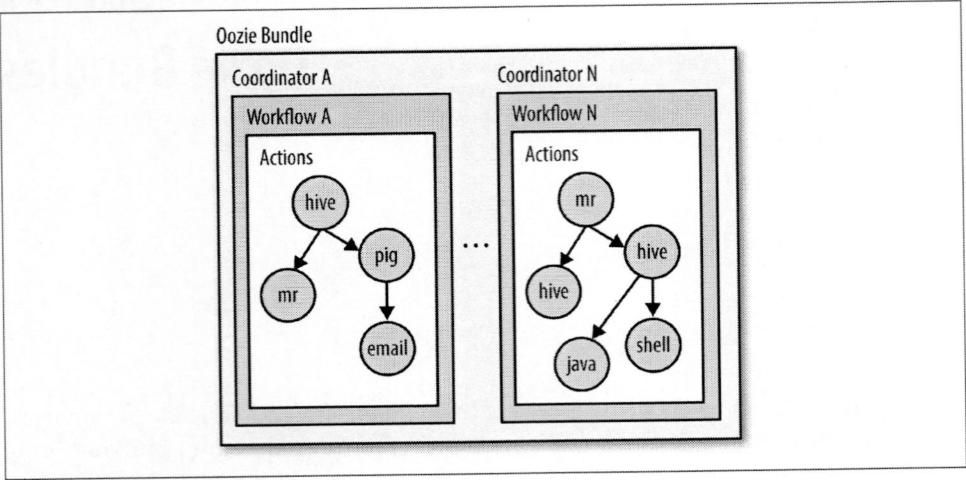

Figure 8-1. Oozie bundle

As the picture suggests, a bundle is designed to contain one or more coordinators. Bundles don't support any explicit definition or management of dependencies between the coordinators, but they can wait on each other implicitly through the data dependency mechanism that the coordinator supports. For example, coordinator C can wait on datasets generated by coordinator A and B. This is how data pipelines are implemented in Oozie using coordinators and bundles.

Why Do We Need Bundles?

Some users, when exposed to the concept of an Oozie bundle for the first time, are a little confused about its usefulness and necessity. Users need and want to run workflows. They also understand the coordinator and its features. But the benefits of an Oozie bundle are not readily apparent. So it might be instructive to go through some concrete use cases and the value of using an Oozie bundle in those example scenarios. bundles are basically available for operational convenience more than anything else.

Let's look at a typical use case of a rather large Internet company that makes its revenue through advertising and ad clicks. Let's say that Apache web logs are collected in a low-latency batch and delivered to the backend. The data pipeline then picks it up and kicks off a variety of processing on it. The list of applications using this input log data include but is not limited to the following workflows:

- There is one workflow that counts ad clicks, calculates the cost to the advertiser account IDs, does some basic comparisons to the same time of the day last week to make sure there are no abnormalities, and publishes a revenue feed. This workflow is called the `Revenue WF` and runs every 15 minutes.
- There is a `Targeting WF` that looks at the user IDs corresponding to the ad clicks and does some processing to segment them for behavioral AD targeting. This workflow also runs every 15 minutes, but it satisfies a completely different business requirement than the `revenue WF` and is developed and managed by another team.
- There is an Hourly workflow called the `AD-UI WF` that rolls up the 15 minute revenue feeds generated by the `revenue WF` and pushes a feed to a operational database that feeds an advertiser user interface. This UI is where advertisers and customers log in and track their AD expenditure at an hourly grain.
- There is a `Reporting WF` that runs daily in the morning to aggregate a lot of the data from the previous day and generate daily canned reports for the executives of the company.
- Last but not the least, the advertiser billing logic and the SOX (Sarbanes–Oxley) compliance checks run monthly because that's when the larger advertisers actually get a bill and are expected to pay. They don't actually pay daily or hourly. This makes up the `Billing WF` and involves monthly aggregations and rollups.

Given the varied use cases detailed here, you can see how the entire, consolidated data pipeline can get rather complex. There are several moving parts and interdependencies, though these individual use cases seem to fit nicely into individual Oozie workflows. There will be corresponding coordinator apps that take care of the necessary time and data triggers for these workflows. The same input dataset (weblogs) drives all of the processing, but different groups within the company actually own specific business use cases. Table 8-1 summarizes these workflows and their time frequency and business owners.

Table 8-1. Business use cases and their workflows

No.	Workflow name	Workflow frequency	Business unit
1	Revenue WF	15 minutes	AD Operations
2	Targeting WF	15 minutes	Behavioral Targeting
3	AD-UI WF	Hourly	AD Operations
4	Reporting WF	Daily	Business Intelligence
5	Billing WF	Monthly	Accounting

In addition to the time frequency, the workflows also have data dependencies among them. For instance, the monthly `billing WF` will be dependent on the entire month's worth of revenue feeds from the `AD-UI WF`, which itself is dependent on the output of the `revenue WF`. These dependencies can be specified via the coordinator app like we saw in Chapter 6. Bear in mind that there is a one-to-one correspondence between a coordinator app and the workflow it runs. So a coordinator by definition cannot run two workflows of different frequencies as part of one job.

Assuming the layout of coordinator and workflow apps as defined in the previous paragraph, let's look at some failure scenarios that are common in such a complex data pipeline. Let's say the operations team finds out at 11 p.m. on March 31 that some of the data for that day is missing. Specifically, there was a network hiccup that caused some silent data loss in the previous four hours starting at 7 p.m. It is finally detected and a high-priority alert is issued. Many operations teams across the organization get into an emergency mode to fix the issue. Once the issue is fixed, the old data that's missing will be delivered to the data pipeline. But the pipeline is long done with hours 7 through 9 and is minutes away from kicking of the hourlies for the 10 p.m. hour. And we are also pretty close to the dailies kicking off and the monthly billing is not too far either, as this is the last day of the month. There is no point kicking off the daily and monthly jobs without completing the reprocessing of the last four hours. The operations team has to stall all those coordinator jobs and reprocess the 15-minute and hourly ones from the last four hours. The coordinator has the right tools and options for suspending, starting, and reprocessing all those jobs, but it's a lot of manual work for the data pipeline operations team responsible for all these coordinator jobs. As we all know, manual processing is quite error-prone.

This is exactly where the bundle comes in. If they had defined the entire data pipeline as a bundle, the life of the operations team becomes a lot easier. They can stop the bundle, and all processing for all coordinators stops right away with one command. They can then handle what needs to be reprocessed through Oozie tools (refer to "Reprocessing" on page 222 for more details). Reprocessing will require some diligent analysis, but some of this reprocessing can happen at the bundle level as well. Bundle level reprocessing features are being developed and released in increments at the time of writing this book. So check your specific Oozie version for details. When it's time to restart the pipeline, they can again do it with one command and Oozie bundle will take care of the rest.

As you can see, bundles are a very powerful abstraction, and for certain high-end use cases, they add a lot of operational flexibility and convenience.

Bundle Specification

Let's now look at the actual bundle specification. As with the other parts of Oozie, bundle specification is also XML based. It borrows and leverages all the concepts of the pipeline definition language, variable substitution, and parameterization that we have covered thus far in the book. bundle specification is a lot less complicated and has fewer elements than the workflow and the coordinator. Figure 8-2 captures the elements that make up a bundle pretty concisely. The optional elements are represented by boxes enclosed by dotted lines.

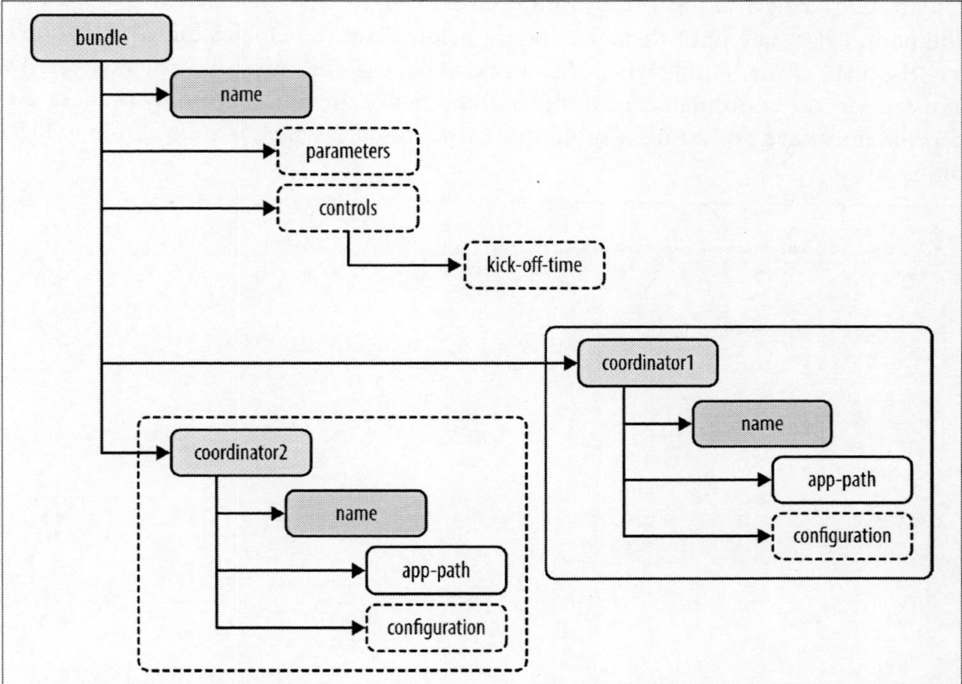

Figure 8-2. Bundle Specification

The optional `<parameters>` section serves the same purpose as it does for the workflows as explained in "The <parameters> Section" on page 92. That's the section where you can declare bundle parameters and optionally add default values so Oozie can check for the variables before running the bundle. The `<controls>` section is optional and the `<kick-off-time>` is when you want the bundle to be started and run. It's explained in detail in the next section. A given bundle can have one or more coordinators as shown in the picture above. Each coordinator has a name and an application path with an optional `<configuration>` section. The `<configuration>` section is similar to what we have seen throughout this book.

Execution Controls

Kick-off time: The only real bundle-specific control element that Oozie supports is the `<kick-off-time>`. This determines when a submitted bundle should actually be run.

Let's assume you are submitting the Oozie jobs via the CLI. Regardless of whether the job is a workflow, coordinator, or a bundle, the interface is the same. You can submit a bundle using ""oozie job -submit" or directly run it using "oozie job -run". If you execute "-run", Oozie will run the bundle regardless of the <kick-off-time>, which will basically be ignored. But if you invoke "-submit", the bundle will be submitted, but Oozie will not run it until the <kick-off-time> is reached. The bundle will be in PREP state until then. The figure below from the Oozie's bundle UI shows you the state of the bundle when the <kick-off-time> has not been reached yet. As you can see, the coordinator list in the bottom half of the figure is empty because the coordinators have not yet been submitted by the bundle, which is still waiting to kick off.

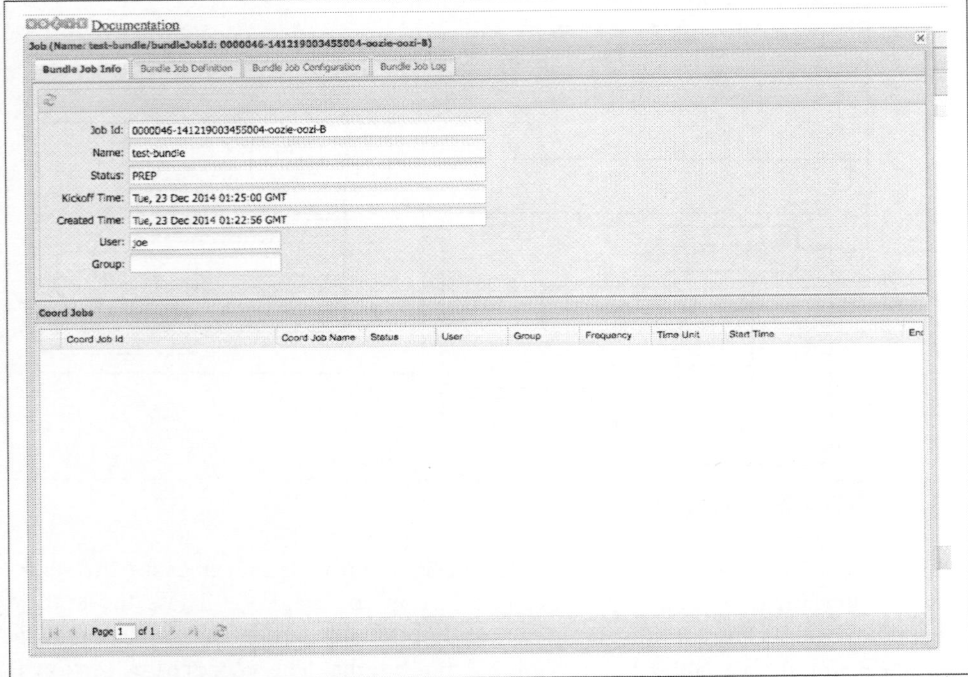

Figure 8-3. Bundle Kick-off Time

If the <kick-off-time> is not specified, the bundle submit and run behave the same and the job will be run "now" as soon as it is submitted. Do keep in mind that the coordinators being invoked by this bundle could also be time triggered. The bundle <kick-off-time> is different from the coordinator start time and orthogonal to the schedule of the coordinator(s) included. The bundle does not even submit the coordinators until the kick-off time. Once submitted, the coordinator instances could run right away or wait depending on the time dependencies at the coordinator level.

Example 8-1 shows an example of a real bundle and as you can see, the specification is pretty simple and straightforward.

Example 8-1. Bundle application

```
<bundle-app name='bundle-example' xmlns:xsi='http://www.w3.org/2001/
                XMLSchema-instance'xmlns='uri:oozie:bundle:0.2'>
  <parameters>
    <property>
      <name>start</name>
    </property>
    <property>
      <name>end</name>
      <value>2014-12-20T10:45Z</value>
    </property>
  </parameters>
  <controls>
    <kick-off-time>2014-12-20T10:30Z</kick-off-time>
  </controls>
  <coordinator name='coord-1'>
    <app-path>${nameNode}/user/apps/coord-1/coordinator.xml</app-path>
    <configuration>
      <property>
        <name>start</name>
        <value>${start}</value>
      </property>
      <property>
        <name>end</name>
        <value>${end}</value>
      </property>
    </configuration>
  </coordinator>
  <coordinator name='coord-2'>
    <app-path>${nameNode}/user/apps/coord-2/coordinator.xml</app-path>
    <configuration>
      <property>
        <name>start</name>
        <value>${start}</value>
      </property>
      <property>
        <name>end</name>
        <value>${end}</value>
      </property>
    </configuration>
  </coordinator>
</bundle-app>
```

When using bundles, make sure the coordinator definition is using the Oozie schema version `0.2` (`xmlns="uri:oozie:coordinator:0.2"`) or higher. Bundle execution will fail if the included coordinators are still conforming to version 0.1.

As always, the bundle specification has to be copied to HDFS. The configuration to the Oozie command line is passed via a *job.properties* file. An example properties file for Example 8-1 is shown in Example 8-2.

Example 8-2. The job.properties file for the bundle

```
nameNode=hdfs://localhost:8020
jobTracker=localhost:8032
oozie.bundle.application.path=${nameNode}/user/apps/bundle/
start=2014-12-20T10:45Z
end=2014-12-30T10:45Z
```

Bundles are invoked just like workflows and coordinators, using the same interfaces. If you are using the Oozie CLI, the commands in Example 8-3 work for bundles, too. The `oozie.bundle.application.path` variable in the *job.properties* tells Oozie that this is a bundle application.

Example 8-3. CLI commands for bundles

```
$ oozie job -config job.properties -submit
  job: 0000056-141219003455004-oozie-oozi-B

$ oozie job 0000056-141219003455004-oozie-oozi-B -run
$ oozie job 0000056-141219003455004-oozie-oozi-B -suspend
$ oozie job 0000056-141219003455004-oozie-oozi-B -resume

$ oozie job -info 0000046-141219003455004-oozie-oozi-B
Job ID : 0000046-141219003455004-oozie-oozi-B
------------------------------------------------------------------------------------------
Job Name : test-bundle
App Path : hdfs://nn.mycompany.com:8020/user/joe/oozie/test_bundle/
Status   : SUCCEEDED
Kickoff time    : Tue Dec 20 10:30:00 UTC 2014
------------------------------------------------------------------------------------------
Job ID                                  Status          Freq Unit
 Started                  Next Materialized
------------------------------------------------------------------------------------------
0000047-141219003455004-oozie-oozi-C    SUCCEEDED       1    DAY
2014-12-20 10:30 GMT    2014-12-20 10:30 GMT
------------------------------------------------------------------------------------------
```

Bundle State Transitions

Figure 8-4 captures the state transitions that an Oozie bundle goes through in detail. `START`, `RUNNING`, `SUSPENDED`, `PAUSED`, `SUCCEEDED`, `FAILED`, and `KILLED` are the most important and the most common states you will encounter. Users are rarely exposed to some of the other states in the picture, though they are all processed internally as part of the state management. The bundle states are pretty self-explanatory and are very similar to the states for the workflow and the coordinator that we have already seen.

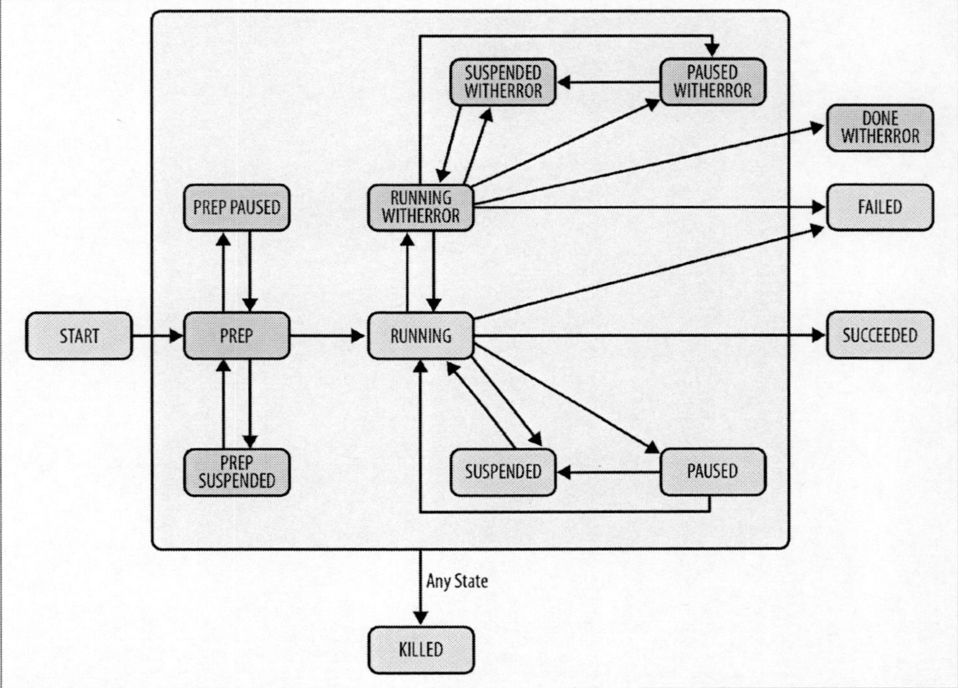

Figure 8-4. Bundle states

Any state management operation you perform on the bundle, like suspending or killing it, will be propagated to the coordinators and workflows that are part of that bundle as well. They will also get killed or suspended or resumed implicitly. This is one of the benefits of using Oozie bundles.

In this chapter, we covered the Oozie bundle in detail. It's not a complicated topic for application developers, but more of an operational concept. We encourage you to use the bundle construct to better manage your data pipelines. With this chapter, we are done covering all of the fundamental Oozie concepts in the form of workflows, coordinators, and bundles. You should be able to write and operate complete Oozie applications at this point. We will now look at more advanced topics starting with the next chapter and through the rest of this book.

CHAPTER 9

Advanced Topics

In the previous chapters, we largely focused on Oozie's three abstractions: workflow, coordinator, and bundle. In particular, we explained the basic and common usage of those abstractions. In this chapter, we discuss some of the advanced concepts concerning the workflow and the coordinator. More specifically, we present how to manage JARs for Oozie workflows and how to execute MapReduce jobs written using the new Hadoop API. We also elaborate on the security features in Oozie. As for the coordinator, we demonstrate how to use cron type scheduling and how to support HCatalog-based data dependency.

Managing Libraries in Oozie

In general, managing different JARs while allowing users the flexibility to include their own custom JARs for their applications is a challenge for any Java-based system. In the previous chapters, we briefly covered some simple examples of JAR management in Oozie. We will discuss a few other important scenarios in this section.

Origin of JARs in Oozie

Before going into the details of JAR management, let's see the different types of JARs Oozie needs to maintain. The JARs in Oozie largely come from the following sources:

System JARs
: This includes Oozie's system JARs that run Oozie services. These JARs are generated during an Oozie build and included as part of the Oozie web application archive (*oozie.war*) file, as discussed in "Install Oozie Server" on page 26.

Hadoop JARs
: These JARs are required for Oozie to communicate to Hadoop services. Hadoop produces these JARs and Oozie injects them into the web application archive

(*oozie.war*) during packaging (also discussed in "Install Oozie Server" on page 26).

Action JARs
: These JARs are required to execute the built-in Oozie actions (e.g., Pig, Hive, DistCp, etc.). The first part of this chapter focuses primarily on these JARs.

User JARs
: These JARs are produced by end users to execute their application logic. For example, `mapper` and `reducer` classes required for MapReduce action, Pig/Hive UDF code, and custom Java classes for Java action. Users usually bundle and deploy their JARs into the *lib/* directory under the workflow application path, as we discussed in "Application Deployment Model" on page 20. In "Supporting the User's JAR" on page 152, we present an alternative and efficient approach to include user JARs into Hadoop applications.

Design Challenges

As mentioned earlier, designing a flexible and intuitive framework for JAR management in a complex system like Oozie is very tricky. Here are some of the reasons for this:

Multiple action types
: Oozie has to deal with different types of built-in and user-defined actions. Each action type needs a different set of JARs and in some cases, they might conflict with each other. For example, Pig and Hive need their respective set of JARs, and some common JARs may not be compatible with each other. In addition, when only one action type is needed for an application, Oozie should include only the required JARs for that action. In other words, Oozie should reduce the overhead of JAR distribution by not including unnecessary JARs.

Multiple versions
: One action type can support multiple versions of the same tool. For example, one user might want to run Pig 0.11 through the Pig action while another user wants Pig 0.13. To address this, Oozie should provide a framework to support the most common versions of each tool it supports.

Different Hadoop versions
: Since most of the actions are directly related to Hadoop, the version of Hadoop plays a critical role in the context of JAR management. For instance, a JAR compiled against Hadoop version 1.x might not run on a Hadoop 2.x cluster. For example, Pig 0.11 compiled against Hadoop 1.x does not work on a Hadoop 2.x cluster. Oozie should provide a framework to handle this type of variability as well.

Seamless jar upgrade

Upgrading JARs is the norm rather than an exception in the Hadoop ecosystem. For example, Oozie supports Pig 0.11. Let's say there is an important bug fix added to Pig 0.11, and Oozie needs to replace or upgrade this JAR. A straightforward replacement of this JAR file can cause running jobs to fail because of the way the Hadoop distributed cache works. Oozie should provide an easy and safe way to upgrade JARs.

Flexibility

It's inconvenient to explicitly include all the common JARs for each application, so Oozie should package these common JARs of each action type at the system level. Furthermore, a user should be able to specify a different JAR version for each action to override the default. Basically, Oozie should support multiple versions of the same tool at the system level, and at the same time, it should allow users to override those system-provided JARs with user-specific JARs. This level of flexibility makes the design and interface complex.

Managing Action JARs

Oozie supports built-in actions such as Pig, Hive, DistCp, Hadoop streaming, Sqoop, and others. These are either independent products in the Hadoop ecosystem or artifacts generated by core Hadoop. For user convenience, it is recommended that Oozie admin provide and manage these JARs. In Oozie, the system-provided JARs are known as `sharelib`. In this section, we describe how an admin can manage the `sharelib` in an Oozie instance.

Although most of the `sharelib` management work is tackled by the Oozie admin, the end user needs to explicitly specify if she wants to use the system-provided `sharelib`. In general, the user defines `oozie.use.system.libpath=true` in the *job.properties* file used during job submission. Since this setting was added much later, Oozie sets the property value to false by default to maintain backward compatibility.

If the action-specific JARs are missing in the classpath, you might see a `java.lang.ClassNotFoundException` or `java.lang.NoClassDefFoundException` message in either the Oozie or the Hadoop job log. The common cause for this type of error is either that the `sharelib` is missing or has not been installed properly for that particular action.

How to get the JARs?

The Oozie distribution's TAR file mentioned in "Build Oozie" on page 25 contains another TAR file (*oozie-sharelib-4.0.1.tar.gz*), which contains all the common JARs required to support different action types. The JARs for each action type are organized under a separate subdirectory. Oozie packages the most commonly used versions of each action type. For instance, the Oozie 4.0.1 `sharelib` by default includes Hadoop-1.x-compatible Pig 0.10.1 and Hive 0.10.0 JARs. If you want to build a different version (e.g., Hadoop-2.x-compatible JARs), you need to build it using specific options in the build command line. For example, if you want Pig 0.12.0 for a Hadoop 2.x cluster, you can do the following to build it:

```
$ bin/mkdistro.sh -DskipTests -Dpig.version=0.12.0 -Phadoop-2
```

For most customers, the bundled `sharelib` JARs are good enough because the Oozie team puts a lot of thought into packaging the most appropriate JARs for the ecosystem tools at the time of the release. However, there are cases where it doesn't work well. Some of the possible problems and their solutions are explained here:

Bundled version versus required version
: In some cases, the version of a product that comes with the Oozie TAR file and the version being used at a particular customer's environment may not match. For example, the customer might only support Pig 0.11 whereas the bundled version with Oozie is Pig 0.12. Administrators can collect the JARs required for Pig 0.11 from the Pig distribution, build the required version from the released source code, or copy from *$PIG_HOME/lib* directory of their Pig 0.11 installation. The same is true for similar products like Hive, Sqoop, and the like.

Hadoop 1.x versus Hadoop 2.x
: For some JARs, Hadoop 1.x and Hadoop 2.x are not compatible. Oozie 4.0.1 by default includes Hadoop-1.x-compliant Pig and Hive JARs. So the admin might have to gather the set of Hadoop-2.x-compliant JARs either by manually building them from the respective code branch, by collecting it from the released artifact, or by using the previously mentioned Oozie build command. In this case, it is recommended that the admin consult the respective product's build and release process.

Installing sharelib

As mentioned in "Shared Library Installation" on page 34, we need to untar the bundled `sharelib` and then upload it to a HDFS directory. For Oozie 4.0.1 and earlier, the following commands, when executed as user *oozie*, would do the task (for version 4.1.0 and later, users can't use these commands and are advised to consult "Sharelib since version 4.1.0" on page 35):

```
$ tar xvf oozie-sharelib-4.0.1.tar.gz
$ hdfs dfs -put share share
```

By default, the `sharelib` points to the HDFS directory */user/${oozie_service_user}/share/lib*. If you want to change the default location, you can do so by overriding the property `oozie.service.WorkflowAppService.system.libpath` in *oozie-site.xml*. You need to make sure the directory has read and write permissions for the Oozie service user (typically *oozie*) and read permissions for all the other users (`hdfs dfs -chmod 755 <PATH>` should work).

Overriding/upgrading existing JARs

As mentioned in "How to get the JARs?" on page 149, there are various reasons for needing to override the bundled JARs after the installation of the `sharelib`. There are two solutions and we illustrate them using Pig JARs as an example. Let's assume for the following example that Pig 0.11 is not bundled with Oozie and the users want to use Pig 0.11:

- The Oozie administrator can manually replace the Pig 0.11 JARs in the HDFS *share/lib* directory (the only risk with this solution is that any running job that's using the original Pig JARs could fail):

```
$ hdfs dfs -rm -r share/lib/pig
$ hdfs dfs -mkdir -p share/lib/pig
$ hdfs dfs -put <local-path-to-pig-0.11>/jars/* share/lib/pig/
```

- The administrator can also create a separate directory for Pig 0.11 JARs and change the default mapping to use the new Pig 0.11 directory (in this case, the original Pig JARs in the `sharelib` are not removed):

```
$ hdfs dfs -put local-path-to-pig-0.11 jars/* share/lib/pig-0.11/
```

  The administrator should then modify the property `oozie.action.sharelib.for.pig` in *oozie-site.xml* and restart the Oozie server. For the Hive action, the admin can follow the same steps and modify the `oozie.action.sharelib.for.hive` property instead.

In general, you can override the `sharelib` of any action at three levels: action, job, and system. For defining at the action level, set the property `oozie.action.sharelib.for.#actionType#` in the configuration section of the action in *workflow.xml*. For job level, you can define it in *job.properties* file as a key-value pair. For a system-level change, the admin can define the property in *oozie-site.xml*.

Supporting multiple versions

In reality, Oozie users might need to use multiple versions of the same tool. For example, some users might want to upgrade to Pig 0.12 while others are still using the older Pig 0.11 version. The Oozie administrator can decide to support both versions. The solution is very similar to the second option described in "Overriding/upgrading existing JARs" on page 151. The administrator can upload the Pig-0.11 library to *share/lib/pig-0.11/* without modifying the *oozie-site.xml*.

Oozie admin is done after multiple versions of JARs are deployed into the *share/lib* directory. Now it is the user's responsibility to pick the right version by defining the appropriate property for her action. For example, if a user needs Pig 0.12, which is the default version installed in the *share/lib/pig* directory, she doesn't need to do anything extra. However, if the user wants to use a nondefault version, Pig 0.11 in this case, she needs to specify the subdirectory through the Pig action's configuration defined in *workflow.xml*. The following example shows how to do this. It also demonstrates how to include multiple subdirectories of JARs for the same action type. The Pig action shown here includes both the Pig 0.11 JARs and the HCatalog JAR:

```
<property>
  <name>oozie.action.sharelib.for.pig</name>
  <value>pig-0.11,hcatalog</value>
</property>
```

Supporting the User's JAR

Oozie users frequently need to use custom JARs for their applications. It includes custom mapper or reducer classes, UDF JAR for Pig or Hive, arbitrary Java code, and more. You might also occasionally want to override the action-specific system JARs with your own version of the product. For example, the deployed Oozie system might support only Pig 0.11 and 0.12, but the user needs Pig 0.10. In this case, you can override the system JARs with your own version of the JARs.

There are many ways to provide your own JARs.[1] Here are two of the most common ways of including JARs in applications:

Through workflow lib/ directory
: As explained in "Application Deployment Model" on page 20, users can copy all the required JARs into the *lib* directory under the workflow application directory. During execution, Oozie will upload those JARs using the Hadoop distributed cache.

1 ShareLib in Apache Oozie.

Using `oozie.libpath`

Although the approach defined above is simple and usually sufficient, it is not efficient in some instances. For example, let's say a user has 100 workflows and all of them need the same set of JARs. In the earlier approach, the user will need to copy the same set of JARs into the *lib/* directories of all 100 workflows. Moreover, when a JAR changes, the user will have to update each one of those 100 directories. Oozie provides a way to include the common set of JARs by defining `oozie.libpath` in the job properties file. This `libpath` can be thought of as a user-level shared library as opposed to the system-level shared library explained in "Installing sharelib" on page 150. In general, a user or a project owner manages the user-level shared library whereas the administrator manages the system-level shared library. In the case of the user-level shared library, Oozie will distribute those JARs from that common location and include them in the application classpath. In addition, for any JAR modification, the user will only have to update the JAR in the common location. The user doesn't have to copy the JAR for each workflow.

JAR Precedence in classpath

As already described, Oozie provides three ways to include the JARs for any workflow action (Oozie ensures the following ordering of these JAR sources in the actual application classpath):

Application lib directory

Any JAR included in the workflow application *lib/* directory receives the highest priority in the classpath.

User-level shared library

The user-level shared library path defined through `oozie.libpath` has the next highest priority in the ordering.

System-level shared library

The action JARs included in the system-defined `sharelib` has the lowest priority among these three options.

Users don't have to do anything special for adding Hadoop JARs. Oozie includes the Hadoop JARs in the classpath by default and gives it the highest priority. If you want to give your JARs higher priority than the Hadoop JARs, you need to specify `oozie.launcher.mapreduce.task.classpath.user.precedence=true` in the action's configuration.

Let's look at an example to describe this ordering. Assume the user includes the Pig 0.12 JARs in the *workflow-app/lib/* directory. She also passes in the `oozie.libpath` that includes the Pig 0.11 JARs. Meanwhile, the administrator uploads the Pig 0.13 JARs into the system's `sharelib` for the Pig action. In this scenario, Oozie will include the Pig 0.12 JARs in the Pig action's classpath, followed by Pig 0.11 and Pig 0.13 JARs.

However, in reality, this is not a recommended way of managing JARs. Users should not use multiple ways of managing the same type of JAR (Pig, in this example). If the user wants to include a custom version, she should include those JARs via the *workflow-app/lib* directory. She should not pass `oozie.libpath` and should not set `oozie.use.system.libpath` to true because these multiple approaches used in conjunction can lead to a lot of confusion.

Oozie Security

Security in the Hadoop ecosystem has become increasingly important, especially for large enterprises. There are multiple layers of security in a distributed data platform like Hadoop. It includes security of the data storage and processing. Since Oozie plays an important role in scheduling and managing Hadoop jobs, guaranteeing the same level of security in Oozie is equally critical. In this section, we describe the various aspects of security in Oozie and see how to implement and manage it.

Oozie Security Overview

Oozie sits right in the middle of Hadoop and its users. Therefore, its security support comes in two forms:

Oozie Service to Hadoop Services
: Oozie ultimately submits the end user's jobs to the JobTracker/ResourceManager and accesses HDFS files. Oozie acts as a Hadoop client and Hadoop only supports Kerberos-based authentication. Therefore, if the Hadoop cluster is secure, Oozie has to present the appropriate Kerberos credentials to those services.

Oozie Client to Oozie Service
: At the other end, when Oozie client communicates with the Oozie service, the client needs to present a valid credential to the Oozie service. By Oozie client we mean the Oozie CLI, REST client, Java client, or any other custom client that accesses Oozie. In this context, users can use any custom security protocol, but we only explain Kerberos based authentication here because that's the most common approach in the Hadoop ecosystem.

Figure 9-1 captures these two forms of security. Security on either side is independent of each other. In other words, Oozie's access to Hadoop could be secure while the connection between the Oozie client and the Oozie server can be insecure. We explain both of them in the rest of this section.

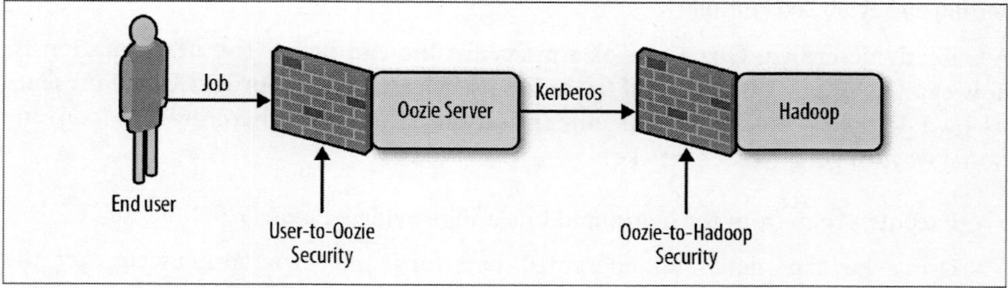

Figure 9-1. Oozie security

Oozie to Hadoop

On a secure Hadoop cluster, every job submission needs to present a valid Kerberos ticket to Hadoop services. The question then becomes, whose Kerberos credential should Oozie present and how will it acquire those credentials? Oozie usually executes a job long after its original submission by the end user. In particular, Oozie coordinator jobs can run for years, periodically scheduling Hadoop jobs during their lifetime. However, Kerberos credentials are generally valid for a limited period of time (e.g., one day). In short, end users can't easily generate the Kerberos ticket for long-running jobs. Due to this, it was decided that Oozie should manage the Kerberos credential on behalf of the end users. Let's now look at all the relevant Hadoop configuration settings that Oozie leverages to implement this special privilege.

Configuring Hadoop services

Oozie utilizes Hadoop's proxy user feature to act as a proxy for its end users and presents Oozie's own credentials to Hadoop services. To achieve this, we must configure Hadoop to allow the Oozie service be a valid proxy. More specifically, Hadoop's *core-site.xml* file should contain these two properties for the Oozie service user (`oozie`):

```
<property>
      <name>hadoop.proxyuser.[OOZIE_SERVICE_OWNER].hosts</name>
      <value>[OOZIE_SERVICE_HOSTNAME]</value>
</property>

<property>
      <name>hadoop.proxyuser.[OOZIE_SERVICE_OWNER].groups</name>
      <value>[OOZIE_SERVICE_OWNER_GROUP] </value>
</property>
```

The example values for `[OOZIE_SERVICE_OWNER]`, `[OOZIE_SERVICE_OWNER_GROUP]`, and `[OOZIE_SERVICE_HOSTNAME]` are *oozie*, *users*, and *localhost*, respectively.

Setting up Keytab and Principal

As already described, Oozie acts as a proxy for the end users. The next question is, how can Oozie authenticate itself to Hadoop services as a valid proxy? Oozie presents its own Kerberos credentials for authentication. In general, there are two conventional ways to get a Kerberos ticket:

- Execute `kinit` from the command line and provide a password.
- Use a `keytab` file as an encrypted password and programmatically get the credentials.

Oozie uses the second option (`keytab` based), which is the widely adopted approach for service authentication. For this, we need two things: a `keytab` file and an associated principal name. Your Hadoop administrator should be very familiar with the standard ways of getting those, but we will explain the basic steps to get a Kerberos principal and the associated `keytab` file here anyway:

Kerberos Principal
: The principal name for the Oozie service usually follows the following syntax: `oozie/<fully.qualified.domain.name>@<REALM>`. Here, `oozie` is the ID of the service user that owns the Oozie web service. `<fully.qualified.domain.name>` determines the hostname where the Oozie web service is running (Oozie server). `<REALM>` specifies the Kerberos domain. One such example of a principal is *oozie/my-host-name.example.com@EXAMPLE.COM*. The output from the following interactive command shows us how to create a principal:

```
$ kadmin
  Authenticating as principal $USER/admin@EXAMPLE.COM with password.
  Password for $USER/admin@EXAMPLE.COM:
 kadmin:  add_principal -randkey oozie/fully.qualified.domain.name
  WARNING: no policy specified for oozie/fully.qualified.domain.name
      @EXAMPLE.COM; defaulting to no policy
  Principal "oozie/fully.qualified.domain.name@EXAMPLE.COM" created.
```

`Keytab` *file*
: After creating the principal, we need to generate a related `keytab` file. The following command-line interactions demonstrate how to create a `keytab` for the same principal:

```
kadmin:  ktadd -k /my/keytab/path/oozie.service.keytab oozie/
                  fully.qualified.domain.name
  Entry for principal oozie/fully.qualified.domain.name with kvno 2,
  encryption type aes256-cts-hmac-sha1-96 added to keytab
  WRFILE:/my/keytab/path/oozie.service.keytab.

  Entry for principal oozie/fully.qualified.domain.name with kvno 2,
  encryption type aes128-cts-hmac-sha1-96 added to keytab
```

```
    WRFILE:/my/keytab/path/oozie.service.keytab.

    Entry for principal oozie/fully.qualified.domain.name with kvno 2,
    encryption type arcfour-hmac added to keytab
    WRFILE:/my/keytab/path/oozie.service.keytab.
kadmin:  exit
```

Testing

There are ways to test if both the principal and the key tab were created correctly. The following commands and the responses demonstrate that both were created successfully:

```
$ klist -kt /my/keytab/path/oozie.service.keytab
   Keytab name: WRFILE:/my/keytab/path/oozie.service.keytab
   KVNO Timestamp         Principal
   ---- ----------------- ------------------------------------------------
   2 09/17/14 00:00:59 oozie/fully.qualified.domain.name@EXAMPLE.COM
   2 09/17/14 00:00:59 oozie/fully.qualified.domain.name@EXAMPLE.COM
   2 09/17/14 00:00:59 oozie/fully.qualified.domain.name@EXAMPLE.COM
$ kinit -kt /my/keytab/path/oozie.service.keytab oozie/
   fully.qualified.domain.name
$ klist
    Ticket cache: FILE:/tmp/krb5cc_5003_VtXj6E
    Default principal: oozie/fully.qualified.domain.name@EXAMPLE.COM

    Valid starting     Expires            Service principal
    09/17/14 00:03:04  09/18/14 00:03:04  krbtgt/EXAMPLE.COM@EXAMPLE.COM
       renew until 09/24/14 00:03:04
```

Configuring the Oozie server

After successfully creating the keytab file and the principal, we are now ready to configure Oozie to support Kerberos security for all Hadoop services. We need to add the following properties to the *oozie-site.xml* file:

```
<property>
  <name>oozie.service.HadoopAccessorService.kerberos.enabled</name>
  <value>true</value>
  <description>
      Indicates if Oozie is configured to use Kerberos. (Oozie to Hadoop)
  </description>
</property>

<property>
  <name>local.realm</name>
  <value>EXAMPLE.COM</value>
  <description>
     Kerberos Realm used by Oozie and Hadoop. Using 'local.realm'
       to be aligned with Hadoop configuration
    </description>
</property>
```

```
<property>
   <name>oozie.service.HadoopAccessorService.keytab.file</name>
   <value>/my/keytab/path/oozie.service.keytab</value>
   <description>
      Location of the Oozie user keytab file.
   </description>
</property>

<property>
   <name>oozie.service.HadoopAccessorService.kerberos.principal</name>
   <value>oozie/fully.qualified.domain.name@EXAMPLE.COM</value>
   <description>
      Kerberos principal for Oozie service.
   </description>
</property>
```

After modifying the configuration, you need to restart the Oozie server using the commands `oozied.sh stop` and `oozied.sh start` . Make sure the service is up and running. In addition, you can open the file *logs/oozie.log* and look for the following type of log messages to confirm that Oozie to Hadoop security is configured correctly:

```
2014-09-11 20:17:21,907  INFO HadoopAccessorService:539 - USER[-] GROUP[-]
   Oozie Kerberos Authentication [enabled]
2014-09-11 20:17:22,338  INFO HadoopAccessorService:539 - USER[-] GROUP[-]
   Got Kerberos ticket, keytab /my/keytab/path/oozie.service.keytab], Oozie
   principal
    principal [oozie/fully.qualified.domain.name@EXAMPLE.COM]
```

When the Oozie server is up, you can submit any Oozie workflow with a Hadoop action to make sure that Oozie can submit jobs to a Kerberized Hadoop cluster.

Oozie Client to Server

As we have seen in the previous section, the Oozie server can act as a proxy for any user. This means that Hadoop services do not check the user's credentials if the job is submitted by the Oozie server. Although Hadoop services execute the job/request as the end user, they authenticate the Oozie service user's credential instead of the end user. Therefore it is very critical that the Oozie server authenticates any user's request before submitting the request to Hadoop.

You can configure the Oozie server to authenticate any Oozie client's request. This way, Oozie checks the client credentials only during job submission. After the submission, Oozie doesn't check the user's credential for any recurrent or delayed scheduling of Hadoop jobs. Both the Oozie server and the client need to take some steps to support this authentication. By default, Oozie supports Kerberos-based authentication between the client and the server. However, it is not unusual that some enterprises may prefer their custom authentication over Kerberos. Oozie supports this requirement through its pluggable authentication framework. Pluggable authentication is covered in Oozie's online documentation in detail. In this section, we cover Kerberos based HTTP authentication for the Oozie web server.

Oozie Server Security

The steps required to secure the Oozie server are very similar to what we followed in "Oozie to Hadoop" on page 155. We have to create a principal for Oozie's HTTP authentication and the corresponding `keytab` file.

Principal and keytab for HTTP: In the following example, we choose `HTTP/fully.qualified.domain.name` as the principal where `HTTP` is required. In addition, we append the corresponding encrypted password into the same `keytab` file, */my/keytab/path/oozie.service.keytab*, that we used in our previous example. Finally, we show the command to test the newly generated `keytab` and the principal:

```
$ kadmin
   Authenticating as principal $USER/admin@EXAMPLE.COM with password.
   Password for $user/admin@EXAMPLE.COM:
  kadmin:  add_principal -randkey HTTP/fully.qualified.domain.name
   WARNING: no policy specified for HTTP/fully.qualified.domain.name@EXAMPLE.COM;
     defaulting to no policy
   Principal "HTTP/fully.qualified.domain.name@EXAMPLE.COM" created.
  kadmin:  ktadd -k /my/keytab/path/oozie.service.keytab HTTP/
                   fully.qualified.domain.name
   Entry for principal HTTP/fully.qualified.domain.name with kvno 2,
    encryption type aes256-cts-hmac-sha1-96 added to keytab
    WRFILE:/my/keytab/path/
      oozie.service.keytab.
   Entry for principal HTTP/fully.qualified.domain.name with kvno 2,
    encryption type aes128-cts-hmac-sha1-96 added to keytab
    WRFILE:/my/keytab/path/oozie.service.keytab.
   Entry for principal HTTP/fully.qualified.domain.name with kvno 2,
    encryption type arcfour-hmac added to keytab
    WRFILE:/my/keytab/path/oozie.service.keytab.
  kadmin:  exit

$ klist -kt /my/keytab/path/oozie.service.keytab
  Keytab name: WRFILE:/my/keytab/path/oozie.service.keytab
  KVNO Timestamp         Principal
 ---- ----------------- --------------------------------------------------------
    2 09/17/14 00:00:59 oozie/fully.qualified.domain.name@EXAMPLE.COM
    2 09/17/14 00:00:59 oozie/fully.qualified.domain.name@EXAMPLE.COM
    2 09/17/14 00:00:59 oozie/fully.qualified.domain.name@EXAMPLE.COM
    2 09/17/14 00:06:27 HTTP/fully.qualified.domain.name@EXAMPLE.COM
    2 09/17/14 00:06:27 HTTP/fully.qualified.domain.name@EXAMPLE.COM
    2 09/17/14 00:06:27 HTTP/fully.qualified.domain.name@EXAMPLE.COM
```

Configuring the Oozie Server

After creating the keytab and the principal, we need to configure the Oozie server to turn on the Kerberos authentication for HTTP communication. After updating the *oozie-site.xml*, we need to restart the Oozie server to make sure the new properties take effect.

Some of the properties needed to support Kerberos authentication between Oozie server and Hadoop look similar to the ones needed for Oozie client-to-server authentication, which can be confusing. One easy way to distinguish these two is as follows: the property names related to Oozie server to Hadoop begin with `oozie.service.HadoopAccessorService` and the property names related to Oozie client to the server start with `oozie.authentication`.

Here's the code we'll need to use:

```
<property>
   <name>oozie.authentication.type</name>
   <value>kerberos</value>
   <description>
     Defines authentication used for Oozie HTTP endpoint.
     Supported values are: simple | kerberos |
     #AUTHENTICATION_HANDLER_CLASSNAME#
   </description>
</property>
<property>
   <name>oozie.authentication.kerberos.principal</name>
   <value> HTTP/fully.qualified.domain.name@EXAMPLE.COM </value>
   <description>
       Indicates the Kerberos principal to be used for HTTP endpoint.
       The principal MUST start with 'HTTP/' as per Kerberos HTTP SPNEGO
        specification.
   </description>
</property>
<property>
   <name>oozie.authentication.kerberos.keytab</name>
   <value/my/keytab/path/oozie.service.keytab </value>
   <description>
       Location of the keytab file with the credentials for the principal.
       Referring to the same keytab file Oozie uses for its Kerberos credentials
       for Hadoop.
     </description>
</property>
```

You might need to copy the property value of `hadoop.security.auth_to_local` from Hadoop's *core-site.xml* into a new property in *oozie-site.xml* called `oozie.authentication.kerberos.name.rules`. In addition, you might also need to add a new rule like `RULE:[2:$1/$2@$0](oozie/.*@EXAMPLE.COM)s/.*/oozie/` as part of its value.

Oozie client

The Oozie client needs to present a Kerberos credential for all its communications to a secure Oozie service. For the Oozie CLI, users typically use `kinit` to get the Kerberos ticket.

If you receive the following error message when you run an Oozie command, it means there is no Kerberos ticket in your environment:

```
Error: AUTHENTICATION :
  Could not authenticate, GSSException:
  No valid credentials provided (Mechanism level:
  Failed to find any Kerberos tgt)
```

You can verify it using `klist` and the following response will confirm the suspected root cause:

```
$ klist
klist: No credentials cache found (ticket cache FILE:
  /tmp/krb5cc_6053)â
```

The resolution is to execute the `kinit` command.

By default, Oozie CLI creates a *~/.oozie-auth-token* token file when you first execute the command with a Kerberos ticket. The subsequent Oozie commands use this token file instead of passing the Kerberos ticket. The user can turn it off by passing the `-Doozie.auth.token.cache=false` argument to the Oozie CLI command.

Oozie Web UI needs HTTP authentication and supports HTTP SPNEGO protocol for web authentication. Some browsers such as Firefox and Internet Explorer already support this type of authentication. Users need to configure their browsers by following the browser-specific instructions (more details can be found in the Hadoop documentation).

Proxy user in Oozie

Much like Hadoop, Oozie server also supports the proxy user facility for its users. In general, any service (e.g., Falcon) that acts as an Oozie client on behalf of its end user needs to be a proxy user to the Oozie service. For each proxy user, the Oozie administrator needs to add the following properties in *oozie-site.xml* and then restart the server (more details can be found in the Oozie documentation):

```
<property>
   <name>oozie.service.ProxyUserService.proxyuser.[OOZIE_USER].hosts</name>
   <value>*</value>
   <description>
      List of hosts the [OOZIE_USER] user is allowed to perform 'doAs'
      operations. The [OOZIE_USER] must be replaced with the username
      of the user who is allowed to perform 'doAs' operations.
      The value can be the '*' wildcard or a list of hostnames.
   </description>
</property>
<property>
   <name>oozie.service.ProxyUserService.proxyuser.[OOZIE_USER].groups</name>
   <value>*</value>
   <description>
      List of groups the [OOZIE_USER] user is allowed to impersonate users
      from to perform 'doAs' operations.
      The [OOZIE_USER] must be replaced with the username o the user who is
      allowed to perform 'doAs' operations. The value can be the '*'
      wildcard or a list of groups.
  </description>
</property>
```

Supporting Custom Credentials

Oozie schedules and executes workflows submitted by users. The workflow ultimately launches the job that communicates with various services in the Hadoop eco-system like the Hive meta-store, HBase service, and so on. For security purposes, each service might need a different type of credential (e.g., a Hadoop token, Hive meta-store token, etc.). These credentials are granted by the corresponding services. Each job needs to present the service-specific credentials (i.e., token) when contacting that service. But who should get the credentials and when? The obvious options are the end user during job submission or the Oozie server during job launch. As mentioned earlier, jobs often run long after the initial submission. During the submission, the end user can get the service token. But the service tokens will expire after some duration. That means the initial token can't be used for the job that runs past token expiration. So the better option is for Oozie to get the service token using Oozie's own credentials just before the launch of the workflow action.

Now that we understand why the job requires the service token and why Oozie must get it on behalf of end users, let's explain how Oozie knows the process/steps required to get any service credential, and which service credential it should get for a given workflow action. By default, Oozie gets and injects the Hadoop services credentials (RM token, HDFS token, etc.) into job conf and Oozie knows how to get them. For other service credentials, Oozie needs to know how to get the credential. The process to get the credential/token is different for each credential type. In other words, the steps required for a Hive meta-store token are different from the steps required for an HBase token.

Oozie provides a unified credential framework to get any custom credential. Oozie admins and users have some responsibilities to support any new credential injection. At first, the admin should specify the mapping in *oozie-site.xml* between the new credential type and the corresponding classes to get the credential. The following example shows how to configure a new credential type called `hive_metastore`, which utilizes the `HCatCredentials` class to gather the token. Admins can define multiple such pairs for other types of new credentials as well. The Apache Oozie documentation demonstrates how to write a new credential gathering class:

```
<property>
  <name>oozie.credentials.credentialclasses</name>
  <value>hive_metastore=org.apache.oozie.action.hadoop.HCatCredentials</value>
</property>
```

By default, Oozie includes two such credential classes, one for the Hive meta-store token and the other for the HBase service token. But they are not configured in the *oozie-site.xml* file by default. In addition, the admin will need to inject the required JARs into the Oozie WAR file to run these credential classes. For `HCatCredentials`, some of the Hive JARs must be included in the Oozie web application path.

Any credential class might need third-party JARs to gather the token from the service. For instance, the `HCatCredential` class needs Hive JARs to get the meta-store token. Without this, you might get the following exception: `java.lang.NoClassDefFoundError: org/apache/hadoop/hive/conf/HiveConf`. In this case, you will need to include `hive-*.jar` and `lib*.jar` from any standard Hive installation *lib/* directory into the *oozie.war* file. You can test it by copying the JARs into the *WEB-INF/lib/* directory of the Oozie web app and restarting the service.

After defining the system configuration, the next question is, how can a user ask Oozie to automatically get and inject this token into an action's configuration? Example 9-1 demonstrates such an action.

Example 9-1. Credentials section

```
<workflow-app xmlns="uri:oozie:workflow:0.2.5" name="hive-with-secirty-wf">
  <credentials>
    <credential name='metastore_token' type='hive_metastore'>
      <property>
        <name>hcat.metastore.uri</name>
        <value>thrift://my_metastore_server:port</value>
      </property>
```

```
      <property>
        <name>hcat.metastore.principal</name>
        <value>hive/fully.qualified.domain.name@EXAMPLE.COM</value>
      </property>
    </credential>
  </credentials>
  <start to="hive-query"/>
  <action name="hive-query" cred="metastore_token">
    <hive xmlns="uri:oozie:hive-action:0.2">
      <job-tracker>${jobTracker}</job-tracker>
      <name-node>${nameNode}</name-node>
      <job-xml>${hiveSite}</job-xml>
      <script>test_query.hql</script>
    </hive>
    <ok to="end"/>
    <error to="fail"/>
  </action>
</worklfow-app>
```

This feature is only supported starting with workflow XSD version 0.2.5. In other words, for the namespace, we should use `uri:oozie:workflow:0.2.5` or higher.

In this example, the user declares a new credential (`metastore_token`) with the necessary configuration to get the token for the credential type `hive_metastore`. This type (`hive_metastore`) needs to pass the two configuration settings (`hcat.metastore.uri` and `hcat.metastore.principal`) to the class (`HCatCredentials`) to get the token. Then the user specifies the name of the credential through the `cred` attribute (i.e., `cred=metastore_token"`) in the action definition. The `cred` attribute can accept a list of comma-separated credentials (i.e., `cred=metastore_token,hbase_cred"`). We summarize the execution steps here:

1. When Oozie sees any action with the `cred` attribute, it looks for and finds the corresponding credential definition with the same name. In this example, Oozie gets the credential definition from the `credentials` section using the name `metastore_token`.
2. Using the `type` attribute in the credential definition, Oozie finds out the corresponding credential class from *oozie-site.xml*.
3. Oozie then passes the configurations provided in the credential section of the workflow and executes the credential class. Note that these configurations are credential-type-specific and can be found in their respective documentations. After this execution, Oozie collects the meta-store service token.

4. At last, Oozie injects this token into the job configuration before submitting the Hive job.

Supporting New API in MapReduce Action

Hadoop supports two similar APIs to write and manage Hadoop MapReduce jobs. The first one is known as the old API or the `mapred` API and is packaged under the `org.apache.hadoop.mapred` package. The second one is known as the new API or the `mapreduce` API, which is included as part of the `org.apache.hadoop.mapreduce` package. MapReduce applications can be written using either API. As we saw earlier, the `<map-reduce>` action that comes with Oozie primarily supports mapper and reducer classes written using the old API out of the box. In this section, we describe a simple approach to run mapper and reducer classes that are written based on the new API using the basic `<map-reduce>` action type.

There is more than one way to use the new MapReduce API because Oozie allows customization at different levels. In the next chapter, we present another way to natively support jobs written using the new API in "Overriding an Asynchronous Action Type" on page 188. Alternatively, developers can also write a new, first-class, MapReduce action type to support the new API following the steps provided in "Creating a New Asynchronous Action" on page 193.

There are a few changes required to support an application using the new Hadoop API through the basic `<map-reduce>` action. We will adapt the MapReduce example written based on the old Hadoop API that comes with the Oozie distribution. We will need to make the following modifications:

- Replace the old API based `wordcount` MapReduce job with the new API based `wordcount` example that comes packaged with the Hadoop distribution. In other words, we need to add the Hadoop example JARs to the *lib/* directory of the workflow.
- Add two new configuration properties named `mapred.mapper.new-api` and `mapred.reducer.new-api` with both values set to `true`.
- Replace two configuration property names as follows: `mapred.map.class` to `mapreduce.map.class` and `mapred.reduce.class` to `mapreduce.reduce.class`.
- Add two new configuration properties: `mapred.output.key.class` and `mapred.output.value.class` with appropriate class names.

The modified *workflow.xml* is shown here:

```
<workflow-app xmlns="uri:oozie:workflow:0.5" name="map-reduce-wf">
  <start to="mr-node"/>
  <action name="mr-node">
  <map-reduce>
    <job-tracker>${jobTracker}</job-tracker>
    <name-node>${nameNode}</name-node>
    <prepare>
      <delete path=
       "${nameNode}/user/${wf:user()}/${examplesRoot}/output-data/${outputDir}"/>
    </prepare>
    <configuration>
      <property>
        <name>mapred.job.queue.name</name>
        <value>${queueName}</value>
      </property>
      <property>
        <name>mapred.mapper.new-api</name>
        <value>true</value>
      </property>
      <property>
        <name>mapred.reducer.new-api</name>
        <value>true</value>
      </property>
      <property>
        <name>mapreduce.map.class</name>
        <value>org.apache.hadoop.examples.WordCount$TokenizerMapper</value>
      </property>
      <property>
          <name>mapreduce.reduce.class</name>
          <value>org.apache.hadoop.examples.WordCount$IntSumReducer</value>
      </property>
      <property>
        <name>mapred.output.key.class</name>
        <value>org.apache.hadoop.io.Text</value>
      </property>
      <property>
        <name>mapred.output.value.class</name>
        <value>org.apache.hadoop.io.IntWritable</value>
      </property>
      <property>
        <name>mapred.map.tasks</name>
        <value>1</value>
      </property>
      <property>
        <name>mapred.input.dir</name>
        <value>/user/${wf:user()}/${examplesRoot}/input-data/text</value>
      </property>
      <property>
        <name>mapred.output.dir</name>
        <value>/user/${wf:user()}/${examplesRoot}/output-data/${outputDir}
        </value>
      </property>
```

```
    </configuration>
  </map-reduce>
  <ok to="end"/>
  <error to="fail"/>
 </action>
 <kill name="fail">
   <message>
    Map/Reduce failed, error message[${wf:errorMessage(wf:lastErrorNode())}]
   </message>
 </kill>
 <end name="end"/>
</workflow-app>
```

Supporting Uber JAR

The term *uber JAR* in this context refers to the Hadoop concept of the same name. In general, users package their application-specific custom classes into a JAR. Additionally, users might need a set of third-party JARs for their application. Hadoop provides a way to include an uber JAR that is comprised of the custom classes as well as the third-party JARs under the *lib/* subdirectory in the JAR. This is purely a convenience feature. This allows the user to include the uber JAR during Hadoop job submission. Hadoop understands this predefined directory structure and includes all the JARs from the *lib/* subdirectory of the uber JAR on to the application classpath.

When users are writing MapReduce code natively in Hadoop, this uber JAR has to be injected using the `conf.setJar()` call. The `setJar()` method in the Hadoop code is a way for the user to set a JAR for the MapReduce job. Oozie also allows this type of MapReduce jobs. To support this, the Oozie administrator has to turn on the feature through the *oozie-site.xml* as shown here (by default, this feature is turned off):

```
<configuration>
   <property>
      <name>oozie.action.mapreduce.uber.jar.enable</name>
      <value>true</value>
   </property>
</configuration>
```

For the workflow job, the user needs to copy the uber JAR into an HDFS location and then define the full HDFS path of the uber JAR through action configuration as shown here (when Oozie launches this MapReduce job, it injects the uber JAR on behalf of the user by calling the `conf.setJar()` method):

```
<map-reduce>
   <job-tracker>${jobTracker}</job-tracker>
   <name-node>${nameNode}</name-node>
   <configuration>
     <property>
       <name>oozie.mapreduce.uber.jar</name>
       <value>${MY_HDFS_PATH_TO_UBER_JAR}/my-uber-jar.jar</value>
```

```
    </property>
  </configuration>
</map-reduce>
```

This feature is only supported in Oozie through the pure `map-reduce` action. It doesn't work for pipe or streaming jobs. Moreover, this feature has a dependency on Hadoop version. The supported Hadoop versions are 1.2.0 or later and 2.2.0 or later.

Cron Scheduling

Oozie coordinator traditionally supports workflow executions at fixed time intervals. In other words, a user can schedule her workflow to run at a regular interval or frequency that can be expressed in minutes, hours, days, or years. This simple and essential feature covers a large number of prevalent use cases. We comprehensively covered this topic in Chapter 6.

While this fixed frequency-based scheduling is very popular, a substantial number of use cases don't follow this regular time pattern. For example, a user might want to schedule her job every hour only on Mondays and Wednesdays from 11 a.m. to 2 p.m. It can get very complicated and unmanageable to schedule and manage her workflow using Oozie's classic, frequency-based coordinator. Oozie addresses this requirement by borrowing from the cron concept, which is widely used in all Linux/Unix systems. In this section, we describe the cron syntax recently adopted by Oozie and how users can flexibly schedule their workflows using this feature.

A Simple Cron-Based Coordinator

Before explaining the details of cron in Oozie, we introduce the concept using a simple example. This example demonstrates how this new feature can be defined and used in the coordinator. We explain Oozie's actual cron specification in the following section.

This example is based on an earlier example in "An Improved Coordinator" on page 113. The original example schedules a workflow every hour of every day from the start time to end time. In this example, we modify the hourly rhythm to every hour from 11 a.m. to 2 p.m. only on Mondays and Wednesdays. Using the cron syntax, we can easily express this restriction by changing the value of the `frequency` attribute in the coordinator definition as shown here (the rest of the coordinator specification remains unchanged):

```
<coordinator-app name="my_second" start="${startTime}" end="${endTime}"
   frequency="0 11-14 * * MON,WED"  timezone="UTC"
   xmlns="uri:oozie:coordinator:0.4">
```

Let's try and broadly understand the example first. The frequency string is obviously different from the traditional coordinator syntax. The first "0" means the workflow will start at 0 minute of the hour and "11-14" limits the execution to the hours between 11 a.m. to 2 p.m. of a day. "MON,WED" means run on Mondays and Wednesdays only.

For instance, if we provide the `startTime` as `2014-07-04T02:00Z` during job submission, the first workflow will not start until July 7 because July 4, 5, and 6 are neither a Monday nor a Wednesday. More specifically, the nominal time of the first coordinator action would be `2014-07-07T11:00Z`. The nominal times of the next four workflow executions (actions 2 through 5) would be `2014-07-07T12:00Z`, `2014-07-07T13:00Z`, `2014-07-07T14:00Z`, and `2014-07-09T11:00Z` in order. In particular, there are two interesting variations to note from this list of nominal times:

- Although the user-defined start time is 2 a.m. on July 4, the first action doesn't materialize until 11 a.m. on July 7. In short, the coordinator will wait for nearly three days after its start time. In a classic frequency-based coordinator, the materialization begins as soon as the start time is hit.
- The fourth action was created for 2 p.m. on July 7. But the fifth one has to wait for nearly two days until July 9 to execute. This type of irregular execution is not possible using the traditional coordinator frequency specification.

Oozie Cron Specification

As discussed earlier, cron is a very powerful and flexible tool commonly used in Unix-like systems. Although the concept is widely understood, there are different variations of the basic cron syntax out there. Oozie's cron implementation is based on the `Quartz Scheduler`. In addition, Oozie has slightly tweaked the Quartz's cron specification to support its use cases. This section describes the details of Oozie's cron syntax using relevant examples. Even if you are an experienced cron user on Unix systems, we still recommend you take some time to review Oozie's cron syntax before using it.

Oozie's cron-based frequency definition is a string of five fields separated by white space. These five fields denote various time components such as `Minute`, `Hour`, `Day-of-Month`, `Month`, and `Day-of-Week`, in that order. Obviously, the missing unit is `seconds` because Oozie doesn't support second-level scheduling. In addition to allowing intuitive numerical or character values in each field, cron also supports special characters for additional flexibility. Table 9-1 and the subsequent examples, adapted from the Apache Oozie documentation, help clarify the concept.

Table 9-1. Oozie's cron syntax

Field name	Allowed values	Allowed special chars
Minute	0-59	Commas (,), dashes (-), asterisks, and slashes (/)
Hour	0-23	Commas (,), dashes (-), asterisks, and slashes (/)
Day of Month	1-31	Commas (,), dashes (-), asterisks, question marks (?), slashes (/), and the letters "L" and "W"
Month	1-12 or JAN-DEC	Commas (,), dashes (-), asterisks, and slashes (/)
Day of Week	1-7 or SUN-SAT	Commas (,), dashes (-), asterisks, question marks (?), slashes (/), hash tags (#), and the letter "L"

Allowed values

The `Allowed Values` in the table above for each field are self-explanatory and similar to other cron specifications, with one exception. While most cron syntaxes support the range 0-6 for the Day of Week field, Oozie supports the values 1-7 instead. Also, each field can have one or more values where multiple values are expressed using special characters described in the next two sections.

Special characters

As shown in Table 9-1, commas (,), dashes (-), asterisks, and slashes (/) are accepted in every field and relatively easy to understand. On the other hand, question marks (?), hash tags (#), and the letters "L" and "W" are used in fewer fields and require careful attention. Let's take a closer look at the standard characters (we cover the nonstandard characters `?LW#` in the next section):

Asterisk (*)
: An asterisk denotes any valid value for the field. For instance, an asterisk (*) in the hour field means Oozie must execute the workflow *every* hour of a day. The user can define a complete frequency string as "* * * * *". This means the workflow will start every minute of every hour of every day between the start and end time.

Comma (,)
: A comma allows users to indicate a list of values in any field. For instance, "2,7,14" in the hour field means the 2, 7, and 14 hour of a day. The frequency string `15` **`2,7,14`** `* * *` tells Oozie to start a workflow at 2:15, 7:15, and 14:15 of each day.

Dash (-)
: A dash describes a range of values in any field. In general, users specify it with a start and an end of a range (both inclusive). For example, "MON-FRI" in the `Day-of-Week` field restricts the valid days to Monday through Friday (both inclusive). Extending the previous example, `15 2,7,14 *` **`FEB-APR`** `*` means start a

workflow at 2:15, 7:15, and 14:15 of each day of the months February, March, and April.

Slash (/)

A slash in any field indicates an increment value for that field. As the continuation of the previous example, **15/30** `2,7,14 * FEB-APR *`, tells Oozie to start the workflow at 2:15, 2:45, 7:15, 7:45, 14:15, and 14:45 of each day of the months February, March, and April. A value of 15/30 in the minute field translates to minute 15 and minute 45 of the hour, as 30 is the increment (15 + 30 = 45). In another example, **15/30** `2/10 * FEB-APR *`, means start the workflow at 2:15, 2:45, 12:15, 12:45, 22:15, and 22:45 of each day of the months February, March, and April.

Nonstandard special characters

Question mark ("?")

The question mark can only be used in the `Day-of-Week` or `Day-of-Month` field. If you want to specify one but not the other among these two fields, you can specify "?" in the field that's not needed. For example, if you want to run a workflow on the 25th of the month (defined using `Day-of-Month`) but you don't care about the `Day-of-Week`, you can specify it as follows: `15 2,7,14` **25** `FEB-APR` **?**. This says start the workflow at 2:15, 7:15, and 14:15 of the 25th day of the months February, March, and April. Alternatively, `15 2,7,14` **?** `FEB-APR` **FRI** tells Oozie to start the workflow at 2:15, 7:15, and 14:15 of each Friday of the months February, March, and April.

Letter "L"

The letter "L" can also be specified only in the `Day-of-Week` or `Day-of-Month` field. It signifies the last day of a week or the last day of a month. For instance, `15 2,7 ? FEB-APR` **L** means start a workflow at 2:15, and 7:15 of the last day of the week (i.e., Saturday) of the months February, March, and April. In a similar example, `0/15 2` **L** `FEB-APR ?` means start a workflow at 2:00 and 2:15 of the last day of the months February, March, and April.

Letter "W"

The letter "W" is only allowed in the `Day-of-Month` field. It refers to the nearest weekday *closest* to a given day. A number usually precedes "W". For instance, "10W" in the `Day-of-Month` field denotes the closest workday to the 10th day of a month. If 10th day is a Tuesday, the workflow will start that Tuesday. However, if the 10th is a Sunday, the workflow will start on Monday, the 11th. If the 10th day of the month is Saturday, the workflow will start on the previous Friday, the 9th.

Hash (#)

This is only allowed in the Day-of-Week filed. In general, it is preceded and followed by a number. For example, 5#4 in Day-of-Week field denotes the 4th Thursday (5th day of the week) of each month.

Apart from this list, there are lots of examples in the Quartz Scheduler documentation that Oozie's cron implementation is loosely based on. We also suggest taking a look at the examples provided in Oozie's documentation.

Emulate Asynchronous Data Processing

Oozie currently supports synchronous data processing. The coordinator basically executes the workflow at regular interval when all of the dependent data is available. This covers a lot of the common use cases. However, there are some use cases that depend on data rather than time. In other words, these use cases require the workflow to be run as soon as some data is available irrespective of the time. Additionally, the dependent data may also be produced at random time intervals without following any regular frequency. Basically, the data could arrive at any time. It may be available in the next five minutes or it may take five more days. Supporting these asynchronous use cases has been in Oozie's wish list for a long time. It's worth noting that the recent addition of support for table-based data dependency described in "HCatalog-Based Data Dependency" on page 174 will make it easier to support such asynchronous processing in future versions of Oozie. Since support for asynchronous processing is not implemented yet at the time of writing this book, we present a rather quick-and-dirty workaround to emulate some aspects of an asynchronous coordinator using the synchronous coordinator.

This is one way of accomplishing this requirement through Oozie, but may not be the most efficient approach. Readers should consider all options, including custom code to implement this logic, as this particular approach can be overkill for some use cases.

The basic idea is to frequently spawn coordinator actions, which will check for data. If the data is available, the workflow will be run. Otherwise, the action will end up in the TIMEDOUT state. In essence, we use a mix of time and data dependency to emulate pure data dependency. However, there are some preconditions required for implementing this approach:

- You need to know the shortest or the most frequent interval when the dependent data can potentially be available. For example, if the range for data being produced is every five minutes to once every five days, the minimum possible frequency is five minutes. We will use this as the value for the rest of our example.

- The dependent dataset should be stored in a directory with the timestamp as part of the HDFS path. And the timestamps of the batch directories should align with the minimum frequency. Even if the actual data creation time doesn't fit the frequency, it should be stored in the directory corresponding to the nearest frequency batch. For example, if minimum frequency is five minutes, the data should be stored under a directory like */tmp/data/$YEAR-$MONTH-$DAY-$HOUR-**05**/*, */tmp/data/$YEAR-$MONTH-$DAY-$HOUR-**10**/*, or */tmp/data/$YEAR-$MONTH-$DAY-$HOUR-**55**/*.

It's important to understand some of the consequences of this approach. If the data is only rarely produced, but the selected minimum frequency is very small, there may be a lot of coordinator actions that aren't doing any work in the system. The action will be created and check for data availability for a `timeout` period of time, and then will end up in `TIMEDOUT` state. For example, if you select a frequency of five minutes and the dependent data doesn't arrive for an entire day, Oozie might end up creating 288 short-lived coordinator actions that don't perform any effective work.

Another important factor is to determine the value of the `timeout` parameter for the coordinator. A very high `timeout` value will keep multiple coordinator actions simultaneously active in the system and that can increase the load and the stress on the Oozie server. For example, if the minimum frequency is five minutes and the `timeout` is one hour, there could be 12 active actions in the system at any time. On the other hand, a very small `timeout` value can cause the action to timeout before the data arrives if the data is even slightly delayed. For example, if the data for 12:05 p.m. comes late to HDFS (say at 12:15 p.m.) and you are running the coordinator with a `timeout` value of five minutes, the coordinator action corresponding to 12:05 p.m. will timeout at 12:10 p.m. This will result in the data from 12:05 p.m. not getting processed at all. In general, a good `timeout` value is usually two or three times the value of the minimum frequency.

Example 9-2 demonstrates how to implement this approach.

Example 9-2. Asynchronous coordinator

```
$ cat coordinator.xml
 <coordinator-app name="SIMULATED_ASYNC_COORD" frequency="${frequency}"
    start="${start}" end="${end}" xmlns="uri:oozie:coordinator:0.4">
   <controls>
    <timeout>10</timeout>
   </controls>
   <datasets>
     <dataset name="simulated_dataset" frequency="${min_frequency}"
        initial-instance="${start}" timezone="${timezone}"> <uri-template>
        hdfs://localhost:8020/tmp/data/${YEAR}/${MONTH}/
        ${DAY}/${HOUR}/${MINUTE}</uri-template>
     </dataset>
```

```
  </datasets>
  <input-events>
    <data-in name="ds_event" dataset=" simulated_dataset ">
      <instance>${coord:current(0)}</instance>
    </data-in>
  </input-events>
  <action>
    <workflow>
      <app-path>hdfs://localhost:8020/${AppBaseDir}/mapreduce/ </app-path>
    </workflow>
  </action>
</coordinator-app>
```

```
$ cat coord-job.properties
  AppBaseDir= hdfs://localhost:8020/user/joe/examples/
  oozie.coord.application.path= hdfs://localhost:8020/user/joe/examples/
    simulated-coord
  frequency=5
  min_frequency=5
  timeout=10
  start=2014-07-30T23:00Z
  end=2014-08-30T23:00Z
  ds_start=2014-07-30T20:00Z
```

HCatalog-Based Data Dependency

As we described in Chapter 7, the Oozie coordinator allows the user to specify HDFS-directory-based data dependency. In this case, when the dependent data is available, Oozie triggers the associated workflow. For each active coordinator action, Oozie periodically checks the HDFS for data availability until the `timeout` period is reached. However, this approach has the following challenges:

- Since Oozie is polling HDFS regularly, it creates a lot of load on the Hadoop NameNode. Although this may be fine for most small- to medium-sized systems, larger systems with a lot of active coordinators can destabilize the `NameNode`.
- This polling-based approach increases the processing load on the Oozie server as well, which can potentially slow down the progress of other jobs and impact Oozie's scalability.
- Due to the polling interval, the workflow might not be started as soon as the dependent dataset is available. For example, if the polling interval is configured to be five minutes, Oozie can be late by as much as five minutes in launching the workflow. In short, longer polling intervals can potentially delay the workflow launch and shorter intervals increases the load on the Oozie server and the Hadoop `NameNode`.

Due to these reasons, the Oozie community has always been interested in some sort of a push model for data availability checks (instead of polling). In particular, Oozie needs to get notified asynchronously as soon as the data is available. HCatalog is a table and storage management layer for HDFS data that can be leveraged by Oozie to eliminate frequent polling. Its table abstraction provides a relational view of data in HDFS. HCatalog also offers JMS based notification as soon as any new data/partition is registered with HCatalog. Oozie exploits these notifications to trigger the workflows to avoid HDFS polling. In summary, Oozie provides two approaches for data triggers:

- HDFS-data-directory-based dependency which is implemented using polling
- HCatalog-table/partition-based data dependency using push notifications.

Although a table/partition-based approach is better, it requires the following additional work:

- HCatalog should be installed in the Hadoop cluster.
- The data producers need to write the data through HCatalog in addition to the conventional HDFS write. It might require some development effort from the data producers to adopt this new approach.
- A JMS-based messaging system such as ActiveMQ should be installed to transmit the notifications.

The pieces listed here are all external to Oozie. In addition, the Oozie installation needs to follow a few extra steps to support table/partition-based data dependency that can be found in the HCatalog configuration.

We present this new paradigm at a very high level in Figure 9-2. From the user's perspective, the main change is to specify a new HCatalog URI for dataset definition in the Oozie coordinator XML. Like HDFS, Oozie supports a similar pattern in URI definition for HCatalog. One such dataset definition is presented here:

```
<dataset name="hcat_dataset" frequency="${coord:days(1)}"
    initial-instance="2009-02-15T08:15Z" timezone="America/Los_Angeles">
  <uri-template>
     hcat://myhcatmetastore:9080/database1/table1/datestamp=${YEAR}
    ${MONTH}${DAY}${HOUR};region=USA
  </uri-template>
</dataset>
```

The key differences in URI definition between directory-based and table-based approaches are as follows.

- HCatalog-based URI uses `hcat` in place of `hdfs` as scheme name.
- It uses the Hive metastore server endpoint, replacing the `NameNode` server.

- HCatalog implements traditional database concepts, which means it can have multiple tables. In turn, each table can have multiple partitions that are defined using partition key-value pairs. In this example, `datestamp` and `region` are two partition keys that identify one logical partition.

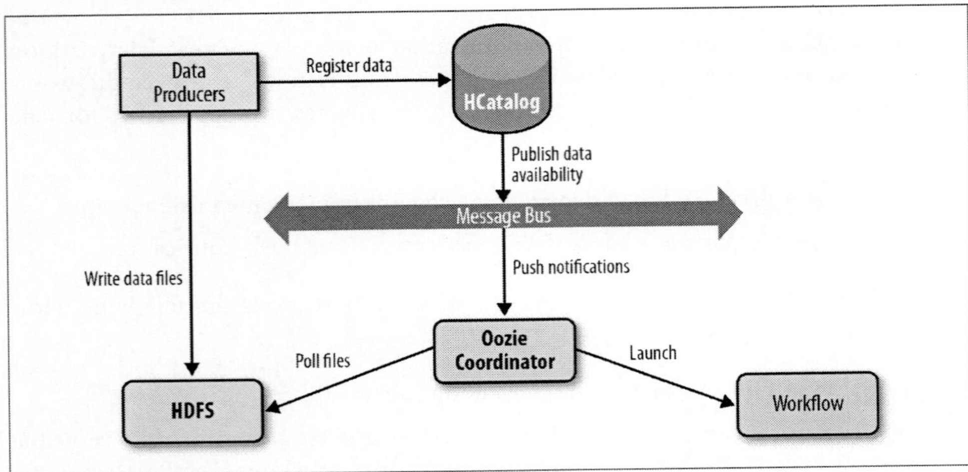

Figure 9-2. Oozie coordinator interactions with HDFS, HCatalog, and Message Bus to support data triggers

This feature is still maturing, but is important for very large and heavily loaded systems (further explanation and usage information can be found in the Apache Oozie documentation).

In this chapter, we covered a few advanced use cases and features of the Oozie workflow and coordinator. We mainly explained Oozie's user and system JAR management and security features. Additionally, we introduced a cron-like scheduling mechanism using the coordinator and explained HCatalog integration with Oozie.

CHAPTER 10

Developer Topics

In previous chapters, we primarily focused on how to use and manage Oozie efficiently. We explained the details of the Oozie service and the various features it supports. Oozie users and administrators were the target audience for those chapters. In this chapter, we cover Oozie from a developer's perspective. In particular, we discuss how to leverage Oozie's extensible framework to expand and broaden its feature set. We see how to add custom EL functions and how to develop new synchronous and asynchronous action types.

Developing Custom EL Functions

The parameterization framework of Oozie enables users to easily build reusable and manageable applications. This feature includes variable substitution and EL functions for workflows, coordinators, and bundles. We discussed this in detail in "Parameterization" on page 86. More specifically, Oozie provides a bunch of built-in EL functions for most of the common use cases. However, users often feel the need for EL functions for new or special use cases. The parameterization framework of Oozie is extensible and allows the addition of new functions with minimal effort. In this section, we describe the steps needed to add an EL function.

Requirements for a New EL Function

Before deciding to write a new EL function, users must first determine whether it is even a good idea to develop a new function. It is highly recommended that the new EL function be simple, fast, and robust. This is critical because Oozie executes the EL functions on the Oozie server. A poorly written function can add unnecessary overhead to the server and threaten Oozie's stability. Also, if the function runs for a long time, it could slow down the Oozie server.

In general, the new function should not perform any resource-intensive operation or be dependent on external systems and services. For these types of requirements, users are advised to use either the Java or shell action defined in "Java Action" on page 52 and "Shell Action" on page 67 instead of an EL function. After due consideration, if it is still determined that implementing a new EL function is the right way to go, it's important that the user makes sure the function is robust, stable, reviewed, and tested. For instance, it will be highly inconvenient if an Oozie application fails due to an unhandled exception caused by some edge case in the new EL function.

Typically, the Oozie administrator in the organization has to approve any new EL function. The Oozie web application archive (*oozie.war*) should contain the new JAR supporting the new EL function. In most organizations, it would be necessary for the administrator to help inject the new JAR into the Oozie server and to configure it accordingly. An Oozie server restart is also required to make the new EL function available. In other words, end users cannot write and deploy their own EL functions without the help of the Oozie administrator.

Implementing a New EL Function

In this section, we describe how to develop and deploy a new EL function into Oozie. We also present a workflow demonstrating the usage of the new EL function.

Writing a new EL function

Oozie doesn't require users to implement a specific interface or extend a particular base class in order to write a new EL function. However, the function should be a `public static` method in a Java class. For example, let's implement a basic utility method to tokenize a string using a specific pattern and return a token at a particular position.

The following Java code shows a sample implementation. We need to compile and package this class into a JAR file (say *oozie-custom-el.jar*):

```
package com.oreilly.oozie.customel;

public class CustomELFunctions {
  public static String splitAndGet(String str, String expr, int pos) {
    if(str == null || expr == null || pos < 0) {
      return null;
    }
    String[] splitArr = str.split(expr, pos + 1);
    if(splitArr.length <= pos) {
      return null;
    }
    return splitArr[pos];
  }
}
```

Deploy the new EL function

To deploy the new EL function on the Oozie server, we need to inject the JAR created in the previous step. The ideal way to do this is to follow the steps described in "Install Oozie Server" on page 26. The only additional step is to copy the custom JAR (*oozie-custom-el.jar*) to the *libext/* directory before executing the command `bin/oozie-setup.sh prepare-war`.

Next, we need to configure the Oozie server by adding these lines to the *conf/oozie-site.xml* file. The property `oozie.service.ELService.ext.functions.workflow` must include all maps of the extended EL function to the associated class and method. Multiple map entries are separated by commas. The following example shows how to add the new function `splitAndGet` to the Oozie system:

```
<property>
  <name>oozie.service.ELService.ext.functions.workflow</name>
  <value>
    splitAndGet=com.oreilly.oozie.customel.CustomELFunctions#splitAndGet
  </value>
  <description>
    EL functions declarations, separated by commas, format is
     [PREFIX:]NAME=CLASS#METHOD. This property is a convenience
     property to add extensions to the built in executors without
     having to include all the built in ones.
  </description>
</property>
```

An optional prefix can be added to the function name in the declaration to help organize the functions into logical groups. For example, we could have used `custom:splitAndGet` as the name. If you choose to use this optional prefix, you'll need to use it in your *workflow.xml* file as well.

After including the JAR and updating the configuration, we need to restart the Oozie server. Alternatively, in the development phase, we can short-circuit the JAR injection and *oozie.war* file re-creation. For testing purposes, we can directly copy the JAR into the *WEB-INF/lib* directory. But we still need to update the configuration and restart the Oozie server.

If users want to support any new EL function at the coordinator level, they need to modify the coordinator-specific property in the *oozie-site.xml* file. Check the *oozie-default.xml* file for more details on a variety of coordinator related properties available to support such extensions.

Using the new function

Now that we have seen how a developer can implement a new function and how an administrator can add it to the Oozie server, we will see how any user on the system can use this EL function in her workflow definition. We borrowed the following example from the `java-main` example that comes with the Oozie distribution. We have added the line `<arg>${splitAndGet("I Installed Apache Oozie!", " ", 2)}</arg>` here to demonstrate the usage of the new EL function. In this example, the EL function returns `Apache` and that is passed as the second argument to the Java main class:

```
<workflow-app xmlns="uri:oozie:workflow:0.5" name="java-main-wf">
   <start to="java-node"/>
   <action name="java-node">
   <java>
     <job-tracker>${jobTracker}</job-tracker>
     <name-node>${nameNode}</name-node>
     <configuration>
       <property>
         <name>mapred.job.queue.name</name>
         <value>${queueName}</value>
       </property>
     </configuration>
     <main-class>org.apache.oozie.example.DemoJavaMain</main-class>
     <arg>Hello</arg>
     <arg>${splitAndGet("I Installed Apache Oozie!", " ", 2)}</arg>
   </java>
   <ok to="end"/>
   <error to="fail"/>
  </action>
  <kill name="fail">
    <message>Java failed, error message[${wf:errorMessage(wf:lastErrorNode())}]
    </message>
  </kill>
  <end name="end"/>
</workflow-app>
```

Supporting Custom Action Types

Oozie provides a set of common action types, which we described in "Action Types" on page 43. Depending on how Oozie executes an action, the workflow actions are broadly divided into two categories, synchronous and asynchronous, as explained in "Synchronous Versus Asynchronous Actions" on page 73. Oozie executes the synchronous action on the Oozie server and blocks the execution thread until it completes. In this model, each execution instance of the action shares resources with the Oozie server and impacts Oozie's performance. Moreover, there is no isolation between the execution of Oozie's services and the execution of the action, which can potentially destabilize the Oozie server. So adding a new synchronous action type is highly discouraged. Users should consider adding it only if the action is simple, runs for a very short period of time, and doesn't execute any user code.

On the other hand, Oozie starts an asynchronous action and immediately returns without waiting for the action to finish. The actual action execution occurs outside the Oozie server on the Hadoop compute nodes. When the spawned action completes, it informs Oozie through a callback. The asynchronous execution model guarantees isolation between the action, which can run user code, and the execution of Oozie's core services. So the recommended way of writing a heavy-duty action is to use the asynchronous model. In this section, we cover how to write both types of actions.

Creating a Custom Synchronous Action

Let's now look at the steps required to support a new synchronous action type. The first step is to write a new `action executor` followed by writing an XML schema (XSD) file for the new action. We should then deploy the new action type onto the Oozie server through the *oozie-site.xml*. Finally, we will show how to write and submit a test workflow using the new action type.

In this example, we will implement a new synchronous action that can execute a SQL statement against any MySQL instance. The output of the SQL can either be stored in a local file on the Oozie server machine or written to `stdout`.

Note that this is merely an example to demonstrate the required steps to write a new synchronous action. Ideally, this specific kind of action should not be a synchronous type.

Writing an ActionExecutor

Every action executor class should extend Oozie's `ActionExecutor` class, which is part of Oozie's core package. Developers should then implement the following methods required by Oozie:

Constructor
: Action developers need to write a no-arg constructor that ultimately calls the super-class constructor passing the new action name (e.g., `super("syncMysql")`). End users will use this name to define the new action type in the workflow XML.

start(ActionExecutor.Context context, Action action)
: Oozie invokes this method when it needs to execute the action. Oozie passes two parameters to this method. The first parameter `context` provides the APIs to access all workflow configurations/variables for this action, set the action status, and return any data to be used in the execution path. The second parameter

`action` includes the action's definition from the workflow XML. All synchronous actions must override this method because this method performs the actual execution. At the end, the method needs to call `context.setExecutionData(externalStatus, actionData)` to pass back the action status and any action-specific data.

check(ActionExecutor.Context context, Action action)
: Oozie calls this method to check the action status. For synchronous actions, Oozie does not need or call this method. Therefore, for this example, it's recommended this method just throw an `UnsupportedOperationException`.

kill(ActionExecutor.Context context, Action action)
: Oozie executes this method when it needs to kill the action for any reason. Typical implementation of this method calls `context.setEndData(status, signalValue)`, passing `Action.Status.KILLED` as the status and `ERROR` as the signalValue.

end(ActionExecutor.Context context, Action action)
: Oozie invokes this method when the execution is finished. In this method, the action executor should perform any cleanup required after completion. The implementation usually calls `context.setEndData(status, signalValue)`. The status and signal value determine the next course of action.

isCompleted(externStatus)
: This utility method is used to determine if an action status is in a terminal state.

These methods are required for Oozie to run any action. Additionally, we implement two new methods for this specific action: `runMySql()` to execute the SQL and `writeResultSet()` to store the output into a file. As mentioned earlier, the `start()` method is the entry point for the execution of a synchronous action. At the very beginning of this method, we need to retrieve the action's definition and parse it using an XML parser. The actual schema of the action definition is defined in the action's XSD file, which we discuss in the next section:

```
public class MySQLSyncActionExecutor extends ActionExecutor {

   private static final String SYNC_MYSQL_ACTION_NS =
                                   "uri:oozie:sync-mysql-action:0.1";
   private static final String ACTION_NAME = "syncMysql";

   protected MySQLSyncActionExecutor() {
     super(ACTION_NAME);
   }

   @Override
   public void start(Context context, WorkflowAction action)
     throws ActionExecutorException {
```

```
      context.setStartData("-", "-", "-");
      try {
        Element actionXml = XmlUtils.parseXml(action.getConf());
        Namespace ns = Namespace.getNamespace(SYNC_MYSQL_ACTION_NS);

        String jdbcUrl = actionXml.getChildTextTrim("jdbcUrl", ns);
        String sql = actionXml.getChildTextTrim("sql", ns);
        String sqlOutputFilePath = actionXml.getChildTextTrim(
          "sql_output_file_path", ns);
        runMysql(jdbcUrl, sql, sqlOutputFilePath);
          context.setExecutionData("OK", null);
      } catch (JDOMException e) {
        throw convertException(e);
      }
  }

  @Override
  public void end(Context context, WorkflowAction action)
    throws ActionExecutorException {
    if (action.getExternalStatus().equals("OK")) {
      context.setEndData(WorkflowAction.Status.OK,
      WorkflowAction.Status.OK.toString());
    } else {
      context.setEndData(WorkflowAction.Status.ERROR,
      WorkflowAction.Status.ERROR.toString());
    }
  }

  @Override
  public void kill(Context context, WorkflowAction action)
    throws ActionExecutorException {
    context.setEndData(WorkflowAction.Status.KILLED, "ERROR");
  }

  @Override
  public void check(Context arg0, WorkflowAction arg1)
    throws ActionExecutorException {
    throw new UnsupportedOperationException();
  }

  private static Set<String> COMPLETED_STATUS = new HashSet<String>();
    static {
      COMPLETED_STATUS.add("SUCCEEDED");
      COMPLETED_STATUS.add("KILLED");
      COMPLETED_STATUS.add("FAILED");
      COMPLETED_STATUS.add("FAILED_KILLED");
    }

  @Override
  public boolean isCompleted(String externalStatus) {
    return COMPLETED_STATUS.contains(externalStatus);
  }
```

```
/*
* Execute a sql statement
*/
private void runMysql(String jdbcUrl, String sql, String sqlOutputFilePath)
  throws ActionExecutorException {
  Connection connect = null;
  Statement statement = null;
  ResultSet resultSet = null;
  try {
    // this will load the MySQL driver, each DB has its own driver
    Class.forName("com.mysql.jdbc.Driver");
    // setup the connection with the DB.
    connect = DriverManager.getConnection(jdbcUrl);
    // statements allow to issue SQL queries to the database
    statement = connect.createStatement();
    // resultSet gets the result of the SQL query
    resultSet = statement.executeQuery(sql);
    writeResultSet(resultSet, sqlOutputFilePath);
  } catch (Exception e) {
    throw convertException(e);
  } finally {
    try {
      if (resultSet != null)
        resultSet.close();
      if (statement != null)
        statement.close();
      if (connect != null)
        connect.close();
    } catch (Exception e) {
      throw convertException(e);
    }
  }
}

private void writeResultSet(ResultSet resultSet, String sqlOutputFilePath)
  throws Exception {
  // resultSet is initialised before the first data set
  PrintWriter out;
  if (sqlOutputFilePath != null && sqlOutputFilePath.length() > 0) {
    out = new PrintWriter(sqlOutputFilePath);
  } else {
    out = new PrintWriter(System.out);
  }
  // Get the metadata
  ResultSetMetaData md = resultSet.getMetaData();
  // Loop through the result set
  while (resultSet.next()) {
    for (int i = 1; i <= md.getColumnCount(); i++) {
      out.println(md.getColumnName(i) + "=" + resultSet.getString(i));
    }
  }
```

```
    out.close();
    }
}
```

The compilation of any action executor class requires at least two Oozie JARs: *oozie-core* and *oozie-client*. The JARs for the most recent versions (starting with version 4.1.0) are published in a Maven repository. If for some reason it is not available, developers will need to get the JARs by building the Oozie source code themselves.

Writing the XML schema

A schema file is required for strict enforcement of the XML syntax of the action definition that the user writes in her *workflow.xml* file. The details of writing a good XML schema can be found online. The following example XSD file is self-explanatory and very similar to any other Oozie action:

```
<?xml version="1.0" encoding="UTF-8"?>
   <xs:schema xmlns:xs="http://www.w3.org/2001/XMLSchema"
     xmlns:sync-mysql="uri:oozie:sync-mysql-action:0.1"
     elementFormDefault="qualified"
     targetNamespace="uri:oozie:sync-mysql-action:0.1">

     <xs:complexType name="SYNC_MYSQL_TYPE">
      <xs:sequence>
       <xs:element name="jdbcUrl" type="xs:string" minOccurs="1" maxOccurs="1"/>
       <xs:element name="sql" type="xs:string" minOccurs="1" maxOccurs="1"/>
       <xs:element name="sql_output_file_path" type="xs:string" minOccurs="0"
         maxOccurs="1"/>
      </xs:sequence>
     </xs:complexType>
     <xs:element name="syncMysql" type="sync-mysql:SYNC_MYSQL_TYPE"/>
   </xs:schema>
```

Readers might remember that some standard Oozie actions like "Java Action" on page 52 and "Shell Action" on page 67 support an element called `<capture-output>` that can be used to pass the output back to the Oozie context. The example action shown here writes the results to an output file (in the `writeResultSet()` function) and does not support the `<capture-output>` feature. This is the right approach for this particular action given that the output generated could be large and not suitable for passing between actions. But developers can implement `<capture-output>` in their custom actions if the use case demands it. The key steps in supporting this feature are to generate the output in a properties file format and write it to a file defined by the system property `oozie.action.output.properties`. Refer to the code sample in "Java Action" on page 52 to see how to implement it (do remember to include the

`<capture-output>` element in the schema just explained if you want your action to support it).

Deploying the new action type

After we develop the code and the XSD file, we have to compile the code and package them both into a JAR file. The XSD file should be at the root level of the new JAR file. Since the preceding code uses the MySQL JDBC APIs to run the query, we would need the `mysql-connector` JAR during compilation and execution. Compilation can use either the IDE's external classpath or the build file to access the JAR. The MySQL JAR can even be included as part of the new JAR we are creating. We can then inject both the JARs (or one "fat" JAR) when creating the Oozie WAR file ("Install Oozie Server" on page 26). The newly created JAR and the MySQL JAR must be copied into the *libext/* directory before executing the `bin/oozie-setup.sh prepare-war` command. However, for testing purposes, we can bypass these standard steps and directly copy the JARs into *$CATALINA_BASE/webapps/oozie/WEB-INF/lib/*.

Next, we need to configure *oozie-site.xml* to enable Oozie to use the new action type. There are two key properties to configure. The property `oozie.service.ActionService.executor.ext.classes` specifies a comma-separated list of new executor classes. For this example, we should append `com.oreilly.oozie.sync.customaction.MySQLSyncActionExecutor` to that list. The `oozie.service.SchemaService.wf.ext.schemas` property defines the additional schema files required for new actions. For this example, we add *sync_mysql-0.1.xsd*. After all these configuration changes, the Oozie server needs to be restarted as always:

```
<property>
  <name>oozie.service.ActionService.executor.ext.classes</name>
  <value>
    org.apache.oozie.action.email.EmailActionExecutor,
    org.apache.oozie.action.hadoop.HiveActionExecutor,
    org.apache.oozie.action.hadoop.ShellActionExecutor,
    org.apache.oozie.action.hadoop.SqoopActionExecutor,
    org.apache.oozie.action.hadoop.DistcpActionExecutor,
    com.oreilly.oozie.sync.customaction.MySQLSyncActionExecutor
  </value>
</property>

<property>
  <name>oozie.service.SchemaService.wf.ext.schemas</name>
  <value>
    shell-action-0.1.xsd,shell-action-0.2.xsd,shell-action-0.3.xsd,
    email-action-0.1.xsd, hive-action-0.2.xsd,hive-action-0.3.xsd,
    hive-action-0.4.xsd,hive-action-0.5.xsd,sqoop-action-0.2.xsd,
    sqoop-action-0.3.xsd,sqoop-action-0.4.xsd,ssh-action-0.1.xsd,
    ssh-action-0.2.xsd,distcp-action-0.1.xsd,distcp-action-0.2.xsd,
    oozie-sla-0.1.xsd,oozie-sla-0.2.xsd, sync_mysql-0.1.xsd
```

```
    </value>
  </property>
```

Using the new action type

Once the new action is deployed, it's time to verify it. We will use the following simple *workflow.xml* to test it. The goal here is to execute an SQL query and write the output to a local file on the Oozie server. The corresponding *job.properties* file is shown here as well. This job assumes that the MySQL server is configured and running properly. Let's also assume that a database named `oozie_book` and a table named `income` are already in place with the right schema and a few records. The name of the DB, login, password, and the table are all defined in the *job.properties* file. The output directory for this Oozie job is configured as *$OOZIE_HOME/my_sync_sqloutput.txt*. Again, this is just an example and a synchronous action is not the best approach for an operation like this:

```
<workflow-app xmlns="uri:oozie:workflow:0.4" name="sync-mysql-wf">
   <start to="sync-mysql-node"/>
   <action name="sync-mysql-node">
      <syncMysql xmlns="uri:oozie:sync-mysql-action:0.1">
         <jdbcUrl>${jdbcURL}</jdbcUrl>
         <sql>${sql}</sql>
         <sql_output_file_path>${SQL_OUTPUT_PATH}</sql_output_file_path>
      </syncMysql>
      <ok to="end"/>
      <error to="fail"/>
   </action>
   <kill name="fail">
      <message>syncMysql failed, error message
         [${wf:errorMessage(wf:lastErrorNode())}]
      </message>
   </kill>
   <end name="end"/>
</workflow-app>

$ cat job.properties
 nameNode=hdfs://localhost:8020
 queueName=default
 examplesRoot=examples

   oozie.wf.application.path=${nameNode}/user/${user.name}/${examplesRoot}/apps/
 sync_mysql
 oozie.use.system.libpath=true
 jdbcURL=jdbc:mysql://localhost:3306/oozie_book?user=oozie_book_user&
 password=oozie_book_pw
 sql=select count(*) from oozie_book.income;
 SQL_OUTPUT_PATH=my_sync_sqloutput.txt
```

Overriding an Asynchronous Action Type

Let's quickly recap Oozie's execution model as described in "Action Execution Model" on page 40. For an asynchronous action, Oozie submits a launcher mapper task to Hadoop along with all the required JARs and configuration for executing the actual action. In particular, there are two important classes involved in executing any asynchronous action in Oozie. The class derived from `ActionExecutor` submits the launcher job to Hadoop. It also includes the required JARs and configuration for the actual action. `ActionExecutor` uses Hadoop's distributed cache to pass the JARs and configuration to the correct compute node. The launcher job ultimately starts a single map task that is implemented by Oozie to execute any action type. This mapper is widely known as the `LauncherMapper`.

The map task (`LauncherMapper`) invokes the `main()` method of the action execution class that runs on the compute node. This class is known as `LauncherMain`. Different action types extend this class to create their own main class that executes action-specific code. For example, the `PigMain` class runs the Pig script and `MapReduceMain` submits the actual MapReduce job. In this section, we discuss how to override these Main classes. Users can write these custom main classes to override the default implementation and package them with their application. This doesn't require any modification on the server side of Oozie. The content in this section will help us understand the next section, where we describe how to write a new asynchronous action from the ground up using the `ActionExecutor` and the associated main class.

The out-of-the-box `<map-reduce>` action supports only the old Hadoop API . In other words, it supports mapper and reducer classes written using the *mapred* (old) API. However, there is a way to use the new `mapreduce` API for the Hadoop job using some special configuration as described in "Supporting New API in MapReduce Action" on page 165. There is also another way to execute a MapReduce job that's written using the new API by overriding the default Main class of the `<map-reduce>` action. In this example, we will see how to replace the old API-based job submission with the new API.

Implementing the New ActionMain Class

As explained earlier, the default `<map-reduce>` main class (`MapreduceMain`) supports executing jobs that are written using `org.apache.hadoop.mapred` package, also known as the old API. In this example, we will create a new main class called `MapReduceNewMain` that submits jobs written using the new API (`org.apache.hadoop.mapreduce`). However, we will still use the default `<map-reduce>` action executor. This allows the users to use the existing `<map-reduce>` action type with minimal changes. This implementation is completely in the user domain and this change doesn't require any modification or restart of the Oozie server. The user can simply replace the original Main class with the new one during job submission.

The implementation of the `MapReduceNewMain` class below is based on the existing `MapreduceMain` class. A lot of boilerplate code is borrowed from the exiting implementation. The main difference is to use the new mapreduce API for job submission. In particular, we replace the `JobClient` class with the `Job` class and the `JobConf` with the `Configuration` class. The complete implementation is shown here:

```
package com.oreilly.oozie.custommain;

import org.apache.hadoop.conf.Configuration;
import org.apache.hadoop.fs.Path;
import org.apache.hadoop.mapreduce.Job;
import org.apache.oozie.action.hadoop.LauncherMain;

import java.util.HashSet;
import java.util.Map;
import java.util.Properties;
import java.io.IOException;
import java.io.FileOutputStream;
import java.io.OutputStream;
import java.io.File;


public class MapReduceNewMain extends LauncherMain {

public static final String OOZIE_MAPREDUCE_UBER_JAR =
   "oozie.mapreduce.uber.jar";

public static void main(String[] args) throws Exception {
  run(MapReduceNewMain.class, args);
}

protected void run(String[] args) throws Exception {
  System.out.println();
  System.out.println("Oozie Map-Reduce action configuration");
  System.out.println("=======================");

  // Loading the action conf prepared by Oozie
  // This is the same action configuration defined in the workflow
  // XML file as pat of the <configuration> section.
  Configuration actionConf = new Configuration(false);
  actionConf.addResource(new Path("file:///", System
   .getProperty("oozie.action.conf.xml")));

  logMasking("New Map-Reduce job configuration:", new HashSet<String>(),
     actionConf);

   System.out.println("Submitting Oozie action Map-Reduce job");
```

```
    System.out.println();
    // submitting job
    Job job = submitJob(actionConf);
    System.out.println("After job submission");
    // propagating job id back to Oozie
    String jobId = job.getJobID().toString();
    System.out.println("Job ID is :" + jobId);
    Properties props = new Properties();
    props.setProperty("id", jobId);
    File idFile = new File(
    System.getProperty("oozie.action.newId.properties"));
    OutputStream os = new FileOutputStream(idFile);
    props.store(os, "");
    os.close();

    System.out.println("======================");
    System.out.println();
  }

  protected void addActionConf(Configuration conf, Configuration actionConf) {
   for (Map.Entry<String, String> entry : actionConf) {
     conf.set(entry.getKey(), entry.getValue());
   }
  }

  protected Job submitJob(Configuration actionConf) throws Exception {
    Configuration conf = new Configuration();
    addActionConf(conf, actionConf);

   // Propagate delegation related props from the launcher job to the MR job.
   // This is critical on secure Hadoop where delegation tokens
   // will be made available through these settings.
    if (System.getenv("HADOOP_TOKEN_FILE_LOCATION") != null) {
      conf.set("mapreduce.job.credentials.binary",
      System.getenv("HADOOP_TOKEN_FILE_LOCATION"));
    }
    Job job = null;
    try {
      job = createJob(conf);
      job.submit();
    } catch (Exception ex) {
      throw ex;
    }
    return job;
  }

  protected Job createJob(Configuration conf) throws IOException {
    @SuppressWarnings("deprecation")
    Job job = new Job(conf);
    // Set for uber Jar
    String uberJar = conf.get(OOZIE_MAPREDUCE_UBER_JAR);
    if (uberJar != null && uberJar.trim().length() > 0) {
```

```
            job.setJar(uberJar);
        }
        return job;
    }

}
```

Testing the New Main Class

After we compile the new main class and package it into a JAR file, we are ready to test this new functionality. The following *workflow.xml* defines the mapper and reducer written using the new `mapreduce` API. Readers are advised to pay close attention to the property names corresponding to the new API in addition to the `oozie.launcher.action.main.class`. This workflow is based on the `wordcount` example that comes with the Hadoop distribution:

```
<workflow-app xmlns="uri:oozie:workflow:0.5" name="map-reduce-wf">
  <start to="mr-node"/>
  <action name="mr-node">
    <map-reduce>
      <job-tracker>${jobTracker}</job-tracker>
      <name-node>${nameNode}</name-node>
      <prepare>
        <delete path="${nameNode}/user/${wf:user()}/${examplesRoot}/
           output-data/${outputDir}"/>
      </prepare>
      <configuration>
        <!-- Using a custom MapReduceMain for new API class-->
        <property>
          <name>oozie.launcher.action.main.class</name>
          <value>com.oreilly.oozie.custommain.MapReduceNewMain</value>
        </property>
        <property>
          <name>mapreduce.job.queuename</name>
          <value>${queueName}</value>
        </property>
        <property>
          <name>mapreduce.job.map.class</name>
          <value>org.apache.hadoop.examples.WordCount$TokenizerMapper</value>
        </property>
        <property>
          <name>mapreduce.job.reduce.class</name>
          <value>org.apache.hadoop.examples.WordCount$IntSumReducer</value>
        </property>
        <property>
          <name>mapreduce.job.output.key.class</name>
          <value>org.apache.hadoop.io.Text</value>
        </property>
        <property>
          <name>mapreduce.job.output.value.class</name>
```

```
            <value>org.apache.hadoop.io.IntWritable</value>
          </property>
          <property>
            <name>mapreduce.input.fileinputformat.inputdir</name>
            <value>/user/${wf:user()}/${examplesRoot}/input-data/text</value>
          </property>
          <property>
            <name>mapreduce.output.fileoutputformat.outputdir</name>
            <value>/user/${wf:user()}/${examplesRoot}/output-data/${outputDir}
            </value>
          </property>
        </configuration>
      </map-reduce>
      <ok to="end"/>
      <error to="fail"/>
    </action>
    <kill name="fail">
      <message>Map/Reduce failed, error message[${wf:errorMessage
      (wf:lastErrorNode())}]</message>
    </kill>
    <end name="end"/>
</workflow-app>
```

Next we need to include the required JARs in the workflow *lib/* directory. We need to copy the JAR that includes `MapReduceNewMain` class. As always, we also need to copy the JAR that includes the mapper (`TokenizerMapper`) and reducer (`IntSumReducer`) classes. Since we reuse the Apache Hadoop example, we have to copy the hadoop-mapreduce-examples JAR into the *lib/* directory to be able to run this example:

```
$ hdfs dfs -put my-custom-main
$ hdfs dfs -lsr my-custom-main
  -rw-r--r--   1 joe jgrp    172 2014-11-15 14:48 my-custom-main/job.properties
  drwxr-xr-x   - joe jgrp      0 2014-11-15 14:48 my-custom-main/lib
  -rw-r--r--   1 joe jgrp 270261 2014-11-15 14:48 my-custom-main/lib/hadoop-
     mapreduce-examples-2.3.0.jar
  -rw-r--r--   1 joe jgrp  19949 2014-11-15 14:48 my-custom-main/lib/
     oozie-extensions.jar
  -rw-r--r--   1 joe jgrp   2452 2014-11-15 14:48 my-custom-main/workflow.xml
```

We will use the following *job.properties* file and commands to run the workflow:

```
$cat job.properties
   nameNode=hdfs://localhost:8020
   #Actually RM endpoint for Hadoop 2.x
   jobTracker=localhost:8032
   queueName=default

   oozie.wf.application.path=${nameNode}/user/${user.name}/my-custom-main
   outputDir=map-reduce-new

$ oozie job -config job.properties -run
   job: 0000001-141115153201961-oozie-joe-W
```

Creating a New Asynchronous Action

In this section, we discuss the steps required to develop a completely new asynchronous action. Most of the steps are already discussed in the previous two sections and we tweak them to develop a new action type. In "Creating a Custom Synchronous Action" on page 181, we described how to implement a synchronous action. In short, we created a new `ActionExcutor`, a new XSD file, and then ultimately deployed it on the Oozie server. Then, in "Overriding an Asynchronous Action Type" on page 188, we explained the steps required to override the `ActionMain` of an existing asynchronous action. To be more specific, the previous example only overrides the `ActionMain` class that runs on the compute node. It doesn't modify the `ActionExecutor` that runs on the Oozie server and is responsible for launching the `LauncherMapper`.

Writing an Asynchronous Action Executor

The asynchronous action executor usually extends the `JavaActionExecutor` that comes with the `oozie-core` package. Most of the common functionalities are already implemented in the `JavaActionExecutor`. This important class basically packages the required classes (e.g., `ActionMain` class) and configuration and kicks off the launcher job on Hadoop. It also passes the JARs and configuration to the launcher mapper through the Hadoop distributed cache. The launcher mapper ultimately invokes the `main()` method of the `ActionMain` class. The `main()` method implements the actual action such as executing a Pig script for the `<pig>` action.

Any action executor that extends `JavaActionExecutor` needs to be implemented under the `org.apache.oozie.action.hadoop` package, though the code can reside outside the Oozie code base. This is required because of a bug/constraint in the `JavaActionExecutor` class where some of the required methods are declared with "*package*" scope instead of "*protected*". So any derived class needs to be under the same package name.

Here we implement the same use case of executing a MySQL query that we described in "Creating a Custom Synchronous Action" on page 181 but using an asynchronous action:

```
package org.apache.oozie.action.hadoop;

import java.util.List;

import org.apache.hadoop.conf.Configuration;
import org.apache.hadoop.fs.Path;
import org.apache.oozie.action.ActionExecutorException;
import org.apache.oozie.action.hadoop.JavaActionExecutor;
import org.apache.oozie.action.hadoop.LauncherMain;
```

```
import org.apache.oozie.action.hadoop.LauncherMapper;
import org.apache.oozie.action.hadoop.MapReduceMain;
import org.jdom.Element;
import org.jdom.Namespace;

public class MySQLActionExecutor extends JavaActionExecutor {

  private static final String MYSQL_MAIN_CLASS_NAME =
    "org.apache.oozie.action.hadoop.MySqlMain";
  public static final String JDBC_URL = "oozie.mysql.jdbc.url";
  public static final String SQL_COMMAND = "oozie.mysql.sql.command";
  public static final String SQL_OUTPUT_PATH = "oozie.mysql.sql.output.path";

  public MySQLActionExecutor() {
   super("mysql");
  }

  @Override
  protected List<Class> getLauncherClasses() {
    List<Class> classes = super.getLauncherClasses();
      classes.add(LauncherMain.class);
      classes.add(MapReduceMain.class);
      try {
        classes.add(Class.forName(MYSQL_MAIN_CLASS_NAME));
      } catch (ClassNotFoundException e) {
        throw new RuntimeException("Class not found", e);
      }
    return classes;
  }

  @Override
  protected String getLauncherMain(Configuration launcherConf,
    Element actionXml) {
    return launcherConf.get(LauncherMapper.CONF_OOZIE_ACTION_MAIN_CLASS,
      MYSQL_MAIN_CLASS_NAME);
  }

  @Override
  @SuppressWarnings("unchecked")
  Configuration setupActionConf(Configuration actionConf, Context context,
    Element actionXml, Path appPath) throws ActionExecutorException {
    super.setupActionConf(actionConf, context, actionXml, appPath);
    Namespace ns = actionXml.getNamespace();

    String sql = actionXml.getChild("sql", ns).getTextTrim();
    String jdbcUrl = actionXml.getChild("jdbcUrl", ns).getTextTrim();
    String sqlOutPath = actionXml.getChild("sql_output_file_path", ns)
      .getTextTrim();

    actionConf.set(JDBC_URL, jdbcUrl);
    actionConf.set(SQL_COMMAND, sql);
    actionConf.set(SQL_OUTPUT_PATH, sqlOutPath);
```

```
    return actionConf;
  }

  @Override
  protected String getDefaultShareLibName(Element actionXml) {
    return "mysql";
  }
}
```

In the preceding class, the constructor just calls its super-class constructor passing the new action name (i.e., `mysql`). This name is what will be used as an action type when the user writes the workflow definition. The method `getLauncherClasses` returns the list of classes required to be executed by the launcher mapper. Oozie server makes these classes available to the launcher mapper through the distributed cache. It includes the `LauncherMain` base class and the actual action main class (`MySqlMain`, described next). The `MapReduceMain` class is included only to support a few utility methods.

The method `getLauncherMain` returns the `ActionMain` class (`org.apache.oozie.action.hadoop.MySqlMain`). The launcher map code calls the `main()` method of this class. The `setupActionConf` method adds the configuration that is passed to the `ActionMain` class through a configuration file. The last method `getDefaultShareLibName` returns the name of the subdirectory under the system `sharelib` directory. This subdirectory hosts most of the JARs required to execute this action. In this example, the *mysql-connector-java-*.jar* file needs to be copied to the *mysql/* subdirectory under the `sharelib` directory.

Writing the ActionMain Class

This example implements the same MySQL use case described in "Implementing the New ActionMain Class" on page 188. The main difference is that this action is asynchronous while the previous example implemented a synchronous action. The `main` class in this example reuses most of the MySQL query execution code from the previous example:

```
package org.apache.oozie.action.hadoop;

import java.io.BufferedWriter;
import java.io.File;
import java.io.OutputStreamWriter;
import java.sql.Connection;
import java.sql.DriverManager;
import java.sql.ResultSet;
import java.sql.ResultSetMetaData;
import java.sql.Statement;

import org.apache.hadoop.conf.Configuration;
import org.apache.hadoop.fs.FileSystem;
```

```
import org.apache.hadoop.fs.Path;
import org.apache.oozie.action.hadoop.LauncherMain;
import org.apache.oozie.action.hadoop.LauncherSecurityManager;

public class MySqlMain extends LauncherMain {

  public static void main(String[] args) throws Exception {
    run(MySqlMain.class, args);
  }

  protected void run(String[] args) throws Exception {
    System.out.println();
    System.out.println("Oozie MySql action configuration");
    System.out
     .println("==============================================");
    // loading action conf prepared by Oozie
    Configuration actionConf = new Configuration(false);

    String actionXml = System.getProperty("oozie.action.conf.xml");
    if (actionXml == null) {
      throw new RuntimeException(
       "Missing Java System Property [oozie.action.conf.xml]");
    }
    if (!new File(actionXml).exists()) {
      throw new RuntimeException("Action Configuration XML file ["
       + actionXml + "] does not exist");
    }

    actionConf.addResource(new Path("file:///", actionXml));
    String jdbcUrl = actionConf.get(MySQLActionExecutor.JDBC_URL);
    if (jdbcUrl == null) {
      throw new RuntimeException("Action Configuration does not have "
        + MySQLActionExecutor.JDBC_URL + " property");
    }

    String sqlCommand = actionConf.get(MySQLActionExecutor.SQL_COMMAND);
    if (sqlCommand == null) {
      throw new RuntimeException("Action Configuration does not have "
       + MySQLActionExecutor.SQL_COMMAND + " property");
    }

    String sqlOutputPath = actionConf
      .get(MySQLActionExecutor.SQL_OUTPUT_PATH);
    if (sqlOutputPath == null) {
      throw new RuntimeException("Action Configuration does not have "
       + MySQLActionExecutor.SQL_OUTPUT_PATH + " property");
    }

    System.out.println("Mysql coomands :" + sqlCommand + " with JDBC url :"
      + jdbcUrl + " sqlOutputPath " + sqlOutputPath);
    System.out
     .println("=====================================================");
```

```
    System.out.println();
    System.out.println(">>> Connecting to MySQL and executing sql now >>>");
    System.out.println();
    System.out.flush();

    try {
      runMysql(jdbcUrl, sqlCommand, sqlOutputPath);
    } catch (SecurityException ex) {
      if (LauncherSecurityManager.getExitInvoked()) {
        if (LauncherSecurityManager.getExitCode() != 0) {
          throw ex;
        }
      }
    }

    System.out.println();
    System.out.println("<<< Invocation of MySql command completed <<<");
    System.out.println();
  }

  public void runMysql(String jdbcUrl, String sql, String sqlOutputPath)
    throws Exception {
    Connection connect = null;
    Statement statement = null;
    ResultSet resultSet = null;
    try {
      // this will load the MySQL driver, each DB has its own driver
      Class.forName("com.mysql.jdbc.Driver");
      // setup the connection with the DB.
      System.out.println("JDBC URL :" + jdbcUrl);
      connect = DriverManager.getConnection(jdbcUrl);

      // statements allow to issue SQL queries to the database
      statement = connect.createStatement();
      // resultSet gets the result of the SQL query
      resultSet = statement.executeQuery(sql);
      writeResultSet(resultSet, sqlOutputPath);
    } finally {
      if (resultSet != null)
        resultSet.close();
      if (statement != null)
        statement.close();
      if (connect != null)
        connect.close();
    }
  }

  private void writeResultSet(ResultSet resultSet, String sqlOutputFilePath)
    throws Exception {
    Configuration configuration = new Configuration();
    Path outPath = new Path(sqlOutputFilePath);
```

```
        BufferedWriter out = null;
        FileSystem fs = null;
        try {
         fs = outPath.getFileSystem(configuration);
         if (fs.exists(outPath)) {
          fs.delete(outPath, true);
         }
         fs.mkdirs(outPath);
         Path outFile = new Path(outPath, "sql.out");
         System.out.print("Writing output to :" + outFile);
         out = new BufferedWriter(new OutputStreamWriter(fs.create(outFile),
          "UTF-8"));

         // Get the metadata
         ResultSetMetaData md = resultSet.getMetaData();
         int recNo = 1;
         // Loop through the result set
         while (resultSet.next()) {
           out.write("Record_No=" + recNo++ + ",");
           for (int i = 1; i <= md.getColumnCount(); i++) {
             out.write(md.getColumnName(i) + "="
               + resultSet.getString(i) + ",");
           }
           out.write('\n');
         }
        } finally {
          if (out != null) {
            out.close();
          }
          if (fs != null) {
            fs.close();
          }
        }
      }
    }
```

The ActionMain class MySqlMain is derived from the LauncherMain class. The run() method actually executes the MySQL query. All of the user-defined properties defined in the *workflow.xml* are passed to MySqlMain class through a file. The action configuration filename is also passed as a system property called oozie.action.conf.xml. After loading the configuration, the main class executes the query and stores the result into the HDFS file passed in as a job property. Alternatively, users can implement and use Oozie's capture-output feature explained in "Java Action" on page 52.

The ActionMain class requires a Hadoop token if it wants to communicate to any service (such as NameNode, JobTracker/Resource Manager) running with Kerberos security enabled. The ActionMain class will need to pass the location of the token file with property name mapreduce.job.credentials.binary in job configuration as shown in the example code in "Implementing the New ActionMain Class" on page 188. If a user wants to pass other kinds of credentials such as Hive meta-store or HBase token, she can follow the instructions provided in "Supporting Custom Credentials" on page 162.

Writing Action's Schema

The XSD file defined in this section is very similar to the one in "Writing the XML schema" on page 185:

```
<?xml version="1.0" encoding="UTF-8"?>
  <xs:schema xmlns:xs="http://www.w3.org/2001/XMLSchema"
  xmlns:mysql="uri:oozie:mysql-action:0.1" elementFormDefault="qualified"
  targetNamespace="uri:oozie:mysql-action:0.1">

  <xs:complexType name="MYSQL_TYPE">
    <xs:sequence>
      <xs:element name="job-tracker" type="xs:string" minOccurs="1"
              maxOccurs="1"/>
      <xs:element name="name-node" type="xs:string" minOccurs="1"
              maxOccurs="1"/>
      <xs:element name="job-xml" type="xs:string" minOccurs="0"
              maxOccurs="unbounded"/>
      <xs:element name="configuration" type="mysql:CONFIGURATION"
              minOccurs="0" maxOccurs="1"/>
      <xs:element name="jdbcUrl" type="xs:string" minOccurs="1" maxOccurs="1"/>
      <xs:element name="sql" type="xs:string" minOccurs="1" maxOccurs="1"/>
      <xs:element name="sql_output_file_path" type="xs:string" minOccurs="1"
              maxOccurs="1"/>
      <xs:element name="file" type="xs:string" minOccurs="0"
              maxOccurs="unbounded"/>
      <xs:element name="archive" type="xs:string" minOccurs="0"
              maxOccurs="unbounded"/>
    </xs:sequence>
  </xs:complexType>
  <xs:complexType name="CONFIGURATION">
    <xs:sequence>
      <xs:element name="property" minOccurs="1" maxOccurs="unbounded">
        <xs:complexType>
         <xs:sequence>
           <xs:element name="name" minOccurs="1" maxOccurs="1" type="xs:string"/>
           <xs:element name="value" minOccurs="1" maxOccurs="1" type="xs:string"/>
           <xs:element name="description" minOccurs="0" maxOccurs="1"
                 type="xs:string"/>
```

```
        </xs:sequence>
      </xs:complexType>
    </xs:element>
   </xs:sequence>
  </xs:complexType>
  <xs:element name="mysql" type="mysql:MYSQL_TYPE"/>
</xs:schema>
```

Deploying the New Action Type

The deployment of a new asynchronous action is very similar to the synchronous action described in "Deploying the new action type" on page 186. If written outside of the Oozie's code base, the first step is to create a JAR that includes `MySqlActionExecutor`, `MySqlMain`, and the *mysql-0.1.xsd* file. Then include this JAR in the Oozie WAR file. After that, we modify the *conf/oozie-site.xml* file to include the new action executor and the new XSD file as shown here:

```
<property>
  <name>oozie.service.ActionService.executor.ext.classes</name>
  <value>
    org.apache.oozie.action.email.EmailActionExecutor,
    org.apache.oozie.action.hadoop.HiveActionExecutor,
    org.apache.oozie.action.hadoop.ShellActionExecutor,
    org.apache.oozie.action.hadoop.SqoopActionExecutor,
    org.apache.oozie.action.hadoop.DistcpActionExecutor,
    org.apache.oozie.action.hadoop.MySQLActionExecutor
  </value>
</property>

<property>
  <name>oozie.service.SchemaService.wf.ext.schemas</name>
  <value>
    shell-action-0.1.xsd,shell-action-0.2.xsd,shell-action-0.3.xsd,
    email-action-0.1.xsd,hive-action-0.2.xsd, hive-action-0.3.xsd,
    hive-action-0.4.xsd,hive-action-0.5.xsd,sqoop-action-0.2.xsd,
    sqoop-action-0.3.xsd,sqoop-action-0.4.xsd,ssh-action-0.1.xsd,
    ssh-action-0.2.xsd,distcp-action-0.1.xsd,distcp-action-0.2.xsd,
    oozie-sla-0.1.xsd,oozie-sla-0.2.xsd,mysql-0.1.xsd
  </value>
</property>
```

If the new action is developed under the Oozie code-base, most of these steps are not required. Those files will then be automatically included as part of the standard Oozie build and the deployment process.

In addition, we need to upload the MySQL JAR into the `sharelib` directory using the following commands (and then restart the Oozie server; also note that commands must be executed by the Oozie service user—that is, (*oozie*):

```
$ hdfs dfs -mkdir share/lib/mysql
$ hdfs dfs -put  ./oozie-server/webapps/oozie/WEB-INF/lib/\
  mysql-connector-java-5.1.25-bin.jar share/lib/mysql/
$ bin/oozied.sh stop
$ bin/oozied.sh start
```

Using the New Action Type

We follow the same steps explained in "Using the new action type" on page 187 to build a workflow that uses the new `mysql` action. The relevant *workflow.xml* and *job.properties* files are shown here:

```
$ cat workflow.xml
  <workflow-app xmlns="uri:oozie:workflow:0.4" name="my-mysql-wf">
    <start to="my-mysql-node"/>
    <action name="my-mysql-node">
      <mysql xmlns="uri:oozie:mysql-action:0.1">
        <job-tracker>${jobTracker}</job-tracker>
        <name-node>${nameNode}</name-node>
        <jdbcUrl>${jdbcURL}</jdbcUrl>
        <sql>${sql}</sql>
        <sql_output_file_path>${SQL_OUTPUT_PATH}</sql_output_file_path>
      </mysql>
      <ok to="end"/>
      <error to="fail"/>
    </action>
    <kill name="fail">
      <message>mysql failed, error message[${wf:errorMessage
      (wf:lastErrorNode())}]</message>
    </kill>
    <end name="end"/>
  </workflow-app>

$ cat job.propeeties
  nameNode=hdfs://localhost:8020
  jobTracker=localhost:8032
  queueName=default
  examplesRoot=examples

  oozie.wf.application.path=${nameNode}/user/${user.name}/${examplesRoot}/
                  apps/mysql
  oozie.use.system.libpath=true
  jdbcURL=jdbc:mysql://localhost:3306/oozie_book?user=oozie_book_user&
                  password=oozie_book_pw
  sql=select * from oozie_book.custom_actions;
  SQL_OUTPUT_PATH=my_sqloutput
```

It's fairly common to see failures with the following exception in the launcher mapper log:

```
Failing Oozie Launcher, Main class
[org.apache.oozie.action.hadoop.MySqlMain], main() threw
exception, com.mysql.jdbc.Driver
java.lang.ClassNotFoundException: com.mysql.jdbc.Driver at
java.net.URLClassLoader$1.run(URLClassLoader.java:202)
```

This is most likely due to missing JARs. In this example, the mysql-connecor JAR was not copied into the *mysql/* subdirectory under the `sharelib` on HDFS. Uploading the correct version of JARs to the correct location will solve this problem.

In this chapter, we focused on Oozie developers and showed how to extend current Oozie functionalities. More specifically, we elaborated on the steps required to write a custom EL function, a new synchronous action type, and a new asynchronous action type. In the next chapter, we will cover the operational aspects of Oozie and other sundry topics concerning managing and debugging Oozie.

CHAPTER 11
Oozie Operations

We covered all the functional aspects of Oozie in Chapters 4 through 8. We learned how to write workflows, coordinators, and bundles, and mastered the fundamentals of Oozie. Chapters 9 and 10 covered advanced topics like security and developer extensions. In this final chapter, we will cover several operational aspects of Oozie. We will start with the details of the Oozie CLI tool and the REST API. We will look at the Oozie server and explore some tips on administering and tuning it for better stability and performance. We will also cover typical operational topics like retry and reprocessing of Oozie jobs. Last but not the least, we will look at debugging techniques and resolutions for some common failures. We will also sprinkle in a few topics that are useful but don't quite fit in any of the previous chapters.

Oozie CLI Tool

The primary interface for managing and interacting with Oozie is `oozie`, the command-line utility that we have used throughout this book (e.g., to submit jobs, check their status, kill them, etc.). Internally, it actually uses Oozie's web service (WS) API, which we will look at in detail in the next section. The CLI is available on the Oozie client node, which is also typically the Hadoop edge node with access to all the Hadoop ecosystem CLI clients and tools like Hadoop, Hive, Pig, Sqoop, and others. This edge node is also usually configured to talk to and reach the Hadoop cluster, Hive meta-store, and the Oozie server. The Oozie client only needs to talk to the Oozie server and it's the server's responsibility to interact with the Hadoop cluster.

Consequently, the CLI has an `-oozie` option that lets you specify the location of the server, which is also the end point for reaching the Oozie server's web service. The CLI also takes the Unix environment variable `OOZIE_URL` as the default value for the server. It's convenient and recommended to define this environment variable on the Oozie client machine to save yourself the effort of passing in the `-oozie` with every command you type on the Unix terminal. Example 11-1 shows how to invoke the CLI command with and without the environment variable. This option lists all the jobs in the system.

The CLI executable `oozie` is available in the *bin/* subdirectory under the oozie client deployment directory. For the remainder of this chapter, we will assume we have the `oozie` executable available in our Unix path and we will skip the absolute path in our examples for invoking the CLI.

Example 11-1. Using the OOZIE_URL environment variable

```
$ oozie jobs -oozie http://oozieserver.mycompany.com:11000/oozie
...

$ export OOZIE_URL=http://oozieserver.mycompany.com:11000/oozie
$ oozie jobs
...
```

The Oozie CLI tool can be finicky when it comes to the order of the arguments. This is a common issue with a lot of the CLI tools in the Hadoop ecosystem. So if you get some unexplained `invalid command` errors, always pay attention to the sequence of the arguments in your command line. For instance, with this example, you might get different results with `oozie jobs -oozie <URL>` and `oozie -oozie <URL> jobs`.

In addition to the `OOZIE_URL` environment variable, `OOZIE_TIMEZONE` and `OOZIE_AUTH` are two other variables that can make using the CLI tool easier, though most users don't need it as often as the server URL.

CLI Subcommands

The `oozie` CLI tool is feature rich and supports a lot of options. It's covered extensively in the Oozie documentation.These options are organized into many subcommands. The subcommands are logical groupings of the different actions and options that the CLI supports, and are listed here (some of these have only one command option that serves one specific function, while the others have several options):

`oozie version`
: Prints client version

`oozie job`
: All job-related options

`oozie jobs`
: Bulk status option

`oozie admin`
: Admin options that deal with server status, authentication, and other related details

`oozie validate`
: Validate the job XML

`oozie sla`
: SLA-related options

`oozie info`
: Print detailed info on topics like supported time zone

`oozie mapreduce`
: Special option to submit standalone MapReduce jobs via Oozie

`oozie pig`
: Special option to submit standalone Pig jobs via Oozie

`oozie hive`
: Special option to submit standalone Hive jobs via Oozie

`oozie help`
: Get help on the CLI and its subcommands

Users can also get help on the CLI tool or specific subcommands by typing in the following commands on the Oozie client machine's Unix terminal.

```
$ oozie help
$ oozie help job
$ oozie help sla
```

Useful CLI Commands

In this section, we will touch on some of the more useful and interesting CLI commands that can make the user's life easier. We will assume that the `OOZIE_URL` is set up appropriately in our environment and hence skip the `-oozie` option in all of the CLI examples we cover the rest of the way.

The validate subcommand

One of the primary complaints about Oozie is that the code-test-debug cycle can be a little complicated with too many steps. Specifically, every time the job XML is modified, it has to be copied to HDFS and users often forget this step and end up wasting a lot of time. Even if they remember to do it, these steps can get annoyingly repetitive if they find errors in the XML after executing the workflow and have to fix the XML and iterate a few times to get it right. The `validate` command can be used to do some basic XML validation on the job file before copying it to HDFS. This won't catch all the errors in the job definition, but it is definitely recommended for every job XML file that users write. Although this only catches some basic syntax errors in the XML, it can and will save some time:

```
$ oozie validate my_workflow.xml
$ oozie validate my_coordinator.xml
```

The job subcommand

The most commonly used CLI options are for submitting and checking the status of jobs as we have seen in earlier chapters. The CLI has been designed for simplicity, and it doesn't matter whether the job in question is a workflow, coordinator, or a bundle; the command tends to be the same. Following are the CLI commands to submit a job (`-submit`) or to submit and run it in one shot (`-run`). The job ID is returned as shown here if the command succeeds:

```
$ oozie job -config ./job.properties -submit
job: 0000006-130606115200591-oozie-joe-W

$ oozie job -config ./job.properties -run
job: 0000007-130606115200591-oozie-joe-W
```

It's the following property during submission, usually defined in the *job.properties* file, that tells the Oozie server what kind of job is being submitted or run. Only one of these three properties can be defined per job submission, meaning a job can be either a workflow, a coordinator, or a bundle:

`oozie.wf.application.path`
: Path to a workflow application directory/file

`oozie.coord.application.path`
: Path to a coordinator application directory/file

`oozie.bundle.application.path`
: Path to a bundle application directory/file

The following commands are commonly used for monitoring as well as managing running jobs. The `-info` option gives you the latest status information on the job and the other options like `-kill` and `-suspend` are self-explanatory. You will need the job ID for all of these commands. We have already seen many of these commands in action throughout this book:

```
$ oozie job -info 0000006-130606115200591-oozie-joe-W
Job ID : 0000006-130606115200591-oozie-joe-W
------------------------------------------------------------------
Workflow Name : identity-WF
```

```
App Path      : hdfs://localhost:8020/user/joe/ch01-identity/app
Status        : RUNNING
Run           : 0
User          : joe
Group         : -
Created       : 2013-06-06 20:35 GMT
Started       : 2013-06-06 20:35 GMT
Last Modified : 2013-06-06 20:35 GMT
Ended         : -
CoordAction ID: -

Actions
------------------------------------------------------------------
ID                                                   Status
------------------------------------------------------------------
0000006-130606115200591-oozie-joe-W@:start:          OK
------------------------------------------------------------------
0000006-130606115200591-oozie-joe-W@identity-MR      RUNNING
------------------------------------------------------------------

$ oozie job -suspend 0000006-130606115200591-oozie-joe-W
$ oozie job -resume 0000006-130606115200591-oozie-joe-W
$ oozie job -kill 0000006-130606115200591-oozie-joe-W
```

The `-info` option for a coordinator job could print pages and pages of output depending on how long it has been running and how many coordinator actions it has executed so far. So there is a `-len` option to control the amount of output dumped onto the screen. The default `len` is 1,000 and the coordinator actions are listed in chronological order (oldest action first). However, this order is reversed and actions are listed in reverse chronological order (newest action first) on the Oozie web UI for better usability:

```
$ oozie job -info 0000084-141219003455004-oozie-joe-C -len 10
```

The other useful option under the job subcommand of the CLI is the `-dryrun`. It is another form of validating the job XML, with the property file taken into account. It might not look like it's telling you much about a workflow, but it is still a good practice to run it before submitting a job. For the coordinators, it tells you things like how many actions will be run during the lifetime of the job, which can be useful information. Here is some sample output:

```
$ oozie job -dryrun -config wf_job.properties
OK

$ oozie job -dryrun -config coord_job.properties
***coordJob after parsing: ***
<coordinator-app xmlns="uri:oozie:coordinator:0.2" name="test-coord"
frequency="1" start="2014-12-22T02:47Z" end="2014-12-23T02:49Z"
timezone="UTC" freq_timeunit="DAY" end_of_duration="NONE">
...
</coordinator-app>
```

```
***actions for instance***
***total coord actions is 2 ***
...
```

Adding the `-debug` flag to the `-job` command can generate a lot of useful information that can help with debugging. One great benefit of the `-debug` option is that it prints the actual web services API that the CLI command calls internally. This can come in handy for users who are trying to develop Oozie client apps using the web services API.

Sometimes users want to tweak and change a few properties of a running coordinator or a bundle job. The `-change` option helps achieve this. Properties like the `end-time` and `concurrency` of a coordinator are ideal for the `-change` option, which only accepts a handful of properties. For instance, users may not want to stop and restart a coordinator job just to extend the endtime. Starting with version 4.1.0, Oozie also supports an `-update` option, which can update more properties of a running job via the *job.properties* file than the `-change` option. Following are a few example commands showcasing both options. Using the `-dryrun` with the `-update` spits out all the changes for the user to check before updating:

```
$ oozie job -change 0000076-140402104721144-oozie-joe-C -value
    endtime=2014-12-01T05:00Z

$ oozie job -change 0000076-140402104721144-oozie-joe-C -value
    endtime=2014-12-01T05:00Z\;concurrency=100\;2014-10-01T05:00Z

$ oozie job -config job.properties -update
    0000076-140402104721144-oozie-joe-C -dryrun
```

We recommend becoming conversant with the `job -rerun` option, as it helps with the important task of reprocessing jobs (we will cover it in detail in "Reprocessing" on page 222).

The jobs subcommand

The `oozie` CLI also provides a `-jobs` subcommand. This is primarily intended to be a monitoring option. It handles jobs in bulk unlike the `-job` option that handles a specific job. The basic `-jobs` command lists all the jobs in the system with their statuses. By default, this lists only the workflow jobs in reverse chronological order (newest first, oldest last) based on the job's creation time. You can add the `-jobtype` flag to get the coordinator or bundle jobs listed. If you print the coordinator jobs using the `jobtype=coordinator` option, the different coordinators will be listed in reverse chronological order based on the next materialization time of the next action in each one of them. This command also takes the `-len` command to control the output printed on to the screen and provides a rich set of filters. You can list the jobs filtered by a specific user, job status, creation time, or some other criteria.

There is also a special `-bulk` option specifically meant for bundles. Oozie bundles in large enterprises can get really hairy to monitor with multiple coordinators. `-bulk` helps monitor the bundles with a variety of filters to organize the information better. This option requires a bundle name, but the rest of the filters are optional.

Listed here are several useful examples of the `-jobs` subcommand:

```
$ oozie jobs
$ oozie jobs -jobtype coordinator
$ oozie jobs -jobtype=bundle
$ oozie jobs -len 20 -filter status=RUNNING
$ oozie jobs -bulk bundle=my_bundle_app
$ oozie jobs -bulk 'bundle=my_bundle_app;actionstatus=SUCCEEDED'
$ oozie jobs -bulk bundle=test-bundle\;actionstatus=SUCCEEDED
```

The `-bulk` option requires bundle name and not the bundle job ID. Also, only the FAILED or KILLED jobs are listed by default. Use the `actionstatus` filter to look at jobs that are in other states, as shown in the preceding example. When using the CLI, escape the ; or quote the entire filter string.

More subcommands

The `admin` subcommand provides users with support for some system-wide administrative actions. One interesting option with this subcommand is the `-queuedump` flag that dumps all the elements in the server queue. The `MapReduce`, `Pig`, and `Hive` subcommands are available for submitting MapReduce, Pig, and Hive jobs right from the command line without having to write a workflow job. These will run as standalone actions and Oozie generates the workflow XML internally, saving some work for the user. All the required JARs, libraries, and supporting files have to be uploaded to HDFS beforehand as always. These jobs are created and run right away. Although these CLI features (which are meant to submit action types) can come in handy occasionally.

The `sla` subcommand has been deprecated starting with Oozie version 4.0 since the new SLA framework explained in "JMS-Based Monitoring" on page 220 has been implemented. Also, the `hive` subcommand is a recent addition to the CLI to go with the `pig` and `mapreduce` commands. As always, double-check the Oozie documentation online to see what options are supported by the particular version of the Oozie CLI you are using.

Oozie REST API

Oozie supports an HTTP-based REST API. This web service API is JSON-based and all responses are in UTF8. Any HTTP client that can make web service calls can submit and monitor Oozie jobs. There is library support in most programming languages like Python for making HTTP REST calls. As you can guess, this API is useful for interacting programmatically with Oozie. The use cases for this include automating the monitoring of your Oozie jobs and building custom web UIs to render all that information. Oozie's own internal services like the Oozie CLI, Oozie's web UI, and the Java client API that we will discuss in "Oozie Java Client" on page 214 use this REST API. Oozie documentation covers this API well, but we will get you up to speed in this section with useful examples, tips, and tricks.

As mentioned earlier, if you run the `oozie -job` with the `-debug` flag, you will actually see the exact REST API call printed for your reference as shown in Example 11-2.

Example 11-2. The -debug option

```
$ oozie job -info 0000025-140522211231058-oozie-joe-C@80 -debug
GET  http://oozieserver.mycompany.com:11000/oozie/v2/job/0000025-
140522211231058-oozie-joe-C@80?show=info
ID : 0000025-140522211231058-oozie-joe-C@80
------------------------------------------------------------------------
Action Number          : 80
Console URL            : -
Error Code             : -
Error Message          : -
External ID            : 0000273-140814212041682-oozie-joe-W
External Status        : -
Job ID                 : 0000025-140522211231058-oozie-joe-C
Tracker URI            : -
Created                : 2014-12-18 01:14 GMT
Nominal Time           : 2014-12-18 01:15 GMT
Status                 : SUCCEEDED
Last Modified          : 2014-12-18 03:13 GMT
First Missing Dependency : -
------------------------------------------------------------------------
```

The URI *http://oozieserver.mycompany.com:11000/oozie* is the *OOZIE_URL* where the Oozie server is running. As of Oozie version 4.1.0, the server supports three different versions of the REST API. Versions v0, v1, and v2 may have slightly different features, interfaces, and responses. The following endpoints are supported in the latest version v2 and the previous versions are not too different, but do check the documentation for the specific details. Readers should be familiar with the listed subcommands from the previous section on CLI.

- /versions
- /v2/admin
- /v2/job
- /v2/jobs
- /v2/sla

Since the Oozie CLI, REST API, and the Java client are all different ways to do the same thing, the examples covered might have some duplicate content. We do try to use different use cases in these examples to minimize overlap and repetition.

Most readers are probably familiar with `curl`, the common command-line tool used on many Unix systems to transfer data to and from a URL. Curl supports the HTTP protocol among several other protocols and is often used for making web service calls from the command line and from scripts on Unix systems. Run `man curl` on your Unix box if you need more information on `curl`. In this section, we will mostly use `curl` for showcasing the Oozie REST API. Following are some simple examples using `curl` with the server's response printed as well to give you a flavor of what's returned by Oozie:

```
$ curl "http://oozieserver.mycompany.com:11000/oozie/versions"
[0,1,2]

$ curl "http://oozieserver.mycompany.com:11000/oozie/v2/admin/status"
{"systemMode":"NORMAL"}
```

Since one of the primary uses for the web services API is enabling programmatic access to the Oozie services, let's take a look at a short and sweet example program in Python that accesses a job status of a particular coordinator action and prints the results:

```
#!/usr/bin/python
import json
import urllib2
url = 'http://oozieserver.mycompany.com:11000/oozie/v2/job/\
0000084-141219003455004-oozie-joe-C?show=info'
req = urllib2.Request(url)
print urllib2.urlopen(req).read()
```

Most of the responses from the Oozie web server are in JSON format. So readers are advised to use JSON formatting and printing utilities to print the server's response in more readable formats. On most Unix systems, piping the JSON output through `python -m json.tool` on the command line generates a readable output, as shown in Example 11-3.

Example 11-3. Handling JSON output

```
$ curl "http://oozieserver.mycompany.com:11000/oozie/v2/jobs?jobtype=bundle" \
   | python -m json.tool
  % Total    % Received % Xferd  Average Speed   Time    Time     Time  Current
                                 Dload  Upload   Total   Spent    Left  Speed
104  2187  104  2187    0     0   146k      0 --:--:-- --:--:-- --:--:--  237k
{
    "bundlejobs": [
        {
            "acl": null,
            "bundleCoordJobs": [],
            "bundleExternalId": null,
            "bundleJobId": "0000083-141219003455004-oozie-joe-B",
            "bundleJobName": "test-bundle",
            ...
            ...
            "createdTime": "Thu, 01 Jan 2015 08:39:10 GMT",
            "endTime": null,
            "group": null,
            "kickoffTime": "Thu, 25 Dec 2014 01:25:00 GMT",
            "pauseTime": null,
            "startTime": null,
            "status": "SUCCEEDED",
            "timeOut": 0,
            "timeUnit": "NONE",
            "toString": "Bundle id[0000083-141219003455004-oozie-joe-B]
                                  status[SUCCEEDED]",
            "user": "joe"
        }
    ],
    "len": 50,
    "offset": 1,
    "total": 1
}
```

The examples so far have shown how to read status and other information from the server using HTTP `GET`. Let's now look at an example that submits or writes something to the server using HTTP `POST`. Oozie's REST API can be used to start and run jobs.

When we submit a workflow or a coordinator (or even an action) using the REST API, we have to send the job configuration as the XML payload via the HTTP `POST`. Similar to what we do with the CLI, artifacts like the JARs for UDFs, other libraries, and job XML like the *workflow.xml* and the *coordinator.xml* have to be copied to HDFS and be in place ahead of the submission. In that sense, the Oozie REST API is not a complete solution for job submissions. However, users can use HttpFS, the REST HTTP gateway for HDFS to upload the files.

We will see a complete example of submitting a Pig action via the REST API. Users can submit Pig, MapReduce, and Hive actions as individual jobs without having to write a *workflow.xml*, which Oozie will generate internally for running the job. This is called proxy job submission and for a Pig job, the following configuration elements are mandatory:

`fs.default.name`
: (the `NameNode`)

`mapred.job.tracker`
: (the `JobTracker`)

`user.name`
: The username of the user submitting the job

`oozie.pig.script`
: The actual Pig code, not a file path

`oozie.libpath`
: HDFS directory that contains any JARs required for the job

`oozie.proxysubmission`
: Must be set to `true`

Let's now build an XML payload with the required configuration for our example Pig job submission (we will keep the job simple with no UDF JARs or other special requirements):

```
$ cat pigjob.xml

<configuration>
    <property>
        <name>fs.default.name</name>
        <value>hdfs://nn.mycompany.com:8020</value>
    </property>
    <property>
        <name>mapred.job.tracker</name>
        <value>jt.mycompany.com:8032</value>
    </property>
    <property>
        <name>user.name</name>
        <value>joe</value>
    </property>
    <property>
        <name>oozie.pig.script</name>
        <value>
               A = load '/user/joe/rest_api/pig/input/pig.data' using
                      PigStorage(',') AS (name:chararray, id:int);
               B = foreach A generate $0 as name;
               store B into '/user/joe/rest_api/pig/output';
```

```
            </value>
        </property>
        <property><name>oozie.libpath
            </name>
            <value>/user/oozie/share/lib/pig/</value>
        </property>
        <property>
            <name>oozie.proxysubmission</name>
            <value>true</value>
        </property>
    </configuration>
```

Given this configuration and the Pig code, let's make the REST API call for the proxy job submission—if it's successful, you will get a job ID returned as shown here:

```
$ curl -X POST -H "Content-Type: application/xml;charset=UTF-8" -d @pigjob.xml \
 "http://oozieserver.mycompany.com:11000/oozie/v1/jobs?jobtype=pig"

{"id":"0000082-141219003455004-oozie-joe-W"}
```

Oozie Java Client

In addition to the REST API, Oozie also supports a Java client API for easy integration with Java code. It supports the same kind of operations and is actually a wrapper on top the REST API. We won't spend a lot of time explaining it here, but readers can refer to the Oozie documentation for more details. The brief example should give you a feel for the client code and the key classes in the Java package (the code shown here should be self-explanatory for most Java programmers):

```
import java.util.Properties;

import org.apache.oozie.client.OozieClient;
import org.apache.oozie.client.WorkflowJob;
import org.apache.oozie.client.WorkflowAction;

OozieClient myOozieClient
    = new OozieClient("http://oozieserver.mycompany.com:11000/oozie");
// Create job configuration and set the application path
Properties myConf = myOozieClient.createConfiguration();
myConf.setProperty(OozieClient.APP_PATH,
    "hdfs://nn.mycompany.com:8020/user/joe/my-wf-app");
myConf.setProperty("jobTracker", "jt.mycompany.com:8032");
myConf.setProperty("inputDir", "/user/joe/input");
myConf.setProperty("outputDir", "/user/joe/output

// Submit and start the workflow job
String jobId = myOozieClient.run(conf);

// Wait until the workflow job finishes printing the status every 30 seconds
while (myOozieClient.getJobInfo(jobId).getStatus() == Workflow.Status.RUNNING) {
        System.out.println("Workflow job running ...");
```

```
        Thread.sleep(30 * 1000);
    }

    System.out.println("Workflow job completed ...");
    System.out.println(myOozieClient.getJobInfo(jobId));
```

If users want to write a client to connect to a secure Hadoop cluster, Oozie's Java API provides another client class (`org.apache.oozie.client.AuthOozieClient`) that they can plug in seamlessly. The client needs to be initialized as shown here:

```
AuthOozieClient myOozieClient  = new
    AuthOozieClient("http://oozieserver.mycompany.com:11000/oozie");
```

This client supports Kerberos HTTP SPNEGO authentication, pseudo/simple authentication, and anonymous access for client connections. Users can also create their own client that supports custom authentication (refer to the Oozie documentation for more details).

The oozie-site.xml File

As is customary with all the tools in the Hadoop ecosystem, Oozie has its own "site" XML file on the server node, which captures numerous settings specific to operating Oozie. A lot of the settings that define operational characteristics and Oozie extensions are specified in this *oozie-site.xml* file. We have been covering a lot of those settings across many chapters of this book if and when the context presented itself; for example, many of the security settings were covered in detail in "Oozie Security" on page 154. But there are several more settings available for tuning various aspects of Oozie. The defaults work well in most cases and users will never have to tune most of these settings. But some settings are more useful than others.

Also, following normal Hadoop conventions, an *oozie-default.xml* is deployed that captures all the default values for these settings and also serves as reference documentation for what the server is actually running. These settings can be overridden with your own setting in the *oozie-site.xml*. Be sure to review the sample *oozie-default.xml* available as part of the Apache Oozie documentation to familiarize yourself with the various settings and options available. We will cover some more of those settings in this chapter, but not all.

It can be very educational to browse through the *oozie-default.xml* file. It can be a quick reference to a lot of the features, options, limits, and possible extensions. Users sometimes are not aware of the options available to them or the system limits that are configurable. So just browsing these "default" files and values can be eye opening for new users of any Hadoop tool in general and Oozie in particular.

The best source of truth for all server configuration is the Oozie web UI of the operational Oozie system (Figure 11-1). Clicking on the System Info tab on the UI lets users see the current configuration that the server is running with. And clicking on the + sign next to the setting of interest expands it and shows the value. This is way easier than fumbling through the site and default XML files trying to figure out which property is where and what value it is set to. The figure below shows the relevant part of the UI. This information is also available via the REST API, though not available through the CLI.

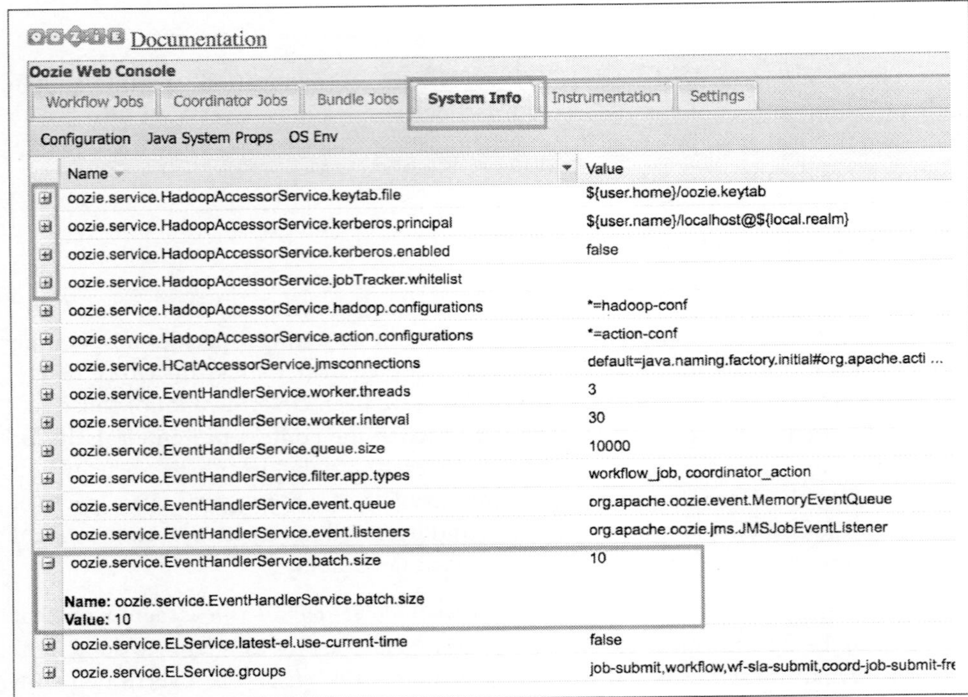

Figure 11-1. Server configuration

One basic setting is the `oozie.services` property. Example 11-4 shows the complete list of services supported by Oozie. You should turn on or off the services of your choice in the *oozie-site.xml* file. This is for the Oozie administrator to define and manage.

Example 11-4. List of Oozie services

```
<property>
    <name>oozie.services</name>
    <value>
         org.apache.oozie.service.SchedulerService,
```

```
            org.apache.oozie.service.InstrumentationService,
            org.apache.oozie.service.MemoryLocksService,
            org.apache.oozie.service.UUIDService,
            org.apache.oozie.service.ELService,
            org.apache.oozie.service.AuthorizationService,
            org.apache.oozie.service.UserGroupInformationService,
            org.apache.oozie.service.HadoopAccessorService,
            org.apache.oozie.service.JobsConcurrencyService,
            org.apache.oozie.service.URIHandlerService,
            org.apache.oozie.service.DagXLogInfoService,
            org.apache.oozie.service.SchemaService,
            org.apache.oozie.service.LiteWorkflowAppService,
            org.apache.oozie.service.JPAService,
            org.apache.oozie.service.StoreService,
            org.apache.oozie.service.CoordinatorStoreService,
            org.apache.oozie.service.SLAStoreService,
            org.apache.oozie.service.DBLiteWorkflowStoreService,
            org.apache.oozie.service.CallbackService,
            org.apache.oozie.service.ShareLibService,
            org.apache.oozie.service.CallableQueueService,
            org.apache.oozie.service.ActionService,
            org.apache.oozie.service.ActionCheckerService,
            org.apache.oozie.service.RecoveryService,
            org.apache.oozie.service.PurgeService,
            org.apache.oozie.service.CoordinatorEngineService,
            org.apache.oozie.service.BundleEngineService,
            org.apache.oozie.service.DagEngineService,
            org.apache.oozie.service.CoordMaterializeTriggerService,
            org.apache.oozie.service.StatusTransitService,
            org.apache.oozie.service.PauseTransitService,
            org.apache.oozie.service.GroupsService,
            org.apache.oozie.service.ProxyUserService,
            org.apache.oozie.service.XLogStreamingService,
            org.apache.oozie.service.JvmPauseMonitorService
        </value>
        <description>
            All services to be created and managed by Oozie Services singleton.
            Class names must be separated by commas.
        </description>
    </property>

    <property>
        <name>oozie.services.ext</name>
        <value>
        </value>
        <description>
            To add/replace services defined in 'oozie.services' with custom
            implementations. Class names must be separated by commas.
        </description>
    </property>
```

The Oozie Purge Service

One of Oozie's many useful services that can be managed through the settings in the *oozie-site.xml* is the database purge service. As you know, Oozie uses a database for its metadata and state management. This database has to be periodically cleaned up so that we don't bump into database-related performance issues. This service—the purge service—can be turned on by enabling `org.apache.oozie.service.PurgeService`. The server allows users to tune several aspects of the purge service (e.g., how soon to purge workflow jobs, how often the purge service should run, etc.). Do keep in mind that the purge service removes only completed and successful jobs; it never touches the failed, killed, suspended, or timed-out jobs. Table 11-1 shows some of the settings that can be tuned to manage the purge service.

Table 11-1. PurgeService settings

Setting	Default value	Description
`oozie.service.PurgeService.older.than`	`30`	Completed workflow jobs older than this value, in days, will be purged by the PurgeService.
`oozie.service.PurgeService.coord.older.than`	`7`	Completed coordinator jobs older than this value, in days, will be purged by the PurgeService.
`oozie.service.PurgeService.bundle.older.than`	`7`	Completed bundle jobs older than this value, in days, will be purged by the PurgeService.
`oozie.service.PurgeService.purge.old.coord.action`	`false`	Whether to purge completed workflows and their corresponding coordinator actions of long-running coordinator jobs if the completed workflow jobs are older than the value specified in oozie.service.PurgeService.older.than
`oozie.service.PurgeService.purge.limit`	`100`	Completed Actions purge: limit each purge to this value. This will make sure the server is not spending too much time and resources purging and overloading the server for other operations.

Setting	Default value	Description
`oozie.service.PurgeService.purge.interval`	`3600`	Interval at which the purge service will run, in seconds. This and the previous setting lets you decide whether you want to run short purges more often or run long purges less often.

With long-term coordinator jobs like the ones that run for a year or two, the purge service by default does not purge completed workflows belonging to that job even past the purge time limits for workflows as long as the coordinator job is still running. This used to be a common source of confusion and problem for users. The solution was to end the coordinator jobs and recycle them every week or month or whatever the DB load dictated. So the setting `oozie.service.PurgeService.purge.old.coord.action` was introduced in version 4.1.0 to allow users to purge successfully completed actions even if they belong to running coordinators.

Job Monitoring

Job monitoring is an integral part of any system for effective operation and management. For a system like Oozie that often deals with time- and revenue-critical jobs, monitoring those jobs is paramount. For instance, if a job fails or runs longer than expected, it is important to know what happened and take remedial action in a timely fashion. Oozie provides multiple ways to monitor the jobs:

User Interface
: Oozie web UI displays the jobs and the associated status and timelines. This UI is very basic and users can only browse jobs.

Polling
: Users can write their own custom monitoring system and poll Oozie using the REST API or Java API that we covered earlier in this chapter to get the latest job information.

Email
: Oozie workflow supports an `Email` action that can send an email when a workflow action finishes.

Callback
: Oozie provides a callback framework where a user can pass the callback URL during workflow submissions. When a job/action finishes, Oozie notifies through the user-defined callback URL and passes the status as payload. This

notification service follows a *best effort* approach and provides no guarantees. More details on this notification feature can be found in the Apache Oozie documentation for both workflows and coordinators.

These approaches implement some parts of an effective job monitoring system, but there are significant shortcomings with each. So the Oozie community decided to implement a monitoring system based on JMS to tackle this problem from the ground up. This is a recent initiative starting with Oozie version 4.0.0.

JMS-Based Monitoring

Oozie supports publishing job information through any JMS-compliant message bus and the consumer can asynchronously receive the messages and handle them using custom processing logic. There are two types of notifications: job and SLA. The first one publishes the job status information that includes when the job started, completed, and so on. Currently, Oozie only supports status change notification for coordinator actions and workflow jobs. There is no support yet for coordinator jobs, workflow actions, and bundle jobs.

The second notification type addresses SLA monitoring. SLAs are very important for mission-critical applications and that information usually feeds daily executive dashboards and other operational reports in large enterprises. Oozie's SLA notifications primarily include various kinds of SLA "met" and "missed" messages. Until version 4.0.0, Oozie supported SLA monitoring in a rather passive way where clients had to poll Oozie to get the SLA information and then determine the status themselves. In post 4.0.0 versions, users can define the expected SLA and the subsequent behavior through workflow and coordinator definition. Oozie pushes the SLA messages through JMS as soon as it is determined. There is also support for a REST API for clients to poll for the status. Moreover, Oozie can send an email when an SLA event occurs. Users can also visually view the SLA status through the new SLA tab of the Oozie UI.

Installation and configuration

The Oozie administrator has to install the JMS-based message bus to support this feature. After the message bus is properly installed, the Oozie server needs to be configured through the *oozie-site.xml* file. The configuration details are covered in the official Apache Oozie documentation.

Most of the testing in Oozie for this feature happened with `ActiveMQ`, but it should work well with any other JMS-compliant message bus. With that said, readers will probably be better off sticking with `ActiveMQ` to the extent possible.

Consuming JMS messages

The main tenet of the JMS-based notification system is that Oozie makes the job and SLA status messages available through a push-based model. The primary focus of this feature is not the presentation or the UI layer. Although Oozie provides a basic and generic UI for all, users are encouraged to design their own UI based on these JMS messages because monitoring UI requirements tends to be quite varied and specific at every deployment.

In order to consume the JMS messages, clients needs to write a conventional JMS consumer. Oozie provides the JMS topic name, message format, and message selectors. Oozie is also flexible in that it allows the users to configure the JMS topic name and selectors. JMS selector is a feature by which the clients can skip the messages they are not interested in. More details on this subject can also be found in the Apache Oozie documentation.

Oozie Instrumentation and Metrics

Oozie code is very well instrumented and it can be used to closely monitor the performance of the server. Several samplers, timers, and counters are generated by this instrumentation, and it can be enabled by turning on the `org.apache.oozie.service.InstrumentationService` service. These metrics are available through the instrumentation log on the server and the web services API using the `admin/instrumentation` endpoint (refer to the documentation for more details). Listed here are some sample JVM variables that can help you manage Oozie server's Java process:

```
free.memory
max.memory
total.memory
```

Starting with Oozie version 4.1.0, a new and improved `metrics` service has been implemented with the intention of eventually replacing the existing instrumentation service. It is turned off by default in 4.1.0, but will become the primary and only source of metrics over the course of the next few releases. This new service is based on the `codahale` metrics package and is API-compatible with the existing instrumentation service. The newer metrics are a lot more accurate and detailed and come with very little changes to the output format. The biggest drawback of the existing instrumentation service is that the metrics are accumulated over time going all the way back to when the Oozie server was started. This can become stale over time. The new metrics don't suffer from this limitation and support a sliding time window for its calculations. Users can turn these metrics on by enabling the following service:

```
<property>
        <name>oozie.services.ext</name>
        <value>
```

```
            org.apache.oozie.service.MetricsInstrumentationService
        </value>
    </property>
```

The two metrics services don't work in parallel and users have to pick one or the other. If the new metrics package is enabled, the `admin/instrumentation` REST endpoint and the Instrumentation tab on the UI will be replaced by the `admin/metrics` endpoint and the Metrics tab, respectively.

Reprocessing

Reprocessing is an important operational undertaking in any complex system. We briefly touched on how bundles help with managing and reprocessing pipelines in Chapter 8. We will now look at reprocessing in detail and see how Oozie supports it at the workflow, coordinator, and bundle levels. In a production environment, job reprocessing is a very common and critical activity. There are three scenarios when a user needs to rerun the same job:

- The job failed due to a transient error.
- The job succeeded but the input data was bad.
- The application logic was flawed or there was a bug in the code.

As you can see, the second and third scenarios can force reprocessing even when the jobs have succeeded. Oozie provides convenient ways to reprocess completed jobs through the CLI or the REST API. Reprocessing is driven through the `job -rerun` subcommand and option of the Oozie CLI. Let's first look at workflow reprocessing.

Workflow Reprocessing

Rerunning a workflow job is fairly straightforward and much simpler compared to the coordinator or the bundle. But Oozie does enforce a few constraints for reprocessing. Workflow jobs should be in a `SUCCEEDED`, `FAILED`, or `KILLED` state to be eligible for reprocessing. Basically it should be in a terminal state. The following command will rerun a workflow job that is already done:

```
$ oozie job -rerun 0000092-141219003455004-oozie-joe-W -config job.properties
```

In order to rerun a workflow on Oozie versions before 4.1.0, you have to specify all of the workflow properties (in the *job.properties* file). This is slightly different from the coordinator and bundle reprocessing, which reuses the original configuration as explained later in this section. This inconsistency has been fixed in Oozie 4.1.0 and workflows can also reuse the original properties now.

While the previous example will try to rerun the workflow, there are a few more details that will determine what exactly happens with that command. We cover some of the key aspects here:

- It's the user's responsibility to make sure the required cleanup happens before rerunning the workflow. As you know, Hadoop doesn't like the existence of an output directory and the `prepare` element introduced in "Action Types" on page 43 exists just for this reason. It's always a good idea to use the `prepare` element in every action in all workflows to make the actions retryable. This may not be useful for normal processing, but will be a huge help during reprocessing.
- There are two configuration properties relevant to rerunning workflows, `oozie.wf.rerun.skip.nodes` and `oozie.wf.rerun.failnodes`. We can use one or the other, not both. As always, they can be added to the *job.properties* file or passed in via the `-D` option on the command line.
- The property `oozie.wf.rerun.skip.nodes` is used to specify a comma-separated list of workflow action nodes to be skipped during the rerun.
- By default, workflow reruns start executing from the failed nodes in the prior run. That's why if you run the command in the preceding example on a successfully completed workflow, it will often return without doing anything. The property `oozie.wf.rerun.failnodes` can be set to `false` to tell Oozie that the entire workflow needs to be rerun. This option cannot be used with the `oozie.wf.rerun.skip.nodes` option.
- There is a workflow EL function named `wf:run()` that returns the number of the execution attempt for this workflow. Workflows can make some interesting decisions based on this run number if they want to.

One of the advantages of the workflow retries requiring the job properties is that you could potentially give it a different workflow application path and different parameters. This can help with one-off fixes for one retry of the workflow without affecting the other runs. But this feature comes with a lot of caveats, so be careful to match up the old and new workflow pretty closely.

Here are a couple of examples (the first command will rerun a workflow that succeeded during the first try; the second command will skip a couple of nodes during reprocessing):

```
$ oozie job -rerun 0000092-141219003455004-oozie-oozi-W
-config job.properties -Doozie.wf.rerun.failnodes=false

$ oozie job -rerun 0000092-141219003455004-oozie-oozi-W
-config job.properties -Doozie.wf.rerun.skip.nodes=node_A,node_B
```

Coordinator Reprocessing

Coordinator actions can be reprocessed as long as they are in a completed state. But the parent coordinator job itself cannot be in a `FAILED` or `KILLED` state. Users can select the coordinator action(s) to rerun using either date(s) or action number(s). In addition, a user also has the option to specify either contiguous or noncontiguous actions to rerun. To rerun the entire coordinator job, a user can give the actual start time and end time as a range. However, a user can only specify one type of option in one retry attempt, either date or action number. For the coordinator reruns, Oozie reuses the original coordinator definition and configuration.

During reprocessing of a coordinator, Oozie tries to help the retry attempt by cleaning up the output directories by default. For this, it uses the `<output-events>` specification in the coordinator XML to remove the old output before running the new attempt. Users can override this default behavior using the `-noCleanup` option.

Moreover, a user can also decide to reevaluate the instances of data (`current()`/`latest()`) using the `-refresh` option. In this case, Oozie rechecks all `current()` instances and recalculates/rechecks the `latest()`.

For example, the following command shows how to rerun a set of coordinator actions based on date. It also removes the old files and recalculates the data dependencies. This command reruns the actions with the nominal time between `2014-10-20T05:00Z` to `2014-10-25T20:00Z` and individual actions with nominal time `2014-10-28T01:00Z` and `2014-10-30T22:00Z`:

```
$ oozie job -rerun 0000673-120823182447665-oozie-hado-C -refresh
-date 2014-10-20T05:00Z::2014-10-25T20:00Z, 2014-10-28T01:00Z,
2014-10-30T22:00Z
```

The next command demonstrates how to rerun coordinator actions using action numbers instead of dates. It also doesn't clean up the old output data files created in the previous run and doesn't recalculate the data dependencies. The command reruns the action number 4 and 7 through 10:

```
$ oozie job -rerun 0000673-120823182447665-oozie-hado-C -nocleanup
-action 4,7-10
```

Bundle Reprocessing

Bundle reprocessing is basically reprocessing the coordinator actions that have been run under the auspices of this particular bundle invocation. It does provide options to rerun some of the coordinators and/or actions corresponding to some of the dates. The options are `-coordinator` and `-date`. It's easier to explain the usage through examples. Refer to the following examples with the responses captured to show what happens when a bundle is reprocessed:

```
$ oozie job -rerun 0000094-141219003455004-oozie-joe-B -coordinator test-coord
Coordinators [test-coord] of bundle 0000094-141219003455004-oozie-joe-B
are scheduled to rerun on date ranges [null].

$ oozie job -rerun 0000094-141219003455004-oozie-joe-B -coordinator test-coord
 -date 2014-12-28T01:28Z
Coordinators [test-coord] of bundle 0000094-141219003455004-oozie-joe-B
are scheduled to rerun on date ranges [2014-12-28T01:28Z].

$ oozie job -rerun 0000094-141219003455004-oozie-joe-B -coordinator test-coord
-date 2014-12-28T01:28Z::2015-01-06T00:30Z
Coordinators [test-coord] of bundle 0000094-141219003455004-oozie-joe-B
are scheduled to rerun on date ranges [2014-12-28T01:28Z::2015-01-06T00:30Z].

$ oozie job -rerun 0000094-141219003455004-oozie-joe-B -date 2014-12-28T01:28Z
All coordinators of bundle 0000094-141219003455004-oozie-joe-B are scheduled
to rerun on the date ranges [2014-12-28T01:28Z].
```

With bundle reprocessing, you are actually rerunning a specific bundle ID, but the `-coordinator` option just needs the coordinator names of interest, not IDs. Oozie will find the specific coordinator action IDs to rerun. As for the `-date` option, enter the exact nominal time of the coordinator action you want to rerun or a date range using the `X::Y` syntax to cover all nominal times in that range. In some versions of Oozie, using a comma-separated list of dates results in some strange behaviors.

Server Tuning

An Oozie server running on decent-sized hardware usually performs well in most deployments. With that said, like any legitimate software service, there are various limits and performance issues that Oozie bumps into once in a while. There are several configurations and settings that can be tuned through the *oozie-site.xml* file that we introduced in "The oozie-site.xml File" on page 215.

JVM Tuning

As we already covered, the Oozie server is a Tomcat web server that runs on a Java Virtual Machine (JVM). Like any JVM application, memory is a major tunable for the Oozie server. By default, the server is configured to run with 1 GB of memory. This is controlled by the following line in the file *oozie-env.sh* under the *<INSTALLATION_DIR>/conf* directory. Oozie administrators can modify and upgrade the memory allocation by editing this line and restarting the server:

```
export CATALINA_OPTS="$CATALINA_OPTS -Xmx1024m"
```

In case of performance issues, monitoring the load on the Oozie server process and analyzing the JVM performance metrics will help. All of the typical JVM concerns (e.g., memory, threads, garbage collection, etc.) apply to the Oozie server as well. The instrumentation and metrics covered in "Oozie Instrumentation and Metrics" on page 221 can be a huge help in debugging these issues.

Service Settings

Oozier server is implemented using the Service Layers Pattern. The server is composed of many distinct services as listed in "The oozie-site.xml File" on page 215. One of the advantage of this design is that these logical services can be independently configured and tuned. Oozie has exposed many settings through *oozie-site.xml* for each of these services. We will look at few important services and their settings in this section.

The CallableQueueService

Of the many services that make up the Oozie service, the `CallableQueueService` is the most important from a performance perspective. This is the core work queue that drives all server-side activity. There are a handful of settings for this specific service in the *oozie-site.xml* file, and Table 11-2 captures the most important ones from a tuning perspective.

Table 11-2. CallableQueueService settings

Setting	Default value	Description
`oozie.service.CallableQueueService.queue.size`	`10000`	Max callable queue size.
`oozie.service.CallableQueueService.threads`	`10`	Number of threads used for executing callables
`oozie.service.Callable QueueService.callable.concurrency`	`3`	Maximum concurrency for a given callable type. Each command is a callable type (submit, start, run, signal, job, jobs, suspend, resume, etc.). Each action type is a callable type (MapReduce, Pig, SSH, FS, sub-workflow, etc.). All commands that use action executors (action-start, action-end, action-kill and action-check) use the action type as the callable type.

The `Queue` in the service name might be slightly misleading. This is not a user-facing queue that manages just the job submissions and other user requests. This is an internal queue that's used by Oozie code during processing. The queue items are various `callables`, which is an Oozie implementation primitive. User actions like scheduling a coordinator or submitting a workflow gets translated into many `callables` internally and that's what this queue manages.

The default value for `oozie.service.CallableQueueService.queue.size` is 10,000, which is a decent size that works for most use cases. But if you notice some poor response times and unsatisfactory performance from Oozie, you can use the `-admin` subcommand of the CLI to look at the queue. The commands here tell us the current size of the queue, in addition to listing all the items that are occupying the queue. There are 549 items in this queue:

```
$ oozie admin -queuedump | wc -l
549

$ oozie admin -queuedump
[Server Queue Dump]:
delay=0, elements=org.apache.oozie.command.coord.CoordActionInput
CheckXCommand@71ab437d
delay=64, elements=org.apache.oozie.command.coord.CoordActionInput
CheckXCommand@e1995a0
delay=26829, elements=org.apache.oozie.command.coord.CoordActionInput
CheckXCommand@6661ee03
delay=7768, elements=org.apache.oozie.command.coord.CoordActionInput
CheckXCommand@3c246ecb
...
...
******************************************
[Server Uniqueness Map Dump]:
coord_action_input_0005771-141217180918836-oozie-oozi-C@241=
Sat Jan 10 23:58:21 UTC 2015
suspend_0056165-140725012140409-oozie-oozi-W=
Fri Jan 09 07:56:57 UTC 2015
action.check_0056171-140725012140409-oozie-oozi-W@pig-node1=
Sat Jan 10 18:31:30 UTC 2015
coord_action_input_0005792-141217180918836-oozie-oozi-C@113=
Sat Jan 10 23:58:52 UTC 2015
suspend_0055992-140725012140409-oozie-oozi-W=
Sat Jan 10 04:05:17 UTC 2015
coord_action_input_0005902-141217180918836-oozie-oozi-C@109=
Sat Jan 10 23:57:57 UTC 2015
action.check_0056156-140725012140409-oozie-oozi-W@pig-node1=
Sat Jan 10 18:31:30 UTC 2015
...
...
```

While the queue size is rarely the problem, Oozie's setting for the number of threads is rather conservative because Oozie cannot make any assumptions about the hardware size and resources at its disposal. In real production systems, users often bump the `oozie.service.CallableQueueService.threads` from 10 to 50 or even 100 depending on the server capacity. For best results, increasing the number of callable queue threads should also be accompanied by increasing the Oozie server's VM heap size and GC parameters. Closely related to the number of threads is the `oozie.service.CallableQueueService.callable.concurrency` setting. Oozie's `callables` have a notion of a callable type. This setting controls the maximum concurrency for any one callable type. The default of 3 means only 3 out of the 10 threads at any give time can be dedicated to any one type of callable. You could potentially list and browse the queue and understand the callable types and tune this concurrency number accordingly. In most cases, just proportionally increasing this to go with the thread count will suffice. For example, if you bump the number of threads to 100, increase the concurrency to 30. There are few more things to tune with the `CallableQueueService`, but these three settings will get you over the performance hump in most deployments.

The RecoveryService

The other interesting service is the Oozie `RecoveryService`. This is also an internal service, is not meant to be user facing, and has nothing to do with user-level job recovery or reprocessing. As you can tell, Oozie is a complicated distributed system that manages jobs on Hadoop, an even more complex system. There are many signaling, notification, and callback systems in place that Oozie leverages for dependency management, data availability checks, and the like. It's almost inevitable that things will go wrong and notifications will be missed or signals will be lost given all the moving parts in play. So Oozie has implemented a recovery service, which keeps an eye on the jobs and the queue and recovers actions and jobs that appear to be hung or lost in space. The service itself runs every 60 seconds and looks for actions older than the configured number of seconds.

Table 11-3 shows the interesting settings that drive the recovery service. In real low-latency pipelines, it might be worthwhile to tune these default numbers down so the recovery happens quicker. Users sometimes complain about how the coordinator is still in the `RUNNING` state for a few minutes even after the corresponding workflow has completed successfully. If these delays bother the user, the following settings are the ones they have to look at closely.

Table 11-3. RecoveryService settings

Setting	Default value	Description
`oozie.service.RecoveryService.interval`	60	Interval at which the RecoveryService will run, in seconds.
`oozie.service.RecoveryService.wf.actions.older.than`	120	Age of the actions which are eligible to be queued for recovery, in seconds.
`oozie.service.RecoveryService.coord.older.than`	600	Age of the coordinator jobs or actions which are eligible to be queued for recovery, in seconds.
`oozie.service.RecoveryService.bundle.older.than`	600	Age of the bundle which that are eligible to be queued for recovery, in seconds.

The other thing to keep an eye on from a performance perspective is the database statistics and tuning. We can't get into the details here (because a lot of it depends on the particular DB system chosen), but having a DBA tune the MySQL or Oracle server and optimize things like DB connections can have a big impact on Oozie's performance.

Oozie High Availability

Oozie introduced high availability (HA) in version 4.1. The idea of the HA feature is to remove the single point of failure, which is the Oozie server. The Oozie server, as you might have noticed throughout this book, is stateless. It stores all state information in the database. When the server process or the server machine goes down, the existing jobs on Hadoop obviously continue to work, but all the new requests to the Oozie server will fail and not get processed. This is where an HA setup helps. In Oozie HA, another Oozie server or a bank of multiple Oozie servers can run in parallel and if one server is down, the system continues to work with the other server handling the requests. These servers work in a true hot-hot fashion and any server can handle any client request.

The multiple Oozie servers are usually fronted by a software load-balancer or a virtual IP or a DNS round-robin solution so that the Oozie CLI or the REST API can use a single address to access the server and the multiple HA servers are hidden behind it. Otherwise, if the clients were talking to one specific server in this HA setup, it would require code or configuration change to switch the server to another when that server fails. This is not desirable nor practical. Using a load-balancer type architecture means that Oozie HA has the added benefit of distributing the load across two or more servers in addition to being fault tolerant.

Oozie HA makes sense only if the database runs in a different machine than the Oozie server and also supports multiple, concurrent connections. The derby database that is shipped with Oozie by default does not work for HA, as it does not support multiple connections. If the crash of an Oozie server also takes down the DB, the Oozie system will be down regardless. That's why it's recommended that the DB runs on other machines and also runs in the database HA mode so the system does not have any single points of failure.

Oozie HA is built on top of Apache Zookeeper, which is an open source server that helps with distributed coordination and Apache Curator, which simplifies the use of Zookeeper. It's beyond the scope of this book to get into the details of these systems.

Apache Zookeeper can be a complicated service to manage and maintain. It is another distinct piece of software that Oozie HA introduces into your environment and some readers may have concerns around that. We recommend that readers gain some working knowledge of Zookeeper if they are interested in running Oozie HA.

While most Oozie client calls are independent requests that can go to any server and the server can respond after consulting the DB, the `oozie job -log` presents some interesting challenges in the HA mode. The Oozie logs are stored on the server where the job runs. So if the `-log` request goes to a specific server, it may or may not find the logs locally. It has to then talk to the other servers to fetch the relevant logs. This feature is also implemented using Zookeeper.

The other problem with `-log` is this: what if the server with the logs is down or unreachable? This scenario has not been handled yet in Oozie 4.1, and can only be solved with a major change to Oozie's logging subsystem in a future release. So even with HA, be prepared to see some failures with `-log` if a server or two are down.

Given the stateless nature of the Oozie server, even in the non-HA mode, a crashed server can be brought back up with very limited loss of functionality except for the requests submitted during the time the server was down. The server can start from where it left off as long as it has access to the DB when it comes back up. There are several approaches to running a couple of Oozie servers in a hot-warm or a hot-cold setup with the DB server deployed on a different box that has been implemented successfully in various enterprises for fault tolerance. Readers are encouraged to understand and evaluate the various trade-offs before jumping all in and enabling Oozie HA.

Example 11-5 shows the required and optional configuration settings for enabling Oozie HA. These settings must be added to the *oozie-site.xml* file on all the Oozie servers running HA (refer to the Oozie documentation for more details on the HA setup).

Example 11-5. Oozie HA settings

```
<property>
    <name>oozie.services.ext</name>
    <value>
        org.apache.oozie.service.ZKLocksService,
        org.apache.oozie.service.ZKXLogStreamingService,
        org.apache.oozie.service.ZKJobsConcurrencyService,
        org.apache.oozie.service.ZKUUIDService
    </value>
</property>
...
<property>
   <name>oozie.zookeeper.connection.string</name>
   <value>localhost:2181</value>
</property>
...
<property>
    <name>oozie.zookeeper.namespace</name>
    <value>oozie</value>
</property>
...
<property>
    <name>oozie.base.url</name>
    <value>http://my.loadbalancer.hostname:11000/oozie</value>
</property>
...
<property>
    <name>oozie.instance.id</name>
    <value>hostname</value>
</property>
```

Debugging in Oozie

Debugging Oozie can be a challenge at times. While Hadoop itself is notoriously complicated when it comes to debugging and error logging, Oozie adds another layer on top and manages jobs through a launcher. New users often find this confusing as most Hadoop actions redirect their `stdout/stderr` to the launcher mapper, but those actions also run their own MapReduce jobs.

In reality, tracking down the job logs is not that hard once users get comfortable with Oozie's execution model, but there is a steep learning curve. Hopefully, this book in general and this section in particular helps clarify and simplify things. The Oozie web UI actually has rich content when it comes to monitoring, though some users may complain that it takes to many clicks and windows to get to the required information. But at least everything is there.

The landing page of the Oozie UI has status information on all the jobs with the focus being on the workflow Jobs tab by default. Users can click and switch to the coordinator or bundle tab and see those jobs as well. This gives a nice overview of all the jobs running in the system. This information is similar to what users can see with `oozie job -info` (as covered in "Oozie CLI Tool" on page 203). This UI also has the System Info tab (as explained in "The oozie-site.xml File" on page 215). Let's look at the job information. Figure 11-2 shows the main Oozie UI.

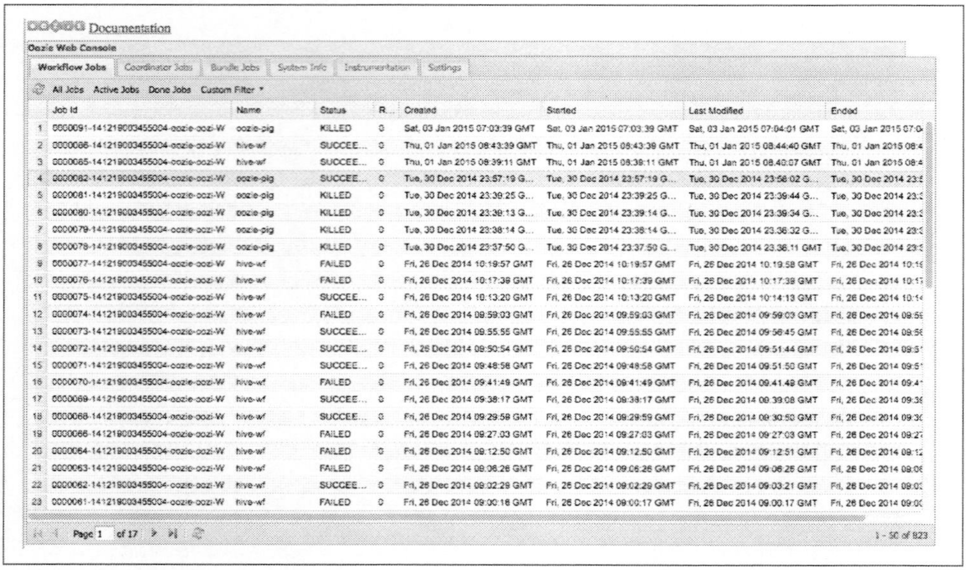

Figure 11-2. Job status

All jobs are clickable, and clicking on a workflow brings up a window with more interesting information. In this page, you are seeing all the information concerning this workflow job. You see the status of all the actions that make up this workflow. You can also see the Job Definition and Job Configuration tabs, which capture the *workflow.xml* and *job.properties*, respectively. This is very convenient, as users have all job-related information in one place. The Job Log tab has Oozie-level job logging and might not be too useful for debugging Hadoop jobs. And the Job DAG tab captures the workflow DAG in a visual fashion. This UI is captured in Figure 11-3 with the main action highlighted.

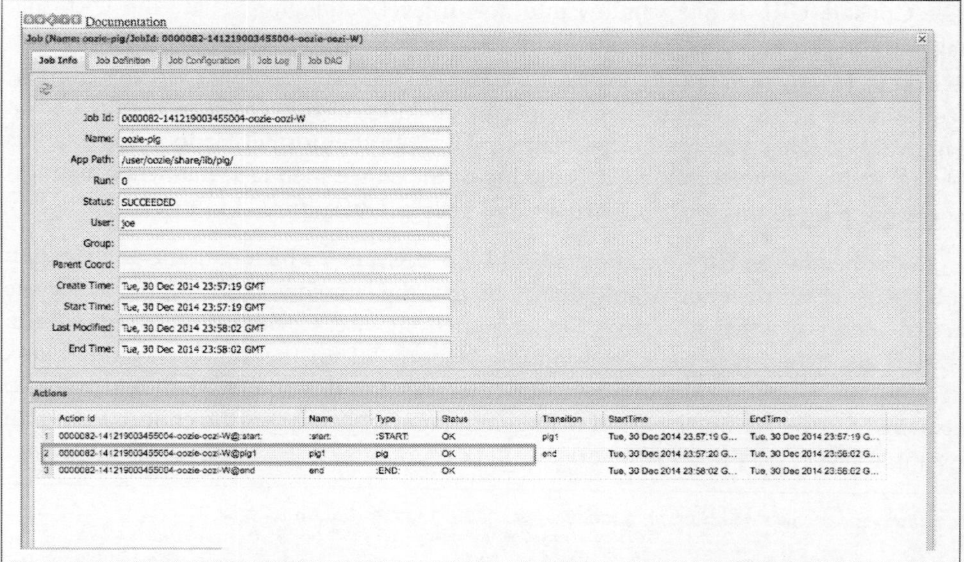

Figure 11-3. Workflow job details

The individual workflow actions are also clickable, and by clicking on the specific action, you get to the most useful action logs. The action-specific UI is captured in Figure 11-4.

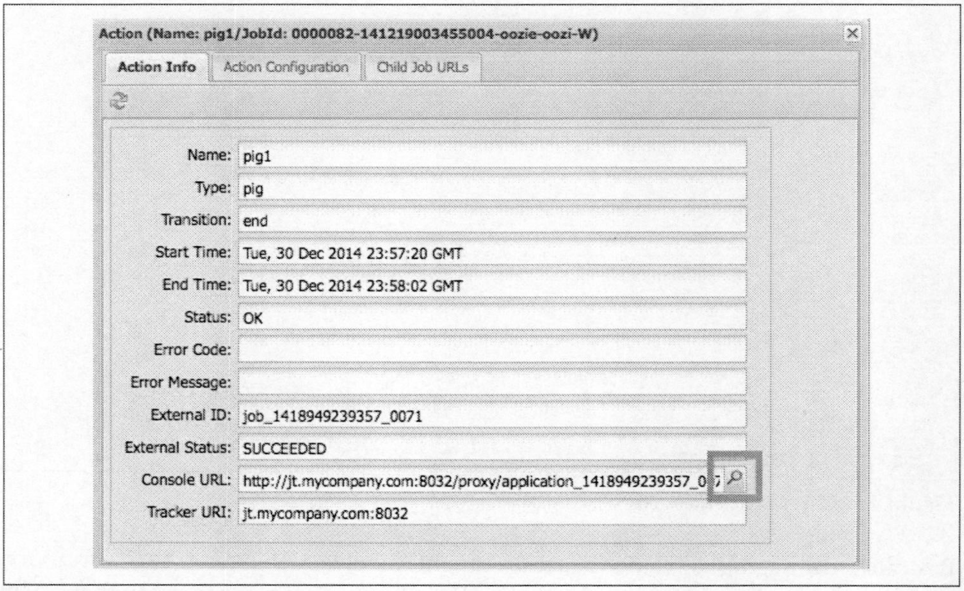

Figure 11-4. Workflow action details

The Console URL is our window into action-level debugging. That's the URL that takes us to the launcher mapper on the Hadoop ResourceManager (RM), the `Job Tracker` (JT), or the Hadoop Job History Server (JHS) if the job has already completed. You can get to the launcher mapper by clicking on the lens icon highlighted in Figure 11-4. Once you are on the Hadoop UI, then the normal Hadoop log analysis begins. What we need to look at is the log of the single map task (launcher mapper) corresponding to this job. Both `stdout` and `stderr` are captured in those logs.

In the same `Action` UI, we can see a Child Job URLs tab, which contains the Hadoop job URLs for all the child MapReduce jobs that the launcher kicks off to execute the actual action, whether it is Hive, Pig, or something else. Clicking on the lens icon in this UI also takes us to the corresponding Hadoop UI for the job. Users should look at both the launcher mapper logs and the logs for the actual MapReduce job(s) spawned for the action as part of debugging. Figure 11-5 shows the child URL for an example action.

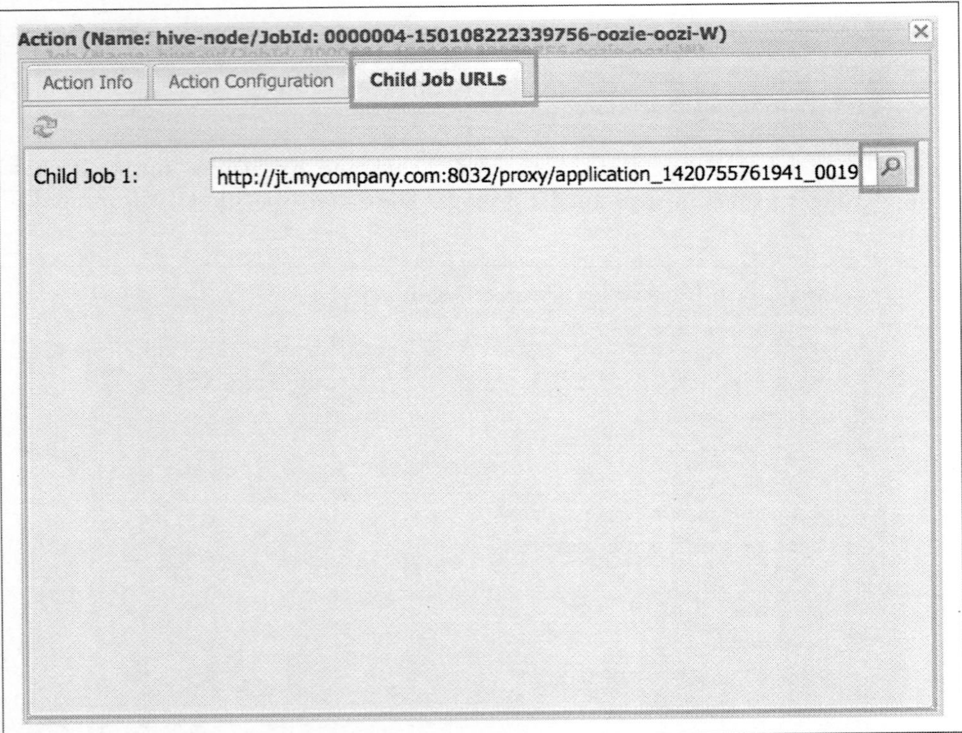

Figure 11-5. Action child URL

Basically, debugging a Hadoop action might involve debugging two (or more) Hadoop jobs, and users can use the Oozie UI as the starting point to get to them. This

UI also has all the information about the bundle, coordinator, workflow, action, job properties, and so on. Users should get comfortable navigating through all this information on the Oozie UI and that will make debugging job failures a lot easier.

Oozie Logs

In "Debugging in Oozie" on page 231, we saw how to get to all the job and action information. In this section, we will see where to find Oozie-level logs on the server. All the Oozie server-side logs can be found under the *<INSTALLATION_DIR>/logs/* subdirectory. The main server log is called *oozie.log* and it gets rotated hourly. The instrumentation log covered in "Oozie Instrumentation and Metrics" on page 221 is another useful resource and it gets rotated daily. The *catalina.** files capture the web-server-level logging and can come in handy for problems related to the Tomcat web server. Following is a sample `ls` from the *logs/* directory showing some of the key logs, both current and rotated logs:

```
$ ls
catalina.2015-01-09.log
catalina.out
oozie-instrumentation.log.2015-01-09
oozie-instrumentation.log
oozie.log-2015-01-10-20
oozie.log-2015-01-10-21
oozie.log
```

The Oozie logs are also available via the CLI command `oozie job -log` and the Oozie web UI. Those logs are just filtered versions of the *oozie.log* file sent to the client for the particular job ID(s).

Developing and Testing Oozie Applications

Given the complexity of deploying and debugging Oozie applications, coming up with an efficient develop-test-debug process is very important. Following are some recommendations on how to approach development of Oozie applications (some of these are just best practices and common sense tips, and you will do well to incorporate these into your development processes):

- Develop Oozie applications in an incremental fashion. It might be too much to expect to write a workflow with 15 actions and test and get it running in one shot. Start with the first action and make sure it works via the workflow. Then expand incrementally.
- Detach Oozie job development from the individual action development. It is a bad idea to debug Hive and Pig issues via Oozie workflows. Make sure you first develop the Hive or Pig code separately and get it working before trying to put it

into an Oozie workflow. It is extremely inefficient to write a brand-new Hive or Pig script and test it through Oozie for the first time. It's a lot easier to catch simple Hive and Pig errors using their respective CLI clients.

- Expanding on the previous suggestion, when you are developing bundles with many coordinators interconnected by data dependencies or complex workflows with many fork/joins, it might be better to make sure the Oozie application logic works as intended before adding complex, long-running actions. In other words, build the shell of your Oozie application with fake actions and see if the control flow works the way you want it to. A simple shell action that just does an `echo Hello` is often good enough to test the Oozie parts of your application. You can then replace these fake shell actions with real actions.
- Develop your job XMLs using an XML editor instead of a text editor. Use the `validate` and `dryrun` options of the Oozie CLI liberally to catch simple errors.
- Write scripts to automate simple steps during development and testing. For example, every time you change your workflow XML, your script could run a validate command, remove the existing file/dir from HDFS, and copy the new file/directory to HDFS and run the app (if that's required). Forgetting to copy the files to HDFS is a common oversight that costs users many minutes during every iteration.
- Parameterize as much as possible. This makes the jobs very flexible and saves time during testing. For example, if you are developing a bundle and have to run it many times to test and fix during development, parameterize the `kick-off-time` control setting. This saves you time because you don't have to reload the bundle XML to HDFS every time just for changing the `kick-off-time`. It can and should be controlled externally, outside the XML, using parameterization.

Application Deployment Tips

As you know, Oozie applications are deployed to HDFS. There are not a whole lot of rules on how the deployment should look except for a couple of conventions that we've already covered in the book. For instance, the workflow, coordinator, and bundle specification files are usually named a certain way and are under the application root directory. The job JARs are usually deployed under the *lib/* subdirectory under the app root and get added to the CLASSPATH automatically. Other than these, there are not a whole lot of rules. New Oozie users always have many questions like whether the bundle, coordinator, and workflow files should be at the top level under the app root directory or should they be under multiple nested directory levels.

We can make it work with any deployment structure we choose, but certain organizing principles are recommended. Ideally, all files can be at the top level for simple bundles with just a handful of files. If the bundle is complex with many coordinators and if each coordinator in turn has many workflows with many JARs, it may be better to organize them in separate multilevel directories to reduce clutter. There may also be cases where the same coordinator might be part of different bundles and the same workflows may be part of different coordinators. Also, JARs are often shared between multiple workflows. For these scenarios, it's important that we don't duplicate and copy files and directories all over HDFS. So a mix of central directories at the top level for the shared components and nested directories for nonshared components will work well. These layouts are captured in Figure 11-6.

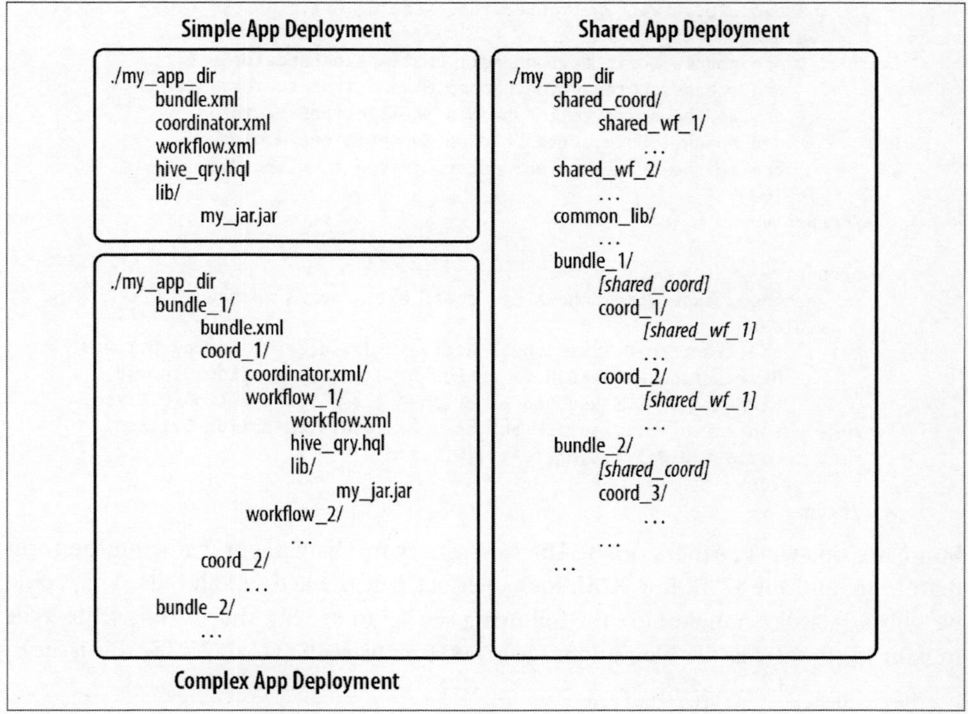

Figure 11-6. Application deployment on HDFS

Common Errors and Debugging

In this section, we cover some common errors and give various tips and solutions. We hope this section will save you some time by being a quick reference guide for some of the common mistakes we have seen repeated on Oozie.

A lot of the Oozie-level errors that the server throws are usually E0710 or E0701. You will see these errors in the Oozie UI and these errors usually mean it's not a Hadoop issue, but something in the Oozie system.

Hive action and/or DistCp action doesn't work: Oozie's out-of-the-box workflow actions are segregated as core actions and action extensions. The extension actions are `<hive>`, `<shell>`, `<email>`, `<distcp>`, and `<sqoop>`; they are all enabled by default on most recent Oozie deployments. But if you do see strange errors running these extension actions, make sure the following setting is enabled in *oozie-site.xml* (you can check this on the Oozie UI as well, like we saw in "The oozie-site.xml File" on page 215):

```
<property>
    <name>oozie.service.ActionService.executor.ext.classes</name>
    <value>
        org.apache.oozie.action.email.EmailActionExecutor,
        org.apache.oozie.action.hadoop.HiveActionExecutor,
        org.apache.oozie.action.hadoop.ShellActionExecutor,
        org.apache.oozie.action.hadoop.SqoopActionExecutor,
        org.apache.oozie.action.hadoop.DistcpActionExecutor
    </value>
</property>

<property>
    <name>oozie.service.SchemaService.wf.ext.schemas</name>
    <value>
        shell-action-0.1.xsd,shell-action-0.2.xsd,email-action-0.1.xsd,
        hive-action-0.2.xsd,hive-action-0.3.xsd,hive-action-0.4.xsd,
        hive-action-0.5.xsd,sqoop-action-0.2.xsd,sqoop-action-0.3.xsd,
        ssh-action-0.1.xsd,ssh-action-0.2.xsd,distcp-action-0.1.xsd,
        oozie-sla-0.1.xsd,oozie-sla-0.2.xsd
    </value>
</property>
```

Some actions work, others don't: The Hive query or DistCp works fine on the command line and the workflow XML looks perfect, but the action still fails. This could be a library issue, so make sure the following setting to use the `sharelib` is set to `true` in your *job.properties* file (you might see a `JA018` error in the Oozie UI for this issue):

```
oozie.use.system.libpath=true
```

Workflow XML schema errors: Always be aware of the XML schema version and features. When you see errors like the one shown here, check the schema:

```
Error: E0701 : E0701: XML schema error, cvc-complex-type.2.4.a:
Invalid content was found starting with element 'global'. One of
'{"uri:oozie:workflow:0.3":credentials, "uri:oozie:workflow:0.3":start}'
is expected.
```

Issues with the <global> section: The example error previously shown relates to support for the `<global>` section. It's only supported in workflow XML version 0.4 or higher, as shown here:

```
<workflow-app xmlns="uri:oozie:workflow:0.4" name="my-test-wf">
```

Also, with some of the extension actions like `hive` or `shell`, the `<global>` section might not work. Remember that the action definitions have their own schema version as well and confirm that you are using supported features both at the workflow level and the action level.

Schema version errors with action types: The action schema versions are different and often a lower number than the workflow schema version. Sometimes, users cut and paste the same version from the workflow header and that may not be the right version number. If you see the following error with a Hive action for instance, you should check the version number (it is probably too high):

```
Error: E0701 : E0701: XML schema error, cvc-complex-type.2.4.c: The matching
wildcard is strict, but no declaration can be found for element 'hive'.
```

Syntax error with the HDFS scheme: Another annoyingly common error is a typo and syntax error in the *workflow.xml* or the *job.properties* file while representing the HDFS path URIs. It is usually represented as `${nameNode}/${wf_path}` and users often end up with a double slash (//) following the `NameNode` in the URI. This could be because the `NameNode` variable has a trailing / or the path variable has a leading / or both. But read the error messages closely and catch typos and mistakes with the URI. For instance, you will see the following error message if the *job.properties* file has a typo in the workflow app root path:

```
Error: E0710 : E0710: Could not read the workflow definition, File does not
exist: //user/joe /oozie/my_wf/workflow.xml
```

Workflow is in a perpetual RUNNING state: You see that all the actions in a workflow have completed either successfully or with errors including the end states (`end` or `kill`), but the workflow is not exiting and is hung in the `RUNNING` state. This can happen if you have a typo or a syntax error in the aforementioned end states. This usually happens due to some error in the message section in the `kill` node as shown here:

```
<kill name="fail">
        <message>Hive failed, error message[${$$wf:errorMessage
        (wf:lastErrorNode())}]</message>
    </kill>
```

Workflow action is running long after the completion of its launcher mapper: Most of the workflow actions utilize a map-only Hadoop job (called *launcher mapper*) to launch the actual action. In some instances, users might find that the launcher mapper has completed successfully according to the ResourceManager or the `Job Tracker` UI. However, the corresponding action in the Oozie UI might still be in a running state long after the launcher mapper has finished. This inconsistency can exist for as long as 10 minutes. In other words, the subsequent actions in the workflow might not be launched for 10 minutes. The possible reason for this delay is some issue with Hadoop's callback that Oozie uses to get the status of the launcher mapper. More specifically, the root cause can be Hadoop not being able to invoke the callback just after the launcher mapper finishes or Oozie missing the Hadoop callback. The more common reason is Hadoop missing the callback due to security/firewall or other reasons. A quick check on the ResourceManager or `JobTracker` log will show the root cause. Oozie admins can also decrease the value of the `oozie.service.ActionCheckerService.action.check.delay` property from the default 600 seconds to 180 seconds or so in *oozie-site.xml*. This property determines the interval between two successive status checks for any outstanding launcher mappers. The reduction of this interval will definitely reduce the duration of the inconsistency between Oozie and the RM/JT. But it will also increase the load on the Oozie server due to more frequent checks on Hadoop. Therefore, it should only be used as an interim solution while the root cause is found and ultimately fixed.

MiniOozie and LocalOozie

There are ways to test and verify Oozie applications locally in a development environment instead of having to go to a full-fledged remote server. Unfortunately, these testing frameworks are not very sophisticated, well maintained, or widely adopted. So users have not had great success with these tools and these approaches may never substitute real testing against a real Oozie server and a Hadoop cluster. But it might still be worthwhile to try to get it working for your application. These approaches should work at least for simple workflows and coordinators:

MiniOozie
: Oozie provides a `junit` test class called MiniOozie for users to test workflow and coordinator applications. IDEs like Eclipse and IntelliJ can directly import the MiniOozie Maven project. Refer to the test case in the Oozie source tree under *minitest/src/test/java* for an example of how to use MiniOozie. MiniOozie uses `LocalOozie` internally.

LocalOozie
: We can think of LocalOozie as embedded Oozie. It simulates an Oozie deployment locally with the intention of providing an easy testing and debugging environment for Oozie application developers. The way to use it is to get an `Oozieclient` object from a LocalOozie class and use it like a normal Java Oozie API client.

Another alternative when it comes to testing and debugging is to run an Oozie server locally against a pseudodistributed Hadoop cluster and test everything on one machine. We do not recommend spending too much time trying to get these approaches working if you bump into issues.

The Competition

You might wonder what other products are available for solving the problem of job scheduling and workflow management for Hadoop. Oozie is not the only player in this field and we briefly introduce a few other products in this section. The overall consensus in the Hadoop community is that these alternatives are not as feature-rich and complete as Oozie, though they all have their own strengths and do certain things well. Most of these products do not have the same widespread adoption and community support that Oozie enjoys. The list is by no means exhaustive or complete:

Azkaban
: The product that's closest to Oozie in terms of customer adoption is Azkaban, an open source batch workflow scheduler created at LinkedIn. It has a lot of usability features and is known for its graphical user interface.

Luigi
: Spotify's Luigi is another open source product that supports workflow management, visualization, and building complex pipelines on Hadoop. It's known for its simplicity and is written in Python.

HAMAKE
: Hadoop Make or HAMAKE is a utility that's built on the principles of dataflow programming. It's client-based and is supposed to be lightweight.

A thorough comparison and analysis of these products are beyond the scope of this book. We do believe Oozie's rich feature set, strong user community, and solid documentation set it apart, but we encourage you to do your own research on these products if interested. Oozie is often accused of being complex and having a steep learning curve, and we hope this book helps address that particular challenge.

Index

C

D

E

F

K

L

M

N

O

P

U

V

W

X

Y

About the Authors

Mohammad Kamrul Islam is currently working at Uber on its Data Engineering team as a Staff Software Engineer. Previously, he worked at LinkedIn for more than two years as a Staff Software Engineer in their Hadoop Development team. Before that, he worked at Yahoo! for nearly five years as an Oozie architect/technical lead. His fingerprints can be found all over Oozie, and he is a respected voice in the Oozie community. He has been intimately involved with the Apache Hadoop ecosystem since 2009. Mohammad has a Ph.D. in computer science with a specialization in parallel job scheduling from Ohio State University. He received his master's degree in computer science from Wright State University, Ohio, and bachelor's in computer science from Bangladesh University of Engineering and Technology (BUET). He is a Project Management Committee (PMC) member of both Apache Oozie and Apache TEZ and frequently contributes to Apache YARN/MapReduce and Apache Hive. He was elected as the PMC chair and Vice President of Oozie as part of the Apache Software Foundation from 2013 through 2015.

Aravind Srinivasan has been involved with Hadoop in general and Oozie in particular since 2008. He is currently a Lead Application Architect at Altiscale, a Hadoop as a service (HAAS) provider, where he helps customers with Hadoop application design and architecture. His association with big data and Hadoop started during his time at Yahoo!, where he spent almost six years working on various data pipelines for advertising systems. He has extensive experience building complicated low latency data pipelines and also in porting legacy pipelines to Oozie. He drove a lot of Oozie's requirements as a customer in its early days of adoption inside Yahoo! and later spent some time as a Product Manager on Yahoo!'s Hadoop team, where he contributed further to Oozie's roadmap. He also spent a year after Yahoo! at Think Big Analytics (a Teradata company), a Hadoop consulting firm, where he got to consult on some interesting and challenging big data integration projects at Facebook. He has a master's in computer science from Arizona State University, and lives in Silicon Valley.

Colophon

The animal on the cover of *Apache Oozie* is a binturong (*Arctictis binturong*), a mostly arboreal mammal that inhabits the dense rainforests of Southeast Asia. The meaning of the name is unknown, having derived from an extinct language. While in fact a member of the civet family, it is commonly referred to as a bearcat, as it resembles a hybrid of the two creatures.

The binturong has a short muzzle, stiff white whiskers, and a long, stocky body cloaked in coarse, dark fur. Five-toed and flat-footed, it stands on its hind legs to walk on the ground, ambling much like a bear. The animal's signature characteristic is its thick, muscular tail; in addition to providing balance, it serves as an extra limb for gripping branches. The tail is nearly the length of the binturong's head and body, which grows to two or three feet long.

Its hind legs rotate backward, allowing the binturong to maintain a strong grip on trees even when climbing down headfirst. Despite being an avid climber, it lacks the acrobaticism of primates and typically must descend to the ground to move between trees. The binturong marks its territory as it roams by producing a distinctive musk, often likened to the smell of buttered popcorn.

The binturong's diet can include small mammals, insects, birds, rodents, and fish, but it favors fruit, particularly figs. Binturongs are one of the only animals capable of digesting the tough seed coat of the strangler fig, which cannot germinate unassisted. The bearcat's role in seed dispersal makes it crucial to its forest habitat.

Many of the animals on O'Reilly covers are endangered; all of them are important to the world. To learn more about how you can help, go to *animals.oreilly.com*.

The cover image is from *Meyers Kleines Lexicon*. The cover fonts are URW Typewriter and Guardian Sans. The text font is Adobe Minion Pro; the heading font is Adobe Myriad Condensed; and the code font is Dalton Maag's Ubuntu Mono.

ISBN	Title	Author	Year	Price
	Shroff / O'Reilly			
9789350236772	#tweetsmart, 124 Pages	McDougall	2012	200.00
9788173669200	.NET Compact Framework Pocket Guide, 122 Pages	Lee	2004	125.00
9788173666544	.NET Framework Essentials, 3rd Edition, 400 Pages	Thai	2003	475.00
9789350236437	20 Recipes for Programming MVC 3, 138 Pages	Munro	2012	250.00
9789350237274	20 Recipes for Programming PhoneGap, 96 Pages	Munro	2012	150.00
9789350234051	21 Recipes for Mining Twitter, 96 Pages	Russell	2011	150.00
9789350239957	21st Century C, 316 Pages	Klemens	2012	550.00
9789350233993	50 Tips and Tricks for MongoDB Developers, 88 Pages	Chodorow	2011	125.00
9789351108450	**60 Recipes for Apache CloudStack, 180 Pages**	**Sebastien Goasguen**	**2014**	**300.00**
9788184041637	**802.11 Wireless Networks: The Definitive Guide,** 2nd Edition (Covers 802.11a, g, n & i), 668 Pages	Gast	2005	625.00
9789351102434	802.11ac: A Survival Guide,172 Pages	Matthew S. Gast	2013	275.00
9789350237267	802.11n: A Survival Guide, 164 Pages	Gast	2012	250.00
9788184049510	97 Things Every Programmer Should Know, 272 Pages	Henney	2010	375.00
9788184048131	97 Things Every Project Manager Should Know, 268 Pages	Davis	2009	400.00
9788184046892	97 Things Every Software Architect Should Know, 236 Pages	Monson	2009	350.00
9789350230503	Access 2010: The Missing Manual, 852 Pages	MacDonald	2010	950.00
9789351101574	Access 2013: The Missing Manual, 886Pages	Matthew MacDonald	2013	1,350.00
9788184043334	Access Data Analysis Cookbook, 384 Pages	Bluttman	2007	375.00
9788173664281	Access Database Design & Programming, 3/ed, 454 Pages	Roman	2002	425.00
9788173666377	Access Hacks: Tips & Tools for Wrangling Your Data, 362 Pages	Bluttman	2005	325.00
9789350238745	Accessibility Handbook, 116 Pages	Cunningham	2012	175.00
9788184042832	ActionScript 3.0 Cookbook, 600 Pages	Lott	2006	475.00
9788184043747	ActionScript 3.0 Design Patterns: Object Oriented Programming Techniques (Adobe Developer Library), 552 Pages	Sanders	2007	500.00
9788184046120	ActionScript 3.0 Quick Reference Guide, The, 508 Pages	Stiller	2008	425.00
9789350236246	ActionScript Developer's Guide to PureMVC, 144 Pages	Hall	2012	450.00
9789350234914	ActionScript Developer's Guide to Robotlegs, 160 Pages	Hooks	2011	250.00
9788173666551	ActionScript for Flash MX Pocket Reference, 152 Pages	Moock	2003	125.00
9788184047103	Active Directory Cookbook, 3/ed: Solutions for Administrators & Developers, 1104 Pages	Hunter	2009	750.00
9789351101727	Active Directory Cookbook, Fourth Edition, 886 Pages	Brian Svidergol	2013	1,250.00
9789351109563	**Active Directory, 5/Ed, 760 Pages**	**Brian Desmond**	**2015**	**1350.00**
9788184046496	Active Directory: Designing, Deploying, and Running Active Directory, 4/ed, 876 Pages	Desmond	2008	600.00
9788184043501	Adding Ajax, 418 Pages	Power	2007	400.00
9788184044980	ADO.NET 3.5 Cookbook, 2/ed (Updated for .NET 3.5, LINQ, and SQL Server 2008), 1,098 Pages	Hamilton	2008	750.00
9788184046441	Adobe AIR 1.5 Cookbook: Solutions and Examples for Rich Internet Application Developers, 460 Pages	Tucker	2008	425.00
9788184045390	Adobe AIR for JavaScript Developers Pocket Guide, 220 Pages	Chambers	2008	150.00
9789350238844	Adobe Edge Animate Preview 7: The Missing Manual, 300 Pages	Grover	2012	475.00
9789350231197	Adobe InDesign CS4 One-on-One, 580 Pages	McClelland	2010	875.00
9788184043563	Adobe Integrated Runtime(AIR) for JavaScript Developers Pocket Reference, 192 Pages	Dura	2007	150.00

ISBN	Title	Author	Year	Price
9789352130900	**Advanced Analytics with Spark, 300 Pages**	**Sandy Ryza,**	**2015**	**525.00**
9788173668302	Advanced Perl Programming, 2/ed, 308 Pages	Cozens	2005	325.00
9788184044409	Advanced Rails, 374 Pages	Ediger	2008	375.00
9789351103172	Agile Data Science, 200 Pages	Russell Jurney	2013	325.00
9788184041576	Ajax Design Patterns, 668 Pages	Mahemoff	2006	500.00
9788184043082	Ajax on Java, 176 Pages	Olson	2007	350.00
9788184042610	Ajax on Rails, 364 Pages	Raymond	2007	350.00
9788184044898	Ajax: The Definitive Guide, 996 Pages	Holdener	2008	800.00
9788184046083	Algorithms in a Nutshell: A Desktop Quick Reference, 376 Pages	Heineman	2008	450.00
9789351109327	**Amazon Fire Phone : The Missing Manual, 388 Pages**	**Preston Gralla**	**2014**	**700.00**
9788173667299	Amazon Hacks: 100 Industrial Strength Tips & Tricks, 312 Pages	Bausch	2003	250.00
9788173667794	Analyzing Business Data with Excel, 276 Pages	Knight	2006	425.00
9788184047332	Android Application Development, 354 Pages	Rogers	2009	525.00
9789350237328	Android Cookbook, 704 Pages	Darwin	2012	700.00
9789351102656	Android Developer Tools Essentials, 272 Pages	Mike Wolfson	2013	450.00
9789351101260	AngularJS,216 Pages	Brad Green	2013	375.00
9789351108016	**AngularJS: Up And Running, 324 Pages**	**Shyam Seshadri**	**2014**	**475.00**
9789351104285	Anonymizing Health Data, 232 Pages	Khaled El Emam	2013	400.00
9789352130917	**Ansible: Up and Running, 356 Pages**	**Lorin Hochstein**	**2015**	**625.00**
9788184040807	ANT: The Definitive Guide, 2/ed (Cover ANT 1.6), 346 Pages	Holzner	2005	475.00
9788184046007	Apache 2 Pocket Reference, 230 Pages	Ford	2008	150.00
9788184044416	Apache Cookbook, 2/ed, 322 Pages	Bowen	2008	475.00
9789352130924	**Apache Oozie, 296 Pages**	**Islam**	**2015**	**500.00**
9788173662270	Apache Security, 428 Pages	Ristic	2005	400.00
9789351103103	Apache Sqoop Cookbook,116 Pages	Kathleen Ting	2013	195.00
9788173665134	Apache: The Definitive Guide, 3/ed, 594 Pages	Laurie	2002	850.00
9789350238530	APIs: A Strategy Guide, 168 Pages	Jacobson	2012	275.00
9788184043549	Apollo for Adobe Flex Developers Pocket Guide, 154 Pages	Dixon	2007	125.00
9789351108603	**App Inventor 2, 384 Pages**	**David Wolber**	**2014**	**675.00**
9789350233962	App Inventor, 352 Pages	Wolber	2011	700.00
9789351100775	Appcelerator Titanium: Up and Running, 174 Pages	Anderson	2013	300.00
9789350239513	Application Security for the Android Platform, 132 Pages	Six	2012	225.00
9788184040395	Applied Software Project Management, 304 Pages	Stellman	2005	550.00
9788184048452	Apprenticeship Patterns: Guidance for the Aspiring Sofware Craftsman, 184 pages	Hoover	2009	275.00
9789350236123	Arduino Cookbook, 2/ed, 752 Pages	Margolis	2012	1,075.00
9789350239490	Arista Warrior, 440 Pages	Donahue	2012	750.00
9789350237588	Art of Community, 2nd Edition, The, 592 Pages	Bacon	2012	600.00
9789351107958	**Ask, Measure, Learn, 356 Pages**	**Lutz Finger**	**2014**	**475.00**
9788173664588	ASP.NET 2.0: Developer's Notebook, 358 Pages	Lee	2005	525.00
9789352130931	**ASP.NET MVC 5 with Bootstrap and Knockout.js, 304 Pages**	**Jamie Munro**	**2015**	**525.00**
9788173669385	AspectJ Cookbook, 364 Pages	Miles	2004	350.00
9789351101567	Asterisk : The Definitive Guide 4th Edition,868 Pages	Russel Bryant	2013	1,350.00
9789350234518	Asterisk Cookbook, 88 Pages	Madsen	2011	150.00
9788184045468	Asterisk: The Future of Telephony, 2/ed, 618 Pages	Meggelen	2008	575.00
9788184042702	Astronomy Hacks, 420 Pages	Thompson	2005	450.00
9789352130160	**Async & Performance, 316 Pages**	**Kyle Simpson**	**2015**	**475.00**
9789351100300	Async in C# 5.0, 124 Pages	Davies	2013	200.00
9789350239711	Atmospheric Monitoring with Arduino, 106 Pages	Gertz	2013	175.00
9789350235607	Automating ActionScript Projects with Eclipse and Ant, 120 Pages	Koning	2011	200.00
9789351108467	**Automating Microsoft Azure Infrastructure Services, 200 Pages**	**Michael Washam**	**2014**	**350.00**
9788184047318	Automating System Administration with Perl, 2/ed, 686 Pages	Edelman	2009	600.00

ISBN	Title	Author	Year	Price
9788184042900	Backup & Recovery, 774 Pages	Preston	2007	600.00
9789350239872	Bad Data Handbook, 282	McCallum	2013	475.00
9789351109907	**Badass : Making Users Awesome, 316 Pages**	**Kathy Sierra**	**2015**	**525.00**
9789350239735	Bandit Algorithms for Website Optimization, 106 Pages	White	2013	175.00
9788184043471	Bash Cookbook, 640 Pages	Albing	2007	875.00
9789350230312	Bash Pocket Reference, 148 Pages	Robbins	2010	225.00
9789350234662	Basic Sensors in iOS, 128 Pages	Allan	2011	200.00
9789352130948	**BeagleBone Cookbook, 372 Pages**	**Mark A. Yoder**	**2015**	**650.00**
9788184046908	Beautiful Architecture, 442 Pages	Gousios	2009	650.00
9788184043556	Beautiful Code: Leading Programmers Explain How They Think, 634 Pages	Wilson	2007	1,075.00
9788184047967	Beautiful Data, 404 Pages	Segaran	2009	700.00
9788184047110	Beautiful Security, 316 Pages	Oram	2009	350.00
9788184047035	Beautiful Teams, 524 Pages	Stellman	2009	475.00
9788184048650	Beautiful Testing, 358 Pages	Goucher	2009	550.00
9789350230510	Beautiful Visualization, 404 Pages	Steele	2010	600.00
9789351108474	**Becoming a Better Programmer, 396 Pages**	**Pete Goodliffe**	**2014**	**675.00**
9789351107071	**Becoming Functional: Steps For Transforming Into A Functional Programmer, 176 Pages**	**Backfield**	**2014**	**300.00**
9789351104650	**Beginning NFC: Near Field Communication with Arduino, Andoid, and PhoneGap, 268Pages**	**Tom Igoe**	**2014**	**400.00**
9788173663956	Beginning Perl for Bioinformatics, 390 Pages	Tisdall	2001	595.00
9789350230657	Being Geek: The Software Developer's Career Handbook, 356 Pages	Lopp	2010	525.00
9789350231142	Best iPhone Apps, 2/ed, 272 Pages	Biersdorfer	2010	375.00
9788173668982	Better, Faster, Lighter Java, 270 Pages	Tate	2004	400.00
9788184040036	Beyond Java, 206 Pages	Tate	2005	200.00
9789350235140	Big Data Glossary, 80 Pages	Warden	2011	150.00
9789350239704	Big Data Now: 2012 Edition, 148 Pages	OReilly Media Inc.	2013	250.00
9789352130955	**BioCoder #7, 68 Pages**	**O'Reilly Media**	**2015**	**100.00**
9788184048988	Bioinformatics Programming Using Python, 540 Pages	Model	2010	750.00
9789351109921	Blockchain : Blueprint for a New Economy, 172 Pages	Melanie Swan	2015	300.00
9789350238400	Book: A Futurist's Manifesto, 336 Pages	McGuire	2012	550.00
9789351101604	Bootstrap,148 Pages	Jake Spurlock	2013	225.00
9788184044393	Building A Web 2.0 Portal with ASP.NET 3.5, 324 Pages	Zabir	2008	350.00
9789350239247	Building a Windows IT Infrastructure in the Cloud, 204 Pages	Rensin	2012	350.00
9789350234488	Building and Testing with Gradle, 136 Pages	Berglund	2011	225.00
9789350231173	Building Android Apps with HTML, CSS, & JavaScript, 204 Pgs	Stark	2010	300.00
9789350236406	Building Android Apps with HTML, CSS, and JavaScript, 2nd Edition, 204 Pages	Stark	2012	375.00
9789351108481	**Building Applications with iBeacon, 104 Pages**	**Matthew S. Gast**	**2014**	**175.00**
9788184047127	Building Embedded Linux Systems, 2/ed: Concepts, techniques, tricks, and traps, 478 Pages	Gerum	2009	525.00
9789351102380	Building Hybrid Android Apps with Java and JavaScript,178 Pages	Nizametting Gok	2013	300.00
9789350235911	Building Hypermedia APIs with HTML5 and Node, 264 Pages	Amundsen	2011	450.00
9789351102984	Building iPhone and iPad Electronic Projects, 352 Pages	Mike Westerfield	2013	600.00
9788184049428	Building iPhone Apps with HTML, CSS, & JavaScript, 202 Pgs	Stark	2010	300.00
9789350237250	Building Mobile Applications with Java, 104 Pages	Marinacci	2012	150.00
9789351102878	Building Modular Cloud Apps with OSGI, 232 Pages	Paul Bakker	2013	400.00
9789350239742	Building Node Applications with MongoDB and Backbone, 224 Pages	Wilson	2013	425.00
9789350234525	Building on SugarCRM, 104 Pages	Mertic	2011	175.00
9789351105213	**Building Polyfills: Web Platform Apis For The Present And Future, 192 Pgs**	**Satrom**	**2014**	**350.00**
9788184041545	Building Scalable Web Sites, 362 Pages	Henderson	2006	500.00
9788184048322	Building Social Web Applications, 452 Pages	Bell	2009	675.00
9789350231906	Building the Perfect PC, 3/ed, 368 Pages	Thompson	2010	825.00

ISBN	Title	Author	Year	Price
9789350230527	Building the Realtime User Experience, 344 Pages	Roden	2010	525.00
9789350237984	Building Web Applications with Erlang, 172 Pages	Kessin	2012	275.00
9789350234471	Building Web Apps for Google TV, 140 Pages	Shen	2011	225.00
9789351107262	**Building Web Apps With Ember.Js, 212 Pages**	**Cravens**	**2014**	**350.00**
9789351107262	**Building Web Apps with Ember.js, 212 Pages**	**Jesse Cravens**	**2014**	**350.00**
9789351105954	**Building Web Apps With Wordpress: Wordpress As An Application Framework, 484 Pages**	**Messenlehner**	**2014**	**900.00**
9789350239865	Building Web, Cloud, and Mobile Solutions with F#, 196 Pages	Mohl	2013	325.00
9789350232897	Building Wireless Sensor Networks, 344 Pages	Faludi	2011	625.00
9788184040494	C in a Nutshell, 618 Pages	Prinz	2005	725.00
9788173666605	C Pocket Reference, 142 Pages	Prinz	2002	200.00
9788173664434	C# & VB .NET Conversion Pocket Reference, 156 Pages	Mojica	2002	125.00
9788184044423	C# 3.0 Cookbook, 3/ed, 902 Pages	Hilyard	2008	650.00
9788184044379	C# 3.0 Design Patterns, 338 Pages	Bishop	2008	550.00
9788184049459	C# 4.0 in a Nutshell, 1064 Pages	Albahari	2010	725.00
9789350230831	C# 4.0 Pocket Reference, 3/ed, 232 Pages	Albahari	2010	225.00
9789350237625	C# 5.0 in a Nutshell, 5th Edition, 1,060 Pages	Albahari	2012	975.00
9789350237632	C# 5.0 Pocket Reference, 240 Pages	Albahari	2012	200.00
9789350236611	C# Database Basics, 134 Pages	Schmalz	2012	200.00
9788173663192	C# Essentials, 2/ed, 224 Pages	Albahari	2002	275.00
9788184040364	C++ Cookbook, 604 Pages	Stephens	2005	400.00
9788173666629	C++ in a Nutshell, (Cover ISO/IEC 14882 STD) 816 Pages	Lischner	2003	500.00
9788173667107	C++ Pocket Reference, 148 Pages	Loudon	2003	175.00
9789350232392	Canvas Pocket Reference, 127 Pages	Flanagan	2011	125.00
9789350231937	Cassandra: The Definitive Guide, 352 Pages	Hewitt	2010	600.00
9788173660450	CGI Programming with Perl 2/ed, 476 Pages	Gundavaram	2000	425.00
9788184042849	Cisco IOS Cookbook, 2/ed, 1,250 Pages	Dooley	2006	900.00
9788173669842	Cisco IOS in a Nutshell, 2/ed: A Desktop Quick Reference for IOS on IP Network, 808 Pages	Boney	2005	500.00
9789351105459	**Citrix(R) Xenmobile(Tm) Mobile Device Management, 132 Pages**	**Phoenix**	**2014**	**225.00**
9789350238837	Civic Apps Competition Handbook, 94 Pages	Carlson	2012	150.00
9788184047134	CJKV Information Processing, 2/ed, 916 Pages	Lunde	2009	700.00
9788173668463	Classic Shell Scripting, 568 Pages	Robbins	2005	800.00
9789351105817	**Client-Server Web Apps With Javasript And Java, 284 Pages**	**Saternos**	**2014**	**500.00**
9789351105589	**Clojure Cookbook: Recipes For Functional Programming, 496 Pages**	**Vanderhart**	**2014**	**875.00**
9789350237151	Clojure Programming, 648 Pages	Emerick	2012	950.00
9789350239667	ClojureScript: Up and Running, 136 Pages	Sierra	2013	225.00
9789350231111	Closure: The Definitive Guide, 616 Pages	Bolin	2010	925.00
9788184047141	Cloud Application Architectures: Building Applications and Infrastructure in the Cloud, 220 Pages	Reese	2009	325.00
9789350239155	Cloud Architecture Patterns, 200 Pages	Wilder	2012	325.00
9788184048155	Cloud Security and Privacy, 352 Pages	Mather	2009	450.00
9789350230152	Cocoa and Objective-C: Up and Running, 436 Pages	Stevenson	2010	650.00
9789350237243	Code Simplicity, 108 Pages	Alexander	2012	175.00
9789350234921	Codermetrics: Analytics for Improving Software Teams, 284 Pages	Alexander	2011	450.00
9789351100331	Coding with Coda, 84 Pages	Gruber	2013	125.00
9788184047455	Complete Web Monitoring, 682 Pages	Croll	2009	975.00
9789351101277	Computer Science Programming Basics in Ruby, 208 Pages	Frieder	2013	350.00
9788184041583	Computer Security Basics, 2/ed, 324 Pages	Lehtinen	2006	450.00
9789351106425	**Concurrency In C# Cookbook, 228 Pages**	**Cleary**	**2014**	**400.00**
9789350234204	Concurrent Programming in Mac OS X and iOS, 80 Pages	Nahavandipoor	2011	125.00
9789351105596	**Continuous Enterprise Development In Java, 278 Pages**	**RUBINGER**	**2014**	**425.00**

ISBN	Title	Author	Year	Price
9788184049473	CouchDB: The Definitive Guide, 288 Pages	Anderson	2010	500.00
9789350233955	Creating a Web Site: The Missing Manual, 3/ed: 604 Pages	MacDonald	2011	725.00
9789351108023	**Creating Apps in Kivy, 212 Pages**	**Dusty Phillips**	**2014**	**375.00**
9789350234990	Creating HTML5 Animations with Flash and Wallaby, 84 Pages	McLean	2011	125.00
9788184048971	CSS Cookbook, 3/ed, 746 Pages	Schmitt	2009	850.00
9788184047165	CSS Pocket Reference: Visual Presentation for the Web, 3/ed: 184 Pgs	Meyer	2009	150.00
9789351102663	CSS Text, 78 Pages	Eric A. Meyer	2013	125.00
9788184042788	CSS: The Definitive Guide, 3/ed, 550 Pages	Meyer	2006	800.00
9788184048124	CSS: The Missing Manual, 2/ed, 580 Pages	McFarland	2009	700.00
9789351100256	CSS3: The Missing Manual, 3rd Edition, 668 Pages	McFarland	2013	800.00
9789352130283	**Customizing Chef, 412 Pages**	**Jon Cowie**	**2015**	**725.00**
9789351109976	**Cython, 296 Pages**	**Kurt W. Smith**	**2015**	**500.00**
9789350231777	Data Analysis with Open Source Tools, 556 Pages	Janert	2010	825.00
9789350238394	Data Journalism Handbook, The, 260 Pages	Chambers	2012	400.00
9789351105800	**Data Push Apps With Html5 Sse, 244 Pages**	**Cook**	**2014**	**450.00**
9789351108498	**Data Science at the Command Line, 236 Pages**	**Jeroen Janssens**	**2014**	**400.00**
9789351102670	Data Science for Business, 432 Pages	Foster Provost	2013	700.00
9789352130962	**Data Science from Scratch, 356 Pages**	**Joel Grus**	**2015**	**600.00**
9789351105343	**Data Structures & Algorithms With Javascript, 268 Pages**	**Mcmillan**	**2014**	**395.00**
9789350237298	Database Design and Relational Theory, 294 Pages	Date	2012	500.00
9788173662362	Database Nation: The Death of Privacy in the 21st Century, 336 Pages	Garfinkel	2000	235.00
9788173662898	Database Programming with JDBC & Java 2/ed, 348 Pages	Reese	2000	575.00
9788184046632	Data-Driven Services with Silverlight 2, 372 Pages	Papa	2009	400.00
9789350230992	Delphi in a Nutshell: A Desktop Quick Reference, 596 Pages	Lischner	2010	900.00
9789350234945	Deploying OpenStack, 108 Pages	Pepple	2011	175.00
9789350236093	Design and Prototyping Drupal for Designers, 184 Pages	Nordin	2012	300.00
9789351109037	**Designing and Developing for Google Glass, 428 Pages**	**Allen Firstenberg**	**2014**	**725.00**
9789352130979	**Designing Connected Products, 744 Pages**	**Claire Rowland**	**2015**	**1300.00**
9789350236840	Designing Data Visualizations, 128 Pages	Steele	2012	200.00
9788184042597	Designing Embedded Hardware, 2/ed, 406 Pages	Catsoulis	2005	600.00
9789351105404	Designing Evolvable Web Apis With Asp.Net: Harnessing The Power Of The Web, 560 Pages	Block	2014	875.00
9789351103868	**Designing for Behavior Change, 416 Pages**	**Stephen Wendel**	**2013**	**700.00**
9789351109020	**Designing for Emerging Technologies, 524 Pages**	**Jonathan Follett**	**2014**	**775.00**
9789351109044	**Designing for Performance, 200 Pages**	**Lara Callender Hogan**	**2014**	**300.00**
9789350234532	Designing for XOOPS, 148 Pages	Ruoyu	2011	225.00
9789351100768	Designing Games, 436 Pages	Sylvester	2013	700.00
9789350232408	Designing Interfaces, 2/ed, 600 Pages	Tidwell	2011	1,025.00
9789350235690	Designing Mobile Interfaces, 608 Pages	Hoober	2011	600.00
9789351105206	**Designing Multi-Device Experiences: An Ecosystem Approach To User Experiences Across Devic, 340 Pages**	**Levin**	**2014**	**700.00**
9789350234006	Developing Android Applications with Adobe AIR, 340 Pages	Brossier	2011	500.00
9789350234129	Developing Android Applications with Flex 4.5, 136 Pages	Tretola	2011	200.00
9789351101437	Developing Backbone.js Applications,396 Pages	Addy Osmani	2013	650.00
9788173662423	Developing Bio-informatics Computer Skills, 504 Pages	Gibas	2001	650.00
9789350234464	Developing BlackBerry Tablet Applications with Flex 4.5, 136 Pages	Tretola	2011	225.00
9789351102229	Developing Business Intelligence Apps for SharePoint, 612 Pages	David Feldman	2013	975.00
9789350236109	Developing Enterprise iOS Applications, 140 Pages	Turner	2012	225.00
9788173669477	Developing Feeds with RSS and Atom, 280 Pages	Hammersley	2005	300.00
9789350235003	Developing iOS Applications with Flex 4.5, 156 Pages	Tretola	2011	225.00
9788184049626	Developing Large Web Applications, 306 Pages	Loudon	2010	475.00

ISBN	Title	Author	Year	Price
9789350237304	Developing Web Applications with Haskell and Yesod: Safety-Driven Web Development, 316 Pages	Snoyman	2012	400.00
9789351109938	**Developing Web Components, 276 Pages**	**Jarrod**	**2015**	**475.00**
9789351100515	Developing with Couchbase Server, 106 Pages	Brown	2013	175.00
9789350238813	Developing with Google+, 124 Pages	Murphy	2012	200.00
9789351103455	Developing with PDF, 240 Pages	Leonard Rosenthaol	2013	400.00
9788184040111	Digital Identity, 266 Pages	Windley	2005	275.00
9789351101796	Disruptive Possibilites: How Big Data Changes Everything,100 Pages	Jeffrey Needham	2013	150.00
9789351100782	Distributed Network Data, 188 Pages	Allan	2013	325.00
9789351101031	DIY Instruments for Amateur Space, 140 Pages	Sandy Antunes	2013	200.00
9789350236628	DIY Satellite Platforms, 110 Pages	Antunes	2012	175.00
9788184041965	DNS & BIND (Covers BIND 9.3), 5/ed, 654 Pages	Albitz	2006	800.00
9788173665677	DNS & BIND Cookbook, 248 Pages	Liu	2002	250.00
9789350234112	DNS and BIND on IPv6, 76 Pages	Liu	2011	100.00
9789350233702	DNS on Windows Server 2003, 3rd Edition, 450 Pages	Liu	2011	650.00
9789350230374	DocBook 5: The Definitive Guide, 568 Pages	Walsh	2010	850.00
9789351103189	Doing Data Science, 428 Pages	Rachel Schutt	2013	725.00
9788184045567	Dojo: The Definitive Guide, 502 Pages	Russell	2008	875.00
9789351104278	Dreamweaver CC: The Missing Manual, 1028 Pages	David Sawyer	2013	1,750.00
9789351108764	**Dreamweaver CC: The Missing Manual, 2nd/Ed, 1052 Pages**	**David Sawyer**	**2014**	**1800.00**
9789350230534	Dreamweaver CS5: The Missing Manual, 1116 Pages	McFarland	2010	1,225.00
9789350238448	Dreamweaver CS6: The Missing Manual, 1052 Pages	McFarland	2012	1,350.00
9788184041200	Dreawweaver 8 Design and Construction, 330 Pages	Campbell	2006	750.00
9789350232958	Droid 2: The Missing Manual, 414 Pages	Gralla	2011	625.00
9789350235225	Droid X2: The Missing Manual, 440 Pages	Gralla	2011	625.00
9789350237236	Drupal Development Tricks for Designers, 108 Pages	Nordin	2012	175.00
9789350238455	Drupal for Designers, 344 Pages	Nordin	2012	550.00
9788184042771	Dynamic HTML: The Definitive Reference, 3/ed, 1,336 Pages	Goodman	2006	800.00
9788173669019	Eclipse (Coverage of 3.0), 344 Pages	Holzner	2004	475.00
9788173669309	Eclipse Cookbook (Cover 3.0), 372 Pages	Holzner	2004	350.00
9788173669941	Eclipse IDE Pocket Guide, 140 Pages	Burnette	2005	125.00
9789351106357	**Ecommerce In The Cloud, 304 Pages**	**Goetsch**	**2014**	**525.00**
9789351102687	Effective Akka, 96 Pages	Jamie Allen	2013	165.00
9789352130368	**Effective awk Programming 4th Edition, 582 Pages**	**Arnold Robbin**	**2015**	**1100.00**
9788173663017	Effective awk Programming, 3/ed, 454 Pages	Robbins	2001	325.00
9789351109051	**Effective Modern C++, 356 Pages**	**Scott Meyers**	**2014**	**625.00**
9789350239858	Effective Monitoring and Alerting, 184 Pages	Ligus	2013	325.00
9789351106432	**Efficient Android Threading: Asynchronous Processing Techniques For Android Applications, 304 Pages**	**Goransson**	**2014**	**525.00**
9789350234679	Elastic Beanstalk, 108 Pages	Paganelli	2011	175.00
9789351100843	Embedded Android, 428 Pages	Karim Yaghmour	2013	600.00
9789350237229	Enabling Programmable Self with HealthVault, 136 Pages	Bhandari	2012	225.00
9789351102373	Enterprise Data Workflows with Cascading, 192 Pages	Paco Nathan	2013	325.00
9788184049886	Enterprise Development with Flex, 700 Pages	Fain	2010	850.00
9789351100287	Enterprise Games, 236 Pages	Hugos	2013	400.00
9789350231135	Enterprise JavaBeans 3.1, 6/ed, 788 Pages	Rubinger	2010	725.00
9788184046137	Enterprise Rails, 366 Pages	Chak	2008	350.00
9789350239698	Enterprise Search, 208 Pages	White	2013	350.00
9788173666780	Enterprise Service Bus, 284 Pages	Chappell	2004	425.00
9788184041446	Enterprise SOA, 468 Pages	Woods	2006	600.00
9789350236444	Environmental Monitoring with Arduino, 124 Pages	Gertz	2012	175.00

ISBN	Title	Author	Year	Price
9789351109983	**Enyo: Up and Running 2nd Edition, 108 Pages**	**Roy Sutton**	**2015**	**200.00**
9789351104230	Enyo: Up and Running, 96 Pages	Roy Sutton	2013	175.00
9788184047493	Erlang Programming, 514 Pages	Cesarini	2009	850.00
9788184040241	Essentail PHP Security, 310 Pages	Shiflett	2005	225.00
9788184045437	Essentail SharePoint 2007, 2/ed, 462 Pages	Webb	2008	475.00
9788184042825	Essentail SNMP, 2/ed, 480 Pages	Mauro	2005	400.00
9788173669316	Essential ActionScript 2.0, 528 Pages	Moock	2004	475.00
9788184043662	Essential ActionScript 3.0, 962 Pages	Moock	2007	800.00
9788184048308	Essential Blogging, 280 Pages	Doctorow	2009	425.00
9788184040104	Essential Business Process Modeling, 362 Pages	Havey	2005	350.00
9788184042757	Essential CVS, 2/ed, 442 Pages	Vesperman	2006	425.00
9789350236260	Essential iOS Build and Release, 144 Pages	Roche	2012	225.00
9788184045277	Essential SQL Alchemy, 242 Pages	Copeland	2008	275.00
9788173666643	Essential System Administration Pocket Reference, 152 Pages	Frisch	2002	125.00
9788173665295	Essential System Administration, 3/ed, 1,178 Pages	Frisch	2002	725.00
9788173660252	Essential Windows NT System Administration, 488 Pages	Frisch	1998	225.00
9789351101246	Ethernet Switches, 98 Pages	Spurgeon	2013	175.00
9789351105398	**Ethernet: The Definitive Guide, 2/Ed, 532 Pages**	**Spurgeon**	**2014**	**800.00**
9788173662492	Ethernet: The Definitive Guide, 528 Pages	Spurgeon	2000	300.00
9789350238806	Ethics of Big Data, 100 Pages	Davis	2012	150.00
9788184047462	Even Faster Web Sites, 274 Pages	Souders	2009	500.00
9788184044058	Excel 2007 Pocket Guide, 2/ed, 180 Pages	Frye	2007	125.00
9789350230541	Excel 2010: The Missing Manual, 916 Pages	MacDonald	2010	900.00
9788184043518	Excel Hacks, 2/ed, Tips & Tools for Streamlining Your Spreadsheets, 428 Pages	David	2007	400.00
9789351109068	**eXist, 604 Pages**	**Erik Siegel**	**2014**	**1100.00**
9789350238240	Exploring Everyday Things with R and Ruby, 276 Pages	Sheong	2012	425.00
9789351109570	**Extreme Programming Pocket Guide,108 Pages**	**Chromatic**	**2015**	**125.00**
9789350233764	Facebook: The Missing Manual, 3rd Edition, 304 Pages	Veer	2011	600.00
9789351104247	Feedback Control for Computer Systems, 352 Pages	Philipp K. Janert	2013	600.00
9789352130351	**Field Guide to Hadoop, 152 Pages**	**Kevin Sitto**	**2015**	**225.00**
9789350238462	FileMaker Pro 12: The Missing Manual, 976 Pages	Prosser	2012	1,500.00
9789352130986	**FileMaker Pro 14: The Missing Manual, 1000 Pages**	**Susan Prosser**	**2015**	**1750.00**
9788184041361	Flash 8 Cookbook, 548 Pages	Lott	2006	400.00
9788184041040	Flash 8 Project for Learning Animation and Interactivity (B/CD), 372 Pages	Shupe	2006	400.00
9789350230985	Flash 8: The Missing Manual, 484 Pages	Veer	2010	725.00
9789350230381	Flash CS5: The Missing Manual, 796 Pages	Grover	2010	725.00
9789350237649	Flash CS6: The Missing Manual, 864 Pages	Grover	2012	1,075.00
9788173667473	Flash Hacks: 100 Industrial Strength Tips & Tools, 504 Pages	Bhangal	2004	400.00
9788173668593	Flash Out of the Box: A User-Centric Beginner's Guide to Flash (B/CD), 264 Pgs	Hoekman	2004	300.00
9788173667312	Flash Remoting MX: The Definitive Guide, 652 Pages	Muck	2003	550.00
9789351106449	**Flask Web Development: Developing Web Application With Python, 280 Pgs**	**Grinberg**	**2014**	**500.00**
9788184048162	flex & bison, 310 Pages	Levine	2009	475.00
9788184045246	Flex 3 Cookbook, 798 Pages	Noble	2008	800.00
9788184048940	Flex 3 with Java, 309 Pages	Kore	2009	525.00
9789350230428	Flex 4 Cookbook, 780 Pages	Noble	2010	900.00
9789351106944	**Full Stack Web Development With Backbone.Js, 212 Pages**	**Mulder**	**2014**	**350.00**
9789351101710	Functional JavaScript,280 Pages	Michael Fogus	2013	475.00
9789350234686	Functional Programming for Java Developers, 112 Pages	Wampler	2011	200.00
9789351107095	**Functional Thinking: Paradigm Over Syntax, 204 Pages**	**Ford**	**2014**	**325.00**
9789350236079	Galaxy S II: The Missing Manual, 456 Pages	Gralla	2012	650.00
9789351107255	**Galaxy S5: The Missing Manual, 476 Pages**	**Gralla**	**2014**	**800.00**

ISBN	Title	Author	Year	Price
9789351107255	**Galaxy S5: The Missing Manual, 476 Pages**	**Preston Gralla**	**2014**	**800.00**
9789350235133	Galaxy Tab: The Missing Manual, 460 Pages	Gralla	2011	525.00
9789350230664	Gamestorming: A Playbook for Innovators, Rulebreakers, and Changemakers, 308 Pages	Gray	2010	550.00
9789350234549	Gamification by Design, 228 Pages	Cunningham	2011	350.00
9788173668685	GDB Pocket Reference, 78 Pages	Robbins	2005	75.00
9789350239445	Geolocation in iOS, 132 Pages	Allan	2012	225.00
9789350237618	Getting Started with .NET Gadgeteer, 108 Pages	Monk	2012	150.00
9789352130399	**Getting Started with Adafruit Flora, 132 Pages**	**Becky Stern**	**2015**	**225.00**
9789351108627	**Getting Started with Adafruit Trinket, 278 Pages**	**Mike Barela**	**2014**	**500.00**
9789351109075	**Getting Started with Arduino 3/ED, 280 Pages**	**Massimo Banzi**	**2014**	**425.00**
9789350235010	Getting Started with Arduino, 2nd Edition 152 Pages	Banzi	2011	250.00
9789351103158	Getting Started with BeagleBone, 164 Pages	Matt Richardson	2013	300.00
9789351108047	**Getting Started with Bluetooth Low Energy, 204 Pages**	**Kevin Townsend**	**2014**	**350.00**
9789350237991	Getting Started with Couchbase Server, 108 Pages	Brown	2012	175.00
9789350238028	Getting Started with CouchDB, 108 Pages	Brown	2012	175.00
9789350238264	Getting Started with D3, 86 Pages	Dewar	2012	150.00
9789350237700	Getting Started with Dwarf Fortress, 256 Pages	Tyson	2012	400.00
9788184045284	Getting Started with Flex 3: An Adobe Developer Library Pocket Guide, 162 Pages	Herrington	2008	175.00
9789350236697	Getting Started with Fluidinfo, 156 Pages	Radcliffe	2012	250.00
9789350234624	Getting Started with GEO, CouchDB, and Node.js, 84 Pages	Thompson	2011	150.00
9789351108634	**Getting Started with Impala, 132 Pages**	**John Russell**	**2014**	**250.00**
9789350239766	Getting Started with MakerBot, 244 Pages	Pettis	2013	425.00
9789350238387	Getting Started with Metro Style Apps, 128 Pages	Dewey	2012	200.00
9789351100003	Getting Started with Mule Cloud Connect, 132 Pages	Carter	2013	225.00
9789350236765	Getting Started with Netduino, 120 Pages	Walker	2012	200.00
9789350236703	Getting Started with OAuth 2.0, 100 Pages	Boyd	2012	150.00
9789351106456	**Getting Started With Openshift: A Guide For Impatient Beginners, 128 Pages**	**Pousty**	**2014**	**225.00**
9789350230596	Getting Started with Processing, 232 Pages	Reas	2010	300.00
9789351108504	**Getting Started with Raspberry Pi 2nd Edition, 220 Pages**	**Matti Richardson**	**2014**	**375.00**
9789350239759	Getting Started with Raspberry Pi, 196 Pages	Richardson	2013	325.00
9789350237212	Getting Started with RFID, 60 Pages	Igoe	2012	100.00
9789350235027	Getting Started with Roo, 84 Pages	Long	2011	150.00
9789351108054	**Getting Started with Sensors, 168 Pages**	**Kimmo Karvinen**	**2014**	**275.00**
9789350238752	Getting Started with Storm, 124 Pages	Leibiusky	2012	200.00
9789350234136	Getting Started with the Internet of Things, 212 Pages	Pfister	2011	275.00
9789351101482	Getting Started with Windows 8 Apps,130Pages	Ben Dewey	2013	250.00
9789351102366	Git Pocket Guide, 252 Pages	Richard E. Silverman	2013	200.00
9788184049503	Google Advertising Tools, 2nd Edition, 452 Pages	Davis	2010	675.00
9789350235881	Google AdWords, 216 Pages	Holdren	2011	350.00
9789350230923	Google Analytics, 240 Pages	Cutroni	2010	375.00
9788184045079	Google Apps Hacks, 396 Pages	Lenssen	2008	525.00
9789351105794	**Google Apps Script, 2/Ed, 240 Pages**	**Ferreira**	**2014**	**450.00**
9789351109297	**Google Compute Engine, 268 Pages**	**Marc Cohen**	**2014**	**475.00**
9788184044942	Google Hacks, 3/ed, Tips & Tools for Finding and Using t he World's Information, 558 Pages	Dornfest	2008	400.00
9788184040876	Google Maps Hacks: Tips & Tools for Geographic Searching & Remixing, 366 Pages	Gibson	2006	350.00
9788173667138	Google Pocket Guide, 144 Pages	Calishain	2003	125.00
9789350234556	Google Power Search, 96 Pages	Spencer	2011	150.00
9789350236390	Google Script: Enterprise Application Essentials, 240 Pages	Ferreira	2012	375.00

ISBN	Title	Author	Year	Price
9788184048285	Google SketchUp: The Missing Manual, 616 Pages	Grover	2009	925.00
9788184042856	Google: The Missing Manual, 2/ed, 478 Pages	Milstein	2006	425.00
9789350236062	Google+: The Missing Manual, 252 Pages	Purdy	2012	375.00
9789351102359	Gradle Beyond the Basics, 100 Pages	Tim Berglund	2013	170.00
9789351102342	Graph Databases,244 Pages	Ian Robinson	2013	400.00
9789350234013	Graphics and Animation on iOS, 104 Pages	Nahavandipoor	2011	150.00
9788184046915	Grep Pocket Reference, 98 Pages	Bambenek	2009	125.00
9789350230398	Hackers & Painters: Big Ideas from the Computer Age, 292 Pages	Graham	2010	450.00
9789350230404	Hackers: Heroes of the Computer Revolution, 540 Pages	Levy	2010	725.00
9789350238066	Hacking and Securing iOS Applications, 376 Pages	Zdziarski	2012	600.00
9788184048148	Hacking: The Next Generation, 314 Pages	Dhanjani	2009	475.00
9789350239261	Hadoop Operations, 316 Pages	Sammer	2012	425.00
9789350237564	Hadoop: The Definitive Guide, 3rd Edition, 704 Pages	White	2012	650.00
9789351107286	**Hands-On Programming With R, 272 Pages**	**Grolemund**	**2014**	**475.00**
9789351107279	**Hands-On Sencha Touch 2, 366 Pages**	**Lee Boonstra**	**2014**	**600.00**
9788173668258	Hardcore Java, 354 Pages	Simmons	2004	300.00
9788184045024	Harnessing Hibernate, 396 Pages	Elliott	2008	575.00
9789350235034	HBase: The Definitive Guide, 576 Pages	George	2011	825.00
9788184048735	Head First 2D Geometry, 372 Pages	Fallow	2009	450.00
9788184045819	Head First Ajax: A Brain-Friendly Guide, 544 Pages	Riordan	2008	650.00
9788184046595	Head First Algebra: A Brain-Friendly Guide, 576 Pages	Pilone	2009	625.00
9789351103530	Head First C# 3rd Edition, 968 Pages	Andrew Stellman	2013	875.00
9789350230350	Head First C#: A Brain-Friendly Guide, 2nd/ed 504 Pages	Stellman	2010	650.00
9789350236925	Head First C, 652 Pages	Griffiths	2012	650.00
9788184047998	Head First Data Analysis, 504 Pages	Milton	2009	650.00
9788173664663	Head First Design Patterns, 688 Pages	Sierra	2004	700.00
9788173665264	Head First EJB: Passing the Sun Certified Business Component Developer Exam, 744 Pages	Sierra	2003	725.00
9788184049893	Head First Excel: A Brain-Friendly Guide, 458 Pages	Milton	2010	525.00
9789350238790	Head First HTML and CSS, 2nd Edition, 782 Pages	Freeman	2012	800.00
9789350235324	Head First HTML5 Programming, 632 Pages	Freeman	2011	750.00
9789350235331	Head First iPhone and iPad Development, 2nd Edition	Pilone	2011	600.00
9789351104254	Head First iPhone and iPad Development, 3rd Edition, 388 Pages	Tracey Pilone	2013	575.00
9788173666025	Head First Java: Your Brain on Java - A Learner's Guide, 2nd Edition (Cover Java 5.0), 730 Pages	Sierra	2005	700.00
9789351105411	Head First Javascript Programming, 724 Pages	Freeman	2014	775.00
9788184044362	Head First JavaScript: A Brain-Friendly Guide, 666 Pages	Morrison	2008	825.00
9789350235164	Head First jQuery, 560 Pages	Benedetti	2011	700.00
9789350236024	Head First Mobile Web, 500 Pages	Gardner	2012	675.00
9788184047301	Head First Networking: A Brain-Friendly Guide, 556 Pages	Anderson	2009	575.00
9788184042214	Head First Object - Oriented Analysis & Design, 648 Pages	McLaughlin	2006	675.00
9788184046588	Head First PHP & MySQL : A Brain-Friendly Guide, 828 Pages	Beighley	2009	895.00
9788184045994	Head First Physics: A Learner's Companion to Mechanics and Practical Physics, 956 Pages	Lang	2008	875.00
9789351104261	Head First PMP, 3rd Edition, 916 Pages	Jennifer Greene	2013	950.00
9788184048766	Head First Programming, 460 Pages	Griffiths	2009	625.00
9789350231883	Head First Python, 516 Pages	Barry	2010	675.00
9788184046571	Head First Rails: A learner's companion to Ruby on Rails, 478 Pgs	Griffiths	2009	525.00
9788184044973	Head First Servlets & JSP, 2/ed (COVER J2EE 1.5): Passing the Sun Certified Web Component Developer Exam, 948 Pages	Basham	2008	775.00
9788184044508	Head First Software Development, 512 Pages	Pilone	2008	575.00
9788184043686	Head First SQL: Your Brain on SQL -- A Learner's Guide, 624 Pgs	Beighley	2007	650.00

ISBN	Title	Author	Year	Price
9788184045826	Head First Statistics: A Brain-Friendly Guide, 732 Pages	Griffiths	2008	850.00
9788184046601	Head First Web Design: A Brain-Friendly Guide, 512 Pages	Watrall	2009	850.00
9789350230671	Head First WordPress: A Brain-Friendly Guide, 386 Pages	Siarto	2010	600.00
9789351103813	Heroku: Up and Running, 124 Pages	Neil Middleton	2013	225.00
9788173669347	Hibernate: A Developer's Notebook, 190 Pages	Elliott	2004	325.00
9789351104711	**High Performance Browser Networking,424 Pages**	**Iiya Grigorik**	**2014**	**825.00**
9789351103448	High Performance Drupal, 282 Pages	Jeff Sheltren	2013	450.00
9788184049909	High Performance JavaScript, 252 Pages	Zakas	2010	375.00
9788173669262	High Performance Linux Cluster with OSCAR, Rocks, OpenMosix, and MPI, 380 Pages	Sloan	2004	350.00
9789350237076	High Performance Mysql, 3/Ed Optimization,Backups, Replication (Covers Version 5.5), 844 Pages	Schwartz	2012	850.00
9788184047189	High Performance MySQL: Optimization, Backups, Replication 2/ed, 724 Pages	Schwartz	2009	875.00
9789351108771	**High Performance Responsive Design, 192 Pages**	**Tom Barker**	**2014**	**325.00**
9788184043808	High Performance Web Sites: Essential Knowledge for Front-End Engineers, 184 Pages	Souders	2007	300.00
9789350238479	HLSL and Pixel Shaders for XAML Developers, 220 Pages	Ritscher	2012	350.00
9789352130993	**Hot Seat : The Startup CEO Guidebook, 340 Pages**	**Dan Shapiro**	**2015**	**600.00**
9788184049527	HTML & CSS: The Good Parts, 368 Pages	Henick	2010	625.00
9788184048995	HTML & XHTML Pockte Reference, 4/ed, 206 Pages	Robbins	2010	250.00
9788184042146	HTML & XHTML The Definitive Guide, 6/ed, 692 Pages	Musciano	2006	775.00
9789350239506	HTML5 and JavaScript Web Apps, 192 Pages	Hales	2012	300.00
9789351101284	HTML5 Canvas, 2nd Edition, 768 Pages	Fulton	2013	1,100.00
9789350235898	HTML5 Cookbook, 304 Pages	Schmitt	2011	475.00
9789350234174	HTML5 Geolocation, 136 Pages	Holdener	2011	175.00
9789350239889	HTML5 Hacks, 520 Pages	Cravens	2013	800.00
9789350234938	HTML5 Media, 160 Pages	Powers	2011	250.00
9789350235041	HTML5: The Missing Manual, 472 Pages	MacDonald	2011	450.00
9789350230824	HTML5: Up and Running, 244 Pages	Pilgrim	2010	375.00
9788184049466	HTTP: The Definitive Guide, 676 Pages	Gourley	2010	975.00
9789351108641	**I ♥ Logs, 82 Pages**	**Jay Kreps**	**2014**	**150.00**
9789350238721	Illustrated Guide to Home Forensic Science Experiments, 468 Pages	Thompson	2012	725.00
9789350233801	iMovie '11 & iDVD: The Missing Manual, 568 Pages	Pogue	2011	850.00
9788184042917	Information Architecture for The World Wide Web, 3/ed, 540 Pgs	Morville	2006	695.00
9789350236277	Information Diet, The, 188 Pages	Johnson	2012	300.00
9789350236116	Inside Cyber Warfare, 2/ed, 332 Pages	Carr	2012	525.00
9788184040388	Integrating Excel and Access, 232 Pages	Schmalz	2005	250.00
9789351105336	**Inside Cyber Warfare, 2/Ed, 332 Pages**	**Buttfield**	**2014**	**650.00**
9789350235195	Integrating PHP Projects with Jenkins, 80 Pages	Bergmann	2011	125.00
9788184043617	Intel Threading Building Blocks Out fitting C++ for Multi-Core Processor Parallelism, 348 Pages	Reinders	2007	350.00
9788184045635	Intellectual Property and Open Source: A Practical Guide to Protecting Code, 406 Pages	Lindberg	2008	525.00
9789351100850	Interactive Data Visualization for the Web, 292 Pages	Murray	2013	500.00
9789350238431	Intermediate Perl, 2nd Edition, 416 Pages	Schwartz	2012	400.00
9789351108061	**Introducing Elixir, 232 Pages**	**Simon St. Laurent**	**2014**	**400.00**
9789351105374	**Introducing Erlang, 228 Pages**	**Laurent**	**2014**	**400.00**
9789350236710	Introducing HTML5 Game Development, 140 Pages	Freeman	2012	225.00
9789351109082	**Introducing iOS 8, 356 Pages**	**Steve Derico**	**2014**	**625.00**
9789351108788	**Introducing Python, 500 Pages**	**Bill Lubanovic**	**2014**	**750.00**
9789350238486	Introducing Regular Expressions, 172 Pages	Fitzgerald	2012	275.00

ISBN	Title	Author	Year	Price
9789350234037	Introduction to Search with Sphinx, 168 Pages	Aksyonoff	2011	250.00
9789350237205	Introduction to Tornado, 156 Pages	Dory	2012	250.00
9789350232934	iOS 4 Programming Cookbook, 664 Pages	Nahavandipoor	2011	800.00
9789350238073	iOS 5 Programming Cookbook, 892 Pages	Nahavandipoor	2012	1,350.00
9789351100270	iOS 6 Programming Cookbook, 996 Pages	Nahavandipoor	2013	1,350.00
9789351103424	iOS 7 Programming Cookbook,1086 Pages	Vandad Nahavandipoor	2013	1,850.00
9789351103431	iOS 7 Programming Fundamentals: Objective-C, Xcode, and Cocoa Basis, 444 Pages	Matt Neuburg	2013	700.00
9789352130375	**iOS 8 Programming Fundamentals with Swift : Swift, Xcode, and Cocoa Basics, 604 Pages**	**Matt Neuburg**	**2015**	**975.00**
9789351109099	**iOS 8 Swift Programming Cookbook, 924 Pages**	**Vandad Nahavandipoor**	**2014**	**1650.00**
9789351105947	**iOS Game Development Cookbook: Simple Solutions For Game Development Problems, 420 Pages**	**Manning**	**2014**	**800.00**
9789350235157	iOS Sensor Apps with Arduino, 148 Pages	Allan	2011	250.00
9789352131006	**iOS Swift Game Development Cookbook, 2E, 432 Pages**	**Jonathon Manning**	**2015**	**750.00**
9788173663376	IP Routing, 244 Pages	Malhotra	2002	250.00
9789350233979	iPad 2: The Missing Manual, 352 Pages	Biersdorfer	2011	500.00
9789350236291	iPad 2: The Missing Manual, 3rd Edition, 380 Pages	Biersdorfer	2012	600.00
9789351103820	iPad: the missing manual 6th Edition, 420 Pages	J.D. Biersdorfer	2013	750.00
9789350239803	iPad: The Missing Manual, 5th Edition, 420 Pages	Biersdorfer	2013	600.00
9789350230336	iPhone 3D Programming, 460 Pages	Rideout	2010	700.00
9789350230329	iPhone App Development: The Missing Manual, 360 Pgs	Hockenberry	2010	550.00
9788184048728	iPhone Game Development, 276 Pages	Zirkle	2009	425.00
9788184046922	iPhone SDK Application Development, 408 Pages	Zdziarski	2009	550.00
9789350239643	iPhone: The Missing Manual, 6/ed, 560 Pages	Pogue	2013	825.00
9789350233818	iPhoto '11: The Missing Manual, 408 Pages	Pogue	2011	600.00
9789350236055	iPod: The Missing Manual, 10/ed, 348 Pages	Biersdorfer	2012	500.00
9789350239919	iPod: The Missing Manual, 11th Edition, 360 Pages	Biersdorfer	2013	550.00
9789351108795	**IPv6 Address Planning, 308 Pages**	**Tom Coffeen**	**2014**	**550.00**
9789351106913	**Ipv6 Essentials 3/Ed, 436 Pages**	**Hagen**	**2014**	**650.00**
9788184042818	IPv6 Essentials, 2/ed, 450 Pages	Hagen	2006	650.00
9788173663024	IPv6 Network Administration, 316 Pages	Murphy	2005	325.00
9788173667374	J2EE Design Patterns, 390 Pages	Crawford	2003	550.00
9788173663437	J2ME in a Nutshell, 474 Pages	Topley	2002	625.00
9788173669293	Jakarta Commons Cookbook, 412 Pages	O'Brien	2004	375.00
9788173669484	Jakarta Struts Cookbook, 536 Pages	Siggelkow	2005	400.00
9788173667145	Jakarta Struts Pocket Reference, 142 Pages	Cavaness	2003	125.00
9788184043068	Java & XML, 3/ed, 496 Pages	McLaughlin	2006	450.00
9788173663796	Java & XSLT, 534 Pages	Burke	2001	350.00
9789351105787	**Java 8 Lambadas: Functional Programming For The Masses, 204 Pgs**	**Warburtpm**	**2014**	**325.00**
9789351105930	**Java 8 Pocket Guide: Instant Help For Java Programmers, 260 Pages**	**Liguori**	**2014**	**325.00**
9788173669361	Java Cookbook (Coverage of 1.5), 2/ed, 872 Pages	Darwin	2004	1,200.00
9789351107040	**Java Cookbook 3E (Covers Java 8), 920 Pages**	**Darwin**	**2014**	**975.00**
9789350232903	Java Cryptography, 388 Pages	Knudsen	2011	625.00
9788173666667	Java Database Best Practices, 304 Pages	Eckstein	2003	275.00
9789350233610	Java Distributed Computing, 408 Pages	Farley	2011	675.00
9789350238820	Java EE 6 Pocket Guide, 224 Pages	Gupta	2012	225.00
9789351102625	Java EE 7 Essentials,384 Pages	Arun Gupta	2013	450.00
9788173665776	Java Enterprise Best Practices, 296 Pages	Eckstein	2002	275.00
9788184042870	Java Enterprise in a Nutshell, 3/ed, 906 Pages	Farley	2005	1,100.00
9788173668630	Java Examples in a Nutshell: A Tutorial Companion to Java in a Nutshell, 3/ed, 728 Pages	Flanagan	2004	400.00

ISBN	Title	Author	Year	Price
9788173666681	Java Extreme Programming Cookbook, 296 Pages	Burke	2003	425.00
9788184042160	Java Generics and Collections, 308 Pages	Naftalin	2006	500.00
9788184041187	Java I/O, 2/ed, 740 Pages	Harold	2006	1,250.00
9789351108511	**Java in a Nutshell 6th Edition, 436 Pages**	**Benjamin J. Evans**	**2015**	**575.00**
9788184042665	Java in a Nutshell, 5/ed, 1,266 Pages	Flanagan	2005	750.00
9788173662713	Java Internationalization, 456 Pages	Czarnecki	1998	675.00
9788184047349	Java Message Service, 2/ed, 348 Pages	Richards	2009	475.00
9789351107446	**Java Network Programming 4th Edition, 524 Pages**	**Elliotte Rusty Harold**	**2014**	**575.00**
9788173663536	Java Network Programming, 3/ed, 770 Pages	Harold	2004	750.00
9788173665110	Java NIO, 308 Pages	Hitchens	2002	275.00
9788173665783	Java Performance Tuning, 2/ed, 600 Pages	Shirazi	2003	800.00
9789351106296	Java Performance: The Definitive Guide, 448 Pages	Oaks	2014	675.00
9788184044881	Java Pocket Guide, 208 Pages	Liguori	2008	200.00
9788184045031	Java Power Tools, 926 Pages	Smart	2008	950.00
9788173663819	Java RMI, 578 Pages	Grosso	2001	450.00
9788173664120	Java Security, 2/ed, 624 Pages	Oaks	2001	750.00
9788173668227	Java Servlet & JSP Cookbook, 756 Pages	Perry	2004	975.00
9788173662850	Java Servlet Programming 2/ed, 786 Pages	Hunter	2001	950.00
9788184047011	Java SOA Cookbook, 756 Pages	Hewitt	2009	1,050.00
9788173665684	Java Swing, 2/ed, 1,288 Pages	Loy	2002	1,750.00
9788173665929	Java Threads (Covers J2SE 5.0), 3/ed, 368 Pages	Oaks	2004	600.00
9788173663444	Java Web Services, 286 Pages	Chappell	2002	425.00
9789351103745	Java Web Services: Up and Running Second Edition, 380 Pages	Marting Kalin	2013	575.00
9788184047196	Java Web Services: Up and Running, 332 Pages	Kalin	2009	375.00
9789350230138	Java: The Good Parts, 212 Pages	Waldo	2010	325.00
9789351102427	JavaMail API,118 Pages	Elliotte Rusty Harold	2013	175.00
9789350235621	JavaScript & jQuery: The Missing Manual, 2nd Edition, 560 Pages	McFarland	2011	550.00
9789351108078	**JavaScript & jQuery: The Missing Manual, 708 Pages**	**David Sawyer**	**2014**	**675.00**
9788184045451	JavaScript and DHTML Cookbook, 2/ed, 620 Pages	Goodman	2008	475.00
9789351109990	**JavaScript Cookbook 2nd Edtion, 656 Pages**	**Shelley**	**2015**	**900.00**
9789350230688	JavaScript Cookbook, 574 Pages	Powers	2010	725.00
9789351100263	JavaScript Enlightenment, 184 Pages	Lindley	2013	325.00
9789351101291	JavaScript for PHP Developers, 178 Pages	Stefanov	2013	300.00
9789350231159	JavaScript Patterns, 260 Pages	Stefanov	2010	400.00
9789350237311	JavaScript Pocket Reference, 3rd Edition, 296 Pages	Flanagan	2012	200.00
9789351101253	JavaScript Testing with Jasmine, 70 Pages	Hahn	2013	125.00
9789350235065	JavaScript Web Applications, 304 Pages	MacCaw	2011	400.00
9789350233948	JavaScript: The Definitive Guide, 6/ed, 1,120 Pages	Flanagan	2011	1,200.00
9788184045222	JavaScript: The Good Parts, 186 Pages	Crockford	2008	325.00
9788184045659	JavaScript: The Missing Manual, 560 Pages	McFarland	2008	675.00
9788173669033	JavaServer Faces, 614 Pages	Bergsten	2004	750.00
9788173665301	JavaServer Pages (Covers JSP 2.0 & JSTL 1.1), 3/ed, 762 Pgs	Bergsten	2003	950.00
9788173663833	JavaServer Pages Pocket Reference, 96 Pages	Bergsten	2001	65.00
9788184040173	JBoss at Work: A Practical Guide, 318 Pages	Marrs	2005	550.00
9788173669460	JBoss: A Developer's Notebook, 182 Pages	Richards	2005	225.00
9788173666711	JDBC Pocket Reference, 160 Pages	Bales	2003	100.00
9789350234563	Jenkins: The Definitive Guide, 448 Pages	Smart	2011	750.00
9788173662508	Jini in a Nutshell, 340 Pages	Oaks	2000	425.00
9788184048759	jQuery Cookbook, 594 Pages	Experts	2009	725.00
9789350234570	jQuery Mobile, 152 Pages	Reid	2011	250.00
9789350236727	jQuery Mobile: Up and Running, 288 Pages	Firtman	2012	375.00
9789350232385	jQuery Pocket Reference, 176 Pages	Flanagan	2011	175.00

ISBN	Title	Author	Year	Price
9789350237182	jQuery UI, 260 Pages	Sarrion	2012	400.00
9788184046427	JRuby Cookbook, 238 Pages	Edelson	2008	300.00
9789350239896	Juniper Networks Warrior, 452 Pages	Southwick	2013	750.00
9789351109105	**Juniper QFX5100 Series, 332 Pages**	**Douglas Richard Hanks,**	**2014**	**600.00**
9789351101956	Juniper SRX Series, 1040 Pages	Brad Woodberg	2013	1,700.00
9788173668609	JUnit Pocket Guide, 100 Pages	Beck	2004	100.00
9788184041163	JUNOS Cookbook, 682 Pages	Garrett	2006	450.00
9788184044997	JUNOS Enterprise Routing, 828 Pages	Marschke	2008	1,000.00
9788184047974	JUNOS Enterprise Switching, 772 Pages	Marschke	2009	1,150.00
9788184048193	JUNOS High Availability, 704 Pages	Sonderegger	2009	1,050.00
9789350231104	Junos Security, 872 Pages	Cameron	2010	1,300.00
9789351106906	**Just Hibernate (Covers 4.0), 160 Pages**	**Konda**	**2014**	**225.00**
9789350237656	Just Spring Data, 88 Pages	Konda	2012	125.00
9789350237090	Just Spring Integration, 118 Pages	Konda	2012	200.00
9789350234716	Just Spring, 84 Pages	Konda	2011	125.00
9788173665158	JXTA in a Nutshell: A Desktop Quick Reference, 422 Pages	Oaks	2002	225.00
9788173665608	Kerberos: The Definitive Guide, 280 Pages	Garman	2003	275.00
9788173669729	Killer Game Programming in Java, 986 Pages	Davison	2005	675.00
9789350236758	Kindle Fire: The Missing Manual, 296 Pages	Meyers	2012	450.00
9789350239483	Kinect Hacks, 300 Pages	Jean	2012	475.00
9789351109112	Knockout.js, 124 Pages	Jamie Munro	2014	225.00
9788184040265	Knoppix Pocket Reference, 104 Pages	Rankin	2005	100.00
9788173666728	LDAP System Administration, 318 Pages	Carter	2003	400.00
9789351100867	Lean Analytics, 456 Pages	Croll	2013	775.00
9789351108085	**Lean Branding, 316 Pages**	**Laura Busche**	**2014**	**475.00**
9789351106470	**Lean Customer Development: Build Products Your Customers Will Buy, 256 Pages**	**Alvarez**	**2014**	**375.00**
9789351109129	**Lean Enterprise, 360 Pages**	**Jez Humble,**	**2014**	**600.00**
9789350231364	Learning ActionScript 3.0: A Beginner's Guide, 2/ed, 480 Pages	Shupe	2010	1,075.00
9789351108986	**Learning Agile, 442 Pages**	**Andrew Stellman**	**2014**	**775.00**
9789350233788	Learning Android, 292 Pages	Gargenta	2011	450.00
9788184040456	Learning ASP.NET 2.0 with AJAX, 536 Pgs	Liberty	2007	400.00
9788184045666	Learning ASP.NET 3.5, 2/ed, 624 Pages	Liberty	2008	400.00
9788184046465	Learning C# 3.0, 708 Pages	Liberty	2008	450.00
9789350238059	Learning CFEngine 3, 204 Pages	Zamboni	2012	325.00
9789351108801	**Learning Chef, 388 Pages**	**Mischa Taylor**	**2014**	**675.00**
9789350239773	Learning Cocoa with Objective-C, 3rd Edition, 380 Pages	Addison	2013	650.00
9789350231890	Learning Flex 4: Getting Up to Speed with Rich Internet Application Design and Development, 500 Pages	Cole	2010	1,125.00
9789351100614	Learning from jQuery, 200 Pages	Macrae	2013	200.00
9788173669637	Learning GNU Emacs, 3/ed, 544 Pages	Cameron	2004	450.00
9789350237083	Learning iOS Programming, 2nd Edition, 448 Pages	Allan	2012	700.00
9789351100737	Learning iOS Programming, 3rd Edition, 472 Pages	Allan	2013	800.00
9788184049718	Learning iPhone Programming, 396 Pages	Allan	2010	600.00
9789351102021	Learning Java 4th Edition, 1030 Pages	Patrick Niemeyer	2013	750.00
9788184047202	Learning JavaScript 2/ed, 412 Pages	Powers	2009	600.00
9789350238707	Learning JavaScript Design Patterns, 268 Pages	Osmani	2012	400.00
9789351104643	**Learning jQuery Deferreds, 156 Pages**	**Terry Jones**	**2014**	**275.00**
9789352131013	**Learning MySQL and MariaDB, 432 Pages**	**Russell J.T. Dyer**	**2015**	**750.00**
9788184042672	Learning MySQL, 632 Pages	Tahaghoghi	2006	825.00
9789350238714	Learning Node, 412 Pages	Powers	2012	475.00
9788184045970	Learning OpenCV: Computer Vision with the OpenCV Library, 592 Pages	Dr. Bradski	2008	725.00

ISBN	Title	Author	Year	Price
9788173663918	Learning Oracle PL/SQL (Covers Oracle9i), 452 Pages	Pribyl	2001	325.00
9789350234341	Learning Perl, 6/ed, 412 Pages	Schwartz	2011	395.00
9788184043716	Learning PHP & MySQL, 2/ed: Step-by-Step Guide to Creating Database-Driven Web Sites, 444 Pages	Davis	2007	550.00
9789351100607	Learning PHP Design Patterns, 384 Pages	Sanders	2013	550.00
9788173667329	Learning PHP 5, 378 Pages	Sklar	2004	475.00
9789352130153	**Learning PHP, MySQL & JavaScript with jQuery, CSS & HTML5, 4th Edition, 828 Pages**	**Robin Nixon**	**2015**	**1200.00**
9789350239988	Learning PHP, MySQL, JavaScript, and CSS, 2nd Edition, 600 Pages	Nixon	2013	650.00
9789351102014	Learning Python 5th Edition,1616 Pages	Mark Lutz	2013	1,200.00
9788184048261	Learning Python, 4/ed, 1,230 Pages	Lutz	2009	775.00
9789351102861	Learning R, 420 Pages	Richard Cotton	2013	650.00
9789350238493	Learning Rails 3, 432 Pages	St. Laurent	2012	675.00
9788184046458	Learning Rails, 458 Pages	St. Laurent	2008	450.00
9788184043341	Learning Ruby, 272 Pages	Fitzgerald	2007	425.00
9789351109945	Learning Spark, 296 Pages	Holden Karau	2015	500.00
9789351103547	Learning SPARQL Querying and Updating with SPARQL 1.1 2nd Edition, 408 Pages	Bob DuCharme	2013	700.00
9789350234594	Learning SPARQL, 280 Pages	DuCharme	2011	400.00
9788184047219	Learning SQL 2/ed, 352 Pages	Beaulieu	2009	450.00
9788184043044	Learning SQL on SQL Server 2005, 342 Pages	Bagui	2006	350.00
9788173668050	Learning the Bash Shell, 3/ed, 362 Pages	Newham	2005	625.00
9788173664236	Learning the UNIX Operating System, 5/ed, 174 Pages	Peek	2001	250.00
9788184045840	Learning the vi and Vim Editors, 7th Edition, 508 Pages	Robbins	2008	400.00
9788173660610	Learning the vi Editor 6/ed, 352 Pages	Lamb	1998	250.00
9788184042689	Learning UML 2.0, 300 Pages	Miles	2006	325.00
9789350239216	Learning Unix for OS X Mountain Lion, 254 Pages	Taylor	2012	400.00
9788184048292	Learning VBScript, 636 Pages	Lomax	2009	600.00
9788184043495	Learning WCF, 624 Pages	Bustamante	2007	650.00
9789351105190	**Learning Web App Development: Build Quickly With Proven Javascript Techniques, 328 Pages**	**Purewal**	**2014**	**600.00**
9789350238912	Learning Web Design, 4th Edition, 640 Pages	Robbins	2012	600.00
9788184048964	Learning XML, 2nd Edition, 436 Pages	Ray	2009	650.00
9788184046472	Learning XNA 3.0: XNA 3.0 Game Development for the PC, Xbox 360, and Zune, 506 Pages	Reed	2008	500.00
9789350232415	Learning XNA 4.0: Game Development for the PC, Xbox 60, and Windows Phone 7, 558 Pages	Reed	2011	850.00
9789350238509	LED Lighting, 88 Pages	Cangeloso	2012	125.00
9788173660627	lex & yacc 2/ed, 392 Pages	Levine	1992	325.00
9789351102328	Lift Cookbook, 276 Pages	Richard Dallaway	2013	450.00
9789351108658	**Lightweight Django, 268 Pages**	**Julia Elman**	**2014**	**475.00**
9788184044904	LINQ Pocket Reference, 188 Pages	Albahari	2008	150.00
9788173668449	Linux Cookbook, 590 Pages	Schroder	2004	825.00
9788184040166	Linux Desktop Pocket Guide, 202 Pages	Brickner	2005	150.00
9788173668494	Linux Device Drivers, 3/ed, 646 Pgs	Rubini	2005	675.00
9788184048278	Linux in a Nutshell 6/ed, 960 Pages	Siever	2009	600.00
9788184043525	Linux Kernel In A Nutshell, 216 Pages	Kroah	2006	300.00
9788173664540	Linux Network Administrator's Guide, 3/ed, 372 Pages	Kirch	2005	550.00
9788184044218	Linux Networking Cookbook, 654 Pages	Schroder	2007	900.00
9789350237144	Linux Pocket Guide, 2nd Edition 248 Pages	Barrett	2012	225.00
9788173667183	Linux Security Cookbook, 340 Pages	Barrett	2003	325.00
9788184042887	Linux Server Security, 2/ed, 556 Pages	Bauer	2005	450.00

ISBN	Title	Author	Year	Price
9788184043105	Linux System Administration, 310 Pages	Adelstein	2007	450.00
9789351107729	**Linux System Programming 2nd Edition, 480 Pages**	**Robert Love**	**2014**	**475.00**
9788184043815	Linux System Programming: Talking Directly to the Kernel and C Library, 404 Pages	Love	2007	450.00
9788173668432	Linux Unwired, 322 Pages	Weeks	2004	300.00
9789350236604	Little Book on CoffeeScript, The, 86 Pages	MacCaw	2012	125.00
9789352131020	**Living Clojure, 264 Pages**	**Carin Meier**	**2015**	**450.00**
9788184048216	Living Green: The Missing Manual, 332 Pages	Conner	2009	475.00
9789350230558	LPI Linux Certification in a Nutshell, 3/ed, 540 Pages	Haeder	2010	750.00
9789351100751	Mac Hacks, 348 Pages	Seibold	2013	575.00
9789350235072	Mac OS X Lion Pocket Guide, 252 Pages	Seibold	2011	250.00
9789350235638	Mac OS X Lion: The Missing Manual, 952 Pages	Pogue	2011	1,475.00
9788184048483	Mac OS X Snow Leopard, 924 Pages	Pogue	2009	1,375.00
9788184048704	Mac OS X Snow Leopard: Pocket Guide, 252 Pages	Seibold	2009	250.00
9789350236741	Machine Learning for Hackers, 340 Pages	Conway	2012	550.00
9789350235652	MacRuby: The Definitive Guide, 268 Pages	Aimonetti	2011	425.00
9789350237953	Maintainable JavaScript, 260 Pages	Zakas	2012	400.00
9789350236130	Make a Mind-Controlled Arduino Robot, 114 Pages	Karvinen	2012	150.00
9789351109136	**Make a Raspberry Pi–Controlled Robot, 192 Pages**	**Wolfram Donat**	**2014**	**325.00**
9789351100324	Make an Arduino-Controlled Robot, 274 Pages	Margolis	2013	450.00
9789351105039	**Make Basic Arduino Projects: 26 Experiments With Microcontrollers And Electronics , 280 Pages**	**Wilcher**	**2014**	**425.00**
9789351104223	Make: 3D Printing, 252 Pages	Anna Kaziunas France	2013	425.00
9789351101376	Make: Analog Synthesizers,206 Pages	Ray Wilson	2013	350.00
9789350233740	Make: Arduino Bots and Gadgets, 320 Pages	Karvinen	2011	650.00
9789351105220	**Make: Avr Programming, 496 Pages**	**Williams**	**2014**	**900.00**
9789350233207	Make: Electronics, 376 Pages	Platt	2011	575.00
9789351105602	**Make: Getting Started With Intel Galileo, 212 Pages**	**Richardon**	**2014**	**375.00**
9789352131037	**Make: Getting Started with the Photon, 224 Pages**	**Simon Monk**	**2015**	**400.00**
9789352131044	**Make: JavaScript Robotics, 292 Pages**	**Backstop Media**	**2015**	**500.00**
9789350239926	Make: Lego and Arduino Projects, 348 Pages	Beckler	2012	600.00
9789351106364	**Make: More Electronics, 416 Pages**	**Platt**	**2014**	**650.00**
9789351109143	**Make: Raspberry Pi and AVR Projects, 274 Pages**	**Cefn Hoile,**	**2014**	**475.00**
9789351106371	**Make: Sensors, 424 Pages**	**Karvinen**	**2014**	**675.00**
9789352131051	**Make: The Annotated Build-It-Yourself Science Laboratory, 360 Pgs**	**Barrett**	**2015**	**625.00**
9789352131068	**Make: The Maker's Manual, 256 Pages**	**Andrea Maietta**	**2015**	**450.00**
9789351109150	**Maker Pro, 180 Pages**	**Altman**	**2014**	**325.00**
9789350236789	Making Android Accessories with IOIO, 88 Pages	Monk	2012	125.00
9789350235706	Making Embedded Systems, 852 Pages	White	2011	490.00
9789350235058	Making Isometric Social Real-Time Games with HTML5, CSS3, and JavaScript, 176 Pages	Pagella	2011	275.00
9789350236734	Making Musical Apps, 140 Pages	Brinkmann	2012	225.00
9789352130382	**Making Simple Robots, 248 Pages**	**Kathy Ceceri**	**2015**	**425.00**
9789350231401	Making Software: What Really Works, and Why We Believe It, 644 Pages	Oram	2010	750.00
9789351102250	Making Things Happen: Mastering Project Management, 428 Pages	Scott Berkun	2013	1,025.00
9789350236284	Making Things See, 464 Pages	Borenstein	2012	725.00
9789351102243	Making Things Talk 2nd Edition,516 Pages	Tom Igoe	2013	900.00
9788173664656	Managing & Using MySQL, 2/ed, 448 Pages	Reese	2002	325.00
9789350234365	Managing Infrastructure with Puppet, 68 Pages	Loope	2011	100.00
9788173669583	Managing Projects with GNU Make, 3/ed, 310 Pages	Mecklenburg	2004	525.00
9789351101420	Managing Start ups : Best Blog Posts,468 Pages	Thomas Eisenmann	2013	795.00
9789350236253	Mapping with Drupal, 176 Pages	Palazzolo	2012	275.00

ISBN	Title	Author	Year	Price
9789350239810	MapReduce Design Patterns, 272 Pages	Miner	2012	475.00
9788173661167	Mastering Algorithms with C (B/CD), 572 Pages	Loudon	1999	500.00
9789351109167	**Mastering Bitcoin, 320 Pages**	**Andreas M. Antonopoulos**	**2014**	**575.00**
9788173664618	Mastering Oracle SQL, 2/ed, 504 Pages	Mishra	2004	800.00
9789351104636	**Mastering Perl 2nd Edition, 420 Pages**	**Brian d foy**	**2014**	**800.00**
9788173666766	Mastering Perl for Bioinformatics, 406 Pages	Tisdall	2003	300.00
9788184043013	Mastering Regular Expressions, 3/ed, 556 Pages	Friedl	2006	690.00
9789350235614	Mastering Search Analytics, 428 Pages	Chaters	2011	650.00
9788184047028	Masterminds of Programming, 510 Pages	Biancuzzi	2009	450.00
9789350230305	Mathematica Cookbook, 848 Pages	Mangano	2010	1,275.00
9788173667916	Maven: A Developer's Notebook, 232 Pages	Massol	2005	350.00
9788184045987	Maven: The Definitive Guide, 484 Pages	Sonatype	2008	675.00
9788184042184	MCSE Core Elective Exams in a Nutshell, 604 Pages	Bhardwaj	2006	500.00
9788184041552	MCSE Core Required Exams in a Nutshell, 3/ed, 750 Pages	Stanek	2006	450.00
9789350235591	Meaningful Use and Beyond, 272 Pages	Uhlman	2011	425.00
9788184047479	Mercurial: The Definitive Guide, 300 Pages	O'Sullivan	2009	550.00
9789351101413	Microinteractions,190 Pages	Dan Saffer	2013	300.00
9789350230565	Microsoft Project 2010: The Missing Manual, 788 Pages	Biafore	2010	825.00
9789351101581	Microsoft Project 2013: The Missing Manual,830 Pages	Bonnie Biafore	2013	1,250.00
9789350234372	Migrating Applications to IPv6, 72 Pages	York	2011	100.00
9789352131075	**Minecraft Modding with Forge, 220 Pages**	**Arun Gupta**	**2015**	**400.00**
9789351103110	Mining the Social Web 2nd Edition, 468 Pages	Matthew A. Russell	2013	695.00
9789350232941	Mining the Social Web, 378 Pages	Russell	2011	575.00
9789350235201	MintDuino, 66 Pages	Kelly	2011	100.00
9789351108092	**Mobile and Web Messaging, 208 Pages**	**Jeff Mesnil**	**2014**	**375.00**
9788184048179	Mobile Design and Development, 352 Pages	Fling	2009	525.00
9789351106388	Mobile Design Pattern Gallery, 2/Ed, 426 Pages	Neil	2014	750.00
9789350236970	Mobile Design Pattern Gallery, 296 Pages	Neil	2012	450.00
9789350237595	Mobile Development with C#, 192 Pages	Shackles	2012	300.00
9789351103943	Mobile HTML 5, 504 Pages	Estelle Weyl	2013	875.00
9789350237960	Mobile JavaScript Application Development, 184 Pages	Kosmaczewski	2012	300.00
9789351109914	Modern PHP: New Features and Good Practies, 292 Pages	Josh Lockhart	2015	500.00
9789350236413	MongoDB and PHP, 104 Pages	Francia	2012	175.00
9789352130146	**MongoDB and Python, 86 Pages**	**Nail O'Higgins**	**2015**	**175.000**
9789351100744	MongoDB Applied Design Patterns, 196 Pages	Copeland	2013	325.00
9789351102694	MongoDB: The Definitive Guide 2nd Edition,452 Pages	Kristina Chodorow	2013	590.00
9789350231128	MongoDB: The Definitive Guide, 240 Pages	Chodorow	2010	350.00
9789351102526	Monitoring with Ganglia,276 Pages	Matt Massie	2013	475.00
9789350234143	Motorola Xoom: The Missing Manual, 444 Pages	Gralla	2011	625.00
9788184042801	MySQL Cookbook, 2/ed, 990 Pages	DuBois	2006	1,200.00
9789350230695	MySQL High Availability, 644 Pages	Bell	2010	800.00
9788173668067	MySQL in a Nutshell, 358 Pages	Dyer	2005	325.00
9788184045444	MySQL Pocket Reference, 2/ed 148 Pages	Reese	2008	125.00
9788184041408	MySQL Stored Procedure Programming, 650 Pages	Harrison	2006	900.00
9789350236666	MySQL Troubleshooting, 284 Pages	Smirnova	2012	300.00
9789351103738	Natural Language Annotation for Machine Learning, 364 Pages	James Pustejovsky	2013	650.00
9788184047486	Natural Language Processing with Python, 522 Pages	Bird	2009	850.00
9788173665240	NetBeans: The Definitive Guide, 662 Pages	Boudreau	2002	825.00
9788184044256	Network Security Assessment: Know Your Network, 2/ed, 520 Pgs	McNab	2007	800.00
9788184042740	Network Security Hacks, 2/ed, 492 Pages	Lockhart	2006	425.00
9789351105244	**Network Security Through Data Analysis: Building Situational Awareness, 360 Pages**	**Collins**	**2014**	**650.00**

ISBN	Title	Author	Year	Price
9788173668395	Network Security Tools: Writing, Hacking, and Modifying Security Tools , 350 Pgs	Dhanjani	2005	350.00
9788173663680	Network Troubleshooting Tools, 370 Pages	Sloan	2005	250.00
9789350234150	Network Warrior, 2nd Edition, 808 Pages	Donahue	2011	975.00
9789350238011	Node for Front-End Developers, 76 Pages	Means	2012	125.00
9789351102236	Node.js for PHP Developers, 308 Pages	Daniel Howard	2013	475.00
9789350237335	Node: Up and Running, 220 Pages	Wilson	2012	350.00
9788173667923	Nokia Smartphone Hacks: Tips & Tools for Your Smallest Computer, 418 Pages	Yuan	2005	400.00
9789351100492	Nook HD 2nd Edition, 500 Pages	Preston Gralla	2013	850.00
9788173667848	NUnit Pocket Reference, 100 Pages	Hamilton	2004	100.00
9788173668265	Office 2003 XML, 596 Pages	Lenz	2004	450.00
9789350230701	Office 2010: The Missing Manual, 976 Pages	Conner	2010	800.00
9789350232880	Office 2011 for Macintosh: The Missing Manual, 840 Pages	Grover	2011	1,250.00
9789351101741	Office 2013: The Missing Manual, 1072 Pages	Nancy Conner	2013	1,475.00
9789351100508	Opa: Up and Running, 184 Pages	Binsztok	2013	325.00
9788184049534	Open Government, 452 Pages	Lathrop	2010	675.00
9788173667725	Open Source for the Enterprise, 246 Pages	Woods	2005	250.00
9788184040296	Open Sources 2.0, 488 Pages	DiBona	2005	425.00
9789351106395	**Openstack Operations Guide, 352 Pages**	**Fifield**	**2014**	**600.00**
9789351108528	**OpenStack Swift, 360 Pages**	**Joe Arnold**	**2014**	**600.00**
9788173667404	Optimizing Oracle Performance, 426 Pages	Milsap	2003	375.00
9788173669286	Oracle Applications Server 10g Essentials, 292 Pages	Greenwald	2004	275.00
9789350237892	Oracle BAM 11gR1 Handbook, 260 Pages	Wang	2012	400.00
9788173667077	Oracle Data Dictionary Pocket Reference, 150 Pages	Kreines	2003	125.00
9788173664175	Oracle DBA Checklist Pocket Reference, 88 Pages	RevealNet	2001	65.00
9788184040005	Oracle DBA Pocket Guide, 164 Pages	Kreines	2005	125.00
9789351101147	Oracle Essentials 5th Edition, 456 Pages	Rick Greendwald	2013	675.00
9788184044201	Oracle Essentials: Oracle Database 11g, 4/ed,422 Pages	Greenwald	2007	400.00
9788173664564	Oracle Initialization Parameters Pocket Reference (Oracle Database 10g), 128 Pages	Kreines	2004	125.00
9788184045413	Oracle PL/SQL Best Practices, 2/ed, 308 Pages	Feuerstein	2008	375.00
9788173661181	Oracle PL/SQL Built-ins Pocket Reference, 78 Pages	Feuerstein	1998	60.00
9788184040357	Oracle PL/SQL for DBAs: Security, Scheduling, Performance & More Includes Oracle Database 10g, 466 Pages	Feuerstein	2005	625.00
9788184045420	Oracle PL/SQL Language Pocket Reference, 4/ed, 194 Pages	Feuerstein	2008	125.00
9789351107309	**Oracle PL/SQL Programming 6th Edition, 1404 Pages**	**Steven Feuerstein**	**2014**	**975.00**
9788184049497	Oracle PL/SQL Programming, 5/ed, 1,246 Pages	Feuerstein	2010	875.00
9788173662409	Oracle PL/SQL Programming: A Developer's Workbook, 576 Pages	Feuerstein	2000	875.00
9788173668111	Oracle Regular Expression Pocket Reference, 74 Pages	Burcham	2003	75.00
9788173661204	Oracle SAP Administration, 208 Pages	Burleson	1999	175.00
9788173666063	Oracle SQL*Plus: The Definitive Guide, 2/ed, 592 Pages	Gennick	2004	400.00
9788173661846	Oracle Utilities Pocket Reference, 136 Pages	Mishra	2003	100.00
9789350237748	Orchard CMS: Up and Running, 148 Pages	Zablocki	2012	250.00
9789351104308	OS X Mavericks: The Missing Manual, 904 Pages	David Pogue	2013	1,500.00
9789350238516	OS X Mountain Lion Pocket Guide, 284 Pages	Seibold	2012	275.00
9789350238653	OS X Mountain Lion: The Missing Manual, 908 Pages	Pogue	2012	1,400.00
9789351109334	**OSX Yosemite : The Missing Manual, 900 Pages**	**David Pogue**	**2014**	**1600.00**
9789350234358	Packet Guide to Core Network Protocols, 180 Pages	Hartpence	2011	300.00
9789350235096	Packet Guide to Routing and Switching, 204 Pages	Hartpence	2011	400.00
9789351100713	Packet Guide to Voice over IP, 260 Pages	Hartpence	2013	450.00
9789351102335	Parallel and Concurrent Programming in Haskell,342 Pages	Simon Marlow	2013	575.00
9789350236802	Parallel R, 140 Pages	Weston	2012	225.00
9789350233771	PayPal APIs: Up and Running, 148 Pages	Balderas	2011	250.00

ISBN	Title	Author	Year	Price
9788184042528	PC Annoyances, 2/ed: How To Fix The Most Annoying Things About Your Personal Computer, Wind & More, 268 Pages	Bass	2005	300.00
9788173667152	PC Hacks: 100 Industrial-Strength Tips & Tools, 316 Pages	Aspinwall	2004	300.00
9788173669736	PC Hardware Annoyances: How to Fix the Most ANNOYING Things About Your Computer Hardware, 276 Pages	Bigelow	2004	275.00
9788173665325	PC Hardware in a Nutshell: A Desktop Quick Reference, 3/ed, 848 Pgs	Thompson	2003	325.00
9788173667121	PDF Hacks: 100 Industrial-Strength Tips & Tools, 308 Pages	Steward	2004	300.00
9789350230169	Perl & LWP, 280 Pages	Burke	2010	350.00
9788173664465	Perl & XML, 224 Pages	Ray	2002	175.00
9788173661075	Perl 5 Pocket Reference, 3/ed, 96 Pages	Vromans	2001	70.00
9788184042764	Perl 6 and Parrot Essentials, 2/ed, 304 Pages	Randal	2004	325.00
9788173667336	Perl Cookbook, 2/ed, 976 Pages	Christiansen	2003	800.00
9789350230183	Perl Graphics Programming, 498 Pages	Wallace	2010	750.00
9788184041385	Perl Hacks, 310 Pages	Chromatic	2006	325.00
9789350234587	Perl Pocket Reference, 5/ed 120 Pages	Vromans	2011	125.00
9788173668364	Perl Testing: A Developer's Notebook, 212 Pages	Langworth	2005	400.00
9789350230411	Personal Investing: The Missing Manual, 268 Pages	Biafore	2010	400.00
9789351101734	Photoshop CC: The Missing Manual, 952 Pages	Lesa Snider	2013	1,350.00
9789350230343	Photoshop CS5: The Missing Manual, 836 Pages	Snider	2010	1,250.00
9789350235300	Photoshop Elements 10: The Missing Manual, 680 Pages	Brundage	2011	875.00
9789351108535	**Photoshop Elements 13: The Missing Manual, 668 Pages**	**Barbara Brundage**	**2014**	**1150.00**
9789350235478	PHP & MySQL: The Missing Manual, 520 Pages	McLaughlin	2011	525.00
9789351107057	**Php Cookbook 3/Ed, 836 Pages**	**Sklar**	**2014**	**900.00**
9788184043006	PHP Cookbook, 2/ed, 842 Pages	Sklar	2006	1,025.00
9789351101307	PHP Web Services,136 Pages	Lorna Jane Mitchell	2013	200.00
9788184040814	PHP Hacks: Tips & Tools for Creating Dynamic Web Sites, 468 Pages	Herrington	2005	400.00
9788184040234	PHP in a Nutshell, 370 Pages	Hudson	2005	450.00
9789350230176	PHP: The Good Parts, 194 Pages	MacIntyre	2010	300.00
9788184040258	PHPUnit Pocket Guide, 88 Pages	Bergmann	2005	100.00
9789351101314	Physics for Game Developers 2nd Edition,596 Pages	David M. Bourg	2013	900.00
9789350235218	Planning and Managing Drupal Projects, 120 Pages	Nordin	2011	175.00
9789350235089	Planning for IPv6, 104 Pages	Hagen	2011	175.00
9788173668715	Postfix: The Definitive Guide, 288 Pages	Dent	2003	275.00
9789350238523	PostgreSQL: Up and Running, 184 Pages	Obe	2012	300.00
9788184042948	PowerPoint 2007 For Starters: The Missing Manual, 325 Pages	Vander	2007	325.00
9788184042566	Powerpoint 2007: The Missing Manual, 502 Pages	Veer	2006	450.00
9788173660306	Practical C Programming 3/ed, 456 Pages	Oualline	1997	400.00
9788173666827	Practical C++ Programming, 2/ed, 582 Pages	Oualline	2002	300.00
9789350238424	Practical Computer Vision with SimpleCV, 272 Pages	Demaagd	2012	425.00
9788184040050	Practical Development Environments, 340 Pages	Doar	2005	325.00
9789350234211	Practical JIRA Administration, 116 Pages	Doar	2011	175.00
9789350234693	Practical JIRA Plugins, 136 Pages	Doar	2011	200.00
9789351107941	**Practical Machine Learning , 84 Pages**	**Ted Dunning**	**2014**	**150.00**
9788173664397	Practical VoIP Using VOCAL, 532 Pages	Dang	2002	450.00
9789351100317	Practical Zendesk Administration, 208 Pages	Vaughan	2013	350.00
9789351101703	Present Yourself,240 Pages	Kit Seeborg	2013	400.00
9789351100089	Privacy and Big Data, 124 Pages	Craig	2013	200.00
9788184042108	Process Improvement Essentials, 364 Pages	Persse, PhD	2006	400.00
9788184040227	Producing Open Sources Software, 302 Pages	Fogel	2005	325.00
9789350239780	Programmer's Guide to Drupal, 180 Pages	Hodgdon	2013	225.00
9788184045673	Programming .NET 3.5, 492 Pgs	Liberty	2008	400.00

ISBN	Title	Author	Year	Price
9788184040340	Programming .NET Components, 2/ed (Covers .NET 2.0 & Visual Studio 2005), 656 Pages	Lowy	2005	425.00
9788173667206	Programming .NET Security, 704 Pages	Freeman	2003	550.00
9788173664380	Programming .NET Web Services, 500 Pages	Ferrara	2002	600.00
9789351105237	**Programming 3D Applications With Html5 And Webgl, 426 Pages**	**Parisi**	**2014**	**800.00**
9789350233757	Programming Amazon EC2, 208 Pages	Vliet	2011	350.00
9788184045055	Programming Amazon Web Services: S3, EC2, SQS, FPS, and SimpleDB, 624 Pages	Murty	2008	900.00
9789350239193	Programming Android, 2/ed, 584 Pages	Meike	2012	600.00
9788184046113	Programming ASP.NET 3.5, 4/ed, 1,178 Pages	Liberty	2008	750.00
9788184043839	Programming ASP.NET AJAX: Build rich, Web 2.0-style UI with ASP.NET AJAX, 490 Pages	Wenz	2007	400.00
9789350239254	Programming ASP.NET MVC 4, 508 Pages	Chadwick	2012	650.00
9788184042085	Programming Atlas, 418 Pages	Wenz	2006	375.00
9789350230855	Programming C# 4.0, 6/ed, 880 Pages	Griffiths	2010	600.00
9788184043709	Programming Collective Intelligence: Building Smart Web 2.0 Applications, 376 Pages	Segaran	2007	650.00
9789350237663	Programming Computer Vision with Python, 272 Pages	Solem	2012	425.00
9789351104322	Programming Elastic MapReduce, 196 Pages	Kevin Schmidt	2014	325.00
9788173660764	Programming Embedded Systems in C & C++, 198 Pages	Barr	1999	295.00
9788184042627	Programming Embedded Systems with C and GNU Development Tools, 2/ed, 340 Pages	Barr	2006	375.00
9789350230862	Programming Entity Framework, 2/ed, 936 Pages	Lerman	2010	1,150.00
9789350235935	Programming Entity Framework: Code First, 216 Pages	Miller	2011	350.00
9789350236673	Programming Entity Framework: DbContext, 276 Pages	Miller	2012	425.00
9788184048490	Programming F#, 424 Pages	Smith	2009	625.00
9788173669699	Programming Flash Communication Server, 842 Pages	Lesser	2005	600.00
9788184047233	Programming Flex 3, 674 Pages	Kazoun	2009	875.00
9789351101369	Programming Google App Engine 2nd Edition, 560 Pages	Dan Sanderson	2013	800.00
9789351101321	Programming Grails,378 Pages	Burt Beckwith	2013	650.00
9789350239148	Programming Hive, 368 Pages	Capriolo	2012	500.00
9789350235904	Programming HTML5 Applications, 164 Pages	Kessin	2011	250.00
9789350236420	Programming Interactivity, 2nd Edition, 752 Pages	Noble	2012	700.00
9788184047981	Programming Interactivity, 756 Pages	Noble	2009	1,125.00
9789350234198	Programming iOS 4, 856 Pages	Neuburg	2011	1,000.00
9789350237137	Programming iOS 5, 2nd Edition, 1,032 Pages	Neuburg	2012	1,500.00
9789351101338	Programming iOS 6 3rd Edition,1208 Pages	Matt Neuburg	2013	1,650.00
9789351104315	Programming iOS 7, Fourth Edition, 954 Pages	Matt Neuburg	2013	1,650.00
9789351109174	**Programming iOS 8, 5/Ed, 1040 Pages**	**Matt Neuburg**	**2014**	**1850.00**
9789350230572	Programming Jabber, 500 Pages	Adams	2010	750.00
9788173668180	Programming Jakarta Struts 2/ed, 470 Pages	Cavaness	2004	575.00
9789350236505	Programming Perl, 4th Edition, 1,204 Pages	Wall	2012	895.00
9789351102113	Programming PHP 3rd Edition, 580 Pages	Kevin Taroe	2013	495.00
9788184042719	Programming PHP, 2/ed, 425 Pages	Lerdorf	2006	500.00
9789350235317	Programming Pig, 242 Pages	Gates	2011	375.00
9789350232873	Programming Python, 4/ed, 1,652 Pages	Lutz	2011	1,150.00
9789350235171	Programming Razor, 140 Pages	Chadwick	2011	225.00
9789351109181	**Programming Scala, 2/Ed, 604 Pages**	**Dean Wampler**	**2014**	**1050.00**
9788184048247	Programming Scala, 464 Pages	Qampler	2009	700.00
9789350235102	Programming Social Applications, 568 Pages	LeBlanc	2011	625.00
9788173667862	Programming SQL Server 2005, 600 Pages	Wildermuth	2006	400.00
9788184048186	Programming the iPhone User Experience, 208 Pages	Boudreaux	2009	300.00

ISBN	Title	Author	Year	Price
9789351101598	Programming the Mobile Web 2nd Edition, 788 Pages	Maximiliano Firtman	2013	1,250.00
9789350230718	Programming the Mobile Web, 532 Pages	Firtman	2010	675.00
9788173662379	Programming the Perl DBI, 372 Pages	Descartes	2000	350.00
9788184047950	Programming the Semantic Web, 320 Pages	Segaran	2009	475.00
9788184045253	Programming Visual Basic 2008, 798 Pages	Patrick	2008	550.00
9789350230947	Programming WCF Services, 3/ed, 936 Pages	Löwy	2010	1,050.00
9788173665738	Programming Web Services with Perl, 492 Pages	Ray	2002	400.00
9788173662041	Programming Web Services with SOAP, 268 Pages	Snell	2001	450.00
9789350230367	Programming Windows Azure, 388 Pages	Krishnan	2010	600.00
9789351105053	**Programming Windows Store Apps With C#, 532 Pages**	**Reynolds**	**2014**	**875.00**
9788184043723	Programming WPF, 2/ed, 880 Pages	Sells	2007	725.00
9789351101697	Propose, Prepare, Present,88 Pages	Alistair Croll	2013	150.00
9789351100904	Pthreads Programming, 308 Pages	Nichols	2013	700.00
9789350239902	Puppet Types and Providers, 112 Pages	Liu	2013	200.00
9789351108740	**Python and AWS Cookbook, 96 Pages**	**Mitch Garnaat**	**2014**	**200.00**
9789351103851	Python and HDF5, 176 Pages	Andrew Collette	2013	275.00
9788173664793	Python Cookbook (Covers Python 2.3 & 2.4), 2/ed, 852 Pages	Martelli	2005	600.00
9789351100065	Python for Data Analysis, 488 Pages	McKinney	2013	550.00
9789351109303	Python for Finance, 628 Pages	Yves Hilpisch	2014	1050.00
9788184045833	Python for Unix and Linux System Administration, 472 Pages	Gift	2008	650.00
9788184045406	Python in a Nutshell, 2/ed, 726 Pages	Martelli	2008	825.00
9788184048506	Python Pocket Reference, 4/ed, 226 Pages	Lutz	2009	275.00
9789351106302	**Python Pocket Reference, 5/ED (Covers Python 3.4 & 2.7), 284 Pages**	**Lutz**	**2014**	**325.00**
9788173668487	qmail, 268 Pages	Levine	2004	275.00
9789350234952	Quick Guide to Flash Catalyst, 96 Pages	Elmansy	2011	150.00
9789351103417	QuickBooks 2014: The Missing Manual, 832 Pages	Bonnie Biafore	2013	1,500.00
9789351108542	**QuickBooks 2015: The Missing Manual, 828 Pages**	**Bonnie Biafore**	**2014**	**1400.00**
9789350233795	R Cookbook, 460 Pages	Teetor	2011	700.00
9789350239827	R Graphics Cookbook, 432 Pages	Chang	2012	725.00
9789350239209	R in a Nutshell, 2nd Edition, 744 Pages	Adler	2012	900.00
9789352131082	**R Packages, 228 Pages**	**Hadley Wickham**	**2015**	**400.00**
9788184049435	RADIUS, 224 Pages	Hassell	2010	325.00
9788184042962	Rail Cookbook, 600 Pages	Orsini	2007	500.00
9788184045956	Rails Pocket Reference, 212 Pages	Berry	2008	150.00
9788184046090	Rails: Up and Running, 2/ed, 232 Pages	Tate	2008	300.00
9789351104339	**RaphaelJS, 144 Pages**	**Chris Wilson**	**2014**	**250.00**
9789351104346	**Raspberry Pi Cookbook, 432 Pages**	**Simon Monk**	**2014**	**750.00**
9789351104292	Raspberry Pi Hacks, 412 Pages	Ruth Suehle	2013	725.00
9788184046489	Real World Haskell: Code You Can Believe In, 710 Pages	O'Sullivan	2008	850.00
9789350231913	Real World Instrumentation with Python: Automated Data Acquisition and Control Systems, 644 Pages	Hughes	2010	975.00
9789351103844	Real World Ocaml, 532 Pages	Yaron Minsky	2013	900.00
9788173666896	Real World Web Services, 230 Pages	Iverson	2004	325.00
9789351106487	**Real-Time Communication With Webrtc, 186 Pages**	**Loreto**	**2014**	**325.00**
9789351108818	**Rebels at Work, 198 Pages**	**Lois Kelly**	**2014**	**350.00**
9789350235119	Redis Cookbook, 96 Pages	Macedo	2011	150.00
9788184045857	Refactoring SQL Applications, 372 Pages	Faroult	2008	350.00
9788184043761	Regular Expression Pocket Reference, 2/ed, 126 Pages	Stubblebine	2007	150.00
9789350238691	Regular Expressions Cookbook, 2nd Edition, 632	Goyvaerts	2012	675.00
9788184047172	Regular Expressions Cookbook, 530 Pages	Goyvaerts	2009	800.00
9789351103837	Releasing HTML5 Games for Windows 8, 184 Pages	Jesse Freeman	2013	300.00
9788184041378	Repairing and Upgrading Your PC, 462 Pages	Thompson	2006	350.00

ISBN	Title	Author	Year	Price
9789351100010	Resilience and Reliability on AWS, 180 Pages	Vliet	2013	300.00
9789350237601	Resource-Oriented Computing with NetKernel, 256 Pages	Geudens	2012	425.00
9789352130863	**Responsive & Fast:Implementing High-Performance Responsive Design, 76 Pages**	**Guy Podjarny**	**2015**	**150.00**
9789351106401	**Responsive Theming For Drupal:Making Your Site Look Good On Any Device, 100 Pages**	**Crittenden**	**2014**	**175.00**
9789351108108	**Responsive Typography, 132 Pages**	**Jason Pamental**	**2014**	**225.00**
9789350235645	REST API Design Rulebook, 136 Pages	Masse	2011	225.00
9789350231166	REST in Practice, 472 Pages	Webber	2010	700.00
9788184046410	RESTful .NET: Build and Consume RESTful Web Services with .NET 3.5, 324 Pages	Flanders	2008	500.00
9789351103806	RESTful Java with JAX-RS 2.0, 412 Pages	Bill Burke	2013	600.00
9788184048698	RESTful Java with JAX-RS, 328 Pages	Burke	2009	500.00
9789351102977	RESTful Web APIs, 424 Pages	Leonard Richardson	2013	700.00
9788184049558	RESTful Web Services Cookbook, 332 Pages	Allamaraju	2010	575.00
9788184043327	RESTful Web Services, 462 Pages	Richardson	2007	700.00
9788184040869	RFID Essentials, 276 Pages	Glover	2006	500.00
9788184047509	Ruby Best Practices, 347 Pages	Brown	2009	550.00
9788184041804	Ruby Cookbook, 920 Pages	Carlson	2006	650.00
9788184041996	Ruby on Rails: Up and Running, 196 Pages	Tate	2006	225.00
9788184043624	Ruby Pocket Reference, 182 Pages	Fitzgerald	2007	150.00
9789350238042	Running Lean, 2nd Edition, 256 Pages	Maurya	2012	400.00
9788184042726	Running Linux, 5/ed, 986 Pages	Welsh	2005	875.00
9789350237670	Safe C++, 160 Pages	Kushnir	2012	250.00
9789350238004	Sakai OAE Deployment and Management, 156 Pages	Whitney	2012	250.00
9788173667053	Samba Pocket Reference, 2/ed, 146 Pages	Eckstein	2003	125.00
9789351102632	Scala Cookbook, 742 Pages	Alvin Alexander	2013	1,050.00
9789350234600	Scaling CouchDB, 92 Pages	Holt	2011	150.00
9789351109556	Scaling MongoDB, 84 Pages	Kristina Chodorow	2015	175.00
9789350239636	SciPy and NumPy, 86 Pages	Bressert	2013	150.00
9788184044935	ScreenOS Cookbook, 854 Pages	Brunner	2008	600.00
9789351102649	SDN: Software Defined Networks, 404 Pages	Thomas D. Nadeau	2013	600.00
9788184047240	Search Engine Optimization for Flash, 294 Pages	Perkins	2009	350.00
9789350238776	Search Patterns, 192 Pages	Callender	2012	400.00
9788173667213	Secure Coding: Principles & Practices, 200 Pages	Graff	2003	225.00
9788184043600	Securing Ajax Applications, 266 Pages	Wells	2007	275.00
9788184040081	Security and Usability, 748 Pages	Cranor	2005	550.00
9788184047257	Security Monitoring, 262 Pages	Fry	2009	300.00
9788184043754	Security Power Tools, 872 Pages	Burns	2007	650.00
9788173668401	Security Warrior, 562 Pages	Peikari	2004	500.00
9788184049572	sed and awk Pocket Reference, 2/ed, 64 Pages	Robbins	2010	100.00
9788173660788	sed and awk, 2/ed, 440 Pages	Dougherty	1997	450.00
9789350239230	Selectors, Specificity, and the Cascade, 104 Pages	Meyer	2012	175.00
9788173669187	SELINUX NSA's Open Source Security Enhanced Linux, 264 Pgs	McCarty	2004	275.00
9789351101383	Sencha Touch 2 Up and Running,296 Pages	Adrian Kosmaczewski	2013	500.00
9788173668234	sendmail Cookbook, 418 Pages	Hunt	2003	400.00
9788184044225	sendmail, 4/ed, 1,324 Pages	Costales	2007	850.00
9788184048674	SEO Warrior, 512 Pages	Jerkovic	2009	775.00
9788173666865	Sequence Analysis in a Nutshell: A Guide to Common Tools & Databases (Covers EMBOSS 2.5.0), 310 Pages	Markel	2003	275.00
9789350236680	SharePoint 2010 at Work, 284 Pages	Miller	2012	450.00
9789350236451	SharePoint 2010 for Project Management, 2nd Edition, 256 Pages	Raymond	2012	400.00

ISBN	Title	Author	Year	Price
9789350237175	SharePoint Apps with LightSwitch, 96 Pages	Ferrill	2012	150.00
9788184046144	SharePoint for Project Management, 266 Pages	Raymond	2008	300.00
9788173669835	SharePoint Office Pocket Guide, 94 Pages	Webb	2005	100.00
9788173667398	SharePoint User's Guide, 158 Pages	IDC	2005	150.00
9789350238646	Shipping Greatness, 244 Pages	Mey	2012	350.00
9789350236048	Sinatra: Up and Running, 144 Pages	Harris	2012	225.00
9788173669507	Snort Cookbook, 296 Pages	Orebaugh	2005	300.00
9788184043693	SOA in Practice: The Art of Distributed System Design, 358 Pgs	Josuttis	2007	525.00
9789351108115	**Spam Kings, 388 Pages**	**Brian McWilliams**	**2014**	**700.00**
9789351105329	**Speaking Javascript: An In-Depth Guide For Programmers, 484 Pgs**	**Rauschmayer**	**2014**	**700.00**
9788173668197	Spidering Hacks: 100 Industrial - Strength Tips & Tools, 436 Pages	Hemenway	2003	350.00
9789351100294	Spring Data, 332 Pages	Pollack	2013	575.00
9788173668371	Spring: A Developer's Notebook, 202 Pages	Tate	2005	300.00
9789350236086	SQL and Relational Theory: How to Write Accurate SQL Code, 2/ed, 472 Pages	Date	2012	750.00
9788184042207	SQL Hacks, 424 Pages	Cumming	2006	400.00
9788184047264	SQL In a Nutshell 3/ed, 606 Pages	Kline	2009	500.00
9789350231920	SQL Pocket Guide, 3/ed, 224 Pages	Gennick	2010	225.00
9788173668241	SQL Tunning (Covers Oracle, DB2 & SQL Server), 356 Pages	Tow	2003	525.00
9788184040685	SQL Cookbook, 640 Pages	Molinaro	2005	775.00
9788184042795	SSH The Secure Shell: The Definitive Guide, 2/ed, 680 Pages	Barrett	2005	525.00
9788184045680	Statistics in a Nutshell: A Desktop Quick Reference, 492 Pages	Boslaugh	2008	250.00
9788173668579	STL Pocket Reference, 136 Pages	Lischner	2003	100.00
9788184045048	Subject To Change: Creating Great Products & Services for an Uncertain World: Adaptive Path on Design, 226 Pages	Merholz	2008	300.00
9789350234617	Supercharged JavaScript Graphics, 304 Pages	Cecco	2011	400.00
9789350238769	Surviving Orbit the DIY Way, 108 Pages	Antunes	2012	175.00
9788184048520	Sustainable Network, The: The Accidental Answer for a Troubled Planet, 364 Pages	Sorensen	2009	575.00
9788184048315	SVG Essentials, 376 Pages	Eisenberg	2009	525.00
9789351108559	**SVG Essentials, Second Edition, 388 Pages**	**J. David Eisenberg**	**2014**	**675.00**
9789351109310	**Swift Development with Cocoa, 496 Pages**	**Jonathon Manning**	**2014**	**850.00**
9789351109198	**Swift Pocket Reference, 204 Pages**	**Anthony Gray**	**2014**	**275.00**
9788173664816	Swing Hacks, 554 Pages	Marinacci	2005	425.00
9789351109952	**Switching to the Mac : The missing Manual, 836 Pages**	**David Pogue**	**2015**	**1450.00**
9789351104872	**Switching To The Mac The Missing Manual (Mavericks Edition), 824 Pgs**	**Pogue**	**2014**	**1,450.00**
9788173665318	Switching to VoIP, 514 Pages	Wallingford	2005	450.00
9789350236031	Tap, Move, Shake , 296 Pages	Moore	2012	475.00
9789350239568	Tapworthy: Designing Great iPhone Apps, 340 Pages	Clark	2012	600.00
9788173660931	Tcl/Tk in a Nutshell: A Desktop Quick Reference, 480 Pages	Raines	1999	240.00
9788173664670	TCP/IP Network Administration 3/ed, 756 Pages	Hunt	2002	775.00
9789350238257	Team Geek, 212 Pages	Fitzpatrick	2012	350.00
9788173666513	Test Driving Linux: From Windows to Linux in 60 Seconds (B/CD), 372 Pages	Brickner	2005	350.00
9789351100881	Testable JavaScript, 292 Pages	Trostler	2013	425.00
9789350234389	Test-Driven Infrastructure with Chef, 111 Pages	Nelson-Smith	2011	175.00
9789351103400	Test-Driven Infrastructure with Chef, 328 Pages	Stephen Nelson-Smith	2013	575.00
9789351101772	Testing in Scala,188 Pages	Daniel Hinojosa	2013	325.00
9788184044232	The Art of Agile Development, 446 Pages	Shore	2007	700.00
9788184046946	The Art of Application Performance Testing, 174 Pages	Molyneaux	2009	350.00
9788184045963	The Art of Capacity Planning, 168 Pages	Allspaw	2008	250.00
9788184048209	The Art of Community, 412, Page	Bacon	2009	625.00
9788184047370	The Art of Concurrency, 321 Pages	Breshears	2009	575.00
9788184046953	The Art of Lean Software Development, 158 Pages	Hibbs	2009	250.00

ISBN	Title	Author	Year	Price
9788173667831	The Art of Project Management, 512 Pages	Berkun	2005	575.00
9789350238677	The Art of SEO, 2/ed, 734 Pages	Enge	2009	700.00
9788184041415	The Art of SQL, 382 Pages	Faroult	2006	400.00
9789350238622	The Connected Company, 324 Pages	Gray	2012	475.00
9788184041811	The Internet: The Missing Manual, 466 Pages	Biersdorfer	2006	350.00
9789351102885	The Makerspace Workbench, 320 Pages	Adam Kemp	2013	550.00
9789350232057	The Myths of Innovation, 268 Pages	Berkun	2011	400.00
9788184047516	The Myths of Security, 280 Pages	Viega	2009	475.00
9788184048711	The New Community Rules, 384 Pages	Weinberg	2009	575.00
9788184049053	The New How: Creating Business Solutions Through Collaborative Strategy	Nilofer	2010	450.00
9788184045581	The Productive Programmer, 238 Pages	Ford	2008	275.00
9788184041989	The Relational Database Dictionary, 126 Pages	Date	2006	150.00
9788184044928	The Ruby Programming Language, 460 Pages	Flanagan	2008	775.00
9789351109211	**The Uncertain Web, 256 Pages**	**Rob Larsen**	**2014**	**450.00**
9788173661303	The Whole Internet: The Next Generation, 576 Pages	Conner/Krol	1999	425.00
9789351102960	Think Bayes, 232 Pages	Allen B. Downey	2013	400.00
9789350238035	Think Complexity, 176 Pages	Downey	2012	300.00
9789350238639	Think Python, 316 Pages	Downey	2012	475.00
9789350234457	Think Stats, 160 Pages	Downey	2011	250.00
9789351108566	**Think Stats, Second Edition, 248 Pages**	**Allen B. Downey**	**2014**	**425.00**
9789351106418	**Thinking With Data: How To Turn Information Into Insights, 112 Pages**	**Shron**	**2014**	**200.00**
9789351107248	**This & Object Prototypes, 196 Pages**	**Simpson**	**2014**	**325.00**
9789351107248	**This & Object Prototypes, 196 Pages**	**Kyle Simpson**	**2014**	**325.00**
9789351108573	**Thoughtful Machine Learning, 258 Pages**	**Matthew Kirk**	**2014**	**450.00**
9788184040302	Time Management for System Administrators, 238 Pages	Limoncelli	2005	250.00
9789351109204	**Time Series Databases, 100 Pages**	**Ted Dunning**	**2014**	**175.00**
9789351103165	Tinkering,388 Pages	Curt Gabrielson	2013	675.00
9788173666032	TOAD Pocket Reference for Oracle, 2/ed, 136 Pages	McGrath	2005	125.00
9788184044041	Tomcat: The Definitive Guide, 2/ed (Cover TOMCAT 6.0), 358 Pgs	Brittain	2007	400.00
9789350234167	Transact-SQL Cookbook, 328 Pages	Gennick	2011	575.00
9788184047271	Twitter API: Up and Running, 429 Pages	Makice	2009	700.00
9789350235973	Twitter Book, The: 2nd Edition, 292 Pages	Milstein	2011	400.00
9789351109969	Type & Grammar , 220 Pages	Kyle Simpson	2015	375.00
9788184041590	Ubuntu Hacks, 462 Pages	Oxer	2006	350.00
9788184040029	UML 2.0 in a Nutshell, 246 Pages	Pilone	2005	250.00
9788184042993	UML 2.0 Pocket Reference, 150 Pages	Pilone	2006	175.00
9789351101390	Understanding and Using C Pointers,246 Pages	Richard Reese	2013	400.00
9789351101680	Understanding Computation, 352 Pages	Tom Stuart	2013	550.00
9789351109228	**Understanding Context, 484 Pages**	**Andrew Hinton**	**2014**	**850.00**
9788184040760	Understanding Linux Network Internals, 1,074 Pages	Benvenuti	2005	900.00
9788184043198	Understanding MySQL Internals, 208 Pages	Pachey	2007	425.00
9789350236383	Understanding PaaS, 76 Pages	McGrath	2012	125.00
9788184040838	Understanding the Linux Kernel (Cover Version 2.6), 3/ed, 954 Pgs	Bovet	2005	825.00
9788184041606	Unicode Explained, 692 Pages	Korpela	2006	525.00
9788173666278	Unit Test Frameworks (B/CD), 222 Pages	Hamill	2004	225.00
9788184046434	Universal Design for Web Applications: Web Applications That Reach Everyone, 214 Pages	Chisholm	2008	300.00
9788184040609	Unix in a Nutshell, 4/ed, 992 Pages	Robbins	2005	1,250.00
9788173665653	Unix Power Tools, 3/ed, 1,162 Pages	Powers	2002	1,600.00
9788173666209	Upgrading to PHP 5 (Covers MySQL 4.1), 358 Pages	Trachtenberg	2004	350.00
9789351108979	**User Story Mapping, 342 Pages**	**Jeff Patton**	**2014**	**600.00**
9789351101345	User-Centered Design,170 Pages	Travis Lowdermilk	2013	300.00

ISBN	Title	Author	Year	Price
9789350237281	Using Drupal, 2nd Edition, 512 Pages	Byron	2012	625.00
9789351108580	**Using Flume, 260 Pages**	**Hari Shreedharan**	**2014**	**450.00**
9788184047363	Using Google App Engine, 282 Pages	Severance	2009	425.00
9788184049008	Using Joomla, 428 Pages	Severdia	2010	650.00
9789350237168	Using Mac OS X Lion Server, 240 Pages	Edge	2012	375.00
9788184043037	Using Samba, 3/ed, 464 Pages	Carter	2007	450.00
9789350233191	Using SANs and NAS, 248 Pages	Preston	2011	375.00
9789351109341	**Using SQLite, 552 Pages**	**Jay A. Kreibich**	**2014**	**1050.00**
9789350234709	Using the HTML5 Filesystem API, 96 Pages	Bidelman	2011	125.00
9789351101352	UX for Lean Startups : Faster, Smarter User Experience Research and Design,256 Pages	Laura Klein	2013	425.00
9789351101673	Vagrant: Up and Running, 176 Pages	Mitchell Hashimoto	2013	295.00
9789350238684	Version Control with Git, 2/ed, 472 Pages	Loeliger	2012	600.00
9788184047288	Version Control with Subversion 2/ed, 446 Pages	Pilato	2009	475.00
9788173662621	vi Editor Pocket Reference, 76 Pages	Robbins	1999	60.00
9789351100454	View Updating and Relational Theory, 280 Pages	Date	2013	475.00
9789350234396	Virtualization: A Manager's Guide, 96 Pages	Kusnetzky	2011	150.00
9788173660962	Visual Basic Controls in a Nutshell, 512 Pages	Dictor	1999	310.00
9789350237687	VMware Cookbook, 2nd Edition, 292 Pages	Troy	2012	600.00
9788184048681	VMware Cookbook, 316 Pages	Troy	2009	475.00
9788184040692	VOIP Hacks: Tips & Tools for Internet Telephony, 326 Pages	Wallingford	2006	325.00
9788184047356	Web 2.0 Architectures: What entrepreneurs and information architects need to know, 292 Pages	Nickull	2009	550.00
9788184045062	Web 2.0: A Strategy Guide: Business thinking and strategies behind successful Web 2.0 implementations, 302 Pages	Shuen	2008	350.00
9789351100799	Web Audio API, 94 Pages	Smus	2013	150.00
9788173669057	Web Database Application with PHP & MySQL (Covers PEAR, PHP 5 & MySQL 4.1), 2/ed, 828 Pages	Willaims	2004	800.00
9788184040982	Web Design in a Nutshell: A Desktop Quick Reference, 3/ed, 826 Pages	Niederst	2006	450.00
9789351107118	**Web Development With Node & Express: Learning The Javascript Stack, 352 Pages**	**Brown**	**2014**	**600.00**
9788184049046	Web Mapping Illustrated, 388 Pages	Mitchell	2005	575.00
9789350230589	Web Operations, 360 Pages	Allspaw	2010	550.00
9789350237977	Web Performance Daybook Volume 2, 244 Pages	Stefanov	2012	400.00
9788184046151	Web Security Testing Cookbook	Hope	2008	600.00
9788173663949	Web Security, Privacy & Commerce, 2/ed, 768 Pages	Garfinkel	2001	650.00
9788173663390	Web Services Essentials, 320 Pages	Cerami	2002	450.00
9788173667626	Web Site Cookbook, 262 Pages	Addison	2006	300.00
9789350237717	Web Workers, 78 Pages	Green	2012	125.00
9789350238738	WebGL: Up and Running, 248 Pages	Parisi	2012	400.00
9788184045628	Website Optimization, 408 Pages	King	2008	450.00
9788173661365	Win32 API Programming with Visual Basic (B/CD), 534 Pages	Roman	1999	700.00
9789350230299	Windows 7 Annoyances, 740 Pages	Karp	2010	900.00
9788184048537	Windows 7: The Definitive Guide, 1008 Pages	Stanek	2009	925.00
9788184049916	Windows 7: The Missing Manual, 924 Pages	Pogue	2010	450.00
9788184048339	Windows 7: Up and Running, 220 Pages	Wei-Meng Lee	2009	450.00
9789350239841	Windows 8 Hacks, 440 Pages	Gralla	2013	750.00
9789351103967	Windows 8.1: Out of the Box, Second Edition, 192 Pages	Mike Halsey	2013	350.00
9789351103950	Windows 8.1: The Missing Manual, 972 Pages	David Pogue	2013	1,400.00
9789350239223	Windows 8: Out of the Box, 160 Pages	Halsey	2012	250.00
9789351100690	Windows 8: The Missing Manual, 948 Pages	Pogue	2013	1,200.00
9789351101048	Windows NT File System Internals: A Developer's Guide, 816 Pages	Rajeev Nagar	2013	1,500.00

ISBN	Title	Author	Year	Price
9789350230930	Windows PowerShell Cookbook, 2/ed, 904 Pages	Holmes	2010	800.00
9789350238417	Windows PowerShell for Developers, 344 Pages	Finke	2012	525.00
9788184045239	Windows PowerShell Pocket Reference, 182 Pages	Holmes	2008	150.00
9789350239797	Windows PowerShell Pocket Reference, 2nd Edition, 196 Pages	Holmes	2013	225.00
9788184045000	Windows Server 2008: The Definitive Guide, 508 Pages	Hassell	2008	775.00
9789350239834	Windows Server 2012: Up and Running, 276 Pages	Lynn	2013	475.00
9788173668838	Windows Server Hacks: 100 Industrial-Strength Tips & Tools , 328 Pages	Tulloch	2004	325.00
9788184042979	Windows Vista For Starters: The Missing Manual, 493 Pages	Pogue	2007	325.00
9788173669668	Windows XP Cookbook, 690 Pages	Allen	2005	500.00
9788184042931	Word 2007 For Starters: The Missing Manual, 372 Pages	Grover	2007	350.00
9788173666926	Word Pocket Guide, 160 Pages	Glenn	2003	125.00
9789350234068	Writing and Querying MapReduce Views in CouchDB, 100 Pages	Holt	2011	150.00
9788173665356	Writing Excel Macros with VBA, 2/ed, 580 Pages	Roman	2002	550.00
9789350234044	Writing Game Center Apps in iOS, 100 Pages	Nahavandipoor	2011	150.00
9788184044430	X Power Tools, 286 Pages	Tyler	2008	325.00
9788184042641	XML Pocket Reference, 3/ed, 198 Pages	Laurent	2005	175.00
9788173666155	XML Hacks: 100 Industrial-Strength Tips & Tools, 490 Pages	Fitzgerald	2004	425.00
9788173668456	XML in a Nutshell (Covers XML 1.1 & XInclude), 3/ed, 724 Pgs	Harold	2005	675.00
9788184047295	XMPP: The Definitive Guide, 324 Pages	Saint	2009	375.00
9788184043181	XQuery, 528 Pages	Walmsley	2007	500.00
9788173664908	XSLT 1.0 Pocket Reference, 188 Pages	Lenz	2005	150.00
9788184040784	XSLT Cookbook (Cover XSLT 1.0 & 2.0, 2/ed, 786 Pages	Mangano	2005	500.00
9789352131099	**You Don't Know JS: Up & Going, 108 Pages**	**Kyle Simpson**	**2015**	**175.00**
9789350237731	YUI 3 Cookbook, 448 Pages	Goer	2012	700.00
9789351102892	Zero to Maker, 238 Pages	David Lang	2013	400.00
9789351100874	ZeroMQ, 536 Pages	Hintjens	2013	900.00
9789351108344	**Zookeeper, 260 Pages**	**Flavio Junqueira**	**2014**	**475.00**

- Prices are subject to change without notice.
- All Prices are in Indian Rupees except where indicated in € (Euro Dollar) $ (US Dollar) and £ (Pound)€
- **Titles Released after January 2014 are marked in Bold.**